WOMEN, POLITICS, AND POWER

Sociology for a New Century Series

SOCIOLOGY FOR A NEW CENTURY

WOMEN, POLITICS, AND POWER
A Global Perspective

PAMELA PAXTON
Ohio State University

MELANIE M. HUGHES
Ohio State University

 PINE FORGE PRESS
An Imprint of Sage Publications, Inc.
Los Angeles • London • New Delhi • Singapore

For information:

Pine Forge Press
A Sage Publications Company
2455 Teller Road
Thousand Oaks, California 91320
E-mail: order@sagepub.com

Sage Publications Ltd.
1 Oliver's Yard
55 City Road
London EC1Y 1SP
United Kingdom

Sage Publications India Pvt. Ltd.
B 1/I 1 Mohan Cooperative Industrial Area
Mathura Road, New Delhi 110 044
India

Sage Publications Asia-Pacific Pte. Ltd.
33 Pekin Street #02-01
Far East Square
Singapore 048763

Printed in the United States of America.

Library of Congress Cataloging-in-Publication Data

Paxton, Pamela.
Women, politics, and power: A global perspective / Pamela Paxton and Melanie M. Hughes.
    p. cm.—(Sociology for a new century series)
Includes bibliographical references and index.
ISBN-13: 978-1-4129-2742-0 (pbk.)
    1. Women in politics. 2. Women in politics—Cross-cultural studies. 3. Representative government and representation. I. Hughes, Melanie M. II. Title.
HQ1236.P39 2007
324.082—dc22

                                        2006030147

This book is printed on acid-free paper.

07   08   09   10   11   10   9   8   7   6   5   4   3   2   1

Acquisitions Editor:	Ben Penner
Associate Editor:	Elise Smith
Editorial Assistant:	Camille Herrera
Project Editor:	Tracy Alpern
Typesetter:	C&M Digitals (P) Ltd.
Cover Designer:	Glenn Vogel

Contents

List of Figures, Tables, and Maps

Figures

Tables

Maps

For our families, with love and gratitude

About the Authors

Pamela Paxton is associate professor of sociology and political science at Ohio State University. She received her undergraduate degree from the University of Michigan in economics and sociology and her PhD in sociology from the University of North Carolina at Chapel Hill. She is affiliated with the Mershon Center for International Security and the John Glenn Institute for Public Service and Public Policy and has consulted for the U.S. Agency for International Development (USAID). She is the author of numerous scholarly articles on women in politics, which focus on statistical models of women's parliamentary representation. Her research has appeared in a variety of journals, including *American Sociological Review, American Journal of Sociology, Social Forces, Comparative Politics, British Journal of Political Science,* and *Studies in International Comparative Development.* Her current work investigates women's inclusion into parliamentary bodies in more than 150 countries from 1893 to 2003. She lives with her husband, Paul von Hippel, in Columbus, Ohio.

Melanie M. Hughes is a PhD student in sociology at Ohio State University. Born in Milwaukee, Wisconsin, she graduated from the University of Texas at Austin in 2001 with a degree in sociology and government. After coming to Ohio State in 2002, she wrote a master's thesis investigating new explanations for women's parliamentary representation in developing countries. She has also researched the lasting impact of colonialism on women's parliamentary representation. She has won multiple university awards, has presented her work on women in politics at several conferences, and has a number of articles forthcoming in journals, including *American Sociological Review* and the *Annual Review of Sociology.* Currently, she is working on her dissertation, which looks at intersectionality through the representation of minority women in national legislatures around the world.

Preface

Imagine your country has 100% women in its parliament or national legislature. How does this make you feel? Are you concerned that men are not being well represented or served by the government? Now add 5% men back into the legislature. Do you feel better about a 95%-5% split? What about 10% men? Are you comfortable yet?

Most readers might feel uncomfortable with a parliament made up entirely of women. But the reverse—the complete dominance of legislatures by men—is actually a reality in some countries. And where men do not completely dominate, they still hold over 90% of parliamentary seats in a wide range of countries. This book focuses on the forces that contribute to such gender inequality in politics. But the story of women's exclusion from politics is changing. Increasingly, women are holding political positions around the world. So in addition to exploring barriers to women's political access, we also show where and how women have been gaining ground.

We open the book by outlining the theoretical and practical reasons to incorporate women in politics formally, descriptively, and substantively. In the early chapters of the book, we track the growth in women's political participation over time beginning with the fight for women's suffrage (Chapter 2) and moving through women's parliamentary representation and ascendance to leadership positions as heads of state or cabinet ministers (Chapter 3). To describe different patterns of growth in women's representation over time, we introduce five basic historical paths to power: flat, increasing, big jump, small gains, and plateau. One point we make in these early chapters is that the West did not necessarily lead the world historically in women's political power and is not currently in the forefront of women's representation.

In Chapters 4, 5, and 6, we explore why women have succeeded in gaining parliamentary representation in some places and not in others. We distinguish between two broad sets of factors that produce different levels of political representation for women across the world: supply-side factors and demand-side factors. Supply factors are those that increase the pool of women with the will and experience to compete against men for political office. Demand factors, on the other hand, are characteristics of countries, electoral systems, or political parties that make it more likely that women will be pulled into office from the supply of willing candidates. Chapter 5 includes an extended discussion of gender quotas, one of the newest developments in the field. In Chapter 6, we also introduce two important overarching influences that cross both supply and demand—armed conflict and international pressure. The central message of these chapters is that we must simultaneously understand cultural beliefs about women's place, the social structural position of women, and the political environment in which women operate, if we are to understand how women can gain political power.

But do women make a difference? Do women in positions of power change anything? Have women changed the style of politics? Chapter 7 attempts to answer these questions by assessing not only women's numbers but also their impact on policy, agenda setting, and legislative style. We argue that understanding women's influence is critical but that we face a variety of challenges in attempting to demonstrate the impact of women. We highlight additional possible sites of influence such as women's movements, we raise concerns about whether a critical mass (30%) of women is necessary for impact, and we point out that many questions about minority women's impact remain.

The next two chapters, 8 and 9, consider women and politics in particular contexts. Chapter 8 looks separately at six regions of the world, drawing out key issues and trends in each. We highlight how the political culture of Scandinavia, as well as other Western industrialized countries, has enabled women to make impressive advances in politics. In Eastern Europe, the focus is on the history and fall of the Soviet Union and the implications for women. Women's activism in movements for democracy, gender quotas, and the Catholic Church are emphasized in the section on Latin America. Turning to sub-Saharan Africa, we must first consider how colonialism undercut women's power, but we also cover land rights, nationalism, and ethnicity. Focusing on 36 diverse countries in Asia and the Pacific, we discuss a wide range of issues, including women's leadership through family connections, Confucianism, and modernization. We close Chapter 8 with a discussion of the Middle East, exploring women's activism and the limitations of Islamic family laws. In Chapter 9, we turn to the United States. In this chapter, we cover women's political involvement as congresswomen, state legislators, governors, and members of the executive branch of government. We also consider gender differences in policy preferences, voting, and other forms of political participation.

The concluding chapter asks where we are going and how we can get there. It introduces the Women Power Index—a new way to measure women's political power. We assess lessons learned and list a number of Internet resources for further reading. We also consider what the world would look like if we lived in a truly 50/50 world, that is, if neither sex dominated political positions.

It is our purpose with this book to explore the experiences of women in politics in countries around the globe. We focus mainly on women's partic-ipation and representation in formal political positions. But throughout the text, we also try to emphasize the importance and power of women's infor-mal political activities, such as participation in social movements. Further, we attempt to remind readers whenever possible that whether we look at the place of women within minority groups, or the place of minorities within groups of women, we must take special care to consider within-group inequalities.

Of course, this book would not have been possible without the support of a wide range of people and institutions. We thank Kira Sanbonmatsu, Clarissa Hayward, Mona Lena Krook, Evan Schofer, Anne Jolliff, Jennifer Green, Josh Dubrow, Sheri Kunovich, Colin Odden, Rachel Lovell, Griff Tester, and Judy Wu for helpful suggestions, comments, or advice at various points in the project. We also thank our reviewers, who provided invaluable suggestions for revision: Hannah Britton (Departments of Political Science and Women's Studies at the University of Kansas), Dianne Bystrom (Carrie Chapman Catt Center for Women and Politics at Iowa State University), Deirdre Condit (Departments of Women's Studies and Political Science at Virginia Commonwealth University), Valentine Moghadam (UNESCO), Barbara Ryan (Departments of Sociology and Women's Studies at Widener University), and Kathleen Staudt (Department of Political Science at the University of Texas at El Paso).

Special thanks go to Vinnie Roscigno, who shepherded our manuscript through its infancy to its completion and provided excellent suggestions throughout the process. We are also grateful to the other series editors, Joya Misra, Gay Seidman, and York Bradshaw, and to Jerry Westby, Ben Penner, Camille Herrera, Elise Smith, and Tracy Alpern, at Sage Publications, as well as copy editor Cheryl Duksta. We also thank the National Science Foundation, the Mershon Center for International Security at Ohio State University, the Coca-Cola Critical Difference for Women program, and the Department of Sociology at Ohio State University for their support of this project. Finally, we thank our friends and families for their encouragement and support and the female politicians of the world for inspiring us to write this book.

1

Introduction to Women in Politics

Women are not well represented in politics. Simply turning on the television to a summit of world leaders, a debate in the British Parliament, or a United Nations Security Council meeting reveals a dearth of female faces. Women make up half of the population of every country in the world. But the worldwide average percentage of women in national parliaments is only 16%. Of the more than 190 countries in the world, a woman is the head of government (president or a prime minister) in only 7. Women are 9% of ambassadors to the United Nations, 7% of the world's cabinet ministers, and 8% of world mayors.

At the turn of the 21st century, there is little overt discrimination against women in politics. Almost every country in the world provides the legal right for women to participate in politics. Women can vote, women can support candidates, and women can run for office. But the lack of visible women in the political life of nation after nation suggests that veiled discrimination against women remains. In some countries, such as Sweden, Argentina, and Rwanda, women have made remarkable progress in their political representation. Unfortunately, in many other countries, the struggle for equal representation proceeds slowly. And some populations, religions, and governments remain openly hostile to the notion of women in politics.

In no country do women make up 50% of the **national legislature**. But a few countries do come close. For years, Sweden reigned as the country with the highest percentage of women in its **parliament**. In 2003, however, Sweden

Figure 1.1   Finding the Six Female World Leaders Among Those Gathered for the United Nations 50th Anniversary Is a Challenge

SOURCE: ©UN/DPI Photo. Reprinted with permission.

was dethroned by Rwanda, which reached 48.8% women in its legislature. The two countries could not be more different. Sweden is a developed Western nation, has been at peace for almost two centuries, and governs through a parliament first established more than 500 years ago (Kelber 1994). In Sweden, women's increasing participation in politics was a long, slow process. Beginning with reforms in the 1920s, Sweden broke the 10% mark for women's legislative representation in 1952, boasted the first female acting prime minister in 1958, and then passed the 20% mark for female legislative presence in 1973 and the 30% mark in 1985.

In contrast, in 2003, Rwanda had just begun to recover from a brutal genocide during which more than a million people lost their lives. Rwanda is a poor nation in Africa that ranks 159th out of 177 countries in its level of "human development" (United Nations 2004). The 2003 election was the inaugural election of a new constitution, which guaranteed women at least 30% of the National Assembly seats. Before that time, women had been less of a presence, never hitting 20% of the parliament before the transition to an interim government in 1994. But even with a guaranteed 30%, voters chose even more women—almost 20% more. The promotion of women by international organizations, the influence of local women's organizations, and the sheer number of men killed during or imprisoned after the genocide help explain the sudden rise of women to substantial political power (Longman 2006).

That Rwanda and Sweden rank first and second in women's legislative presence suggests that one cannot assume that women do better in Western, industrialized nations. Indeed, there is substantial variation across regions of the world, and many highly developed Western countries fall far behind developing countries in their representation of women as political leaders. For example, as of June 2005, the United States ranked 61st of 185 countries in percentage of women, falling behind Bosnia and Herzegovina, Ecuador, and Zimbabwe. Britain ranks 52nd and is behind Mexico, Namibia, and Vietnam. Spain, Italy, and the United States have never had a female president, whereas Sri Lanka, the Philippines, and Indonesia have. It is also important to recognize that Sweden and Rwanda are two of only a handful of true success stories for women's presence in politics. Of all countries, 73% have less than 20% women in their national legislatures. And 10 countries have no women representatives at all.

The story of women, politics, and power is therefore different than that of women in education or women in the labor force. Although women have made remarkable inroads into both higher education and traditionally male occupations, the political sphere remains an arena where women have far to go. Altogether, when we talk about women and politics, women remain just a "blip on the male political landscape" (Reynolds 1999:547).

Arguments for Women's Representation in Politics

Why should we care about a lack of women in politics? First, politics is an important arena for decision making. Individuals who hold official positions in government get to decide how to allocate scarce resources, such as tax revenues. Politicians make political decisions that may help some people at the expense of others. Decisions by politicians even affect people's individual choices by encouraging some behaviors and outlawing others. Second, political power is a valuable good. Politicians hold power over other social institutions, such as the family or education, and are able to codify particular practices into law (Martin 2004). Politicians have the power to enforce their decisions, sometimes with force. Third, holding a political position is to hold a position of authority. Looking at the makeup of political figures in a country highlights who is legitimated to make societywide decisions in that society.

But does it matter if all political decision makers are male? In principle, the answer could be no. But in practice the answer is often yes. In principle, most laws are gender neutral, and elected representatives pay attention to all of their constituents equally. In practice, however, **feminist** political theorists have argued that the appearance of neutrality toward gender or equality between men and women in government actually hides substantial gender inequality. If gender-neutral language is used in principle, but in practice only men appear in politics, then women are not equal but rather invisible. Theorists such as Anne Phillips, Carol Pateman, and Iris Young have shown that abstract terms used in political theory, such as *individual* or *citizen*, though having the appearance of being gender neutral, actually signify White males (Pateman 1988, 1989; Phillips 1991, 1995; Young 1990). Even more forceful arguments say that the state was structured from its inception to benefit men and that it has a continuing interest in the maintenance of male domination, both in Western countries (Lerner 1986; MacKinnon 1989) and in non-Western countries (Charrad 2001).

Without women, the state, being populated only by men, could legislate in the male interest. That is, if women are not around when decisions are made, their interests may not be served. Golda Meir was an Israeli cabinet minister before she became prime minister of Israel. She related the following story: "Once in the Cabinet we had to deal with the fact that there had been an outbreak of assaults on women at night. One minister (a member of an extreme religious party) suggested a curfew. Women should stay at home after dark. I said: 'but it's the men attacking the women. If there's to be a curfew, let the men stay at home, not the women.'" Golda Meir's presence on the cabinet allowed her to point out the unfairness of making women stay home rather than men. If she had not been there, who would have pointed this out?

In general, male lawmakers are less likely to initiate and pass laws that serve women's and children's interests (Berkman and O'Connor 1993; Bratton and Haynie 1999; Childs and Withey 2004; Schwindt-Bayer 2006; Swers 1998; Taylor-Robinson and Heath 2003; Thomas 1991). They less often think about rape, domestic violence, women's health, and child care. But in democracies, the points of view of all groups need to be taken into account. Therefore, the views and opinions of women as well as men must be incorporated into political decision making.

These arguments are interesting in theory, but what about in practice? What might it mean to women around the world to be underrepresented in politics?

Case Study: The Story of Mukhtaran Bibi—Village Council Justice

In June 2002, in Meerwala, a remote village in Pakistan, Mukhtaran Bibi's 12-year-old brother was accused of having an affair with a woman of a higher caste. The village council ruled that her brother had committed a crime and sentenced Mukhtaran Bibi to be gang-raped by four men as punishment. The four men stripped her naked and took turns raping her. She then had to walk home almost naked in front of several hundred people.

The expectation was that now Mukhtaran Bibi would commit suicide. Indeed, because they are now considered deeply dishonored and stigmatized, this is the typical path taken by the hundreds of Pakistani girls gang-raped every year due to family or tribal rivalries. Instead, Ms. Mukhtaran defied tradition by testifying against her attackers, resulting in six convictions. Government investigators now say that the accusation against her brother was false. Instead, members of the higher caste tribe actually sexually abused Mukhtaran Bibi's brother and tried to cover it up by falsely accusing him of the affair.

Mukhtaran Bibi's story has a mostly happy ending. She received compensation money from Pakistani President Perrez Musharraf and used it to start two schools in her village, one for boys and the other for girls. When the government detained her for planning to visit the United States in June 2005, international attention and outcry forced her release. Her round-the-clock guards provided by the government afford her some protection from her attackers, who were released after their convictions were overturned in March 2005.

The stories of many other young girls in Pakistan do not have such happy endings. They are beaten for not producing sons, raped, disfigured for trying to choose a husband for themselves, or killed as a matter of family honor. In a society that does not acknowledge rape in marriage, approximately 50% of women who do report a rape are jailed under the 1979 Hudood Ordinances. These Ordinances allow courts to view a woman's charge of rape as an admission of illegal sex unless she can prove that the intercourse was nonconsensual. Such proof requires multiple male witnesses to the crime, as in some circumstances the testimony of a woman is worth only half that of a man.

SOURCES: Kristof (2004, 2005) and Human Rights Watch (1999).

Case Study: Wife Beating in Nigeria—Legal Under the Penal Code

In December 2001, Rosalynn Isimeto-Osibuamhe of Lagos, Nigeria, wanted to visit her parents. Her husband, Emmanuel, told her she had to stay home. Their argument ended when Emmanuel beat Rosalynn unconscious and left her lying in the street outside their apartment. This was hardly the first time she'd been beaten. During the course of their 4-year marriage, Emmanuel beat her more than 60 times.

This story is not an unusual one in Africa, where domestic violence is endemic. Chronic underreporting, cultural acceptance, and women's shame make it difficult to provide hard and fast numbers on the extent of wife beating in Africa. But a recent study suggests that one half of Zambian

...ᴖᴖn report being physically abused by a male partner. An earlier Nigerian survey explains that 81% of married women reported being verbally or physically abused by husbands. Few African countries have domestic violence laws on the books.

What could Rosalynn Isimeto-Osibuamhe do? Domestic violence is entrenched in Nigerian law. Section 56 of the Nigerian Penal Code allows husbands to use physical means to chastise their wives, as long as the husbands do not inflict grievous harm, where grievous harm is defined as loss of sight, hearing, power of speech, facial disfigurement, or other life-threatening injuries. Nigeria, a country of 350,000 square miles, has only two shelters for battered women. Police do not pursue domestic violence as assault, and Rosalynn's pastor told her not to make her husband angry and to submit to him. Indeed, many of Isimeto-Osibuamhe's female neighbors believe that husbands have a right to beat wives who argue, burn dinner, or come home late.

Rosalynn Isimeto-Osibuamhe is unusual in that she was able to leave her husband. She is university educated and the founder of a French school. And she did find a shelter and stayed there for weeks. Still, she is unsure whether she wants a divorce. And many other women in Africa, unable to leave their husbands, are not so lucky.

SOURCES: LaFraniere (2005), Kishor and Johnson (2004), and Odunjinrin (1993).

Case Study: Delaying the Clarence Thomas Vote—Female Representatives Speak Out

For many people in 1991, the television image of 16 White men interrogating Anita Hill during Senate Judiciary Committee hearings epitomized the lack of women's presence in American politics. But that hearing might not have taken place at all if not for the swift and decisive actions of a small group of female congresswomen.

In the fall of 1991, Clarence Thomas was close to being confirmed as a U.S. Supreme Court justice. But on October 6th, 2 days before the Senate was scheduled to vote on his nomination, a distinguished law professor, Anita Hill, accused Thomas of sexually harassing her in 1981. The story exploded in the media and various groups began calling for a delay on the confirmation vote until the charges of sexual harassment could be fully investigated.

But on Tuesday morning, the 8th of October, it looked like the Senate vote on Thomas would go forward as planned. The men of the Senate (at the time the Senate had 98 men and 2 women) did not plan to investigate the charges of sexual harassment and appeared ready to confirm Thomas's nomination to the Supreme Court. This continued a month-long pattern, as Hill had told the Senate Judiciary Committee about her allegations in early September, but the committee had not pursued it. The male senators seemed ready to take Judge Thomas's word over Professor Hill's without formal or detailed examination of the evidence.

Because 98% of the Senate was male, congresswomen were concerned that women's perspectives on sexual harassment were not being fully considered. Therefore, a number of congresswomen decided to take action. They began by speaking on the floor of the House of Representatives, reminding their colleagues that justice required that Hill's allegations be taken seriously. As argued by Barbara Boxer, "Mr. Speaker, imagine yourself dependent on another human being for your livelihood. Imagine the power that person holds over you. Imagine that person making suggestive comments to you, and beyond that, telling you in detail about pornographic materials he had seen. Would you be intimidated? Yes, especially if you are in your 20s and you are a woman in a man's field. . . . And, which court is that final protection of women from this kind of harassment? . . . The Supreme Court of the United States of America."

When procedural rules were used to stop these speeches, the congresswomen decided to go further and take their concerns directly to the Senate. In a march immortalized in photographs, seven congresswomen left Congress and strode over to the Senate side of the Capitol to speak with Senate Democrats during their regular Tuesday caucus meeting. High heels clicking as they advanced up the steps of the Capitol, these elected representatives were determined to emphasize that the women's point of view might be very different from the view of these male senators. To them, these charges were serious and worthy of genuine consideration.

The congresswomen were turned away from the closed-door caucus meeting, despite repeated pleas to be allowed in. The Senate majority leader ultimately agreed to meet with the women separately, and they stated their case. That night, facing mounting public pressure, he announced that a confirmation vote on Thomas would be delayed so hearings on Anita Hill's charges could be held.

Thus, seven elected female representatives, Patricia Schroeder of Colorado, Barbara Boxer of California, Louise Slaughter of New York, Jolene Unsold of Washington, Patsy Mink of Hawaii, Nita Lowey of Massachusetts, and Eleanor Holmes-Norton of the District of Columbia, played a critical role in helping America and the Senate understand that women's concerns were important in the halls of power.

This story also has a mostly happy ending. Although many felt that the Anita Hill hearings were ultimately a farce, public resentment of that farce helped to send Barbara Boxer, one of the marchers, and three other women to the Senate the following year—a Senate that would not have a women's bathroom until 1993. The Anita Hill hearings also helped increase awareness of sexual harassment of women in the workplace, which was only incorporated into the guidelines set by the Equal Opportunity Commission (the body responsible for adjudicating sexual harassment claims) in 1980.

SOURCES: Boxer (1994), Dowd (1991), and Winess (1991).

Ultimately, all of these situations lead to the question, if a government chronically underrepresents women, are we positive the rules of the game are fair? The same question can be asked about any historically marginalized or oppressed group—for example, a racial or ethnic group. Indeed, it is difficult to separate the stories of oppressed women in this chapter from their racial and ethnic status. For our purposes here, we generally focus on women alone, while acknowledging that race, class, and gender are intertwined in the lives of women around the world.

Justice Arguments for Women's Representation

Women make up half of the population of every country in the world. A simple justice argument would therefore suggest that women and men should be equally represented in politics. But what does *equal representation* mean? Arguments for women's equal representation in politics fall into one of three types—each type with a different conception of *representation*. These types are formal, descriptive, and substantive representation.

The earliest and most basic formulation of equal representation is **formal representation**, meaning that women have the legal right to participate in politics on an equal basis with men. Formal representation requires that any barriers to women's participation in decision making be removed. Women must have the right to vote and the right to stand for office. Discrimination against women in the arena of politics must be eradicated. Men and women must be equal before the law. In short, women must have the same opportunity as men to participate in politics.

This may sound straightforward to people who have voted their whole life, but the fight for the formal representation of women in politics was long, difficult, and occasionally bloody. In the early part of the 20th century, as women fought for the right to vote, it was not always clear that they would get it. Furthermore, this struggle continues into the present: Multiple votes were taken before women got the vote in Kuwait in 2005, proof of education is required for a woman to vote in Lebanon, and women still cannot vote in Saudi Arabia.

Kuwait, Lebanon, and Saudi Arabia are anomalies in the present day. The idea that women require formal representation in politics has become nearly universally accepted over the last 100 years. Women's political rights are now seen as human rights, and statements about women's political participation are set out in the resolutions, codes, and formal conventions of most international bodies as well as in the law of many individual countries. The United Nations (UN; 1946) adopted the first of a number of resolutions dealing with women's political rights in 1946 when, during its first session, the UN General Assembly recommended that all member states fulfill the aims of its charter "granting to women the same political rights as men" (resolution 56 (I)). At the time, only about 50% of UN member states allowed women the vote.

Today, women can formally participate in politics almost everywhere, and resolution statements are much stronger, taking for granted the notion that women can and should participate. For example, at the fourth UN World Conference on Women held in Beijing in 1995, 189 countries agreed to a platform for action stating, "No government can claim to be democratic until women are guaranteed the right to equal representation" (United Nations 1995). Ultimately, these arguments for formal representation are about equal opportunity for women. The goal of formal representation is the absence of direct and overt discrimination against women in politics.

But observation suggests that formal representation does not necessarily result in substantial numbers of women in positions of political power. Even though most countries of the world grant women the equal opportunity to vote and to participate in politics, women remain substantially underrepresented in positions of political decision making. More than 98% of countries in the world have granted women the formal right to vote and the formal right to stand for election. But as noted earlier, few countries have more than 20% women in their legislative bodies. Equal opportunity through formal representation does not appear to automatically produce large numbers of women in politics.

For this reason, in the last decades of the 20th century, feminist political theorists began to argue that a different conception of equal representation was needed. Equal representation can also require **descriptive representation**—that there must be descriptive similarity between representatives and constituents. If women make up 50% of the population, they should also make up roughly 50% of legislative and executive bodies.

Arguments for descriptive representation suggest that it is not enough to have formal political equality in politics. This is because simply extending the legal right to pursue public office to women does not ensure that they will. Rights alone do not remedy the substantial social and economic inequalities that prevent women from taking advantage of their political opportunities. Instead, their past and continued exclusion from elites reinforces the idea of women's inferiority in the political arena (Phillips 1995).

Advocates of descriptive representation therefore view formal political equality as only the first step in achieving equal representation for women. In principle, laws can ensure that women have an equal opportunity to vote and to pursue political careers. In practice, however, women may not come to the starting line with the same resources or skills as men, and this can result in differences in outcomes, even without differences in opportunity.

In discussing the limits of equal opportunity, an analogy to a foot race is often used. Perhaps the most famous example is President Lyndon Johnson's 1965 speech to the graduating class of Howard University: "You do not take a man who for years has been hobbled by chains, liberate him, bring him to the starting line of a race, saying, 'you are free to compete with all the others,' and still justly believe you have been completely fair." It is easy to substitute *woman* for *man* in this speech and understand the critique of simple formal representation. The present effects of past discrimination can prevent laws ensuring equal opportunity from translating into equal outcomes.

Instead, something more is required: "Those who have been traditionally subordinated, marginalized, or silenced need the security of a guaranteed voice and . . . democracies must act to redress the imbalance that centuries of oppression have wrought" (Phillips 1991:7). Further action must be taken—electoral laws changed, gender quotas introduced—to ensure that women are represented in politics in numbers more proportionately similar to their presence in the population.

Arguments for descriptive representation hinge on the notion that racial, ethnic, and gender groups are uniquely suited to represent themselves in democracies. Social groups have different interests due to varied economic circumstances, histories of oppression, and cultural or ideological barriers they continue to face. In principle, democratic ideals suggest that elected representatives will serve the interests of the entire community and be able to transcend any specific interests based on their own characteristics, such as sex, race, or age. But in practice, "while we may all be capable of that imaginative leap that takes us beyond our own situation, history indicates that we do this very partially, if at all" (Phillips 1991:65). Although elections make representatives accountable to their constituents, they are sporadic enough to allow representatives to pursue private preferences or party loyalties.

If groups cannot be well represented by other groups, they need to be represented themselves among political elites (Williams 1998). In the case of women, the argument is that due to different socialization and life experiences, women are different from men. Thus, "women bring to politics a different set of values, experiences and expertise" (Phillips 1995:6). Women have different interests than men do, and those interests cannot be represented by men; therefore, women must be present themselves in the political arena. When asked why there should be more women in politics, Sirimavo Bandaranaike, the world's first female prime minister, replied "because they are not considered. Women's problems are not considered now ... women have to work very hard, not necessarily at a desk in an office ... they have ... family problems that are different than what the men have" (Liswood 1995:109).

Arguments for descriptive representation are not essentialist (Phillips 1995:55–6; Williams 1998:5–6). They do not assume that, by definition, all women share an essential identity with the same interests and concerns. Instead, these feminist writers make it clear that women have a common interest because of their social position. Because of women's historically marginalized position, their general relegation to certain economic roles, and their primary responsibility for child and elder care, women have shared experiences and therefore common interests. And because women can best represent themselves, the argument continues, they need to be numerically represented in politics, not simply formally represented. Descriptive representation requires that women have a legislative presence (Williams 1998).

Arguments for descriptive representation are becoming more common in international statements on women's political position. For example, the 1995 Beijing Platform for Action states, "Women's equal participation in decision-making is not only a demand for simple justice or democracy but can also be seen as a necessary condition for women's interests to be taken into account" (United Nations 1995, paragraph 181). This statement suggests that equal participation, or representation, must go beyond simple justice and move toward the incorporation of women's interests.

Even if we accept that women have different interests than men do and therefore cannot be represented by men, a question remains: Can women represent women? This question leads to a third type of equal representation: **substantive representation**, which means that women's interests must be advocated in the political arena. Substantive representation requires that politicians speak for and act to support women's issues.

Going even further than the numerical representation of women outlined in descriptive representation arguments, advocates of substantive representation point out that *standing for* is not the same as *acting for* (Pitkin 1972). Getting higher numbers of women involved in politics is only a necessary but not sufficient condition for women's interests to be served. Instead, for women's interests to be represented in politics, female politicians have to be willing to and able to represent those interests.

But what does it mean to represent women's interests, needs, or concerns? There are a variety of answers to that question:

- Female politicians could state that they view women as a distinct part of their constituencies or that they feel a special responsibility to women (Childs 2002; Reingold 1992).

- Female politicians could draft or support legislation that directly attempts to promote social, educational, or economic equity for women. Examples include the U.S. 1963 Equal Pay Act, which worked to end the pay differential between men and women and Mozambique's 2003 New Family Law that allows wives to work without the permission of their husband (Disney 2006).

- Female politicians could prioritize, support, or vote for "women's issues"—issues of particular interest and concern to women. These issues may be directly related to women—for example, Namibia's 2003 Combating of Domestic Violence Act, which supports victims of domestic violence and aids the prosecution of crimes against women (Bauer 2006). Or women's issues may be indirectly related to women through their greater responsibility for child and elder care. Examples include the U.S. Family and Medical Leave Act, which mandates that employers allow employees up to 12 weeks of unpaid leave to care for a newborn child or a sick immediate family member, such as a parent, or to recuperate from a serious illness.

- Female politicians may also prioritize, support, or vote for policies of particular interest to feminists, such as abortion or contraception (Molyneux 1985b; Tremblay and Pelletier 2000). For example, a female politician in South Africa may have supported the 1996 Choice on the Termination of Pregnancy Act, which allows abortion for all women on demand (Britton 2006).

Talking about substantive representation raises three distinct issues. First, female politicians may not have the desire to act "for women." Second, even if they want to, female politicians may not be able to act "for women." Finally, female politicians of a particular race, ethnicity, class, or caste may not desire to or be able to act "for all women."

To begin, women who reach positions of political power may not have any desire to act for women in one or all of the ways described earlier. Women vary in their interest in advancing equality for women or in their commitment to feminist concerns, such as access to abortion. Not all women feel moved to devote special attention to the interests of women, children, and families. For example, Margaret Thatcher, prime minister of Britain from 1979 to 1990, was famously antifeminist and pursued policies that many deemed detrimental to the women and children of England and Scotland.

Even if they want to act in the interests of women, female politicians may not be able to. Simply being a politician does not mean that one's interests can be effectively pursued. There are a number of reasons why female politicians may be unable to initiate or support legislation related to women's interests. First, as Joni Lovenduski (1993) warns, institutions may change women before women can change institutions. Female legislators are embedded in political institutions where male behavior—for example, forcefulness, detachment, and impersonality—is considered the norm. Thus, women may need to change or adapt to conform to those norms. Consider what a female legislator from Southern Europe has to say: "politics may change women because, in order to survive politically, women may copy the men in their methods and behavior" (Inter-Parliamentary Union 2000:23).

Even if women do not change their behavior, they may be sanctioned if they act in the interests of women. Relating the experience of members of parliament (MPs) from the Labour Party in Great Britain, Childs (2002) explains:

> The most common perception is that women who seek to act for women act *only* for women. This results in a tension between a woman MP's parliamentary career and acting for women. If an MP desires promotion, she cannot afford to be regarded as acting for women too often or too forcefully. (p. 151, emphasis added)

If women act for women, they may be relegated to "female" committees such as health or social services. A desire to break out of these roles and gain more prestigious "masculine" committee assignments can lead to the disavowal of gender ("I'm a politician not a woman") (Sawer 2000:374).

Finally, as members of political parties, female politicians are beholden to party stances on various issues. Indeed, for many issues relevant to women, party differences may be greater than differences between men and women. Many studies of male and female legislators have demonstrated that women tend toward the **political left**, prioritize women's issues more highly, and espouse feminist ideals more often than men. But much of the difference between men and women disappears if political party is taken into account. So, for example, women may tend to support women's issues, such as public funding for day care or equality between the sexes, more than the men of their own party. However, the men of left parties may espouse more support for such issues than the women of parties on the

political right (Burrell 1994:160–1; Dolan 1997; Swers 1998, 2002a; Tremblay 1993).

Still, having more women in politics unquestionably makes the government more receptive to the interests of most women. Advocates of substantive representation therefore argue that not only must the numbers of women in politics increase but those women must also receive support when they attempt to act for women's interests. For example, women's caucuses can help achieve substantive representation by supporting women and providing them with resources. As an example, the bipartisan U.S. Congressional Caucus for Women's Issues adopts legislative priorities, plans strategies to move women's issues forward, and links like-minded congressional members to each other and to outside groups. Some advocates of substantive representation argue that rather than simply electing women to political office voters should elect feminists, either women or men, who are more likely to be directly supportive of women's interests (Tremblay and Pelletier 2000).

But can female politicians represent all women? Women are not just women—they are women of a particular race, ethnicity, religion, class, sexual orientation, or linguistic group. Although women's unique relationship to reproduction and the family cuts across all other social categories, women are not a monolithic group. The interests of a woman from a lower class may be different from those of a woman from an upper class. The problem arises when the women who attain political power are of only certain classes, races, or ethnicities—when they are elite women. For example, all 18 women currently serving in the Israeli Knesset are Jewish (not Arab) (A. Ben-Arieh, personal communication, December 21, 2005). Therefore, it is vital to ask whether these female politicians can represent all women, or whether they can represent only rich, or White, or Western interests. We return to this critical issue at the end of this chapter.

Utility Arguments for Women's Representation

Arguments for why women should be represented in politics are not restricted to justice arguments. Other arguments focus on the utility, or usefulness, of having women represented in politics. These arguments can be divided into two types: the argument that increasing women's participation improves the quality of representation and deliberation and the argument that visible women in politics act as role models for younger women.

Including women in politics can increase the quality of political decision making. When women are included among potential politicians, it doubles the pool of talent and ability from which leaders can be drawn. When women are not included, valuable human resources are wasted (Norderval

1985:84). Without women's full participation in politics, political decision making will be of lower quality than it could be or should be.

The quality of political decision making should also increase with greater inclusion of women because including women increases the overall diversity of ideas, values, priorities, and political styles. Introducing women to the political realm should introduce new ideas because women have different interests. In his philosophical work, John Stuart Mill (1859, 1861) argued that allowing diverse and competing views in the marketplace of ideas helps societies determine what is true and what is not true. If certain ideas are not allowed in the marketplace, then they cannot be proven right and used to change policy, or proven wrong and used to bolster existing ideas.

Diversity is certainly good in and of itself, but it should also make political decision making more flexible and capable of change. The analogy here is to diversity of species in ecological niches. Biologists know that ecological niches dominated by a single species are more vulnerable to changes in the environment than niches with a diversity of species. In a similar manner, having only the ideas and perspectives of men represented in a country's polity could make a country less flexible to changes in its internal or international environment.

A final utility argument is that female political leaders act as role models for young girls and women. Having a visible presence of women in positions of leadership helps to raise the aspirations of other women (Burrell 1994:173; Campbell and Wolbrecht 2006; Mansbridge 1999; Wolbrecht and Campbell 2005). For example, High-Pippert and Comer (1998) found that women in the United States who were represented by a woman reported more interest in politics than did women who were represented by a man. In Uganda, following the implementation of a law requiring that women make up at least 30% of local councils, women also began participating more in community events (Johnson, Kabuchu, and Vusiya Kayonga 2003). Alternatively, if groups are excluded from politics, this creates the perception that persons in these groups are "not fit to rule" (Mansbridge 1999:649). Without the presence of women in politics, there are no role models to inspire the next generation.

A female legislator from Central Europe puts it well:

Because of cultural differences women often have different experiences and different views on certain issues. That means that as women move into previously male-dominated positions, new perspective and new competence are added. . . . The presence of women in parliament means new skills and different styles in politics. . . . It also brings a new vision, which ultimately leads to revision of laws in order to improve existing ones. Most of all, they [women] serve as role models for future generations. (Inter-Parliamentary Union 2000:41)

But women can hardly affect dominant political values if their numbers are small. If there are only a few women in a country's national legislature, they will be under pressure to behave like men. With only a few other women for support, any efforts by a woman legislator to raise a "women's issue" are likely to be denigrated, and the woman who raises them is likely to be marginalized. Some argue that women need to be at least a large minority to have an impact (Kanter 1977). In fact, the United Nations has stated that to make a difference women need to have a critical mass of at least 30% of a legislature.

Consider the view of a female politician from North Africa:

> The central committee of the RCD [Democratic Constitutional Rally] has included 21.3 percent women. The change is tangible. In meetings, when a woman speaks in favor of a proposal which concerns women, the applause is louder and more sustained, at least from her female colleagues. They can have a decisive influence during debates and on decisions. A significant percentage can sway a vote. (Inter-Parliamentary Union 2000:68)

We discuss critical mass and the impact of women in greater detail in Chapter 7.

A Brief Overview of Women's Participation in Politics

Women's modern-day participation in politics begins with the acquisition of voting rights (**suffrage**). The first country to fully enfranchise women, and the only country to give women's suffrage in the 19th century, was New Zealand in 1893. In 1902, Australia was the second country to give women's suffrage and was followed by a variety of Western and Eastern European states. By 1945, 46% of the world's countries allowed women to vote. Today, only a single country, Saudi Arabia, allows men to vote but not women. We discuss the fight for women's suffrage in detail in Chapter 2.

Today, the average percentage of women in national legislatures around the world is 16% (Inter-Parliamentary Union 2005a). There is substantial variation across nations, however. Table 1.1 presents a sample of countries and their world rank in female representation in parliament. As discussed earlier, Rwanda currently has the highest percentage of women in its national legislature, followed by Sweden in the second position. Cuba is tied with Spain at seventh in the world (36%), followed closely by Costa Rica and Mozambique. Iraq, under its new constitution, is ranked 15th in the world in women's representation with 31.6%. The United Kingdom and the United States are in the middle of the world rankings, 52nd and 61st, respectively. Toward the bottom, we find Brazil and India, with 8.6% and 8.3% women in their legislatures, and Turkey, ranked 115th with 4.4% women. Kuwait and Micronesia are among the countries tied in 128th position for having no women in their national legislatures.

Table 1.1   World Rankings for Women in Parliament for Select Countries, 2005

Rank	Country	% Women
1	Rwanda	48.8
2	Sweden	45.3
3	Norway	38.2
4	Finland	37.5
5	Denmark	36.9
6	Netherlands	36.7
7	Cuba	36.0
7	Spain	36.0
8	Costa Rica	35.1
9	Mozambique	34.8
10	Belgium	34.7
15	Iraq	31.6
19	New Zealand	28.3
20	Vietnam	27.3
21	Namibia	26.9
26	Australia	24.7
27	Mexico	24.2
41	China	20.2
42	Poland	20.2
52	United Kingdom	18.1
61	United States	15.2
62	Israel	15.0
66	Ireland	13.3
72	France	12.2
79	Botswana	11.1
82	Zimbabwe	10.7
89	Russian Federation	9.8
95	Brazil	8.6
97	India	8.3
102	Japan	7.1
115	Turkey	4.4
116	Iran	4.1
122	Egypt	2.9
128	Kuwait	0
128	Micronesia	0

The sampling of rankings in Table 1.1 demonstrates that highly ranked countries can come from any region. For example, the top 10 countries come from Africa, Europe, and Latin America. But regional difference in women's representation, on average, is still a reality. Table 1.2 shows how the percentage of seats held by women in national legislatures (**lower** and **upper houses**) varies by region. As would be expected from the rankings, Scandinavia has the highest average rate of female participation, followed by the Americas (which includes the United States) and Europe. Other regions have averages below the worldwide average, for example, Asia, sub-Saharan Africa, and countries in the Pacific. The Middle East has the lowest levels of women's participation of any region.

Currently, 11 countries have no women in their national legislature. Four of these countries are in the Middle East—Saudi Arabia, Bahrain, the United Arab Emirates, and Kuwait. It would not be expected that women would be well represented in these countries, as women do not have the vote in Saudi Arabia and only gained the vote in Bahrain in 2002 and Kuwait in May 2005. In the United Arab Emirates, neither men nor women can vote. The other six countries without women in their national legislature are all small Asian-Pacific island nations—the Solomon Islands, Micronesia, Nauru, Palau, Tonga, and Tuvalu. Of these, Micronesia and Palau have never had women represented in their national legislatures. The others have had women before, up to 8% in Tuvalu.

Women are less well represented as heads of government or in high-level appointed offices, such as cabinet ministers. There are currently seven female heads of government around the world: Helen Clark, prime minister of New Zealand; Gloria Macapagal-Arroyo, president of the Philippines; Khaleda Zia, prime minister of Bangladesh; Ellen Johnson-Sirleaf, president of Liberia; Angela Merkel, chancellor of Germany; Michelle Bachelet, president of Chile; and Portia Simpson-Miller, prime minister of Jamaica. Unfortunately, in several of these cases, the female leader gained legitimacy

Table 1.2   Regional Percentages of Women in Parliament, 2005

Region	Single House or Lower House	Upper House or Senate	Both Houses Combined
Scandinavia	39.9%	—	39.9%
Americas	18.8%	19.5%	18.9%
Europe	16.9%	16.9%	16.9%
Asia	15.2%	13.5%	15.1%
Sub-Saharan Africa	15.0%	14.2%	14.9%
Pacific	11.2%	26.5%	13.3%
Arab States	8.8%	5.6%	8.1%

because a male relative previously held the top position in the country. In those countries, there are few women in the national legislature, suggesting that these are mainly figurehead women. We return to the issue of women in leadership positions, as well as women in parliaments, in Chapter 3.

Orienting Theories

Before continuing with our exploration of women in politics around the world, it is important to first introduce a number of key concepts and theories that we use throughout this volume. To understand women in politics, we must understand power, gender, and the interaction between the two.

Power

Sociologists often use a classic definition of *power* developed by Max Weber: the ability to impose one's will on others, even in the face of opposition. Specifically, Weber argued that "'power' is the probability that one actor within a social relationship will be in a position to carry out his own will despite resistance, regardless of the basis on which this probability rests" (Weber 1978:53). According to this definition, power is a valued resource that cannot be held by all. If one person has power, another does not. Power is overt—applied directly and visibly.

However, theorists do not agree on the proper way to define or conceptualize power, and scholars such as Michel Foucault, Antonio Gramsci, C. Wright Mills, and Talcott Parsons have debated the nature of power for decades. Although we do not discuss the various definitions and debates here, we do suggest that in the field of women in politics, it may be especially important to conceptualize power in a way that accounts for ways of exercising power that are less visible or overt. Thus, we employ a three-fold definition of power developed by Stephen Lukes (1974), who is also especially useful because his work specifically addresses primarily political (rather than economic) components of power. In short, Lukes's definition includes three dimensions:

- Dimension 1: prevailing in a conflict over overt political preferences
- Dimension 2: preventing the preferences of others from reaching the agenda
- Dimension 3: shaping the preferences of others to match yours

First, Lukes (1974) agrees with Weber that in some cases, power is explicit and direct. But he distinguishes a particular form of direct power often termed the *pluralist view*, which follows the work of theorists such as Robert A. Dahl and Nelson Polsby. This first, one-dimensional view of power focuses on actual and observable behavior, decision making, and conflict. We can evaluate the first dimension of political power by looking at the policy preferences, and political participation of legislators or other actors, how they behave, and who prevails (p. 15).

The second dimension of power involves preventing the preferences of others from even reaching the agenda. This dimension is developed partly as a critique of the first dimension's focus on observable decisions, arguing that, alternatively, power can be exercised by setting limits on the scope of decision making to include only certain issues. According to this perspective, demands for change can sometimes be "suffocated before they are even voiced; or kept covert; or killed before they gain access to the relevant decision-making arena; or, failing all these things, maimed or destroyed in the decision-implementing stage of the policy process" (Bachrach and Baratz 1970:44, cited in Lukes 1974:19). This dimension of power can include a variety of mechanisms for controlling the agenda, including agenda setting, influence, authority, and manipulation.

Finally, Lukes (1974) introduces a third dimension of power that supplements both of the first two dimensions. The third dimension, unlike the first two, recognizes that one person may exercise power over another not only by getting the person to do what he or she does not want to do but also by influencing or shaping what the person even wants. The mechanisms of this process include the control of information, mass media, and socialization. This dimension allows us to recognize that perhaps "the most effective and insidious use of power is to prevent conflict from arising in the first place" (p. 23). Lukes acknowledges that this dimension is the hardest to study, but in the case of women's political power it is especially important to try to understand.

Before we finish our discussion of power, it is important to go beyond Lukes's dimensions, which compare the power of one actor or group over another, to consider the social structure in which individuals and groups operate. Structural theorists argue that power does not come just from an individual's or group's intrinsic qualities but from the roles and social relationships that structure power relations. For example, in schools, the structure of the education system creates an uneven distribution of power between teachers and students who each have a different set of social powers (Isaac 1987, cited in Hayward 2000). Other structural theorists have pointed to the importance of individuals or norms outside of the immediate relationship that contribute to the power of one side (e.g., Wartenberg 1990, 1992). For example, the teacher–student power relation is affected by parents, university admissions officers, and companies who take cues from the teacher. The teacher's power is thus reinforced by these other actors. A teacher's power is also reinforced by social norms—for example, expectations that he or she will be addressed formally, with the title Mr. or Ms. Similarly, when thinking about women in politics, one must think about how women's power relations are affected by political parties, pressure groups, cultural beliefs, and even global forces.

Addressing gendered power directly, feminist theorists further emphasize the process of personal transformation as a form of power—power within rather than power over. That is, when women, or men, come to better understand themselves and their position in an unequal world, they can be inspired to challenge gender inequality (Kabeer 1994; Rowlands 1997). And feminist theorists stress the ability to work collectively with others as another form of power—power with others to bring about political change (Kabeer 1994; Parpart, Rai, and Staudt 2002). A useful example of the dimensions of power and how they relate to gender appears in Box 1.1.

Box 1.1   Adam, Betsy, and the Cereal Power Struggle

To further understand the dimensions and structure of power, we discuss this simple example. Suppose there are two siblings named Adam and Betsy. Every week their mother allows them to pick one breakfast cereal at the grocery store that the two will then eat on weekday mornings before going to school. The first week, Adam decides that he wants the frosted O's, but Betsy really prefers the rice squares. While in the cereal aisle, Adam stands over Betsy and tells her that because he is bigger he should get what he wants. Even though Betsy still wants the rice squares, she agrees, and the family goes home with the frosted O's. In this example, Adam has one-dimensional power over Betsy.

Before the family's next trip to the store, however, Adam begins to worry that his sister may put up a fight the next week to get the rice squares. But while eating his frosted O's the following morning, Adam finds a solution—a coupon on his frosted O's box for $1 off wheat flakes, chocolate grahams, or frosted O's. He clips the coupon off of the box and takes it to his mother. When the family goes to the store, the mother sends Adam and Betsy down the cereal aisle with the coupon. Faced with the choice of only three cereals, Betsy cannot get her rice squares, so she again acquiesces to her brother's will, and the family goes home with frosted O's. In this case Adam has exercised two-dimensional power, preventing rice squares from even entering the realm of decision making.

(Continued)

(Continued)

Later that day, Adam is very nervous. He looked at the frosted O's box, and this time there is no coupon. He is sure that after 2 weeks of frosted O's, Betsy might finally get her way. So Adam devises a plan. Over the next week, while watching television with his sister, every time the commercial for frosted O's comes on the TV, he proclaims, "Mmmmmm, frosted O's. Those look soooo good." And every morning as he walks to school with his sister, he hums the song from the frosted O's commercial. The next week at the grocery store, standing in the cereal aisle, Adam begins to hum the song from the frosted O's commercial. "Yum, those frosted O's are good," he says. Betsy replies, "Hmmm. Let's get frosted O's again. They are so good!" In this example, Adam exercised three-dimensional power over his sister Betsy.

Faced with this example, structural theorists would likely argue that it is not just the interaction between Adam and Betsy that is important for understanding power. One must consider their roles within the larger social structure that is their family. For example, as the older brother, Adam may believe that he knows what is best for his sister, and Betsy is used to looking to her older brother for advice and guidance. Thus, the power is not just a function of Adam's forceful or scheming ways but also is grounded in the older brother–younger sister relationship of Adam and Betsy.

Finally, it is important to consider why this situation did not play out differently. When threatened by her brother the first week at the grocery store, why did Betsy not put up a fight? Why did Betsy not pick up a box of breakfast bars and throw them at Adam, demanding that the family buy the rice squares? To understand this question, we have to consider who Adam and Betsy are and how they were raised. What messages have they received from their parents, their teachers, and the outside environment about how to behave properly? To understand Adam and Betsy, we must talk about gender.

Gender and Gender Stratification

Any discussion of gender usually begins by distinguishing sex and gender. *Sex* typically refers to biological differences between men and women, whereas *gender* refers to socially constructed differences between men and women. Why do we prefer to talk about gender instead of sex? Because sex is typically not socially interesting. Gender is. Think about comparing Hillary Clinton, senator from New York since 2000, to a male senator. What difference does it make that Hillary Clinton is a woman? Answering the question by pointing to obvious physiological differences between Senator Clinton and the male senator will not get one very far (D'Amico and Beckman 1995). What interests us is Senator Clinton's socially constructed gender: Does her gendered upbringing lead her to have different attitudes than men? Will she adhere to or break out of the roles and behaviors expected of her? What stereotypes will other senators, or the public, bring to bear in evaluating her performance?

So what is gender? To begin, gender is difference. Even though human beings are among the least sexually dimorphous of species, most cultures actively work to distinguish men and women through dress, ornamentation, and exaggeration of physiological differences (Lorber 2003). Similarly, gender character traits are often defined in opposition so that if a particular trait, such as aggressiveness, is attributed to one gender, it is typically determined to be lacking in the other. Men and women are polar opposite sexes. In Western cultures, we often find male–female pairings, such as rational–emotional, aggressive–passive, competitive–cooperative, or assertive–compliant (D'Amico and Beckman 1995:3).

Gender is created. Gender characteristics are cultural creations that get passed on from generation to generation through socialization. From birth, individuals are taught their gender. For example, today in the United States, infant girls are dressed in pink and described as cute or adorable, whereas male infants are dressed in blue and described as big or strong. Children begin to refer to themselves as members of their gender as soon as they learn to speak (Lorber 2003). When moving from infancy to childhood, toddlers are encouraged to move from baby to either big boy or a big girl. Researchers point out that these categories mean different things—in the United States, boys are taught to manipulate their surrounding environment using strength, whereas little girls learn the importance of physical appearance (Cahill 1986; West and Zimmerman 1987). And during playtime in the Philippines, girls enact mother-child scenarios and play house (*bahay-bahayan*) but are cautioned against boys' games, such as ball games (*larong bola*) and wandering about (*paggala-gala*) (Sobritchea 1990). Throughout childhood, parents and other authority figures often interact with children differently based on sex, encouraging appropriate gendered behavior while discouraging transgressive behavior. As Simone de Beauvoir said, "One is not born, but rather becomes, a woman; it is civilization as a whole that produces this creature which is described as feminine" (1952:267 cited in Lorber 2003).

Gender is recreated. We "do gender" by constantly creating and recreating it in our interactions with each other (West and Zimmerman 1987). We behave like a man or a woman, thereby practicing being a man or a woman every day. Thus, gender is not complete when a young person is fully socialized; instead it must be practiced on a daily basis. Grown individuals are not socialized robots. They are active agents who choose to display, perform, and assert their gender in any given interaction (Martin 2004). But choice is constrained—if someone chooses not to "do" gender appropriately, then he or she will likely be sanctioned (West and Zimmerman 1987:146). The sum of countless individual displays of gender across social interactions creates an overarching gendered social landscape and helps to maintain a conception of gender difference as normal and natural.

But gender is not fixed. Gender varies across countries and over time and even within a single woman's lifetime. The characteristics or behaviors expected of women in one country may be very different from those expected of women in another (Costa, Terracciano, and McCrae 2001). What it means to be a man or woman has also changed over time (Connell 1987:64). Hansen (1994) demonstrated that in the 19th century men as well as women made quilts and wrote passionate letters to each other. A century ago, women were not meant to participate in politics, whereas today they are presidents and prime ministers. The meaning of gender can even change dramatically within a single person's lifetime. Over a 50-year period in the United States, men began to take care of children and even stay at home. Women have succeeded in occupations that were considered inappropriate to their nature 75 years ago.

Gender can be hard to notice. Because people are socialized to perform gender since infancy and because they recreate gender on a daily basis, people often take gender for granted (Lorber 2003). Gender is a part of everything people do. But because gender is internalized, people often do not notice its impact on their perceptions or actions. Therefore, gender can be a powerful background identity that colors people's judgments about one another in very subtle ways (Ridgeway 2001). Because gender is in the background, people may consciously focus on more obvious characteristics of a person's personality or actions without noticing that, unconsciously, they are bringing gender assumptions into their evaluations. Thinking back to the previous section and our discussion of three-dimensional power, it is important to consider forces that may shape a person's perceptions, actions, and desires without the person's knowledge.

Gender is an institution. Like other institutions, gender is a persistent and pervasive social form that orders human activity (Acker 1992; Martin 2004). It is an overarching system of social practices for making men and women different in socially significant ways (Ridgeway and Smith-Lovin 1999). A set of social positions is defined by gender and characterized by rules for conduct and procedures for interactions. Gender has a legitimating ideology that constrains and facilitates behavior on the part of individuals. Gender is tightly linked to other institutions, such as the family, the economy, and education. Conceiving of gender as an institution helps to highlight power and the unequal allocation of resources, privilege, and opportunities (Acker 1992; Martin 2004; Risman 2004).

Gender is ranked. Gender is a socially constructed relationship of inequality where the gender categories of male and female are linked to unequal prestige and power (D'Amico and Beckman 1995). The gender differences created and maintained through socialization, everyday performance, and social practice are not neutral but instead create unequal power relationships and ultimately translate into omnipresent gender hierarchy. Gender as rank crosscuts all other social categories—wealthy, powerful women are disadvantaged compared to wealthy, powerful men.

Gender and Power Concepts: Patriarchy, Public Versus Private, and Intersectionality

So far we have discussed how gender is both institutionalized and ranked. The combination of these factors means that, worldwide, women have less power than men do. Women's lower levels of power and status can be described in many ways, but common terms include *gender stratification, gender inequality, female disadvantage, sexism,* and *patriarchy* (Chafetz 1990). Patriarchy is a term used to describe the social system of male domination over females, where male domination is built into the social, political, and economic institutions of society. Patriarchal societies are characterized by male control of economic resources, male domination of political processes and positions of authority, and male entitlement to sexual services. According to the feminist perspective, though some societies are more patriarchal than others, all modern societies have a patriarchal structure.

Women's power relative to men varies not only across cultures but within societies as well. Specifically, under patriarchy women almost always have more power in the home than in political or economic environments outside of family life. To distinguish between these domains, we use the terms **public sphere** and **private sphere**. Throughout history and in many societies in the modern world, it is considered natural or proper for women's concerns to be in the home, or the private sphere. Women may still lack control over important decisions regarding how resources should be allocated within the home, but the private sphere is generally considered a female domain. According to this perspective, women should be focused on their family and children and making their husbands happy.

One form of this belief, the Cult of True Womanhood, was present in the United States during the 1800s. According to this ideal, women's proper behavior involved four virtues: piety, purity, submissiveness, and domesticity. Clearly none of these virtues suggested that women should engage in public political participation or try to run for office. Instead, women were encouraged to assist the church, a task that did not threaten to take women away from their proper sphere or make women less domestic or submissive. If any woman wanted more than the four virtues, she was thought to be tampering with society, undermining civilization, and unwomanly. For example, early women's activists such as Mary Wollstonecraft, Francis Wright, and Harriet Martineau were considered "semi-women" or "mental hermaphrodites" (Welter 1966).

Although it is clear that women have been oppressed throughout history, some people may think patriarchy is an outdated concept. Over the past few decades, women across a wide range of societies have made remarkable gains in literacy, life expectancy, education, the labor force, and control over reproduction. For instance, in the United States women were once excluded from the most prestigious universities but now often outnumber men. Around the world, professional and managerial classes are now composed of both men and women. And in some countries men are taking on more responsibilities in the home. So do men really still dominate, oppress, and exploit women?

Michael Mann (1986) argues that though gender inequality still exists, patriarchy is an outdated concept. Mann's reasoning is that patriarchy is fundamentally based on a male-dominated household. And as gender roles have changed over time, public and private boundaries between men and women have dissolved. But feminist theorists have countered that patriarchy is not just about public/private distinctions. The concept of patriarchy posits that there is "systematically structured gender inequality" (Walby 1996:28). And as the household form of patriarchy diminishes, other forms of patriarchy arise (Walby 1996). Although women may now work alongside men, in the United States they still earn 80 cents to every male dollar, and this figure has not changed in 20 years (General Accounting Office 2003). And in relation to the state and policy, politics is not only historically a male institution, but it also continues to be "dominated by men and symbolically interpreted from the standpoint of men in leading positions" (Acker 1992:567).

The public/private distinction has also received criticism from researchers focusing on non-Western countries. In many African countries, for example, women engage in economic activities outside of the home, such as trade; women and men often both have control over household finances; and women form collectives with one another for mutual benefit (Staudt 1986). Many of the public/private distinctions that do exist in these African countries came about during colonialism, when Western powers engaged in trade solely with men, undercutting female influence. Thus, although women across the world have less power than men do in the public realm, there are still important cultural distinctions to keep in mind.

When talking about women in Africa and other countries of the **global south** (formerly known as the Third World), feminists often point out that these women must manage multiple forms of disadvantage or oppression. Not only do they suffer the universal subordination shared by women across the world, but also they must contend with living in poorer or less-developed countries. Therefore, to reiterate the discussion in the earlier section on women's substantive representation, it is important to realize that, although women may share a common identity grounded in reproduction or status, they are not a monolithic group. Women have differential amounts of power based on factors such as region, class, religion, race, and ethnicity.

When talking about these multiple sources of power or disadvantage, feminists use the term **intersectionality** (Crenshaw 1991; Hill Collins 2000; hooks 2000). The idea of intersecting disadvantage is useful because it is difficult to average or add up the situation of being a racial, ethnic, or religious minority and the situation of being a woman to equal the experience of being a minority woman. Nor can you privilege either gender or minority status as the defining category for identity (Hancock 2005). Intersectionality research asks one to consider that women who are also poor, minority, or from the global south face multiple sources of oppression that may not combine in simple ways.

Earlier in this chapter, we introduced the work of feminist political theorists who argue that gender-neutral terms such as *individual* or *citizen* actually signify White males. Similarly, intersectionality researchers find that statements about women as citizens, activists, or politicians are often truly statements about White women, whereas research on minorities focuses on minority men. But as Kimberlé Crenshaw (1994) articulated, "[W]omen of color experience racism in ways not always the same as those experienced by men of color, and sexism in ways not always parallel to experiences of white women" (p. 99). And politically, women may be situated in multiple groups that pursue conflicting agendas (Crenshaw 1994). Without focusing on the intersections of disadvantage, the unique obstacles faced by minority women seeking rights, opportunities, or representation may simply be ignored altogether.

Throughout this volume, we attempt to incorporate research on women at the intersection of a wide variety of social positions. For instance, we discuss how across many countries, White women received political rights before women of color (see Chapter 2). In our discussion of the impact of female legislators, we consider how the underrepresentation of minority women may lead to policies that marginalize women of color (see Chapter 7). In discussing the United States, we highlight differences in the voting behavior and political participation of women across class and minority status (see Chapter 9). And in Chapter 5 we introduce the story of the first trans-sexual member of parliament in New Zealand.

But our efforts to present information about women at the intersections of disadvantage are also complicated by the fact that countries and political parties do not keep good records of the race, ethnicity, and class backgrounds of their politicians. We may know that a country has 10% women in its parliament, but we do not know whether those women are all of one ethnic group or caste. Although we have little information about the race, ethnicity, religion, and social class of female legislators across the world, having more women should increase the chance that the range of views across women is replicated in the political arena (Kanter 1977). But it is appropriate to end our discussion by highlighting the importance of keeping difference among women in mind, even when we are unable to directly talk about it.

2

Women Struggle for the Vote

The History of Women's Suffrage

It requires philosophy and heroism to rise above the opinion of the wise men of all nations and races.

—Elizabeth Cady Stanton

Today in the United States, women vote in federal, state, and local elections more often than their male counterparts. For example, according to the U.S. Census Bureau, more than 11 million more women than men voted in the 2004 presidential election. During campaigns, non-partisan organizations seek to increase women's registration and turnout, political pundits talk about the influential vote of groups such as "soccer moms" and "security moms," and candidates and political parties develop strategies designed to address women's interests. And women's importance as a group of voters is not unique to the United States. Countries such as Barbados, Chile, Finland, Malta, and the United Kingdom all have witnessed women turning out in higher numbers than men in recent elections (International Institute for Democracy and Electoral Assistance 2005). In fact, women have been an important force since they began voting. In the first election after women in New Zealand were granted the right to vote in 1893, 78% of women voted compared with 69% of men (Catt 1918).

Today, people often take for granted that women have the right to vote, but this was not the case across the globe just a century ago. Since the time of the world's first democracy in ancient Greece through the mid-1800s, political thinkers excluded women from notions of citizenship and male law-makers from extensions of democratic rights. Politics was the domain of men, and women were thought to lack the qualities and capabilities necessary for equal citizenship. Furthermore, religious doctrine or practice and cultural traditions regarding women's proper place in society served as barriers to women's political participation (see Chapter 5). It was only following decades of struggle that women in many countries achieved **suffrage**, or the right to vote. The enfranchisement of women was the primary goal of **first-wave feminism**, which generally covers the time from the late 19th through the early 20th century. The term *first wave* is used to distinguish early women's movements from the women's liberation movements of the 1960s and 1970s. Although women in many countries won the right to vote during feminism's first wave, in parts of the world the struggle continues.

At the beginning of this chapter, Box 2.1 introduces three important theoretical concepts used in research on social movements to provide for a better understanding of the struggle for female suffrage. The chapter itself begins the exploration of the struggle for women's suffrage with the U.S. case. Because the struggle for female enfranchisement is one of the largest and well documented in the United States, we discuss at length the progression of the suffrage movement in America. First, we discuss how the American political system evolved from the colonial period to formally exclude women from voting. We then discuss the political activity of women during the Progressive Era, stressing the importance of women's connections to other social movements of the period. We also apply the concepts of social movement theory to understand why state suffrage movements experienced quite different outcomes. Finally, we outline the events leading up to the extension of the franchise to women at the national level through the 19th Amendment of the U.S. Constitution. Following the detailed discussion of the U.S. case, we address how other suffrage movements around the world compare with those of the United States across a number of dimensions, including movement size, ideology, and tactics. We conclude with a discussion of the international women's movement and struggles for suffrage following World War II.

Box 2.1   Social Movement Concepts

To better understand the struggle for women's suffrage, we borrow a few important concepts from the study of social movements. In recent years, scholars in this field have come to agree that there are at least three interdependent factors that affect the emergence and development of social movements: resource mobilization, framing processes, and political opportunities (McAdam, McCarthy, and Zald 1996). First, **resource mobilization** refers to the ability of social movement participants to organize and effectively use both financial and human resources to their benefit. Resource mobilization often refers to the organizational structure of the movement, including the number and size of organizations, ties to other social movements, the skill level of leadership, the movement's ability to raise funds, or the varied tactical strategies used by movement actors. Resource mobilization research has shown that disrupting public order can often be a successful tactic for social movements (Gamson 1990; Jenkins 1983; McAdam 1983).

Second, a social movement is often a struggle over meanings and beliefs. Individuals participate in social movements because they are dissatisfied with some aspect of their lives or surroundings and believe that they can promote change through organized group effort. Therefore, one should not ignore the psychological, cognitive, or ideational components of movement participation. To address this area, movement scholars use the concept of **framing processes**. *Framing* refers to the "conscious strategic efforts by groups of people to fashion shared understandings of the world and of themselves that legitimate and motivate collective action" (McAdam et al. 1996:6). From a strategic standpoint, movement leaders and activists often seek to link their ideals to popular or widely held beliefs to expand the support for their cause.

Finally, the origin, development, and outcome of a social movement are shaped by the wider context in which the movement operates. Changes that are favorable for movement advancement or success and occur in the broader environment are termed **political opportunities**. Looking across regions or countries, different political systems or environments may also be more or less open to social movement activity, resulting in a different political opportunity structure. For example, authoritarian governments may be more likely to suppress movement activity than democracies, making it more likely that movements will develop and grow in democratic systems. In addition, how politicians are elected in democratic systems may make them more or less responsive to the pressure exerted by social movements. Although the structure of political opportunities is sometimes defined narrowly in terms of the interaction between social movements and institutionalized politics, it is also often applied more generally. For example, suffrage researchers have argued that changing gender relations can create gendered opportunities (McCammon et al. 2001). According to movement scholar Doug McAdam (1982), a shift in political opportunities is "*any* event or broad social process that serves to undermine the calculations and assumptions on which the political establishment is structured" (p. 41).

Suffrage in the United States

Female Suffrage and the U.S. Constitution

As Thomas Jefferson penned the famous words, "All men are created equal," the right to vote in most American colonies was not based on sex but on land ownership. Thus, in some colonies, such as Massachusetts and Connecticut, female property holders did have voting privileges. However, the Declaration of Independence enshrined the belief that governing was a male activity, that "governments are instituted among Men, deriving their just powers from the consent of the governed." At the time there was no organized women's movement in America, and the founding fathers of the United States were able to largely avoid the discussion of women's rights (Kelber 1994).

Despite the overall absence of a women's movement during this period, a small number of prominent women were arguing for women's rights. For example, in March 1776, Abigail Adams wrote to her husband in the Continental Congress in Philadelphia, "In the new code of laws . . . I desire you would remember the ladies, and be more generous and favorable to them than your ancestors. Do not put such unlimited power into the hands of husbands. Remember, all men would be tyrants if they could." She followed this statement with the first threat of female revolt for the denial of suffrage: "If particular care and attention are not paid to the ladies, we are determined to foment a rebellion, and will not hold ourselves bound to obey any laws in which we have no voice or representation" (Stanton, Anthony, and Gage 1887:32). Unfortunately, however, her pleas went unheeded. Her husband, future U.S. President John Adams, replied, "Depend upon it, we know better than to repeal our Masculine systems" (Kelber 1994:3). Women's struggle for suffrage in the United States had just begun.

Although the Constitution did not extend suffrage to women, it also did not preclude it. Whereas the Declaration of Independence used gendered terms such as *men*, the Constitution was more inclusive, using the term *persons*. After the Constitution was ratified, women's suffrage was still somewhat of an open question. From 1776 to 1807, for example, women had the right to vote under the New Jersey Constitution. Ironically, it was the extension of the vote to former slaves under the 14th and 15th Amendments that first codified women's exclusion from voting in the U.S. Constitution. Although the 14th Amendment established the universality of U.S. citizenship for "all persons born or naturalized in the United States," it then set up penalties against states that denied the right to vote to significant numbers of adult male citizens. Thus, women were considered citizens but denied inclusion in the electorate. When it became clear that the 14th Amendment would be insufficient to force the rebel states of the Confederacy to grant votes to freed slaves, the 15th Amendment was introduced. Ratified in 1869, the 15th Amendment authorized congressional action to guard against disfranchisements by the states on the basis of "race, color or previous condition of servitude." Once again, women were excluded.

Women and Progressive Movements: The Struggle Begins

Although women generally spent their time and energy maintaining their homes and families during the 18th and 19th centuries, women also increasingly worked outside of mainstream channels to influence government. Women participated in crowd actions, circulated petitions, founded reform organizations, and lobbied legislatures. Women often concentrated their efforts on matters connected to the well-being of the home, family, children, women, and the community (Baker 1994). Yet even on these issues, some argued women should abstain from public participation. As one lady's journal stated in 1847, "It is woman's mission. Let her not look away from her own little family circle for the means of producing moral and social reforms, but begin at home" (Arthur 1847:178, cited in Welter 1966:163).

Despite perceptions about women's "proper place," women were active participants in the abolitionist (antislavery) movement. And in the early 20th century, the fight for women's suffrage became aligned with the Progressive Movement. The Progressive Movement was a response to the dramatic changes that were taking place in American society during the latter half of the 19th century. The frontier had been tamed, cities began to sprawl, and powerful men like Andrew Carnegie and John D. Rockefeller had risen to dominate the business world. Yet not all citizens shared in the country's new wealth and prestige. In response, social activists undertook the reform of working conditions, sought to humanize the treatment of mentally ill people and prisoners, and worked to outlaw the consumption of alcohol, perceived as a central cause of society's problems.

The importance of women's participation in the reform movements of the 19th and 20th centuries for the rise of female suffrage cannot be underestimated. From a resource mobilization perspective, suffragists not only gained experience through participating in other movements, but they could draw on the financial and organizational resources of other progressive organizations. In Montana, for example, women's suffrage and temperance groups were successful allies in the fight for suffrage (Cole 1990). However, the presumed alliance between women's suffrage and prohibition movements also caused the suffrage movement to inherit many enemies, including organized liquor interests and retail saloon operators. By analyzing the voting patterns of men in referendums on suffrage, McDonagh and Price (1985) also found that German Catholics, whose culture was heavily tied to alcohol consumption, were more likely to oppose suffrage.

Early on, the themes of the antislavery movement led women to draw conclusions about their own status in society. Paradoxically, women's exclusion from full participation in the antislavery movement also served as a wake-up call. In 1840, two founders of the American suffrage movement, Lucretia Mott and Elizabeth Cady Stanton, traveled to London to attend an antislavery convention. After being denied the right to participate in the convention, the women decided that when they returned to America, they would organize a women's rights convention. They followed through in 1848 by organizing the **Seneca Falls Convention** in New York (see Figure 2.1). Three hundred women and men attended, and for the first time a formal demand was made in the United States for women's right to vote: "it is the duty of the women of this country to secure for themselves their sacred right to the elective franchise" (Stanton 1848).

The Leadership, Organization, and Tactics of the Early Suffrage Movement

The women's suffrage movement in the United States was spearheaded by a number of passionate and influential women. Two especially prominent women in the struggle for suffrage in the United States were Elizabeth Cady Stanton and Susan B. Anthony. Stanton and Anthony met in 1851 and quickly established a life-long friendship. As the better writer, Stanton crafted many of the pair's speeches, whereas Anthony focused on movement organization and tactics.

Stanton and Anthony fought for women's suffrage in a number of ways. In 1866, Elizabeth Cady Stanton tested women's right to stand for election by running for Congress, receiving 24 of 12,000 votes cast. And in 1872, Susan B. Anthony was arrested and stood trial for casting a Republican vote in the presidential election. In 1869, Stanton and Anthony founded the National Woman's Suffrage Association (NWSA). NWSA sought a federal

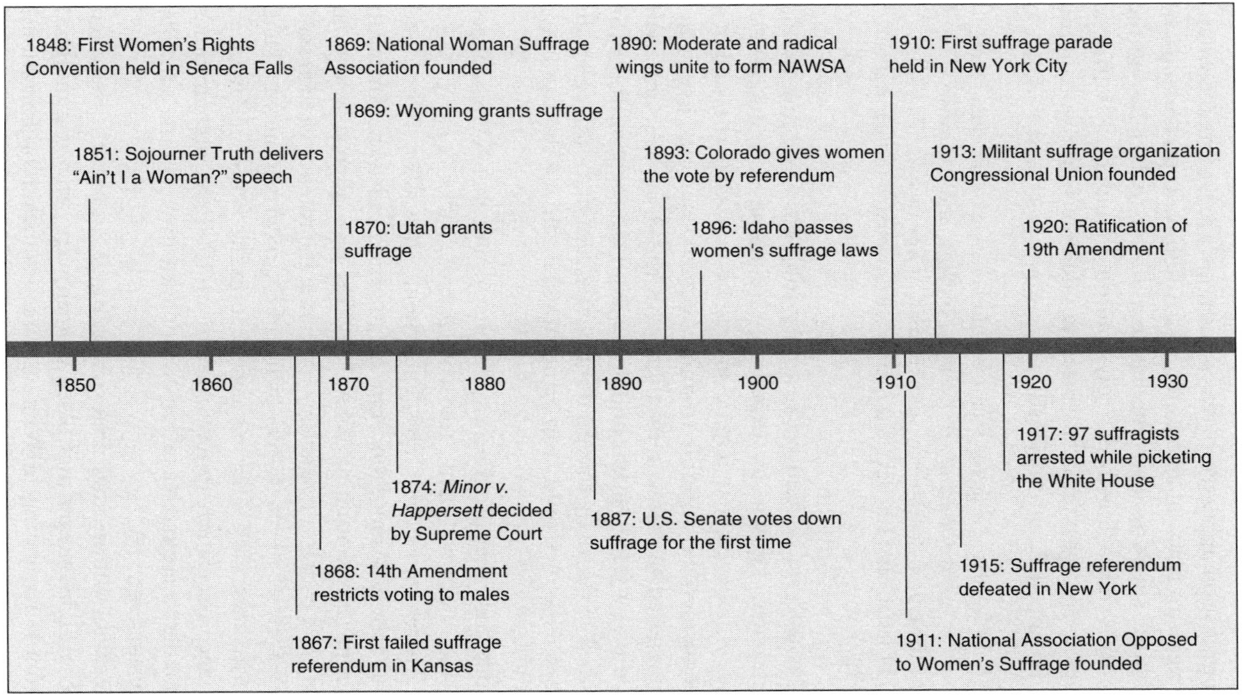

Figure 2.1 Timeline of the American Women's Suffrage Movement

1848: First Women's Rights Convention held in Seneca Falls

1851: Sojourner Truth delivers "Ain't I a Woman?" speech

1869: National Woman Suffrage Association founded

1869: Wyoming grants suffrage

1870: Utah grants suffrage

1890: Moderate and radical wings unite to form NAWSA

1893: Colorado gives women the vote by referendum

1896: Idaho passes women's suffrage laws

1910: First suffrage parade held in New York City

1913: Militant suffrage organization Congressional Union founded

1920: Ratification of 19th Amendment

1867: First failed suffrage referendum in Kansas

1868: 14th Amendment restricts voting to males

1874: *Minor v. Happersett* decided by Supreme Court

1887: U.S. Senate votes down suffrage for the first time

1911: National Association Opposed to Women's Suffrage founded

1915: Suffrage referendum defeated in New York

1917: 97 suffragists arrested while picketing the White House

1850 1860 1870 1880 1890 1900 1910 1920 1930

constitutional amendment to guarantee women's suffrage, and in addition to advocating votes for women, NWSA also advocated easier divorce and an end to discrimination in employment and pay.

However, a gulf soon appeared between suffragists regarding the extension of voting rights to Black men. Stanton and Anthony accused abolitionist and Republican supporters of emphasizing Black civil rights at the expense of women's rights. Elizabeth Cady Stanton, though herself an abolitionist, expressed outrage that other races should receive the vote while White women remained disenfranchised:

> If Saxon men have legislated thus for their own mothers, wives and daughters, what can we hope for at the hands of Chinese, Indians, and Africans? . . . I protest against the enfranchisement of another man of any race or clime until the daughters of Jefferson, Hancock, and Adams are crowned with their rights. (hooks 1981:127)

NWSA was considered radical because they took on a "by any means necessary" approach, known as **expediency** (Giddings 1996:124–25). Movement leaders believed that female suffrage would cure the nation's ills. So it was considered justifiable to allow women's suffrage organizations to be segregated by race or to align with the Women's Christian Temperance Union (WCTU), even though the WCTU sought suffrage for vastly different reasons than the predominantly feminist suffragists in NWSA. In short, NWSA would stop at nothing to achieve the franchise for women.

But Lucy Stone and other prominent suffragists argued that NWSA tactics were too extreme, and civil rights for women and Blacks could proceed hand in hand. Therefore, later in 1869, Lucy Stone, Julia Ward Howe, and Josephine Ruffin formed a more moderate organization called the American Woman's Suffrage Association (AWSA). AWSA was aligned with the Republican Party and concentrated solely on securing the vote for women state by state. However, by 1890, the two branches of the movement were willing to put aside their differences. They merged to form the National American Woman's Suffrage Association (NAWSA), and in 1900 the organization's national headquarters were established in New York City under the direction of Carrie Chapman Catt.

Still, the tension within the women's suffrage movement between women's and civil rights meant that Black women were often marginalized or excluded from participating in White women's suffrage organizations. Southern White women were the most vehement in their opposition to Black women joining their organizations, but Northern White women also supported organizational segregation. Black women therefore often formed their own suffrage associations. By the 1900s, Black women suffrage clubs were active in Tuskegee, St. Louis, Los Angeles, Memphis, Boston, Charleston, and New Orleans (Giddings 1996).

Although White women outnumbered Black women in the suffrage movement (Chafetz and Dworkin 1986), a number of prominent Black women were active in the women's suffrage movement and questioned the exclusion of Black women. For instance, in 1851, Sojourner Truth gave a now famous speech titled "Ain't I a Woman?" (see Box 2.2). Abolitionists such as Harriet Tubman and Frances Ellen Harper were active in the movement, addressing women's suffrage meetings. And Ida Wells-Barnett, an antilynching crusader and journalist, challenged segregation in the women's movement. In a massive 1913 suffrage march, Wells-Barnett refused to march separately from White Chicago delegates (Giddings 1996).

It is also important to note that Black women were actually more likely to support universal suffrage following the Civil War than were White women (Giddings 1996). Black women viewed suffrage as the vehicle through which to gain influence with school boards and improve education. And because the majority of Black women worked, voting rights could allow Black women to seek labor protection legislation (Giddings 1996).

Box 2.2   "Ain't I a Woman?" by Sojourner Truth, 1851

Sojourner Truth was born Isabella Baumfree, one of 13 children of slave parents. When she was 29 years old, she ran away with her infant son after her third master reneged on a promise to free her. Seventeen years later, Isabella experienced a spiritual revelation, and changing her name to Sojourner Truth, began walking through Long Island and Connecticut preaching about God. Later, she began speaking about abolitionism and women's suffrage, drawing on her life experiences as a slave. In 1851, at the age of 54, she gave a now legendary speech at a women's convention in Akron, Ohio:

"Well, children, where there is so much racket there must be something out of kilter. I think that 'twixt the negroes of the South and the women at the North, all talking about rights, the white men will be in a fix pretty soon. But what's all this here talking about?

"That man over there says that women need to be helped into carriages, and lifted over ditches, and to have the best place everywhere. Nobody ever

(Continued)

(Continued)

helps me into carriages, or over mud-puddles, or gives me any best place! And ain't I a woman? Look at me! Look at my arm! I have ploughed and planted, and gathered into barns, and no man could head me! And ain't I a woman? I could work as much and eat as much as a man—when I could get it—and bear the lash as well! And ain't I a woman? I have borne thirteen children, and seen most all sold off to slavery, and when I cried out with my mother's grief, none but Jesus heard me! And ain't I a woman?

"Then they talk about this thing in the head; what's this they call it? [member of audience whispers, "intellect"] That's it, honey. What's that got to do with women's rights or negroes' rights? If my cup won't hold but a pint, and yours holds a quart, wouldn't you be mean not to let me have my little half measure full?

"Then that little man in black there, he says women can't have as much rights as men, 'cause Christ wasn't a woman! Where did your Christ come from? Where did your Christ come from? From God and a woman! Man had nothing to do with Him.

"If the first woman God ever made was strong enough to turn the world upside down all alone, these women together ought to be able to turn it back, and get it right side up again! And now they is asking to do it, the men better let them.

"Obliged to you for hearing me, and now old Sojourner ain't got nothing more to say."

SOURCES: Sandburg (1939) and Truth (1851).

The State Suffrage Movement: Why the West Was Best

In December 1869, Wyoming territory became the first modern legislative body to grant suffrage to women. There was no active suffrage movement in Wyoming at the time (McCammon 2001, 2003), so some might wonder why suffrage came first to Wyoming. In the early days, it was often said that the passage of female suffrage in Wyoming was a joke. Edward M. Lee, Secretary of the Territory in 1869, wrote:

Once, during the session, amid the greatest hilarity, and after the presentation of various funny amendments and in the full expectation of a gubernatorial veto, an act was passed enfranchising the Women of Wyoming. The bill, however, was approved, became a law, and the youngest territory placed in the van of progress. . . . How strange that a movement destined to purify the muddy pool of politics . . . should have originated in a joke. (printed in Cheyenne's *Wyoming Tribune*, October 8, 1870; cited in Larson 1965:58)

Although it is unlikely that women's suffrage passed only as a joke, Lee's quote does suggest another reason—legislators wanted Wyoming to appear modern (Larson 1965). Research also suggests that the legislators wanted to publicize the territory to the rest of the country and that the heavily male population may have wanted to attract more women. In 1890, when Wyoming was admitted to the Union, it also became the first state in America to allow women to vote. Congress wanted to refuse statehood to Wyoming as long as it allowed women to vote, but the legislature wired back to Washington: "We'll stay out a thousand years rather than come in without our women." To this day, Wyoming's leadership on female suffrage is a part of its identity, calling itself the Equality State.

Although Wyoming was first, other western states soon followed suit, granting women the right to vote. Utah was right on Wyoming's tails, passing female suffrage only 2 months later, and the Dakota Territorial Legislature failed by one vote to pass female suffrage in January of that year (Larson 1965). Furthermore, by 1920, most western states had passed bills allowing female suffrage, whereas most nonwestern states had not. See Map 2.1 for a map of state **ratification** of women's suffrage.

As evident in Map 2.1, suffrage movements were much more successful in western states. Except for Michigan and Kansas, Midwestern states were willing only to offer women the vote for presidential elections. Of the southern and eastern states, only Oklahoma and New York granted full female suffrage. Explanations for the regional differences in the success of suffrage movements are numerous. For example, in 1967, Alan P. Grimes advanced the Puritan ethos hypothesis, asserting that the White, male voters of the West were reacting to the social instabilities of frontier culture. The men thought women voters could bring order to public life.

In a series of studies researching the American women's suffrage movement, however, Holly J. McCammon and her colleague Karen Campbell (2001) were able to dismiss Grimes's claim, along with a number of other possible explanations for why state suffrage movements were so much more successful in the West. For example, suffrage organizations in the West were no larger or more numerous than those in other parts of the country. By collecting and analyzing more than 650 secondary accounts of suffrage movements in 48 states, McCammon and Campbell found that the success of women's suffrage movements in the West was likely a product of political opportunities, resource mobilization, and framing processes.

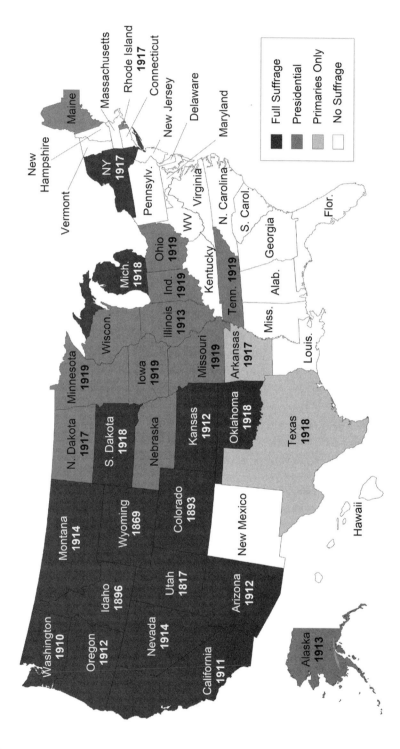

Map 2.1   States That Ratified Women's Suffrage Before 1920

Full Suffrage
Presidential
Primaries Only
No Suffrage

New Hampshire
Vermont
Maine
Massachusetts
Rhode Island 1917
Connecticut
New Jersey
Delaware
Maryland

NY 1917
Pennsylv.
WV
Virginia
N. Carolina
S. Carol.
Flor.

Mich. 1918
Ohio 1919
Ind. 1919
Kentucky
Tenn. 1919
Georgia
Alab.

Wiscon.
Illinois 1913
Missouri 1919
Arkansas 1917
Miss.
Louis.

Minnesota 1919
Iowa 1919
Kansas 1912
Oklahoma 1918
Texas 1918

N. Dakota 1917
S. Dakota 1918
Nebraska

Montana 1914
Wyoming 1869
Colorado 1893
New Mexico

Washington 1910
Oregon 1912
Idaho 1896
Utah 1817
Nevada 1914
Arizona 1912
California 1911

Hawaii

Alaska 1913

First, societies in the West were newly formed and constantly changing, allowing women more opportunities than they could have in eastern states. Women in the West had higher educational enrollments, and the region had more women in law and medicine. There were also a good number of female homesteaders—women who owned property. Where the separate spheres of men and women became blurred, it may have been perceived as more justifiable for women to participate in government (McCammon and Campbell 2001). Therefore, in social movement terms, the changing definition of proper female behavior in the West created political opportunities for the women's suffrage movement. Though evident first in the West, research suggests that the increase in female labor force participation likely helped lead to the suffrage movement's eventual overall success (Cornwall, Dahlin, and King 2005).

Second, the women's suffrage movement also pursued different tactical strategies in the West. Across the country, suffragists used both outsider tactics—parades, fair booths, leaflet distribution, canvassing, attempting to vote—and insider tactics such as legislative lobbying and candidate campaigning (King and Cornwall 2004). In the West, suffragists often avoided visible outsider tactics, such as large public demonstrations (McCammon and Campbell 2001). For example, Abigail Scott Duniway, an activist in the Northwest, coined the term *still hunt,* which meant that she sought to persuade influential voters, not the public at large (McCammon 2003). This technique may have succeeded in part because it did not inspire as much opposition.

Although large, vocal movements were not more successful in the state ratification movement, public tactics became more frequent as state ratification lagged. Movement scholars note that **suffragists** were more likely to use these outsider tactics after suffering setbacks, such as a loss in a state referendum (King and Cornwall 2004; McCammon 2003). Women stood on soapboxes or on the backs of open cars, and after 1908 women began marching in parades. Given that women's proper place was still considered the home, parades were very controversial. Some women even chose to quit the movement rather than marching in public (Blatch and Lutz 1940).

In addition to differences in movement strategies, female activists in different regions framed the goal of female suffrage differently. McCammon and Campbell (2001) distinguished two approaches used by state suffrage movements: justice and expediency. **Justice frames** suggest that it is a woman's right to vote. According to these arguments, women should not be treated differently from men, and women's political participation is better for women and women's interests. Voting privileges allow women both to influence the passage of favorable legislation and to pressure for the removal of laws that are unjust. Because these frames challenged the public versus private distinction and asserted gender equality, they were often met with fierce resistance.

On the other hand, **expediency frames** suggest that women are different and bring special skills to the political arena (Fischer 1994; McCammon and Campbell 2001). (Expediency frames are distinguishable from the strategy of expediency, discussed earlier in this chapter.) Because women were perceived as less corrupt, female suffrage could make it harder to elect notoriously bad candidates. Because women were perceived as law abiding and moral women's participation in the political process could remediate social problems, leading to more moral, educational, and humane legislation and laws that would protect children. McCammon and Campbell (2001) found that expediency frames were used more frequently as time marched on, were used more often in western states, and more often led to movement success.

Opposition to Female Suffrage

Although suffrage movements in western states were more successful prior to 1920, female suffrage never proceeded unopposed. For example, in Wyoming in 1871, women's suffrage was challenged. Due to accounts that women more often voted for Republicans in the previous election, Democrats in the legislature voted to repeal the vote for women. Although Governor Campbell vetoed the bill, the legislature responded by attempting to override his veto. Ultimately, the veto failed by only one vote (Larson 1965).

Although less common in the West, antisuffragists formed several organizations to advance their cause. As early as 1882, women took the lead in establishing the Boston Committee of Remonstrance to oppose women's suffrage in Massachusetts. There was also a Women's Anti-Suffrage Association, founded by the wives of two popular Civil War commanders. They declared: "If women gain the vote, it upsets the natural order and sows 'division and discord' in the family unit and in the country" (Clift 2003:65). Antisuffrage organizing by both men and women grew as time passed, and as the suffrage movement made gains. After the vote was won in California in 1911, numerous antisuffragist organizations joined forces to form the National Association Opposed to Woman Suffrage (see Figure 2.2).

Many opponents of suffrage grounded their arguments in the ideas of separate male and female spheres. Antisuffragists predicted that family life would collapse if women were allowed out of their preordained sphere of house and home. In 1889, 104 women published "An Appeal against Female Suffrage," claiming that men were developing a "new spirit of

Figure 2.2   National Association Opposed to Woman Suffrage

SOURCE: Courtesy of the Library of Congress, Prints and Photographs Division.

justice and sympathy" which had caused them already to address the "principal injustices of the law toward women . . . by means of the existing constitutional machinery" (Ward et al. 1889:413, cited in Thomas 2003:49). With men sympathetically taking care of women's interests, there was no reason for women to subvert their proper role in society as wives, mothers, and guardians of the home.

Suffrage movements in the West, however, did not have to contend with some of the major oppositional forces of female suffrage. In big cities, for example, the belief that women were reformers often led political machines to oppose their enfranchisement. Researchers also suggest that textile and manufacturing interests often opposed female suffrage because they wanted to keep women as a source of cheap labor (McDonagh and Price 1985). Railroad magnates and meatpackers supported antisuffragist organizations through financial contributions (Barber 1997). Finally, suffrage was largely opposed in the South, where the expansion of voting rights was hindered by opposition to suffrage for Black women.

Women Gain the Vote: The Events Leading to the Passage of the 19th Amendment

Although the radical and moderate branches of the American women's suffrage movement had joined forces under NAWSA in 1890, a new militant group called the Congressional Union, known later as the National Woman's Party (NWP), was organized in 1913 by Alice Paul and Lucy Burns. Scholars often credit this more militant wing with carrying the movement forward during a period when the mainstream movement was suffering after a number of major setbacks in state referenda (Flexner 1975). Social movement researchers often find that radical wings are beneficial to social movements through what they call radical flank effects. The presence of radical or extremist groups operating within the same movement as more moderate social movement organizations tends to strengthen the bargaining position of moderate groups politically and to increase their funding as a way of undercutting radical influence (McAdam et al. 1996).

The first radical move by Alice Paul and her militant suffrage organization was to organize a parade of 5,000 on the day before Woodrow Wilson's inauguration. One newspaper account recounted the event:

> The women had to fight their way from the start and took more than one hour in making the first ten blocks. Many of the women were in tears under the jibes and insults of those who lined the route. . . . It was where Sixth Street crosses the avenue that police protection gave way entirely and the two solid masses of spectators on either side came so close together that three women could not march abreast. (*Baltimore Sun,* March 4, 1913, cited in Flexner 1975:273)

Although difficult for the suffragists, the event received much coverage in the press and brought national attention to the cause.

The NWP sought a constitutional amendment, believing that the state suffrage movement had gone as far as it could. To force the adoption of a suffrage amendment in Congress, Alice Paul and the NWP held the Democrats, the controlling party in Congress and the party of the president, responsible for enacting change. Beginning in 1914, the group began campaigning against Democratic candidates for Congress, regardless of their position on suffrage (Flexner 1975). In 1914, women's suffrage came to the floor of the Senate, failing to pass by a vote of 34 to 35. The following year, the measure was also defeated in the House of Representatives, 204 to 174. The struggle for women's suffrage continued.

In 1917, Alice Paul and the NWP staged the first political protest ever to picket the White House. Known as Silent Sentinels, the pickets marked the first nonviolent civil disobedience campaign in the United States. Following months of protest, the picketers were arrested on charges of obstructing traffic. Many, including Alice Paul, were convicted and incarcerated. Viewing themselves as political prisoners, the women began a hunger strike to protest the conditions at the prison. Paul, along with several of the women, were moved to the psychiatric ward and fed forcibly through tubes in their noses. News of the forced feedings, along with the continuing demonstrations and attendant press coverage, kept pressure on the Wilson administration to grant women the vote.

As relations with Germany were deteriorating and the possibility of war loomed greater, suffragists were uncertain about how the war would influence the movement. Although suffrage was still the organization's primary concern, Catt committed the services of NAWSA to the Wilson administration in the event of war. Women were brought out of their homes into new spheres of action. Women rushed into industrial work and public service, sharply altering their standing in the community and proving their competence to assume political responsibility (Flexner 1975). In January 1918, the president announced that women's suffrage was urgently needed as a war measure. Thus, World War I provided an important shift in the political opportunity structure of the women's suffrage movement.

The passage of the **19th Amendment**, called the Anthony Amendment in honor of Susan B. Anthony, was scheduled in the House of Representatives for January 10, 1918. Despite the call by the president for the passage of the amendment, his party was divided almost evenly, and the vote would be close. Knowing this, Representative Hicks from New York followed what would have been the wishes of his wife, a devoted suffragist, who had just passed away. He left her deathbed to go to Washington for the vote, returning afterward for her funeral (Flexner 1975). The amendment passed with exactly the two thirds majority required.

After another fight in the Senate, on June 4, 1919, the U.S. Congress voted to amend the Constitution with the following words: "The right of citizens of the United States to vote shall not be denied or abridged by the United States or by any State on account of sex. Congress shall have power to enforce this article by appropriate legislation." In both the House and Senate, most of "nay" votes came from representatives of the South, making it a surprise, therefore, that the suffrage movement reached its final success in that region.

Before the amendment could become law, it required ratification by 36 states. Alabama was the first state to defeat the measure, quickly followed by Georgia. But 11 states ratified the amendment within 1 month and 22 within 6 months. After 35 states ratified the amendment, the issue came before the Tennessee State Legislature in August 1920.

Suffragists knew the battle would be a tough one. The notion that Black women would also get the vote under the amendment was enough to inspire opposition by both men and women. Carrie Chapman Catt, the president of NAWSA at the time, stated, "We now have 35½ states. We are up to the last half of the last state. . . . The opposition of every sort is here fighting with no scruple, desperately. Women . . . are here, appealing to Negrophobia and every other cave man's prejudice" (Flexner 1975:335). Antisuffragists had good reason to hope that if Tennessee failed to pass the 19th Amendment, the amendment would never become law. Catt joined forces with movement leaders in Tennessee to organize a vigorous fight for the cause. Tennessee women from different social classes and races worked together in writing letters, making speeches, and lobbying legislators (Hiers 2004).

The battle that ensued would come to be remembered as the War of the Roses. Proponents of the suffrage amendment united under the symbol of the yellow rose, and antisuffragists adopted the red rose. Even the legislators displayed their intentions by wearing roses on their lapels. By counting the number of red roses worn by legislators, the suffragists knew they were in trouble for the vote on August 18. It looked as though the amendment would be defeated, 47 for and 49 against. In the first roll call, however, one representative came over to the suffragist's side and the vote was 48–48. The second roll was taken, and the vote remained dead-locked. During the third roll call, with a red rose pinned to his jacket, Harry Burn—the youngest member of the legislature—suddenly broke the tie (Hiers 2004).

Burn was asked by journalists to explain his yellow-rose vote. He replied that although he was wearing a red rose, his breast pocket contained a telegram from his mother in East Tennessee, which read, " . . . vote for suffrage, and don't keep them in doubt. . . . Don't forget to be a good boy and help Mrs. Catt put the Rat in ratification!" (Baltimore Sun, August 22, 1920, cited in Flexner 1975:336). Burn stated, "I changed my vote in favor of ratification because a mother's advice is always safest for her boy to follow, and the opportunity was mine to free millions of people from political bondage" (Braun 2003). Women had finally won their struggle.

On August 18, 1920, the 19th Amendment was ratified, and women won the right to vote. After decades of organizing, the women's movement no longer had a unifying goal and quickly declined. Although women had achieved suffrage, they did not initially move forward to demand large-scale political representation, and at the time women were no more willing to vote for female candidates than men were. The struggle for female political representation was still to come.

Suffrage Movements
Outside the United States

Three years after Wyoming was admitted to the United States as the first state with women's voting rights, New Zealand became the first country to introduce universal suffrage. Similar to the western United States, New Zealand was a colonial farming society with a heavily male population (Grimshaw 1994). The movement in New Zealand was not particularly large, indicating again that movement size was not necessarily related to women's success. The most prominent member of the women's suffrage movement in New Zealand was Katherine Sheppard, who famously called for equality and justice: "All that separates, whether of race, class, creed, or sex, is inhuman, and must be overcome." Sheppard was also a founding member of the WCTU, reiterating that ties to other social movements provided an important organizational resource for women's movements in other countries as well.

Although the movement for female suffrage in the United States has much to teach, it is important to remember that the battle for female suffrage occurred across the globe. As women were organizing in the United States, women marched, lobbied, and agitated for political rights in many countries, often struggling for years to gain access to the rights men were handed without dispute. The United States was not the first to grant female suffrage, nor was it the last. (Figure 2.3 presents the dates suffrage was acquired in the countries of the world.) The American suffrage movement was exceptional in some respects—the size of the movement, for example, was only rivaled by the movement in the United Kingdom. Yet there are also similarities between the suffrage movement in the United States and in other countries, such as the education and social class of movement members. Overall, the United States provides a good reference point from which to compare other suffrage movements. We focus on five ways women's suffrage movements varied around the world: time period; movement size, composition, and alliances; goals and ideology; oppositional forces; and level of militancy.

Time Period

As evident in Figure 2.3, there was a great deal of variation in the years countries granted female suffrage. The year women's movements developed also differs. The United States and United Kingdom were the locations for the first women's movements. Around the time that Elizabeth Cady Stanton and Lucretia Mott were planning a women's convention to advance female

1893	New Zealand
1902	Australia*
1906	Finland
1913	Norway
1915	Denmark, Iceland
1917	Canada*
1918	Austria, Estonia, Georgia, Germany, Ireland*, Kyrgyzstan, Latvia, Poland, Russia, United Kingdom*
1919	Belgium*, Belarus, Kenya*, Luxembourg, Netherlands, Sweden, Ukraine
1920	Albania, Czech Republic, Slovakia, United States
1921	Armenia, Azerbaijan, Lithuania
1924	Kazakhstan, Mongolia, St. Lucia, Tajikistan
1927	Turkmenistan
1928	Ireland**, United Kingdom**
1929	Ecuador, Romania*
1930	South Africa*, Turkey
1931	Portugal*, Spain, Sri Lanka
1932	Maldives, Thailand, Uruguay
1934	Brazil, Cuba
1935	Myanmar
1937	Philippines
1938	Bolivia*, Uzbekistan
1939	El Salvador
1941	Panama*
1942	Dominican Republic
1944	Bulgaria, France, Jamaica
1945	Croatia, Indonesia, Italy, Japan, Senegal, Slovenia, Togo
1946	Cameroon, Djibouti, Guatemala, Liberia, Macedonia, North Korea, Panama**, Romania**, Trinidad & Tobago, Venezuela, Vietnam, Yugoslavia
1947	Argentina, Malta, Mexico, Pakistan, Singapore
1948	Belgium**, Israel, Niger, Seychelles, South Korea, Suriname
1949	Bosnia and Herzegovina, Chile, China, Costa Rica, Syria*
1950	Barbados, Haiti, India
1951	Antigua and Barbuda, Dominica, Grenada, Nepal, St. Kitts and Nevis, St. Vincent & the Grenadines
1952	Bolivia**, Cote d'Ivoire, Greece, Lebanon
1953	Bhutan, Guyana, Hungary, Syria**
1954	Belize, Colombia, Ghana
1955	Cambodia, Ethiopia, Eritrea, Honduras, Nicaragua, Peru

├─1956	Benin, Comoros, Egypt, Gabon, Mali, Mauritius, Somalia
├─1957	Malaysia, Zimbabwe
├─1958	Burkina Faso, Chad, Guinea, Laos, Nigeria
├─1959	Madagascar, San Marino, Tunisia, United Republic of Tanzania
├─1960	Canada**, Cyprus, Gambia, Tonga
├─1961	Bahamas, Burundi, Malawi, Mauritania, Paraguay, Rwanda, Sierra Leone
├─1962	Algeria, Australia**, Monaco, Uganda, Zambia
├─1963	Congo, Equatorial Guinea, Fiji, Iran, Kenya**, Morocco
├─1964	Libya, Papua New Guinea, Sudan
├─1965	Afghanistan, Botswana, Lesotho
├─1967	Democratic People's Republic of Yemen, Democratic Republic of the Congo, Kiribati, Tuvalu
├─1968	Nauru, Swaziland
├─1970	Andorra, Yemen Arab Republic
├─1971	Switzerland
├─1972	Bangladesh
├─1973	Bahrain
├─1974	Jordan, Solomon Islands
├─1975	Angola, Cape Verde, Mozambique, Sao Tome and Principe, Vanuatu
├─1976	Portugal**
├─1977	Guinea-Bissau
├─1978	Republic of Moldova
├─1979	Micronesia, Marshall Islands, Palau
├─1980	Iraq
├─1984	Liechtenstein
├─1986	Central African Republic
├─1989	Namibia
├─1990	Samoa
├─1994	South Africa**
├─2005	Kuwait

Suffrage was sometimes granted to women with restrictions—for example, only women of a certain racial or ethnic group could vote. When women's enfranchisement proceeded in stages, a single asterisk (*) denotes the first time women in a country were allowed to vote nationally, and two asterisks (**) signify universal suffrage.

Figure 2.3   The Worldwide Progression of Female Suffrage

SOURCE: Data from Paxton, Hughes, and Green (2006b).

suffrage, the women's movement was beginning in the United Kingdom. In 1847, Ann Knight, a Quaker, produced the first recognizable women's suffrage pamphlet, and the first British suffrage organization was formed 4 years later in 1851. The first wave of the women's movement in France and Germany began during the 1860s and developed slightly later in the Nordic countries (1870s and 1880s). Women's movements in Asia, Latin America, and the Middle East often lagged slightly behind, developing movements in the first decades of the 20th century. The development of first-wave women's movements was inhibited by forces such as political authoritarianism, Catholicism, or both (Randall 1987:211).

Movement Size, Composition, and Alliances

Most countries had only small or incipient first-wave women's movements. Others, such as Canada, Cuba, France, Holland, and Mexico, reached an intermediate size, and some were slightly larger—Denmark, Germany, Iceland, Japan, and Sweden (Chafetz and Dworkin 1986). The United States and the United Kingdom were the only countries to reach the mass movement level. Yet even where movements were small, women were often involved in some form of protest about their exclusion, making it hard to ignore them completely (Hannam, Auchterlonie, and Holden 2000). A smaller number of active women may also have the advantage of failing to inspire widespread opposition, and tactics like the still hunt could have been effective with movements of any size.

One of the most striking similarities between suffrage movements before World War II is the education and social status of those involved. Across the world, the leaders and rank-and-file members of suffrage organizations were largely educated, urban, middle-class women. Such women had the resources to organize, lead, and participate in social action. Furthermore, suffrage leaders frequently had links with Europe through birth and education. For example, Sarojini Naidu, an Indian nationalist and vocal supporter of women's education and suffrage rights, was from a Brahmin (a Hindu priestly caste) family, was educated at Cambridge, and married a doctor.

Women's education was a key factor in the struggle for suffrage. Where literacy rates were high, women often organized first to fight for higher educational opportunities (Hannam et al. 2000). In Latin America, Asia, and the Middle East, Westernized males usually first raised the issue of basic education, followed by small groups of women who were often the first to be educated (Chafetz and Dworkin 1986). As women struggled for the right to education and challenged their relegation to the home, they recognized the importance of the vote in the ability to secure their demands and further women's status in their societies. Chafetz and Dworkin suggested that movements failing to grow beyond the incipient stage often lacked a pool of educated women to fuel movement membership.

First-wave feminist movements were often also comprised mainly of middle- or upper-class women. For example, Bertha Lutz, the president of the Brazilian Federation for the Progress of Women, was the daughter of a pioneer of tropical medicine. In Egypt, women formed a federation in 1923 to defend the right of women to education and advocate for reforms such as women's suffrage; however, according to Morgan (1984), the federation consisted of exclusively upper-class women and had no links to the working classes. In Sri Lanka, middle-class women fought for education, suffrage, and equal political rights, and the working women of the country struggled for material gains, equal wages for men and women, and more humane conditions at work (Chafetz and Dworkin 1986). This does not mean that working-class women did not take part in suffrage movements. School-teachers and journalists were important, often serving as a bridge between upper and working classes. Working-class participation also increased when suffrage organizations developed closer ties to the labor movement (DuBois 1998).

Goals and Ideology

Both between and within countries, movements also disagreed regarding their primary goal. Although women in many countries demanded universal suffrage, some countries still placed education or property restrictions on male suffrage. In these nations, therefore, women often demanded rights on the same terms as men. In some instances where men did have universal suffrage, movements still carefully weighed whether imposing voting restrictions on women would aid their cause. In Norway, for example, Gina Krog supported a limited franchise for women even after men had achieved adult suffrage because she believed that gradualism would be a more effective policy. In the United States, some suffrage movement leaders wanted to restrict the vote to educated women, and similarly in 19th-century Britain there were disagreements within the movement over whether the demand for the vote should include married women.

For former colonies, suffrage often came later for indigenous women than for White women living in the colonies. For example, in Kenya, a British colony, a legislative council was established in 1907. European women were given the vote in 1919, and Asian men and women were granted suffrage in 1923. Black African voters had to wait until 1957 when a wide franchise was introduced, one still restricted by property and educational qualifications. Still excluded, Arab women from Mombasa protested that the legislation had denied them the franchise. Finally, upon independence in 1963, universal adult suffrage was introduced. This phenomenon was not unique to British colonies or to sub-Saharan Africa. In Indonesia, for example, Dutch women, but not local women, were given municipal voting rights in 1941.

Arguments that suffrage should be limited to educated or propertied women were labeled by socialists as bourgeois suffrage and contributed early on to a split between suffrage movements and socialist women. *Bourgeois* is a term used to refer to wealthy or propertied social classes in a capitalist society. The split between socialist and bourgeois women was actively promoted by socialists as "anti-collaborationism" (DuBois 1998: 263). Yet in some cases, such as Puerto Rico and Austria, socialist and working-class women took the lead in the suffrage campaign (Azize-Vargas 2002). Alliances were also sometimes made between bourgeois and socialist working women. In Mexico in the 1930s, for example, an umbrella suffrage organization, Frente Único Pro-Derechos de la Mujer, recruited at its height 50,000 members from a wide array of backgrounds.

Despite the separation of many socialist women from Western suffrage movements, the adoption of Marxist ideas by governments was often quickly followed by female suffrage. As we discuss in Chapters 3 and 8, communist governments espoused an ideal of a genderless state. And women were expected to participate in all areas of social, political, and economic life. Thus, several countries, such as China and Democratic Yemen, adopted suffrage in their first year of Communist rule. And Yugoslavia, though independent in 1918, did not adopt female suffrage until 1946 after declaring itself a socialist state (Paxton et al. 2006a). Socialist women also played important roles in organizing for women's rights. German political activist Clara Zetkin, for example, organized the first International Conference of Socialist women in 1907, and she proposed March 8th as International Women's Day in 1911.

Still, because of the prominence of women's movements in the West, Marxists and nationalists worldwide denounced feminism as Western imperialism, and suffragists in non-Western countries sometimes faced opposition on these grounds. Thus, women in these countries developed indigenous feminist forms. Although the women's suffrage movement is often considered a Western phenomenon, movements for women's emancipation in China, India, and other parts of Asia can be traced back to the 19th century. Women "participated in social and political movements, in nationalist and patriotic struggles, in working-class agitations and peasant rebellions" and formed autonomous women's organizations (Jayawardena 1986:254).

Movement Opposition

Perhaps the most obvious similarity between the United States and other social movements is that no matter where they were, proponents of female suffrage faced opposition. Women around the world confronted the belief that they lacked the necessary qualities or capabilities to participate in politics. In the Third World, these beliefs were often reinforced by European Colonialism, which carried notions of separate spheres backed by political philosophers of the Enlightenment. Women themselves feared that changing the status quo would disrupt the family and lead to the loss of male economic and social protection.

Oppositional groups were stronger in some countries than in others. In countries with strong suffrage movements like the United Kingdom, anti-suffrage organizations were formed, while in countries like Australia and New Zealand, women faced much less opposition. Women in many countries also faced opposition from both sides of the political spectrum. In France, for example, republicans feared women would vote according to Catholic lines, and conservatives thought women were more likely to support progressive reform interests like temperance.

Women often faced unique obstacles grounded in distinctive cultural, political, or religious circumstances. In Latin America, for example, traditional values and machismo served to hinder women's progress (Lavrin 1994). In Uruguay, one opponent to suffrage invented a new term, *machonismo*, to describe the desire to copy men and divert women from their natural path (Hannam, Auchterlonie, and Holden 2000). Authoritarian regimes and conservative parties tended to oppose democratization and the extension of voting rights. For example, Japan had a small women's movement that emerged in the 1880s but it was silenced by the government until the 1920s (Chafetz and Dworkin 1986). Direct government suppression of independent women's organizations occurred at various times in France, Russia, China, Japan, Indonesia, Iran, Brazil, and Peru (Randall 1987).

In addition to traditional values or political authoritarianism, a country's dominant religion often influenced the development and success of first-wave women's movements. Specifically, Catholic countries are often seen as more resistant to suffrage than Protestant countries. For example, Ehrick (1998) argues that a liberal-feminist movement developed in Uruguay in part because the Catholic Church was not as strong as in Chile, where the suffrage movement was less successful. Of 14 nations which may have had suffrage movements beyond an incipient, or beginning level, 10 were predominantly Protestant (Chafetz and Dworkin 1986:160).

Scholars do not all agree, however, on why Catholicism presented a barrier to women's suffrage. One argument is that the Catholic Church often discouraged women from involvement in public affairs, while Goode (1963) suggests that feminism is the logical, philosophical extension of Protestant notions about the rights and responsibilities of the individual (p. 56, cited in Randall 1987:213). Chafetz and Dworkin (1986) argue that the religion effect is not direct, but indirect through education: Protestantism emphasizes education more than other religions. They point out that the Quakers, a religious group that emphasized education and individualism for both sexes, were influential in the early American and British movements. Furthermore, many of the women's movement leaders in Asian countries were educated in Christian schools, their education serving as the catalyst for future mobilization.

Hannam, Auchterlonie, and Holden (2000) report that the negative "Catholic effect" was partially fueled by women's rights activists themselves, who feared that women would vote Catholic. In France, activists feared female suffrage would lead to political Catholicism and a return to monarchy; some argued that women needed a secular education first that would liberate them from the church. The same pattern is evident in Belgium, where Socialists and Liberals dropped suffrage due to fear of religious fanaticism. In Italy, support for suffrage dropped further after WWI with the rise of a mass Catholic political party.

Tactics and Level of Militancy

Another factor that varied both within and across suffrage movements is women's use of militant tactics. The term *militancy* was first applied to the activities of the Women's Social and Political Union (WSPU), a suffrage organization in the United Kingdom, to distinguish them from more constitutional methods, including lobbying, petitioning, and letter writing. The term is associated with a wide range of tactics including the disruption of meetings, tax resistance, refusing to fill in census forms, breaking windows, arson attacks on public buildings, other forms of property destruction, imprisonment, hunger striking, and forcible feeding.

The WSPU in Britain is the most well-known of militant suffrage organizations. Just as women's protests in the United States grew more public over time, the WSPU's tactics changed as well. The first act of militancy occurred in October 1905, when WSPU leaders Christabel Pankhurst and Annie Kenney interrupted an election meeting by standing up and shouting "Votes for women!" They were subsequently arrested when Christabel spat at a policeman. After 1908 the militancy of the WSPU escalated to include symbolic acts, such as women chaining themselves to the Ladies Gallery in Parliament, and threats to public order, such as groups of women rushing the House of Commons and destroying property. For example, in early March 1912, suffragettes launched two window-breaking campaigns. The first, on March 1st, involved women making coordinated raids throwing stones to break windows throughout London at fifteen-minute intervals.

The second incident, three days later, involved more than one hundred women smashing all panes of glass along a street in Knightsbridge (Jorgensen-Earp 1999). By the summer of 1912, 102 British **suffragettes** were in prison, and 90 were being forcibly fed.

Box 2.3   Buffeting, Violent Responses to Female Suffragettes

While the idea of militant, stone-throwing suffragettes may be shocking, it is also important to note the use of violence by the government and individual men. It is simultaneously important to recognize the reluctance of some women to use these militant tactics. The following story, related by Cheryl Jorgensen-Earp (1999), illustrates both these points:

Despite its symbolic beginning, stone throwing was quickly adopted by WSPU members as a practical response to meet the second exigency often encountered during suffrage protests. Before they would arrest suffrage speakers or members of suffrage deputations, the police would subject women to a period of "buffeting." Buffeting was a term used at the time to describe a delay of arrest during which time the suffragettes would be pummeled and manhandled by police and angry male crowds. Injuries to Union members were inevitable, and it was clearly the hope of the government and police that the threat of such injury would dissuade suffrage activism. Then, too, the practice of buffeting allowed the police to inflict maximum physical punishment while simultaneously claiming that they arrested the suffragettes only when absolutely necessary. Quickly, Union members discovered that if they threw a stone (even if it did not reach its target) or committed simple assault (dry "spitting" or slapping a policeman), they would be arrested in short order and not subjected to as much physical damage. This initial step into illegal action caused such mental anguish for many of the suffragettes that they swaddled the stones in heavy paper and even took the precaution of tying long strings from stone to wrist, thus avoiding injury to bystanders. Despite their scruples, union members came to agree with Sylvia Pankhurst's assertion, "Since we must go to prison to obtain the vote, let it be the windows of the government, not the bodies of women, which shall be broken." (Jorgensen-Earp 1999:101)

The actions of the WSPU often inspired women in other movements. Alice Paul, for example, spent several years in the WSPU before leading women in militancy in the United States. In the UK, however, militancy was used earlier and was more widespread. Figure 2.4 depicts the perceived contrast in tactics between the two movements.

Figure 2.4   Political Cartoon Depicting British and American Suffragists

SOURCE: *Utica Saturday Globe*, March 1913. Courtesy of BoondocksNet.com.

Although militancy is most well known in the UK, women in other countries also organized demonstrations and stormed legislatures (Jayawardena 1986; Randall 1987). For example, in 1911, Tang Junying founded the Chinese Suffragette Society in Beijing and led women to the first meetings of the National Assembly. When they were refused the vote, the women launched an attack, and by the third day the assembly had to send for troops for protection. Similarly, in Guangdong, the provisional government promised women the vote but retracted it, and women invaded the legislature (Hannam et al. 2000; Morgan 1984). Women also used militancy in Japan (1924), Egypt (1924), Iran (1917), and Sri Lanka (1927).

On the other hand, women in some countries were very reluctant to use militant tactics. In Europe, many women shied away from street demonstrations, and in South America many movements distanced themselves from militancy to avoid being called unwomanly or too radical. Women also may have been reluctant because militancy was not necessarily perceived as more successful. Many movements, such as those in New Zealand, Canada, and Scandinavia, were successful in achieving suffrage before the United Kingdom without using militant tactics. Figure 2.5 satirizes this point in a political cartoon, showing women in the Netherlands gaining suffrage before their more militant English counterparts.

Figure 2.5   Political Cartoon Depicting Women in the Netherlands Gaining the
Vote Before the More Militant British

SOURCE: *Minneapolis Journal,* November 1913. Courtesy of BoondocksNet.com.

The International Women's Movement

In addition to the struggles that took place at the national level in countries
across the world, women also organized at the international level. In 1878,
the first international women's congress convened in Paris, attended by
11 foreign countries and 16 organizations (Moses 1984; Rupp and Taylor

1999). The better-known first International Congress of Women (ICW) was founded a decade later by Susan B. Anthony, May Wright Swell, and Frances Willard and held its first convention in Washington. The convention was attended by representatives of Canada, Denmark, Finland, France, Great Britain, India, and Norway. Though the congress's primary goal was the advancement of women, it initially did not demand female suffrage so as not to alienate its more conservative members. The early international conferences were extensively covered by the press, especially the 1899 meeting in which Anthony met Queen Victoria.

Early years of organizing at the international level also included Latin America. In 1910, the first International Feminist Congress was held in Buenos Aires, and in 1916 the International Conference of Women convened in the Yucatán. Often these events in the international movement had profound implications for women active in local movements. For example, according to Morgan (1984), the International Feminist Congress was a watershed moment for Argentina's suffrage movement, inspiring women across the country.

Despite the varied geography of international meetings, the international movement was composed of mostly Western, upper-class, educated, White women. Groups such as the International Woman Suffrage Alliance sought to convert non-Western women to the suffrage campaign (Hannam et al. 2000). Yet, as discussed earlier, women were engaged in indigenous women's movements across the globe. International Woman Suffrage Alliance (IWSA) president, Carrie Chapman Catt, expressed surprise when, as a result of her travels in 1911 and 1912, she found that woman in Asia already had a movement of considerable strength. Socialist women participated in the international movement with the International Socialist Women's Conference in 1907 and the International Communist Conference of Working Women in 1920.

Besides encouraging national-level women's movements, as the international women's movement grew in strength it actively began to pressure international organizations such as the League of Nations and the United Nations. Berkovitch (1999) argued that the League of Nations and the International Labor Organization (ILO) "opened a new arena for women's mobilization by offering a central world focal point that theretofore had been lacking" (p. 109). In 1931, 10 of the largest women's organizations joined forces to form the Liaison Committee of Women's International Organisations, which in 1937 lobbied the League of Nations to collect data on women's legal status around the world (Berkovitch 1999). These international women's groups successfully placed a women's rights issue, the nationality of married women, on the agenda of the ILO. In 1946, the General Assembly of the United Nations recommended that all member states fulfill the aims of its charter "granting to women the same political rights as men" (resolution 56 (I)). As discussed in the next section, the international women's movement helped to make women's suffrage, once considered unacceptable by both politicians and the public, a taken-for-granted requirement of a modern country. See also Chapter 6 for a longer discussion of the international women's movement and its impact.

Women's Suffrage After 1945

Up to this point, we have focused on women's struggle to be recognized as men's political equals. In some countries, this struggle took decades, and in some women were even willing to destroy property and endure prison, hunger strikes, and forced feedings. Women were fighting against the belief held for centuries that they lacked the capacity to participate politically. They worried that simply by voting they might damage the institution of the family and the very fabric of their society. Despite these challenges, women won the vote in New Zealand and in the United States, Sweden, Spain, Chile, and Myanmar. And as increasing numbers of countries increasingly granted women suffrage, the pressure on surrounding countries that had not yet extended rights to women mounted.

With the end of World War II, the world landscape changed. France, Italy, Romania, Yugoslavia, and China immediately granted women the right to vote, and others soon followed. As empires began to dismantle, and colonies around the world struggled for independence, new countries began to enter the world system. With only a few exceptions, these new countries granted both men and women the right to vote in their constitutions. Varying national debates about women's rights gave way to an internationally recognized universal belief in women's enfranchisement. The gendered definition of political citizenship had changed (Ramirez, Soysal, and Shanahan 1997).

Interestingly, it was sometimes countries with longer histories of democratic principles that held out, continuing to deny women rights. Switzerland, for example, did not allow women to vote in federal elections until 1971, and the last canton (similar to a county in the United States) was finally forced to grant women suffrage at the local level in 1990. Another group of holdout countries resided in the Gulf region of the Middle East. Yet these countries often had not extended political rights to men or women. Whether women would be allowed to vote when democracy was first instituted was a question that remained to be answered. In 1999, women secured voting rights in the country of Qatar, followed by Bahrain in 2001 and Oman in 2003. Women's most recent success took place in Kuwait, when, following a drawn out battle and several failed attempts, women were finally granted the right to vote in May 2005 (see Box 2.4).

Box 2.4   The Struggle for Suffrage in Kuwait: Success in 2005

The passage of women's suffrage in Kuwait on May 16, 2005, marked the culmination of 40 years of struggle by women's rights activists and their allies. Kuwait is located on the Persian Gulf, bordering both Iraq and Saudi Arabia. Approximately 85% of the population is Muslim, the majority of which are Sunni. Roughly the size of New Jersey, Kuwait is home to 10% of the world's oil reserves. The country's oil wealth has allowed the state to guarantee free public education through the university level, as well as free health care.

Compared to other countries in the Middle East, women in Kuwait have a good deal of freedom. Unlike Saudi Arabia, for example, Kuwaiti women drive and are allowed to travel without a male escort. Contraception is available without prescription, and in 1982 Kuwait became the first country in the Middle East to legalize abortion. The literacy rate of Kuwaiti women is 77.5%, and women are a majority of university graduates. The country has the highest female labor force participation rate in the Gulf region—around 33%.

Women's first claims to suffrage arose out of the country's 1962 constitution, which mandates equality before the law for all citizens. However, electoral law passed in the same year restricted the vote to men. In 1981, the prime minister promised that Kuwaiti women would soon be allowed to vote in parliamentary elections. The following year, however, a bill proposing women's suffrage was defeated by a vote of 27 to 7. Before the vote, the legislature proclaimed that "the time is not opportune for receiving the idea in the light of well-established traditions" (Morgan 1984:409). A week later, 10,000 women demonstrated for suffrage, sent messages to the assembly, and organized delegations to confront members who voted against the bill. Their efforts to sway the National Assembly were unsuccessful.

In August 1990, Kuwait was invaded by neighboring Iraq. Kuwaiti women reacted immediately. Two days after the occupation began, women organized their first demonstration against the occupation. Throughout the war, Kuwaiti women participated in the underground struggle against Iraq just as their male counterparts did. Those captured faced prison, torture, rape, and death. As Dr. Alqudsi-Ghobra (2002), a professor at the University of Kuwait, stated, "The high percentage of Kuwaiti women among those executed or imprisoned during the occupation is a matter of shocking record." When the Iraqi occupation ended, Kuwait's emir, Sheik Jaber Al Ahmed Al Sabah, returned from exile with praise for his country's women and promises of equality. But in 1999, when he decreed women could vote and run for parliament, a powerful coalition of tribal interests and Islamists in the legislature overruled him.

One might expect that Islam was the primary barrier to the extension of political rights to women, but research suggests otherwise. By surveying a representative sample of 1,500 Kuwaiti citizens in 1994, a group of researchers found that Islamic beliefs are not incompatible with the extension of women's political rights. Meyer, Rizzo, and Ali (1998) reported: "Both between and within Islamic sects, there were respondents who favored increased participation for women in political life" (p. 142). Muhammad, the founder and prophet of Islam, taught that both sexes were to be treated with justice. Therefore, Sunni and Shia citizens who strongly believed in Islamic orthodoxy were supportive of women's suffrage. Alternatively, individuals favoring traditional Islamic practices regarding dress were less inclined to extend rights to women. See Chapter 4 for further discussion of Islam and women in politics.

Despite continual failures to convince the parliament to extend rights to women, protests and other social agitation for women's suffrage continued. On February 1, 2000, for example, hundreds of women marched to voter registration centers and demanded to be registered as voters. Although female activists and women's groups were the primary force in the fight for women's suffrage, research suggests that among the general population in Kuwait men held far stronger opinions regarding women's political rights than did women. Rizzo, Meyer, and Ali (2002) believe that women's comparative neutrality likely reflects women's socialization to be apolitical.

In 2005, the emir issued a second decree calling for women's suffrage, but in early May the parliament again overruled him. After exerting considerable pressure on the members of the legislature, the emir forced another vote on May 16. This time, however, the outcome was different. By a vote of 35 to 23 with one abstention, a bill for women's suffrage finally passed in the National Assembly. Still, of the 35 votes cast in favor of extending political rights to women, 15 were votes of the emir's cabinet ministers. If the vote had been determined by only parliamentarians, the bill would once again not have passed. Conservative interests also succeeded in attaching an amendment to the bill requiring women to abide by Islamic law. Although the exact implications of the amendment are still unclear, many suggest female voters will be required to wear conservative dress and use separate polling locations.

After the vote, women danced and sang in the streets. Sheikha Soad al-Sabah, a well-known Kuwaiti poet from the al-Sabah ruling family, told reporters, "I have been struggling for this moment for more than 20 years through my writings, the media, conferences, and through all sorts of activities." Roula al-Dashti, Kuwaiti activist, remarked, "We made it. This is history."

SOURCES: Alqudsi-Ghobra (2002), Central Intelligence Agency (2005), United Nations Development Programme (2004a), "Quote of the Day" (2005), Meyer et al. (1998), Morgan (1984), and Rizzo et al. (2002).

Despite these recent victories, however, women's equal citizenship is not yet universal. In Lebanon, proof of education is required for a woman to vote, whereas a man is not subject to any education restrictions. Women's vote is optional, whereas men are required to vote by law. In Bhutan, only one vote per family is allowed at the village level, meaning that oftentimes women are excluded. As of 2005, Saudi Arabia still refuses altogether to allow women the right to vote.

In February 2005, men took part in Saudi Arabia's first municipal elections. Although the country's election law does not explicitly ban women from taking part in the electoral process, women were excluded from participation. Women's exclusion also came somewhat as a surprise because in 2000 Saudi Arabia ratified an international treaty pledging to "ensure to women, on equal terms with men, the right to vote in all elections." It is important to understand, therefore, that establishing women's political rights in law does not mean in practice that women will be allowed to exercise those rights. Women's political future in Saudi Arabia is uncertain. The head of the Election Committee, Prince Mut'ab bin Abdul Aziz, said, "I expect women to participate in elections in future stages, after conducting studies to assess whether it is useful or not" (Amnesty International 2004). Unfortunately, it is exceptionally difficult for women to organize to demand reform in Saudi Arabia because women are not allowed to drive or even appear in public without being accompanied by an immediate male relative, or *Mahram*.

Today, many people cannot imagine women lacking the ability to participate in the electoral process. When one heads to the polls, men and women are seen casting ballots alongside each other to choose a leader. It is important not to forget, however, that women's right to vote came only after decades of struggle by thousands of brave men and women and that some women in the world still lack this basic right.

3

Women Struggle
for Representation

Accessing Positions of Power

O nce women had the vote, they had a voice in politics for the first time. They were formally represented in power, having the legal right to participate in politics on an equal basis with men. But as discussed in Chapter 1, formal political equality is only the first step in achieving equal representation. Women now needed to fight for descriptive representation in the traditional halls of power. Slowly, over the course of the 20th century, women began to make inroads into areas of power typically held by men: Pioneering women became the first to hold political office, others led the way as presidents and prime ministers, and women began to fill cabinet positions and advise leaders on public policy.

But though women successfully stormed the male political castle in some countries, they remained encamped on the outside in others. In some countries, women became commonplace as members of parliament, reaching 15, 20, and even 30% of legislatures. In many other countries, however, the struggle for descriptive representation has proceeded slowly, and women remain barely visible in political life. Still other countries demonstrate that women can lose political power even after they have gained it. The pace of women's access to positions of power was also very different from country to country. In some countries, women were appearing in politics in substantial numbers by the 1970s, whereas in others it would take until the 1990s to gain political clout. And women are still waiting for minimal levels of descriptive representation in a substantial block of countries.

This chapter provides an overview of women's struggle to access a variety of positions of political power. It begins with a look at the vanguard group of women who first held elected office. It then turns to a historical overview of the growth of women's participation in national legislatures. Then female world leaders and female cabinet members are discussed.

First Female Members of Parliament

In Chapter 2 we described how New Zealand led the world to become the first country to grant women suffrage; however, New Zealand did not capture all "firsts" for women in politics. In 1907, Finland became the first country to elect a female member of parliament. Although this was a truly historic event, we cannot tell you the story of the first female parliamentarian because there was not one woman elected in 1907 to Finland's new unicameral parliament, nor were there two women. In the world's first election to allow women to contest seats alongside men, 19 women were elected. See Box 3.1 for a more detailed account of this historic event.

Box 3.1   Finland: The First Country to Elect Women to Parliament

In the early 20th century, Finland was an autonomous grand duchy of the Russian empire. The region had been conquered in 1808 by the armies of Emperor Alexander I. Although Finland had a legislative assembly called the Diet of Four Estates, which had roots extending back into the 17th century, it did not hold regular meetings during most of Russia's occupation, and the authority to manage Finland's internal affairs was often granted to Russian ministers. When Russia went to war with Japan in 1904, however, political unrest spread from Russia to Finland in the form of massive strikes.

To ease the unrest, the Russian emperor consented to radical parliamentary reform, and, in 1906, Finland replaced the Diet of Four Estates with a unicameral legislature, or single house, of 200 members. Suffrage became universal and equal, and women could vote and run for election against men. According to some accounts, women's participation in the massive strikes, risking life and limb, was an important reason they were granted the vote in Finland.

The first general elections to select representatives to the new parliament were held in March 1907. Election advertisements directed at women stressed the importance and historical significance of the general elections.

Organizations affiliated with the women's movement urged every Finnish woman to ensure that a sufficient number of women was elected into office, using the argument that women are best at interpreting women's wishes. In a historic moment for both the country and the world, 19 women were elected to the new legislative body. Nine of the women members were socialists, and 10 represented bourgeois parties. However, the majority of women cast ballots for men candidates.

During the first parliament, 26 bills were presented by women members. The legislation covered topics such as the legal rights of married women, maternity insurance, women's property rights, female employment, and funding for school children. However, women from the suffrage movement still expressed disappointment that female members of parliament (MPs) appeared more loyal to their parties than to a common women's cause. After the 1907 election, Finland would not elect so many women to its parliament again until 1954. Women candidates fared worst in the general election of 1930, when women's representation fell to less than 6%. The number of female MPs began rising in 1966, when women's share of seats exceeded 15% for the first time.

SOURCES: "Finnish Women" (1911), Gronlund (2003), and Manninen (2004).

The ability of women to run for political office went hand and hand with female suffrage in the vast majority of countries. Typically, when women were granted the vote, they were also granted the right to run for political office and be elected. Yet voting and obtaining initial representation were sometimes separate struggles. For example, though women in New Zealand could vote in 1893, they did not receive the right to stand for election until 1919 and could not sit in the upper house until 1941. In Djibouti, women could vote in 1946, prior to the country's 1977 independence, but women were not able to run for office until 1986. Often the gap was shorter, such as in Turkey (4 years) and Mexico (5 years).

In some countries, the opposite was true—women were allowed to hold political office before they could vote. In the United States, for example, women could in theory run for office from the ratification of the Constitution in the late 1700s. However, it took almost 100 years for a woman to test the theory that she could run for political office. In 1866, Elizabeth Cady Stanton did run for Congress, although she only received 24 votes. America's first female MP was Jeannette Rankin, elected to the U.S. House of Representatives from Montana in 1917, 3 years before the passage of the 19th Amendment (see Box 3.2). Women were elected to legislatures before they could officially vote in Brazil, Hungary, the Netherlands, and Yugoslavia (Inter-Parliamentary Union 1995).

Box 3.2   Jeannette Rankin: First Woman in the United States Congress

Jeannette Rankin was a native of Missoula, Montana; a suffragist; and a lifelong pacifist. She was active in the suffrage movement and in 1914 helped women win the right to vote in Montana, 6 years before the 19th Amendment was passed. After winning the vote, Rankin promptly ran for the House of Representatives on the Republican ticket. Thus, alone among her fellow suffragists, she was able to declare, "The first time I voted . . . in 1916 . . . I voted for myself" (Hoff 1985).

Rankin won the election and entered the House of Representatives on April 2, 1917, to cheers and applause. Only a few days later, on April 6, 1917, following her pacifist beliefs, she—along with only 50 representatives—voted against U.S. entry into World War I. Despite receiving harsh criticism, she was adamant that women and peace were inseparable, saying, "The first time the first woman had a chance to say no against war she should say it" (Jeannette Rankin Peace Center 2006). Probably as a result, she lost her reelection bid in 1918. But before leaving office she amended a bill to secure equal employment for women, helped reform working hours for women in the Bureau of Printing and Engraving, and worked for a federal constitutional amendment to give women the right to vote. After leaving office, she remained active in pacifist issues.

Rankin ran for Congress again in 1940, winning a second term. But in 1941, she stood alone as the sole vote against U.S. entry into World War II, a vote that drew immediate hostility. On the way back to her office, she had to take refuge in a phone booth to escape an angry crowd. The vote ended her political career. Throughout the rest of her life, she was active in the peace movement and today is remembered as the only member of Congress to oppose U.S. entrance into both world wars.

Figure 3.1   Jeannette Rankin Planting a Montana Fir Tree, Arbor Day 1917

Photo: Montana Historical Society Archives.

SOURCES: Hoff (1985), Jeannette Rankin Peace Center (2006), and Josephson (1974).

Once women had the vote and the right to run for public office, public opinion was still hard to change. Citizens were sometimes not ready to elect women, and often women were no more willing to vote for female candidates than were men. Women were still considered inferior and viewed as belonging in the home. In New Zealand, after women won the right to run for political office, three women contested seats, but none was successful in getting elected. The first female member of parliament in New Zealand was not elected until 1933, when the Labour Party's Elizabeth McCombs was chosen by the electorate to fill the seat of her deceased husband, James McCombs, in a by-election.

Because of continuing concern about women's abilities and qualifications, less than 30% of the world's countries actually elected a woman to parliament in the election following female enfranchisement. Table 3.1 presents the list of the 53 countries (out of 182) that elected a woman to parliament within 3 years of universal suffrage, along with the year the women were elected.

Not all women had to run as candidates to achieve political office. The appointment process allowed some women to gain entry to legislative bodies before they were perceived as viable candidates by the electorate. For example, in Jordan, women first voted in parliamentary elections in 1989. Of the 10 women who presented their candidature in these elections, not one won a seat, but one woman was appointed to the senate (Abu-Zayd 1998; Lane 2001). Although this pattern occurred most frequently in the Middle East, women were appointed before they were elected in all regions of the world and throughout the 20th century. Other examples include Norway (1911), Lithuania (1920), Belgium (1921), Turkey (1935), Thailand (1948), Colombia (1954), Uganda (1962), and Bahrain (2002). According to the Inter-Parliamentary Union (1995), about 12% of countries appointed a woman to their parliament before one was elected.

Women Access Parliaments: Patterns of Representation

Once the first woman was elected to political office, others typically followed. When did women achieve other milestones of descriptive representation? When did women reach 10% of parliaments, or 20%? The answer is "it depends." Some countries experienced steady growth in the number of women in parliaments over time. Others had no growth at all. Some countries have only recently encountered women in politics in large numbers. Other countries had higher levels of female participation in the past than in the present.

Table 3.1 Countries Electing a Woman to Parliament Within 3 Years of Universal Suffrage by Year Woman Elected

1907 Finland	**1919** Austria Luxembourg Poland	**1921** Sweden	**1931** Spain Sri Lanka	**1942** Dominican Republic	**1944** Jamaica	**1945** France
1946 Italy Japan Panama Romania	**1946 (cont.)** Trinidad & Tobago Venezuela	**1947** Malta Pakistan	**1948** North Korea South Korea	**1949** Chile Israel	**1951** Barbados	**1952** Greece India Nepal
1953 Guyana	**1954** Colombia	**1956** Peru	**1957** Egypt Ethiopia Honduras	**1958** Laos	**1959** Malaysia Tunisia	**1962** Algeria Uganda
1963 Congo Monaco Paraguay	**1964** Sudan	**1965** Afghanistan Lesotho	**1971** Switzerland	**1973** Bangladesh	**1975** Cape Verde Sao Tome & Principe	**1977** Mozambique
1980 Iraq	**1986** Liechtenstein	**1987** Central African Republic	**1989** Namibia			

NOTE: If there are two houses of parliament, the number of women elected to the lower house is reported.

To provide an overview of women's growth and decline in descriptive representation across countries, we have divided country parliamentary histories into five basic paths: (1) Flat, (2) Increasing, (3) Big Jump, (4) Small Gains, and (5) Plateau. In this section, we describe each of these historical paths, which run from 1945 to 2005. We present a general picture of each type of path, discuss the countries that follow each pattern, and provide a brief explanation of the path.

Flat Countries: Women's Representation Does Not Change Over Time

The first category, Flat, includes a diverse array of countries whose numbers of women are fairly stable or constant across time. Unfortunately, the largest number of countries in this grouping never elected a significant number of women to their parliament, hovering at less than 5%. This group of countries is indicated by the dotted line in Figure 3.2. Many of these countries are in the Middle East and North Africa, including Algeria, Bahrain, Egypt, Iran, Jordan, Kuwait, Lebanon, Libya, Turkey, United Arab Emirates, and Yemen. Other countries in this group are mostly from Asia and sub-Saharan Africa, including Myanmar, Nepal, South Korea, Sri Lanka, Thailand, Kenya, Madagascar, Niger, Nigeria, and Zaire.

The concentration of countries that have never incorporated women into politics in a few regions of the world suggests that there is something in these regions that acts as a barrier to women's political representation. Research suggests that this barrier is culture. As discussed in Chapter 4, negative cultural beliefs toward women are based in either religious traditions or cultural attitudes that suggest that women should not participate in the political realm.

Although arguments for the equality of all people regardless of sex are manifest across all major world religions, Islam in particular has been used in many countries in the Middle East to keep women out of politics. The most recent examples of this approach took place in both Kuwait and Saudi Arabia, where antisuffragists used the *Shari'a*, the Islamic law or code of conduct, to combat women's agitation for political rights. Once suffrage is granted, these societies often still resist women's election to office. As noted earlier, women were first appointed to office rather than elected in most Middle Eastern countries.

Alternatively, some of these low performers may have been hindered by large breaks in their parliamentary histories. For example, Nigeria has had a functioning parliament for only a few years since it became sovereign in 1960, reaching a maximum of only 4.9% women in parliament in 2003.

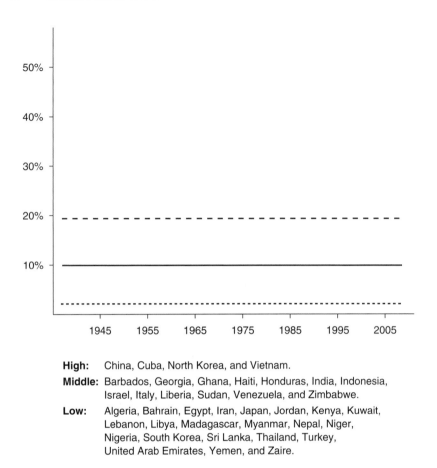

High: China, Cuba, North Korea, and Vietnam.
Middle: Barbados, Georgia, Ghana, Haiti, Honduras, India, Indonesia, Israel, Italy, Liberia, Sudan, Venezuela, and Zimbabwe.
Low: Algeria, Bahrain, Egypt, Iran, Japan, Jordan, Kenya, Kuwait, Lebanon, Libya, Madagascar, Myanmar, Nepal, Niger, Nigeria, South Korea, Sri Lanka, Thailand, Turkey, United Arab Emirates, Yemen, and Zaire.

Figure 3.2   Patterns of Representation: Flat

NOTE: These are generalized examples of country histories. Individual countries may have slight variations away from the general trend. Also ignored are periods of crisis or war when a parliament was dissolved, and for countries independent after 1945 we only look at the percentage of women in parliament following the country's independence. Each graph includes three lines that demonstrate variations of the same basic configuration; the best performing group is indicated by a dashed line, the middle group receives a solid line, and the lowest performing group is marked with a dotted line.

In an environment fraught with conflict and instability, women can have a difficult time gaining momentum over time and building on previous gains. However, as we discuss in Chapter 6, conflict and instability can also provide unique opportunities for women to make large jumps in accessing positions of power typically denied to them.

The second group of Flat countries, marked by the solid line, also elects a fairly constant number of women to parliament over time, but the number of women is higher, around 5–10%. A good example of this trajectory is Israel, which elected 10.8% women to their first parliament in 1949 and continued to hover around 2 to 4 percentage points below that number for the next 50 years. This group of countries in this Middle Flat group exhibits the greatest regional variation of any historical path, including countries in Asia (India and Indonesia), the Caribbean (Barbados and Haiti), Eastern Europe (Georgia), Latin America (Honduras and Venezuela), the Middle East (Israel), sub-Saharan Africa (Ghana, Liberia, Sudan, Zimbabwe), and even the West (Italy). Around the world, therefore, a steady level of women's participation at about the 10% level is a typical pattern.

Finally, the world's remaining communist countries—China, Cuba, North Korea, and Vietnam—appear together in the High Flat group and are indicated by the dashed line. This group has high and very steady levels of women's participation in parliaments. For the 30 years between 1975 and 2005, for example, China held steady around 21% women in their parliament, deviating from that number by less than 2% in either direction. North Korea was even more stable during the same period, vacillating between 19.5% and 21.1% women to parliament over the whole time period. Cuba and Vietnam both did slightly better in women's descriptive representation, breaking the 25% barrier.

Although women appear to have successfully stormed the halls of power in communist countries such as China and Vietnam, parliaments in these countries are not the true seats of power. Unlike in democratic systems, where legislatures are the voice of the people, legislatures under communism serve only as "rubber stamps" on the decisions made by party elites, positions where women are "noticeably absent" (Matland and Montgomery 2003:6). Although women may not have real political power, communism uses a language and ideology of gender equality. Regimes call for the dissolution of public and private spheres, institute higher levels of education for women, and enforce female participation in the labor force and in politics. Further, scholars generally agree that Marxist-Leninist governments actively attempt to erase gender differences (Gal and Kligman 2000:5; Matland and Montgomery 2003).

However, in reality, women living under communism are still marginalized by the patriarchal system (Fodor 2002). For example, although extensive welfare programs may allow women to participate in the labor force, women are concentrated in lower prestige positions that earn lower wages, and women are still expected to perform the bulk of household and child-rearing duties (Gal and Kligman 2000). Thus, although communist systems use the language of feminist emancipation, power is not shared equally between men and women. Women appear in such high numbers in communist systems because their political participation is considered mandatory, and states reserve a certain share of parliamentary seats for women. It is this policy that produces the high, flat trajectories visible in Figure 3.2. Still, although women may not be truly powerful in communist countries, women are symbolically powerful there.

Increasing Countries: Women Make
Steady Gains in Representation

We label the next general pattern that countries follow Increasing. Many countries in the West fall into this category, along with a few from Latin America and Africa. Looking at Figure 3.3, it becomes clear that countries with generally increasing trajectories vary across two main dimensions: the height of the curve (what percent of the parliament women eventually attain) and where the increase started (the time period when women started making substantial gains). The main classifying dimension is height, or the largest percentage women in parliament the country reached. For example, the High Increasing category includes five of the six countries with the highest female parliamentary representation in the world in 2005: Sweden (45.3%), Norway (38.2%), Finland (37.5%), Denmark (36.9%), and the Netherlands (36.7%). The Middle Increasing category includes countries that reached between 25% and 35%, and countries in the Low Increasing category end up between around 18% and 24%. Countries with increases that did not reach 18% are often in the Small Gains category, which is discussed later.

The second dimension for classifying countries in the Increasing category is when women began making gains in descriptive representation—the point in time where the graph's curve begins to increase. Among this group of countries, the timing of women's gains in political power goes hand-in-hand with what percent of the legislature they ultimately attained. That is, of the countries that follow a general increasing pattern, higher per-forming countries often had an earlier inflection point—beginning to make significant gains earlier in time than countries in the lower performing groups. Figure 3.3 shows that countries in the High Increasing group often started their steep incline in the late 1970s and early 1980s. Finland and Sweden pretty closely follow this trajectory, both crossing the 30% women in parliament threshold by 1985. Middle Increasing countries, marked by the solid line, often began their incline a little bit later. Iceland started to grow in the late 1980s, whereas Austria did not make significant gains until the early 1990s. Several countries in the Low Increasing group, such as Bolivia, Burundi, and Portugal, did not cross the threshold of 10% women in parliament until the mid-to-late 1990s.

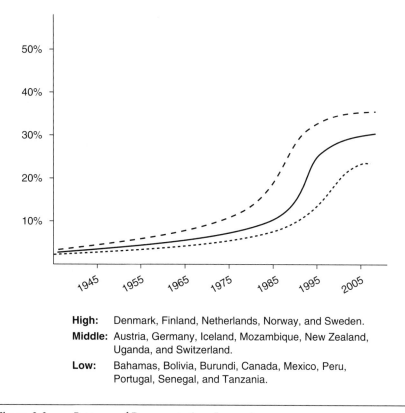

High: Denmark, Finland, Netherlands, Norway, and Sweden.
Middle: Austria, Germany, Iceland, Mozambique, New Zealand,
         Uganda, and Switzerland.
Low: Bahamas, Bolivia, Burundi, Canada, Mexico, Peru,
         Portugal, Senegal, and Tanzania.

Figure 3.3   Patterns of Representation: Increasing

Why did women do so well in these countries? First, with the exception
of the Netherlands, all of the countries in the High Increasing category
are Scandinavian countries, and this reaffirms the importance of regional
differences, and culture, in women's representation. Heckscher (1984:172)
notes, "it is no exaggeration to say that the fundamental principle of equality between men and women is more widely accepted in Scandinavia than
in most other countries of the world; this is seen in legislation, in the apparent attitudes of the public, and in actual practice."

But more is going on than simply a culture of equality. All of the High
Increasing countries, and all but one of the Middle Increasing countries,
also have a **proportional representation system.** Proportional representation
systems are different from the majoritarian systems found in the United
States and Britain. In proportional representation systems, citizens vote for
parties, rather than individuals. That is, a party puts forward a list of candidates and voters vote for the party, rather than any one candidate. Then,

a party gets the percent of seats in the legislature equal to the percent of votes it received. If a party receives 30% of votes, it takes the top 30% of candidates on its list, and they get seats in the legislature. Proportional representation electoral systems are good for women's representation because they are not zero-sum contests between men and women. In majoritarian systems, a woman must run directly against a man for a seat in the legislature. This may put her at a disadvantage if voters prefer male candidates. But in a proportional representation system, if a party list was all men, it might look equally undesirable to voters. The importance of proportional representation electoral systems, and other political factors, is discussed in Chapter 5.

Big Jumps: Women Make Sudden Gains

The third historical pattern of women's parliamentary representation is the Big Jump. Countries in this group experience extremely large gains in women's representation in short periods of time—often a single election cycle. In Figure 3.4, we classify countries by the level of women's parliamentary representation following the jump. We use thresholds similar to the Increasing category described earlier, where High Jump countries finished their big jump above 35% women in parliament, Middle Jump countries reached between 25% and 35% women, and countries in the Low Jump category achieved between 16% and 24%. The Low and Middle Jump categories include a range of countries from around the world, both old and new, both industrialized and less developed. Rwanda is the only country in the High Jump category, ousting Sweden to become the most gender balanced parliament in the world in 2003 with 48.8% women.

But doesn't where a country started make a difference for how high it can jump? Yes. There are two kinds of jumps a country can make: absolute jumps and relative jumps. Absolute jumps are the simple percentage increase in women's parliamentary representation. Rwanda's representation, for example, jumped from 25.7% to 48.8% in 2003, an absolute gain of 23.1% in a single year. No matter where a country starts in its level of female representation, be it 2% women or 30% women, large absolute gains create significant changes to the gender composition of a parliament.

Relative gains, on the other hand, take into consideration where a country started. Big relative jumps are seen when a country starts with few women in its parliament. It is easier for a country with 2% women in its legislature to double women's numbers to 4% than it is for a country to double 20% women to 40%. Relative jumps also signify important changes to parliamentary composition. If the number of women in parliament doubles or triples, this represents a significant change to the status quo, even if

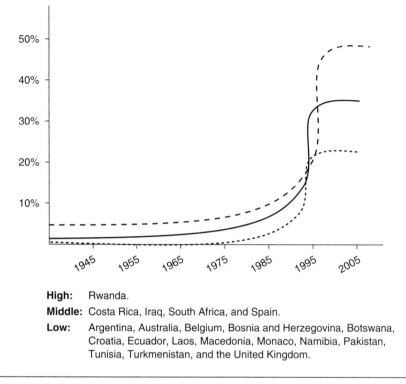

High: Rwanda.
Middle: Costa Rica, Iraq, South Africa, and Spain.
Low: Argentina, Australia, Belgium, Bosnia and Herzegovina, Botswana,
         Croatia, Ecuador, Laos, Macedonia, Monaco, Namibia, Pakistan,
         Tunisia, Turkmenistan, and the United Kingdom.

Figure 3.4   Patterns of Representation: Big Jump

it does not represent an especially large absolute gain or bring the number of women to a particularly high level. Relative gains are easier to make if the prior percentage of women in parliament was low, so they often identify when women made their first significant gains in representation.

To illustrate the difference, let's return to the case of Rwanda. Before the 23.1% gain in 2003, Rwanda experienced its first big jump in 1997, from 4.3% to 17.1%, almost quadrupling the percentage of women in parliament. Thus, in an absolute sense, the 2003 gain was much larger, but in a relative sense the 1997 gain is more significant.

Table 3.2 presents the absolute and relative jumps in women's parliamentary representation in select Big Jump countries. Countries with the largest absolute gains appear at the top of the list.

Notice that the countries in Table 3.2 often experienced their big jump from the mid-1990s through the early 21st century. This is no coincidence. During that period, countries around the world began to implement **gender quotas**, where individual parties or country constitutions mandate a certain percentage of female candidates or parliamentarians. In fact, the vast majority of countries

Table 3.2   Absolute and Relative Gains in the Percentage of Women in Parliament of Select Big Jump Countries

Country	Start (%)	End (%)	Absolute (%)	Relative (%)	Years
Iraq	7.6	31.6	24.0	4.16	2003–2005
South Africa	1.2	25.0	23.8	20.83	1994–1995
Rwanda	25.7	48.8	23.1	1.90	2002–2003
Pakistan	2.3	21.1	18.8	9.17	1999–2002
Monaco	5.6	22.2	16.6	3.96	1997–1998
Argentina	5.8	21.8	16.0	3.76	1992–1995
Costa Rica	19.3	35.1	15.8	1.82	2001–2002
Spain	21.6	36.0	14.4	1.67	1999–2004
Ecuador	3.7	17.4	13.7	4.70	1997–1998
Turkmenistan	4.6	18.0	13.4	3.91	1993–1994
Australia	8.8	21.6	12.8	2.45	1995–1998
Rwanda	4.3	17.1	12.8	3.98	1996–1997
Croatia	7.9	20.5	12.6	2.59	1999–2000
Laos	9.4	21.2	11.8	2.26	1996–1997
Singapore	4.3	16.0	11.7	3.72	2000–2001
Tunisia	11.5	22.8	11.3	1.98	2003–2004
Namibia	6.9	18.1	11.2	2.62	1993–1994
Belgium	12.7	23.3	10.6	1.83	1998–1999
Macedonia	7.5	17.5	10.0	2.33	2001–2002
Bosnia & Herzegovina	7.1	16.7	9.6	2.35	2001–2002
United Kingdom	9.5	18.2	8.7	1.92	1996–1997

on this list introduced gender quotas into law just before large gains were made. For example, South Africa, the country with the largest relative gain, achieved these results via a gender quota. After the major political party in South Africa, the African National Congress (ANC), adopted a 30% quota for women, women's share of parliamentary seats rose by 23.8%, increasing by more than 20 times. Similar is the Iraq case, whose 2004 interim constitution introduced a quota requiring that one quarter of parliamentary seats be filled by women. The 25% quota in Iraq led to the largest absolute increase in women's parliamentary representation ever seen. We explore the different types of gender quotas and their effects in Chapter 5.

Small Gains: Women Catching Up?

The fourth pattern of women's representation over time is the Small Gain. In these countries, women truly remain just a "blip on the male political landscape" (Reynolds 1999:547). Unlike the Flat category, Small Gains countries experience change over time (Figure 3.5). But they did not experience either the steady increases or big jumps that resulted in a substantial percentage of female parliamentarians. Percentages of women remain relatively low in Small Gains countries, and women's smallish gains came generally fairly late. In 2005, women's parliamentary representation in Small Gains countries ranged from 7.7% women in Ethiopia to 15.2% women in the United States.

Because these countries have not experienced large gains, the Small Gains category only has two subsets: low and middle. Low Gains countries have come close to, but not yet achieved, 10% women in parliament. In fact, many of these countries could be placed in the Low Flat category if not for recent evidence that women's participation in politics is on the rise. Bhutan, for example, did not elect more than 2% women to their parliament for most of the country's history, but in 2000 the country reached 9.3%. Countries in the Middle Gains category have reached between around 10% and 15%. France, Ireland, and the United States fall into this category, as none has enough women in power as of 2005 to be placed in the Low Increasing group.

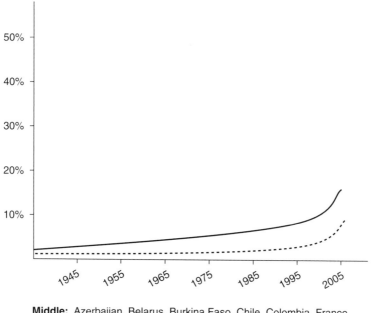

Middle: Azerbaijan, Belarus, Burkina Faso, Chile, Colombia, France, Ireland, Lesotho, Mali, Morocco, Sierra Leone, Syria, Tajikistan, United States, and Uruguay.

Low: Bhutan, Brazil, Ethiopia, Greece, Malaysia, and Malta.

Figure 3.5   Patterns of Representation: Small Gains

There is no single explanation for why women were unable to make gains until the very recent past in this group of countries. For example, the explanation for Chile might be a combination of **machismo**, a patriarchal ideology that exaggerates masculinity (see Chapter 8) and a history of parliamentary interruptions. In the United States, however, as discussed in Chapter 9, the forces of incumbency, zero-sum contests between men and women, and a lack of willing female candidates until recently better explain women's lack of progress. A variety of forces can combine to keep women from achieving political power.

Plateaus: Women Fall Back

Women can also lose the power they have gained over time. The countries classified as Plateau demonstrate this pattern. Countries in the Plateau category often experience an early jump in women's parliamentary representation followed by a period of general stability and then a sharp decline. Of the five general patters, this is the only one associated with a major decline in the percentage of women in parliament.

Most of the Plateau countries are formerly communist countries, including Albania, Cambodia, Bulgaria, Czechoslovakia, Hungary, Mongolia, Poland, Romania, and the Soviet Union. During their communist period, these countries espoused the same ideology as the communist countries (China, Cuba, North Korea, and Vietnam) discussed earlier. But, as in the current communist countries, female politicians in these Plateau countries were not in truly powerful positions. When these countries transitioned to democracy around 1990, their legislatures became politically powerful for the first time, and women's participation dropped sharply. For example, Hungary had between 20% and 30% women in its legislature between 1979 and 1989. As in other communist countries, this legislature was not the seat of ultimate authority. When Hungary transitioned to democracy in 1990, 13 parties fought for seats in the newly powerful legislature. After those true elections, women's participation in politics dropped to 7%. The unique history of women's representation in Eastern Europe and the former Soviet Union is covered in more detail in Chapter 8.

The other Plateau countries have similar stories. Some of the Plateau countries, such as Guyana and Guinea-Bissau, were not formally communist but did have Leftist authoritarian governments. Like the communist countries, these governments kept the number of women in politics artificially high. Once free and fair democratic elections were held, the percentage of women in parliament declined sharply. The complicated relationship between women and democracy is covered in Chapter 5.

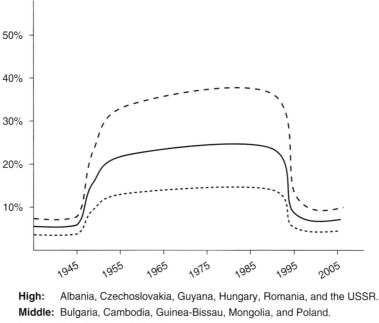

High: Albania, Czechoslovakia, Guyana, Hungary, Romania, and the USSR.
Middle: Bulgaria, Cambodia, Guinea-Bissau, Mongolia, and Poland.
Low: Bangladesh and Chad.

Figure 3.6   Patterns of Representation: Plateau

The Plateaus in Figure 3.6 vary in several important ways. First, like the
other patterns, they differ by height. High Plateaus (the dashed line) peaked
at around 30% to 35%, Middle Plateaus ranged at their highest point
from about 20% to 25%, and Low Plateaus reached around 10% to 15%.
Second, within High, Middle, and Low Plateaus, individual countries differ
by the length of time spent at the peak of the plateau. Chad, for example,
spent only 4 years at 16.4% women in parliament before dropping down
to 2.4%. On the other end of the spectrum, Bulgaria crossed 15% women
in parliament in 1949 and gradually increased for a full 40 years (to 21%)
until 1990, when it dropped to 8.5%.

A final way that Plateaus vary is that some countries have rebounded in
women's representation since their sharp declines, whereas others have
not. Of the 11 Plateau countries that still exist (many countries, such as the
Soviet Union, have dissolved), only Bulgaria and Poland rebounded to
levels close to their prior peaks. See Chapter 8 for an in-depth discussion of
rebounding.

Women in Top Leadership Positions

Women's representation in legislative bodies is only one of the many ways that women can access power. Women can also ascend to the highest levels of politics as the primary national leader of their country—such as President Corazon Aquino of the Philippines or Prime Minister Margaret Thatcher of Britain. But a female in the top leadership position of a country is an extremely rare creature. In 1980, Jean Blondel estimated that 5 out of the 1,000 leaders in the contemporary world were women (Blondel 1980:116). Today, a few more female leaders have appeared on the world stage, but numbers are still small. Since 1960, when Sirimavo Bandaranaike became the first female to lead a modern country, only 30 women have become the top political executive of their country.

Table 3.3 lists these 30 female political executives over the last 50 years. Although it might seem simple, it is not an easy matter to determine who is a political leader of a country and who is not. National leaders may be called a head of state, a head of government, or both—and a title in one country means something very different in another. For example, in some countries the head of state is a very powerful position. George W. Bush is the head of state of the United States of America. In other countries, the head of state is a purely ceremonial position—for example, Elizabeth II, Queen of Great Britain and Northern Ireland.

Looking down the list of leaders, some have held the title "prime minister," and others have held the title "president." In all cases, these women are the leaders of their respective countries; what differs is the form of government of their country. In a parliamentary system, the top political leader is often called a prime minister. In a presidential system, that person is usually known as a president. Understanding the distinction is important because it can help us to distinguish women who truly hold positions of power from those who hold largely ceremonial roles. "It is clear that one wants to define leaders by their real activities, not by a title which they possess" (Blondel 1980:11). A person holding the title of president in a parliamentary system is not the leader of the country but holds a position that is typically ceremonial and boasts little power. A person holding the title "prime minister" in a presidential system at best shares power with the president.

To understand the distinctions, consider three different female prime ministers:

> Gro Harlem Brundtland was prime minister in a parliamentary democracy. In the Norwegian government, the prime minister acts as both the executive and legislative head of the government. He or she holds the most powerful

Table 3.3   Female National Leaders

	Title	Country	Dates of Rule	Relationship to Powerful Male?	Level of Development
Sirimavo Bandaranaike	prime minister	Sri Lanka	1960–65, 1970–77	Yes, husband	Developing
Indira Gandhi	prime minister	India	1966–77, 1980–84	Yes, father	Developing
Golda Meir	prime minister	Israel	1969–74	No	
Isabel Peron	president	Argentina	1974–76	Yes, husband	Developing
Margaret Thatcher	prime minister	UK	1979–90	No	
Lydia Gueiler Tejada	president[t]	Bolivia	1979–80	No	Developing
Eugenia Charles	prime minister	Dominica	1980–95	No	Developing
Gro Harlem Brundtland	prime minister	Norway	1981, 1986–89, 1990–96	No	
Corazon Aquino	president	Philippines	1986–92	Yes, husband	Developing
Benazir Bhutto	prime minister	Pakistan	1988–90, 1993–96	Yes, father	Developing
Violeta Chamorro	president	Nicaragua	1990–96	Yes, husband	Developing
Ertha Pascal-Trouillot	president[t]	Haiti	1990–91	No	Developing
Khaleda Zia	prime minister	Bangladesh	1991–96, 2001–present	Yes, husband	Developing
Kim Campbell	prime minister	Canada	1993	No	
Silvie Kinigi	president[t]	Burundi	1993–94	No	Developing
Tansu Ciller	prime minister	Turkey	1993–96	No	Developing
Reneta Indzhova	prime minister[t]	Bulgaria	1994–95	No	

(Continued)

Table 3.3 (Continued)

	Title	Country	Dates of Rule	Relationship to Powerful Male?	Level of Development
Chandrika Kumaratunga	president	Sri Lanka	1994–2005	Yes, mother and father	Developing
Ruth Perry	president[t]	Liberia	1996–97	No	Developing
Sheikh Hasina Wajed	prime minister	Bangladesh	1996–2001	Yes, father	Developing
Jenny Shipley	prime minister	New Zealand	1997–99	No	Developing
Janet Jagan	president	Guyana	1997–99	Yes, husband	Developing
Mireya Moscoso de Arias	president	Panama	1999–2004	Yes, husband	Developing
Helen Clark	prime minister	New Zealand	1999–present	No	
Megawati Sukarnoputri	president	Indonesia	2001–04	Yes, father	Developing
Gloria Macapagal-Arroyo	president	Philippines	2001–present	Yes, father	Developing
Angela Merkel	chancellor	Germany	2005–present	No	
Ellen Johnson-Sirleaf	president	Liberia	2005–present	No	Developing
Michelle Bachelet	president	Chile	2006–present	No	Developing
Portia Simpson-Miller	prime minister	Jamaica	2006–present	No	Developing

t = interim or acting

NOTE: Ruth Dreifuss served as president of Switzerland between 1998 and 1999 as part of a seven-member chief executive with a rotating chair.

political position in the country. While in office Brundtland pursued strong economic and foreign policy agendas and will be remembered for bringing environmental issues to the top of the nation's political agenda.

Edith Cresson was the prime minister of France from 1990 to 1992. France has a mixed political system with a strong president and a potentially powerful prime minister. The prime minister is chosen by the president from the dominant party in the parliament. If the dominant party in the parliament is different from the party of the president, then the prime minister can be a very strong political figure (this is called cohabitation). However, if the dominant party is the *same* as the president's party, then the prime minister is generally viewed as subservient to the president and holds little independent power. Edith Cresson was of the same party as Francois Mitterrand, a strong President. Indeed, as Cresson herself explains: " . . . you are not entirely free to choose [your] ministers (far from it). As far as I [was] concerned, my freedom was certainly limited" (Liswood 1995:122). In a list of leaders of France in the twentieth century, Francois Mitterrand would appear from 1990 to 1992, but not Edith Cresson.

Elisabeth Domitien held the position of prime minister of the Central African Republic from 1975 to 1976. She was appointed to the position by the dictator Jean-Bédel Bokassa when he formed a new government and decided to include a prime minister. But when Bokassa began discussing making the country a monarchy and crowning himself emperor (which he ultimately did), Domitien publicly spoke out against his plans and was promptly fired. Domitien cannot be considered to have had any substantial political power: she "was only a puppet." (Opfell 1993:65)

Changing political systems and mother-daughter succession can make titles even more interesting. In Sri Lanka, the title indicating the most powerful position in the country has changed over time. If you look at Table 3.3, you see two women from Sri Lanka on the list of powerful women—a mother, who was prime minister, and her daughter, who was president. When Sirimavo Bandaranaike became prime minister of Sri Lanka in 1960, Sri Lanka's political system was a Westminster-style parliamentary system with a powerful prime minister. Thus, Sirimavo Bandaranaike was a powerful leader in Sri Lanka from 1960 to 1965 and again from 1970 to 1977. But in 1978, Sri Lanka's president was given much greater power. Thus, Bandaranaike's daughter, Chandrika Kumaratunga, was also a powerful leader because she held the title "president" from 1994 to the present. In a further twist, Chandrika Kumaratunga appointed her mother as prime minister from 1994 to 2000. But because Bandaranaike now held the position of prime minister in a presidential system, she could not be classified as the leader of the country. Her daughter held that honor.

Another important group of female leaders are not the top executive in their country but can be viewed as holding a type of dual leadership role. As discussed in the case of Edith Cresson, in some political systems, a president holds much of the power but the prime minister is an important leader in government, especially if she is from the opposition party. Table 3.4 lists all female prime ministers who have served in such systems. Although not listed here, in some countries women may hold the top position in a legislature without holding the title "Prime Minister." For instance, Nancy Pelosi, recently elected Speaker of the House in the United States, is an important leader of the U.S. government.

Table 3.3 contains only those women who have held truly top political positions, either as prime minister in a parliamentary system or president in a presidential system. Table 3.4 contains women who have shared power in a dual leadership system. This means that there are some famous female leaders who do not appear on either list. For example, Ireland is often highlighted as exemplary in having had two female presidents in a row. But neither Mary Robinson, president of Ireland from 1990 to 1997, nor Mary McAleese, current president of Ireland, are allowed to suggest legislation or even make partisan statements. Similarly, Vigdis Finnbogadottir of Iceland held a largely ceremonial position as president from 1980 to 1996. Table 3.5 contains female leaders who only held ceremonial, or symbolic, power. As noted earlier, the tables also do not include hereditary heads of state, such as Queen Elizabeth II of Great Britain and Northern Ireland or Queen Beatrix of the Netherlands. In most countries today, such positions are entirely ceremonial.

Table 3.4   Female Prime Ministers in Presidential Systems

	Country	Dates in Office
Maria de Lourdes Pintasilgo	Portugal	1979
Milka Planinc	Yugoslavia	1982–86
Edith Cresson	France	1991–92
Hanna Suchocka	Poland	1992–93
Sirimavo Bandaranaike	Sri Lanka	1994–2000
Claudette Werleigh	Haiti	1995–96
Tarja Halonen[a]	Finland	2000–present
Madoir Boye	Senegal	2001–02
Maria das Neves Ceita Batista de Sousa	Sao Tome and Principe	2002–04
Luisa Dias Diogo	Mozambique	2004–present
Yuliya Tymoshenko	Ukraine	2005
Han Myung-Sook	South Korea	2006–present

a. Halonen is the president of Finland but shares power with the prime minister.

Table 3.5   Female National Leaders Holding Mainly Symbolic Power

	Title	Country	Dates in Office
Elisabeth Domitien	prime minister	Central African Republic	1975–76
Vigdis Finnbogadottir	president	Iceland	1980–96
Agatha Barbara	president	Malta	1982–87
Sabine Bergmann-Pohl	president	Germany (Dem Rep)	1990
Mary Robinson	president	Ireland	1990–97
Agathe Uwilingiyimana	prime minister	Rwanda	1993
Mary McAleese	president	Ireland	1997–present
Vaira Vike-Freiberga	president	Latvia	1999–present

NOTE: Tables 3.3–3.5 do not include female leaders of states that are not recognized as independent. For example, Pamela Gordon, Premier of Bermuda (a British territory), in 1997–1998 is not included. Neither is Kazimiera Prunskiene, prime minister of Lithuania.

This is not to say that symbolic leaders do not play a very important role for women in politics. When men dominate formal politics, it perpetuates ideas that politics is the domain of men. Long lists of female leaders therefore help make it seem normal that women would participate in politics (Phillips 1995) and may inspire more girls to consider politics as a career (Burrell 1994). Especially in countries where women's representation is particularly low, a female in a ceremonial leadership position can provide a boost of confidence for women.

How Women Attain Top Leadership Positions

What paths to power do women take to gain top political office? To answer that question we begin by describing the earliest women to gain political power. Before 1980, there were only six women who attained substantial leadership positions in their country: Sirimavo Bandaranaike of Sri Lanka, Indira Gandhi of India, Golda Meir of Israel, Isabel Peron of Argentina, Margaret Thatcher of Great Britain, and Lydia Gueiler Tejada of Bolivia. These women truly broke stereotypes, and their backgrounds and rise to power provide a glimpse into the themes that matter for women achieving such rarified positions of power.

In 1960, Sirimavo Bandaranaike became the world's first prime minister of Sri Lanka (called Ceylon at that time). Born Sirimavo Ratwatte to an aristocratic family in 1916, Sirimavo was 24 years old when her parents arranged her marriage to Solomon West Ridgeway Dias Bandaranaike, a rising politician who also came from a wealthy landowning family. In the early years of their marriage, she raised children and was active in the Ceylon women's association, which had the aim "to ameliorate rural conditions and improve the social and economic life of the people, particularly in the rural areas" (Opfell 1993:3). Meanwhile her husband was elected to the nation's house of representatives and advocated policies of socialism and nationalism. In 1956, her husband became prime minister when a coalition of his party, the Sri Lanka freedom party (SLFP), with independent and leftist parties won the majority of seats in the national legislature. Under his leadership, the state began to nationalize a number of industries and antagonized the Tamil-speaking Hindu population by introducing legislation to make Buddhism the national religion. On September 25, 1959, tragedy struck. Solomon was assassinated in their villa, practically before Sirimavo's eyes. New elections were set and the widow, known as "Mrs. Banda," was asked to campaign on behalf of her husband's party.

Sirimavo campaigned tirelessly and in May became the head of the party. She had little political experience before this point and only reluctantly agreed to accept the party's nomination.

> I had no intention to take up politics during his life. Except after he died, people wanted me. I was more or less forced to take it up competitively . . . to lead the party after his death. I did not want to. But after much consideration, I agreed to take up the leadership of the party. (quoted in Liswood 1995:47)

In July, the SLFP won 75 of 151 seats, and Sirimavo Bandaranaike was appointed prime minister. She immediately began to follow through on some of her husband's policy priorities, such as nationalization and encouragement of Buddhism. She also began to enforce the use of Sinhalese, rather than English, as the national language. This last move created dissent among the Tamil minority, and she had to send troops into the Tamil provinces. In 1965, her party lost power, but she regained the position in 1970. In 1972, she presided over the ceremonies when Ceylon became the Socialist Republic of Sri Lanka. Her party lost power again in 1977. She remained in politics after that point, running a failed bid for president in 1988 and ultimately retaking her seat in the national assembly and heading the opposition. In 1994, her daughter, Chandrika Kumaratunga, became president and appointed her as prime minister once again.

The story of Sirimavo Bandaranaike's rise to political prominence introduces our first important theme. As would many of the female leaders that followed her, the world's first female prime minister gained power originally as a surrogate for her husband. This is hardly a rare occurrence. Fifty percent of the women listed in Table 3.6 have famous husbands or fathers who preceded them in political life. To name just a few: Indira Gandhi's father was India's founding prime minister, Corazon Aquino's husband was viewed as a national martyr, and in Bangladesh the widow of a former president replaced the daughter of a former prime minister. The phenomenon of daughters or wives standing as surrogates for their fathers or husbands is particularly apparent in regions of the world where women in leadership positions would be least expected (Jalalzai 2004). For example, Asia has generally low levels of female participation in other areas of politics, but it accounts for 30% of female national leaders and 75% of countries with more than one female leader over time. However, every woman who has held high political office in Asia is part of a political dynasty.

D'Amico (1995:18) labels this the "widow's walk to power" and Burn (2005:234) explains that the surrogate route to power may be most common where attitudes toward women are especially traditional. In places where women are seen as helpmates to their husbands, it is easy to visualize them as stand-ins for their husbands. The husband or father may have been assassinated, hanged, or have spent a great deal of time in prison, thereby making him a martyr in the eyes of the public and the surrogate wife or daughter a symbol of the continuing struggle.

There is nothing subtle about women's surrogacy. During campaigns, references to the husband or father are repeated time and again, with the spoken or unspoken implication that the female candidate would simply continue his legacy. Benazir Bhutto referred often to her father in speeches and made sure his picture was in the background of her official portraits (Anderson 1993:52). During her campaign, Violeta Chamorro repeatedly invoked her assassinated husband, who was viewed as a national martyr: "I am not a politician, but I believe this is my destiny. I am doing this for Pedro and for my country" (Boudreaux 1991, quoted in Saint-Germain 1993). On hearing of Indira Gandhi's election in 1966, the crowds cried out not only "long live Indira" but also "long live Jawaharlal" [her father] (Moraes 1980:127, quoted in Everett 1993).

Of course, family dynasties in politics are not restricted to women following their husbands or fathers. Asia, in particular, has a strong legacy of family politics. For example, in India, Indira Gandhi's son followed her into politics, cementing a Gandhi-Nehru dynasty lasting for most of the last half of the 20th century. But relationship to a former politician is definitely one way that women have been able to reach the highest echelons of political life.

As mentioned, Indira Gandhi, the second woman to achieve the highest political office of a country, was also related to a famous political father, Jawaharlal Nehru. Nehru had worked with Mahatma Gandhi to achieve independence from Britain and, in 1947, was the newly independent India's first prime minister. But Gandhi exemplifies an important clause in the surrogate path to power: Female widows of politically powerful husbands often have little political experience before standing in as a surrogate for their husband. In contrast, daughters of political figures may have substantial political experience before taking power (see Genovese 1993:212–3). Indira Gandhi had a great deal of political experience of her own. She had been a member of the Congress Party, headed by her father since 1952. She was elected to the Congress Parliamentary Board in 1958 and become the president of the Congress Party in 1959. In 1966, 2 years after the death of her father, she became prime minister. During her time in office, she faced economic crises, war, and political intrigue. She also declared emergency rule when her leadership was challenged, imposed authoritarian rule, and censored newspapers. She was assassinated in 1984 and was succeeded in the prime minister's office by her son, Rajiv Gandhi (Carras 1995; Everett 1993; Opfell 1993).

Together, Bandaranaike and Gandhi introduce another theme in women's path to power—that women have done better gaining high-level positions of power in developing nations than in more developed nations. Until 1979, when Margaret Thatcher ascended to the top political position in Britain as prime minister of the House of Commons, the only women to have achieved leadership positions were in developing nations. Looking at all of the women who have ever held the highest political positions of a country, 73% of them are from the developing world. As we already pointed out, it is also in these developing nations that women leaders are more likely to be surrogates. But even among the women who do not have any powerful male relation, 53% are from the developing world. The West does not lead the world in elevating women to highest political office.

Golda Meir, the third woman to hold a national leadership position, had no family connections. Hers was solely a rise through the ranks. Born in 1898 in Kiev, Ukraine, Golda Meir had early experiences with both the pain of being a Jew in Russia and the passion of politics. By the time she left for the United States at 8 years old, Golda had many opportunities to see violence and discrimination from her gentile neighbors. For example, a drunken man once terrified Golda and a friend by banging their heads together and shouting that all Jews should be so treated (Opfell 1993:34). But, sitting on a shelf above the big coal stove, Golda was inspired by the passionate political rhetoric of the clandestine political meetings held by her older sister in the family kitchen. After her family's move to Milwaukee, Wisconsin, she had her first political success "as the main organizer and keynote speaker, at age 10, of a benefit show to raise money for her classmates who could not afford the nominal charge for textbooks. In hindsight, one can see patterns that would be repeated time and again: identification or wrong that needed to be rectified, a focus on fundraising, diligent organizing and persuading (including talking the owner of the hall into renting it on the promise of payment after the event), and delivery of a major address ad-lib" (Thompson 1995:137).

By the time she was 20 years old, Golda had married and was increasingly active in the Zionist movement, which advocated for a Jewish state in Palestine. At 23 years of age, she left America for Palestine with some members of her family, lived briefly on a kibbutz, and settled in Tel Aviv. She became increasingly involved in Zionist politics but simultaneously estranged from her husband who had difficulty with her political work. From 1928 to 1968, Golda moved up the ranks into the political elite, acting as fundraiser, signer of the proclamation of the State of Israel in 1948, ambassador, and ultimately both minister of labor and foreign minister. In 1968, at age 70, she officially retired from politics—a retirement that was to last only a little over a year. In 1970, Israel's prime minister suffered a fatal heart attack and Golda was asked to return to politics, first as interim prime minister and then as the nationally elected prime minister. She served until 1975 and during her term contended with economic problems, terrorism, and the Yom Kippur war with Egypt and Syria.

As the third woman to ever hold the highest political office, Golda Meir exemplifies how women can climb through the ranks of political systems to achieve high office (D'Amico 1995). Other women have followed a similar path. Margaret Thatcher, the fifth woman to hold office, worked her way through Britain's Conservative Party ranks, was elected to the House of Commons in 1959, was elected leader of the Conservative Party in 1975, and finally became prime minister in 1979. Kim Campbell of Canada also took this route, as did Eugenia Charles of Dominica and Portia Simpson-Miller of Jamaica.

But it can take a special circumstance for even these political insiders to achieve high office over a male. To return to Golda Meir's life, she was called out of retirement to lead the country when Israel's prime minister died suddenly of a heart attack. But it is unlikely that this would have occurred had the governing party not been split with personal and political rivalries. Meir was seen as a compromise interim leader to keep the current balance of power until new elections could be held (Thompson 1995:148). Similarly, Margaret Thatcher's election to the head of the Conservative Party was "the result of a series of accidents" (Harris 1988:32) caused by political maneuvering by more powerful party members that left few candidates to oppose her. Indira Gandhi was chosen by a small group of party leaders (called the Syndicate) because they loathed the most obvious candidate, Morarji Desai (Opfell 1993:25) and felt Gandhi would be more malleable.

The last female to lead a country before 1980 illustrates how women have risen to positions of prominence in situations of extreme social or political instability (Genovese 1993). Often, in this case, their time in office is very short. Lydia Gueiler Tejada of Bolivia exemplifies this path to power. The years between 1978 and 1980 were very unstable in Bolivia, with multiple elections, coups, countercoups, and caretaker governments. In 1979, Wálter Guevara Arze was elected president but almost immediately overthrown in a military coup. However, the leader of the coup also stepped down because he was not accepted by the military, civilians, or the United States. Thus, Lydia Gueiler was appointed interim president to arrange fresh elections. Before these elections were finalized, however, Bolivia's first female president was overthrown by General Luis García Meza. She had not been president for even a year.

Other female leaders who took power under situations of extreme social or political unrest include Ruth Perry of Liberia and Silvie Kinigi of Burundi. Both of of these women led their countries briefly during civil wars. In fact, Ruth Perry was appointed to her position by an outside body of neighboring African states because Liberia was under a state of anarchy at the time. When women are placed into leadership positions during times of substantial social upheaval, it may be because they are viewed as symbols of reconciliation. Kinigi, for example, was an ethnic Tutsi originally appointed by an ethnic Hutu to build unity between Burundi's two ethnic groups.

As suggested by reviewing the biographies of the first female leaders, there are many similarities among the women in Tables 3.6 and 3.7. But there is great diversity among them as well. Sirimavo Bandaranaike and Indira Gandhi were from wealthy and privileged backgrounds, whereas Golda Meir and Margaret Thatcher were not. Female leaders from exceptionally privileged backgrounds are more likely in developing countries, but this trend is not universal.

Female leaders also vary in age and level of education. Benazir Bhutto entered office at 35 years old, whereas Janet Jagen of Guyana first entered office at 77 (Jalalzai 2004). Some of the women who have held the highest political office of a country had less than a high school education, whereas others held PhDs. Some were in office less than a year, whereas Margaret Thatcher was Britain's longest serving prime minister of the 20th century.

Difficulties Faced by Female Leaders

Leaders of any gender are expected to behave in certain ways. Traditionally, effective leadership is associated with aggression, competitiveness, dominance, and decisiveness. As discussed in Chapter 1, people also have expectations of women and men. Male stereotypes suggest that men are assertive, aggressive, dominant, independent, and competitive. Women, on the other hand, are stereotyped as nurturing, helpful, likeable, gentle, and polite.

The match between stereotypes of men and leaders is much better than the match between women and leaders. For this reason, women face prejudice as leaders because people tend to assume that leadership is a masculine trait (Eagly and Karau 2002). Further, because women have traditionally been in a subordinate position to men, cultural beliefs lead people to assume that men are more competent and legitimate as leaders than are women (Ridgeway 2001). This prejudice is even more likely to emerge when the leadership position in question is typically male, as in the case of military leaders or political leaders.

Female leaders in highly visible leadership positions therefore must live with assumptions that they are less competent than their male counterparts. They may be held to higher standards than men to obtain and retain their leadership position. Maria Liberia-Peters, prime minister of the Netherlands Antilles (a British protectorate), explains:

> . . . and you had to put all into it, and everybody expected you to put everything into it, because nobody questions the [preparedness] of a man over [a] female . . . when you're a woman, you hear, oh, she's a kindergarten teacher, she's this, she's that and she's the other, and suddenly you are being questioned, so you have to put 100 percent, 200 percent in your work. (quoted in Liswood 1995:68)

Female leaders face an additional problem because they must serve two roles: their role as a leader and their role as a woman. The two sets of expectations can be very different and, in fact, conflict with each other. This puts a female leader in a difficult position. Should she act the way people expect her to act as a woman? Should she be nurturing, supportive, and gentle? Or should she act the way people expect a leader to act? This may require exhibiting "masculine" behavior, such as aggressiveness and dominance. If female leaders choose the second path, research demonstrates that they will be negatively evaluated. In a review of research, Eagly, Makhijani, and Klonsky (1992) found that people evaluate autocratic behavior by women more negatively than the same behavior by men. Women who act assertively violate the expectations of those around them and subsequently get penalized for this behavior (Ridgeway 2001). For example, Margaret Thatcher, a very assertive and aggressive politician, was called Attila the Hen. This puts female leaders in a real catch-22: "Conforming to their gender role can produce a failure to meet the requirements of their leader role, and conforming to the leader role can produce a failure to meet the requirements of their gender role" (Eagly and Johannesen-Schmidt 2001:786).

Consider how Corazon Aquino's early socialization led her into a conflict between her role as a woman in Philippine society and her role as president:

Aquino: In school you're always taught to be polite, and you always ask—you don't command or you don't order. So, I remember, I guess in the first few months of my presidency, I would call in a cabinet member, or maybe a general or somebody working under me, and I would say, well, I would like to ask you to do this. And then, of course, I'm sure they were very shocked. And then, later on, one of my advisers pointed out to me, he said, "Look, perhaps that was all right when you were not president, you know, to be polite and to ask instead of ordering." . . . I guess, as president, you're not expected to be polite, or you're not expected to be too concerned about good manners, etc. . . . You don't ask, you order. And so, well, I certainly learned that fast enough. But in the beginning . . . I guess from the time I went to school, and during my time, there was always what I would refer to as an etiquette class. . . . There was this lady would come to us, and the class was called Lessons in Charm and Good Manners, or something like that. We were taught how to sit and what to do in social engagements, which is, of course, so very different from what it is when you are president.

Interviewer: They didn't teach you how to order generals?

Aquino: No, they did not. (from Liswood 1995:91–92)

Women may also have to overcome social expectations about a woman's proper place. Golda Meir ultimately separated from her husband, at least partly due to her choice of career. She also struggled with her role as mother: "At work, you think of the children you've left at home. At home, you think of the work you've left unfinished. Such a struggle is unleashed within yourself, your heart is rent."

Benazir Bhutto, a female politician in a conservative Muslim country, had to marry to pursue her political career:

I was under so much scrutiny. If my name had been linked with a man, it would have destroyed my political career. Actually, I had reconciled myself to a life without marriage or children for the sake of my career. And then my brothers got married. I realized I didn't even have a home, but in the future I couldn't do politics when I had to ask for permission from their wives as to whether I could use the dining room or the telephone. I couldn't rent a home because a woman living on her own can be suspected of all kinds of scandalous associations. So keeping in mind that many people in Pakistan looked to me, I decided to make a personal sacrifice in what I thought would be, more or less, a loveless marriage, a marriage of convenience. (quoted in Liswood 1995:70)

Bhutto was able to turn her need to marry into political advantage. Her opponents claimed that she was too Western. So she agreed to an arranged marriage, the accepted norm in her society, to emphasize her identity as an Asian woman (Anderson 1993:58). Her opponent countered by timing elections to coincide with the birth of her first child. It was "the first election to be timed for gynaecological considerations" (Singh 1988, quoted in Anderson 1993:59).

Bhutto's use of her need to marry for political advantage suggests that women can use cultural expectations about masculinity and femininity to their advantage. Margaret Thatcher is an example of a female leader who was very aware of the impact of her femininity on the men around her. She dressed attractively and would coax, cajole, and flatter to get her way (Genovese 1993:207). But she also adopted traditionally masculine behavior in a way that men found difficult to counter. Thatcher was aggressive, tough, ruthless, and rude—behavior that men did not expect from a woman. Harris (1995:62) related an interview with a member of Thatcher's first cabinet:

If any male Prime Minister had said things to me in cabinet in the terms and tone that she often adopted, I would have gone to him privately afterwards, given him a blasting, and told him that if he did that again I'd resign. But you can't treat a woman like that. (Liswood 1995:67)

Similarly, because of unwritten but rigorous codes of chivalry, Poland's male-led parties were hesitant to intrigue against Hanna Suchocka, their female prime minister (Liswood 1995). And a recently elected female leader, Ellen Johnson-Sirleaf of Liberia, ran on a gendered platform, claiming that she was free of corruption and would "bring a motherly sensitivity and emotion to the presidency" as a way of healing the wounds of war" (BBC News 2005a).

Gender and Leadership: Are Female Leaders Different From Men?

These women were female leaders. Does that make a difference in how they act? People expect female leaders to be concerned about the welfare of

other people (Eagly and Johannesen-Schmidt 2001). And women live up
to this expectation when in leadership positions (Moskowitz, Suh, and
Desaulniers 1994). For example, Gro Harlem Brundtland, prime minister of
Norway, argued:

> If you don't understand the type of situation that a family in a local commu-
> nity is meeting every day, then how can you sum up and have a total picture?
> Every person in a society is a detail, but the sum of all the details, or the sum
> of all the people, is how society functions. (quoted in Liswood 1995:82)

The depth of caring that some female political leaders express for their
constituents can be inspiring. Corazon Aquino described people at one of
her campaign rallies in the following way:

> They were poor, and certainly they needed every peso, and yet, they would be
> passing out this plastic pail. . . . it was only later when I realized . . . they were
> dropping money there. . . . and, you know, my heart really went out to them,
> because, I thought, if these people are willing to sacrifice for me, then certainly
> I should also be prepared, you know, to undergo whatever sacrifices are
> demanded of me. I think in a way it was the people who really inspired me to
> continue with this. Without them I don't think I would have dared challenge
> somebody as formidable as Mr. Marcos. (quoted in Liswood 1995:101)

While Aquino's heart may have gone out to her constituents, Margaret
Thatcher was famously known as "Maggy Thatcher the Milk Snatcher" for
spearheading the repeal of subsidies for schoolchildren's milk.

Women also tend to be more democratic and participatory in their
leadership style than are men, for example, allowing subordinates to participate in decision making (Eagly and Johnson 1990). Men, in contrast,
tend to be more autocratic and directive. Studies of female legislators do
suggest that women tend to be more collaborative in their leadership styles
than men are, answering more positively when asked whether they "try
hard to find a fair combination of gains and losses for all sides," "pull
people together," and "share power with others" (Rosenthal 1998a:855).
Consider the following account of interviews with state legislators in Ohio:

> One chairwoman emphasized the desire to be more inclusive of as many points
> of view on an issue as possible, to find a win-win solution, and to use nontra-
> ditional decision-making strategies such as facilitator-mediated dispute resolu-
> tion. By contrast, one of her male colleagues preferred to "develop my own
> solution to problem, have it drafted, drop in the hopper and watch everyone
> scream." (Rosenthal 1998a:858–9)

Biographies of women at the highest levels of political leadership suggest that some, such as Corazon Aquino and Violetta de Charmorro, worked for participation and consensus. Others, however, were famously autocratic. Margaret Thatcher was a self-described conviction politician, rather than a consensus politician. She surrounded herself with "yes" men and limited debate and discussion during cabinet meetings. Thatcher would enter a cabinet meeting, tell her cabinet members what she wanted, and then try to bully them through fear, intimidation, control of the agenda, and "sheer force of personality and conviction" (Genovese 1993:199). Indira Gandhi seriously endangered India's 28-year-old democracy by declaring emergency rule when her leadership was challenged. Declaration of emergency rule essentially transformed India into a dictatorship, and Gandhi, as the head of the central government, was able to arrest opposition leaders, censor the press, ban political organizations, and jail more than 100,000 people without trial (Everett 1993).

Are women more peaceful as leaders than men? Stereotypes suggest that men are the aggressive perpetrators of war, whereas women are the peacemakers who try to stop wars. A substantial body of research has demonstrated that women in the general population are less likely to advocate violence and aggression in international affairs. For example, in the United States in the last century, women were less supportive than men of U.S. involvement in wars by approximately 8 percentage points (Conover and Sapiro 1993).

But female leaders may not be different from men in their attitudes about aggression. McGlen and Sarkees (1993) found that women working in the U.S. State Department and Defense Department advocated aggression and violence at the same rate as men. And female leaders may not be able to be more peaceful as they act on the world stage. If male leaders perceive female leaders as weak, countries led by female leaders may be more likely to be attacked by nearby neighbors. Caprioli and Boyer (2001) argued that, of the 10 international crises involving female leaders between 1960 and 1990, the female leaders never initiated a crisis.

But female leaders have been involved in wars. Historically, there have been many warrior queens. For example, Queen and General Tomyris of the Massagetae (in what is now eastern Iran) used her forces to crush the Persians. The legendary and historical Queen Boudica led a warlike society of Celtic heritage in present-day England. And in 17th-century Angola, Queen Nzinga was a cannibal who personally beheaded and drank the blood of prisoners (Goldstein 2001). In the contemporary period, Indira Gandhi, Golda Meir, and Margaret Thatcher were all involved in wars, and Benazir Bhutto and Tansu Ciller were involved in crises that that did not lead to full-scale war. Though women may be seen as symbols of peace and reconciliation when they come to power (as has occurred in Africa), once in power they are willing to use force if necessary. For example, Margaret Thatcher did not hesitate to respond to Argentina's invasion of the British-controlled Falkland Islands. And, like a male leader, Margaret Thatcher experienced a huge rise in popularity after Britain's successful defense of the islands.

Still, although we cannot know their innnermost thoughts, it may be that female leaders do feel differently about war than their male counterparts do. Golda Meir explained:

> I have given instructions that I be informed every time one of our soldiers is killed, even if it is in the middle of the night. When President Nasser leaves instructions that he is to be awakened in the middle of the night if an Egyptian soldier is killed, there will be peace.

Regardless of potential differences between female and male leaders, the fact remains that there have been very few female leaders in history. Simone de Beauvoir put it well: "Perseus, Hercules, David, Achilles, Lancelot, the French warriors Du Geslin and Bayard, Napoleon—so many men for one Joan of Arc." Young men growing up today have plenty of heroes to emulate. But who can women look up to? Luckily for today's young woman, there are more examples of powerful female leaders for them to follow. Female national leaders act as prominent exceptions to the rule that "men govern." Today's young women can look to today's leaders as examples, just as Gro Harlem Brundtland looked to Golda Meir (Liswood 1995:99) and Margaret Thatcher looked to Indira Gandhi.

Women in Cabinet Positions

Women can also fill the appointed positions that advise government leaders. Typically called the **cabinet**, members of these executive positions are responsible for generally running a country. In 2005, examples of cabinet officials included Condoleezza Rice, the U.S. Secretary of State; Donald Rumsfeld, the U.S. Secretary of Defense; and Charles Clarke, the UK Secretary of State for Home Affairs. Descended from the groups of advisors surrounding kings and emperors, "cabinet positions are some of the most powerful political positions in the world" (Davis 1997:12).

As in other areas of politics, women hold only a low percentage of cabinet positions. Reynolds (1999) surveyed cabinet ministers in more than

180 countries in 1998 and found that only 9% were female (302 out of 3,486). Thirty-eight countries out of 180 do not have any women cabinet ministers at all. This number has increased over time. Rebecca Davis tracked 15 countries in Western Europe over time and found that the percentage of female cabinet officials increased from only 3% in 1968 to 13% in 1992 (Davis 1997).

There is substantial regional variation in women's representation as cabinet officials. In Western Europe, 20% of cabinet officials are women, compared with only 2% in the Middle East. Table 3.6 compares the percentage of cabinet officials who are women across the major regions of the world. Women are also better represented as cabinet officials in countries that are predominantly Christian (Catholic, Protestant, or Orthodox) compared with countries with other dominant religions, such as Buddhism or Hinduism.

In most countries, each cabinet official is given responsibility for a specific government department, such as labor or foreign policy. These departments, and the officials that lead them, are not necessarily equal. The prime minister or the president, at the center of the circle of advisors, may have a core group of trusted advisors around him or her. This core usually includes cabinet officials covering finance and foreign affairs (Davis 1997:12–13). Other cabinet officials, farther out in the circle of advisors, may play less of a role in creating and implementing policy.

Women are highly overrepresented in some cabinet positions and underrepresented in others. Female cabinet ministers tend to be given positions in "softer" areas—health, family, education—that are less prestigious and less likely to be in the core of advisors (Blondel 1988). Table 3.7 lists the percentage of female cabinet officials holding 20 types of cabinet positions in 1998. Of the varied types of departments women could tackle, they are most often in health (14% of the time) or women's affairs (13% of the time). Education, culture/arts, and family and children are the next three most common. In contrast, women are substantially less likely to appear in

Table 3.6   Percentage of Women in Cabinets by Region, 1998

Africa	7.8
Asia	5.9
Central and Eastern Europe	5.3
Middle East	2.1
North America & Caribbean	14.7
Oceania	3.9
Central and South America	10.5
Western Europe	20
Total	8.7

SOURCE: Data from Reynolds (1999).

the more prestigious cabinet positions, such as defense, finance, or home affairs. In each of these cases, only 1% of female cabinet officials hold these positions. Unfortunately, it is these more prestigious cabinet positions that can be viewed as stepping-stones to greater power.

Women have rarely been able to achieve prestigious cabinet positions. Between 1968 and 1992 in Western Europe, roughly 50% of female cabinet appointments were in the areas of health, social welfare, education, family, culture, or consumer affairs. And women never held positions associated with economic affairs, defense, relations with parliament, employment, equipment, and budget (Davis 1997).

Why do we see low numbers of women in cabinet positions? One important explanation is the lack of women in legislative positions. In

Table 3.7   Percentage of Female Cabinet Ministers Holding Types of Cabinet Positions

Type of Cabinet Position	%
Health/Social Welfare	14
Women's Affairs	13
Education	9
Culture/Arts/Heritage	9
Family and Children	8
Labor/Employment	6
Environment/Energy	6
Planning and Development	5
Law/Justice/Security	4
Communication/Information	4
Trade/Industry/Science	4
Foreign Affairs	3
Agriculture/Fishing/Sea	3
Regional/Local/Minority	3
Sport	3
Transport	2
Finance/Treasury	1
Home Affairs	1
Defense	1
Oil	1
Civil Service	1
Housing	1
Tourism	1
Displaced Persons	1

SOURCE: Data from Reynolds (1999).

parliamentary systems, cabinet ministers are almost always drawn from among parliamentarians (Blondel 1991). Loyal party members come to the attention of prime ministers and get choice cabinet appointments as a reward. This means that when there are few women in a country's parliament, there are few women available for potential appointment to the cabinet.

Rebecca Davis created a hierarchy of Western European regions based on their percentage of female cabinet ministers. Scandinavia does the best in women's representation in cabinets, followed by the continental countries (the Netherlands, Belgium, France, Germany, and Austria). The United Kingdom and Ireland and countries in southern Europe do worse, rarely achieving more than 10% women. This hierarchy mirrors almost perfectly the percentage of women in parliaments in those regions (see Davis 1997:16, 35). The same pattern appears when one considers countries around the world—higher percentages of females in parliament are related to higher percentages of females in cabinet positions (Reynolds 1999).

Why are women overrepresented in the softer cabinet positions? The explanation may again start with their experience as legislators. National legislatures often divide their work into **legislative committees** to prepare or review legislation in a particular area. There are also committees that serve very specific functions, such as the rules committee, which does not focus on a particular policy arena but instead makes decisions about how the legislation submitted by other committees will be debated on the house floor. Subsets of legislators belong to legislative committees of different types—defense, finance, and so on. And committee members often have significant influence over the legislation proposed in their committee's area.

But female legislators are more likely to be assigned to "women's issues" committees and social issues committees. Women are seldom assigned to the so-called power committees, such as treasury, budget, or foreign relations (Heath, Schwindt-Bayer, and Taylor-Robinson 2005). It is by serving on these power committees that legislators get the important experience that helps channel them to top cabinet posts. Because women serve on power committees at much lower rates than men do, women get channeled to power cabinet posts at lower rates.

And why are women getting assigned to social issues committees instead of power committees? As relative newcomers to politics, these women pose a serious threat to traditional male power on these committees (Duverger 1955). In most legislative bodies it is a small number of people who make committee assignments (e.g., the party leaders). If male party leaders can, therefore, they will sideline women into unimportant committees to preserve their own power (Heath et al. 2005). Other explanations for low numbers of women in cabinet positions include the supply of qualified candidates and the different demand for women across political parties. These explanations are discussed in Chapters 4 and 5.

4

Explaining the
Political Representation
of Women—Culture
and Social Structure

The previous two chapters outlined women's struggle to participate as equals in political decision making. Why has it been such a struggle? And why have women succeeded in gaining political power in some places and not in others? In this section of the book (Chapters 4–6), we address three broad explanations for differences in women's participation—culture, social structure, and politics—and consider how they interact to influence women's chances.

Women-in-politics researchers often distinguish between two sets of factors that produce different levels of political representation for women across the world: supply-side factors and demand-side factors (Norris 1993; Paxton 1997; Randall 1987). Supply factors are those that increase the pool of women with the will and experience to compete against men for political office. **Demand factors,** on the other hand, are characteristics of countries, electoral systems, or political parties that make it more likely that women will be pulled into office from the supply of willing candidates. Although it is not cut and dry, you can begin by thinking of culture and the social structure as creating a supply of women (discussed in this chapter) and political systems as creating a demand (discussed in Chapter 5). Of course, in reality this distinction is not so simple—these factors combine and interact to influence women's chances (as we explain in Chapter 6).

To understand the overall picture of women's political representation, it is useful to begin with the **political recruitment model**—a model of how individual citizens become politicians. Figure 4.1 presents the political recruitment model developed by Pippa Norris and refined by Richard Matland (Matland 2002; Norris 1993). As Richard Matland explained, women need to pass three critical barriers to attain elected office. First, they need to decide to run for elected office. Second, they have to get selected as a candidate by a party. Finally, they need to be chosen by the voters. As women pass through those barriers they move from simply being eligible to run for office (eligibles) to aspiring to hold political office (aspirants) to being selected by a party to run for office (candidates) to finally being elected by voters (legislators).

In this chapter, we begin by thinking of the supply-side factors that impact the pool of both eligible women and political aspirants. Cultural traditions and social structure influence women's decisions to run for political office. If cultural traditions suggest that women are not mentally or emotionally capable of handling politics, or that a woman's place is at home, then women are unlikely to have the personal ambition to run for political office. Similarly, if a society's social structure limits women's attainment of personal financial and educational resources, there will not be many women who can run for office.

But once women do decide that they would like to run for office, they must also pass the other two barriers. Political parties may work to recruit or nominate different levels of female candidates, and voters may or may not support those female candidates. In Chapter 5, we discuss the political demand for female aspirants, candidates, and legislators. Finally, in

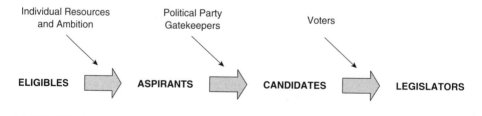

Figure 4.1   The Political Recruitment Model

SOURCES: Matland (2002) and Norris (1993).

Chapter 6, we turn to additional explanations of women's political power and how culture, social structure, and politics combine to influence women's chances.

Beliefs Have Consequences: Culture

What people think about women and a woman's place matters for women's ability to attain political power. If women are considered irrational, apolitical, or incapable of acting apart from a male, they will not be taken seriously as contenders for power. If societal norms suggest that women should stay at home, then women acting in the public sphere may be perceived as rebels harming their families and perhaps even the very fabric of society. If women are told they are incompetent, then they may choose to avoid public life and defer to their fathers and husbands for guidance. Overall, **culture** can help explain women's complete exclusion from politics in the past and their difficulty in attaining power in the present. We begin by examining the arguments that have been used to justify women's exclusion from politics for centuries. These arguments continue to resonate through the present and affect women as they attempt to gain power.

A Women's Place in History: Women in Political Philosophy

Women have been barred from the political process throughout much of human history, and arguments against women's political participation have been remarkably similar across both time and place. Generally, there are two sets of reasons offered for women's political exclusion: assumptions about women's inherent nature or capabilities and beliefs regarding women's proper place in society. Each of these reasons was deeply embedded in the cultures of past societies and was likely used by ordinary people to justify women's lack of power. But each set of reasons was also codified in the political philosophy written by men throughout the ages, helping to legitimize women's exclusion from political power.

The first set of arguments against women in politics asserts that women naturally do not have the temperament or capabilities necessary for political participation. According to this perspective, women's biological difference is thought to extend to differences across moral, intellectual, and emotional dimensions. Aristotle is credited with offering the first comprehensive theoretical account of the superiority of men's virtues, reason, and status (Gardner 2006). Aristotle's theory that women were deformed or inferior versions of men influenced thinkers around the world (Ahmed 1992:29; Okin 1979). Ideas about women's inferiority carried through the Middle Ages, a period that transmitted an image of woman as "lacking judgment and reason; as vain, duplicitous, capricious, seductive, weak-minded, generally inferior and, often, as downright evil" (Coole 1988:70).

In the 18th and 19th centuries, as philosophy began again to tackle questions of man's natural rights, women were still perceived to lack man's rationality. In 18th-century England, for example, Sir William Blackstone grouped women with lunatics, idiots, minors, aliens, perjurers, and criminals as people that should not be allowed to vote (Kelber 1994). Political philosophers of the Enlightenment, such as Hegel, Rousseau, and Schopenhauer, viewed women as lacking the reason and judgment necessary to participate as citizens. For example, in 1762, Jean-Jacques Rousseau argued, "By the law of nature herself, women, as much for themselves as for their children, are at the mercy of men's judgment," and "opinion is the tomb of man's virtue and the throne of woman's." Similarly, in 1821, German philosopher G. W. F. Hegel wrote, "If women were to control the government, the state would be in danger, for they do not act according to the dictates of universality, but are influenced by accidental inclinations and opinions" (Hegel 1977:167). Thus, even as ideas about politics, ethics, and natural rights were advanced and debated during the Enlightenment, women remained conceptualized as inferior.

Philosophical arguments about women's inferior nature were not restricted to Western philosophy (Giele and Smock 1977:chap. 2, 3). In non-Western philosophy, too, women were portrayed as inferior in reasoning and intellect. For example, Walda Heywat, an Ethiopian teacher writing in the 17th century, cautions, "O man, remember that a woman is weak by nature and less intelligent than man" (Bonevac and Phillips 1992). On another continent and in a different century, Avicenna, an Islamic metaphysician, states, "For in reality [woman] is not very rational and is quick to follow passion and anger" (Avicenna [~1000] 1963). Nizamu'l-Mulk Tusi, writing around the same time, warns his king not to allow women's influence because women are by nature inferior to men in the field of politics and administration (Sherwani 1977).

A second set of arguments against female political power stress that politics is simply out of women's proper sphere or domain. Women's concerns are properly in the home, and women should be focused on the family— caring for their children and making their husbands happy. Thus, even if women could be accorded equality in intellect or reason, they must remain narrowly relegated to the private sphere, their wishes and desires supposedly known and acted on by the male head of the family.

As discussed in the introduction, the distinction between the public and private sphere is a crucial one for women's power (Pateman 1989). In Western philosophical and political thought, the public sphere is the place where laws are contested, contracts honored, and political principles debated. The private sphere, in contrast, is the family, the home, and the site where the daily needs of life are met. The male, the head of the family, is the traditional public political subject, and his wife, daughter, mother, and sister are responsible for providing comfort, support, and training for the next generation. For Aristotle and the philosophers that followed him, man belonged to the *polis,* the public sphere, whereas woman belonged to the private (Coole 1988; Okin 1979).

Although the vast majority of early political philosophy asserted that women lacked the qualities necessary for political participation, there have of course been exceptions, often voiced by women. During the French Revolution, for example, educated and upper-class women fought the battle of ideas, putting forth feminist conceptions of the political future of their country. One woman, Olympe de Gouges, argued that women were entitled to the full exercise of liberty, property, security, justice, political and civil freedom, and free speech and assembly, and, in October 1789, she proposed a feminist reform agenda to the National Assembly (Kelber 1994). In 1792, Mary Wollstonecraft published *Vindication of the Rights of Women,* the first systematic treatise on the rights of women. She argued:

> Let an enlightened nation then try . . . allowing them [women] to share the advantages of education and government with man, see whether they will become better, as they grow wiser and become free. They cannot be injured by the experiment; for it is not in the power of man to render them more insignificant than they are at present. (p. 42)

There have also been men that stood for women. In 1792, the same year that Mary Wollstonecraft published her treatise, Theodore Gottlieb von Hippel published *On Improving the Status of Women.* Speaking to men, von Hippel argued:

> Even less should women be forbidden to take part in the inner workings of the state, since at present they are entrusted with the management of their entire household, and their performance at these duties, even in the judgment of us men, is commendable. . . . If anyone denies that the female sex possesses the ability to perceive matters in a larger context; to set up regulations for whole kingdoms and then carry them out on a large scale; to comprehend far-reaching laws and, in short, to raise its ideas to the level of the universal, he betrays very little familiarity with the way of the world. (Pp. 156–7)

Nice.

John Stuart Mill and Frederick Douglass also famously supported women's political rights. The views of John Stuart Mill were influenced by his wife, Harriet Taylor. In 1869, he published *On the Subjection of Women*, which attacked the legal and social position of women and argued there was no reason that women should not have equal suffrage. He argued that only the vote would ensure just and equal consideration of women's interests and that women's suffrage should be granted at both the parliamentary and municipal levels on equal terms with men. The work was rapidly published in multiple languages and influenced educated women across the world. But though Mill may have tackled the question of women's innate inferiority, he did not directly challenge the sexual division of labor and the separation of women in the public and private spheres (Coole 1988; Okin 1979). Frederick Douglass also voiced support for female suffrage and the women's movement through his newspaper, *North Star*, published in the mid-1800s. Indeed, even the paper's motto began, "Right is of no sex. . . ."

But men outside of the Western world also crafted and advanced ideas favorable to women. Vladimir Lenin, one of the founding fathers of communism, often wrote and spoke about the women's emancipation (Krupskaya 1938). Though the role of women was often downplayed in revolutions, Lenin held the firm conviction that no revolution is possible without the participation of women. Further, he encouraged men to support women's participation in politics.

But overall, most political philosophy, from the beginning of written records through the early 20th century, articulated serious obstacles to the political participation of women. These obstacles stemmed from problems within women—their inferior intellect, rationality, and so on. And women's "natural" unfitness for public life helped justify their relegation to the private sphere. Worse yet, most of this was not explicit. Historically, political actors were assumed to be men, and women were simply ignored (Coole 1988; Okin 1979). When political philosophers spoke of the principles of equality in nature, they were speaking of equality among men. Recently, however, feminist political theorists have demonstrated that although the language of political philosophy was technically gender neutral, women's absence was critical (MacKinnon 1989; Phillips 1995). One reason is because the family was considered the basic political unit in that men's participation in the public was predicated on women's labor in the private sphere (Coole 1988; Okin 1979). If women manage the family and home, men are freed to come together to decide the workings of the community.

Box 4.1   Women, Stay at Home! The Cult of True Womanhood in 19th-Century America

Woman's place in the home has been glorified both subtly and overtly during different times in the past. Perhaps not surprisingly, just around the time that Mary Wollstonecraft and Elizabeth Cady Stanton began to speak about women in the public sphere, ladies' journals advised women to subscribe to the Cult of True Womanhood. According to the Cult of True Womanhood, a woman's proper place was in the home. To satisfy this ideal, women's proper behavior involved four virtues: piety, purity, submissiveness, and domesticity. Clearly none of these virtues suggested that women should engage in public political participation. If any woman wanted more than the four virtues, she was tampering with society and undermining civilization, and she was considered unwomanly. For example, early women's activists, such as Mary Wollstonecraft, Francis Wright, and Harriet Martineau, were considered "semiwomen" or "mental hermaphrodites."

An example of the messages put forth during this period about women's proper behavior can be found in the women's magazine *The Ladies Wreath,* which offered a $50 prize for the best essay titled "How May an American Woman Best Show Her Patriotism." In the winning essay, the wife asks the husband's opinion, and he informs her that voting was no asset because it would result only in "a vast increase of confusion and expense without in the smallest degree affecting the results." Besides, if "we were to go a step further and let children vote, their first act would be to vote their mothers at home." The essay continued, "Most women would follow the lead of their fathers and husbands" and the few that would "fly off on a tangent from the circle of home influence would cancel each other out." The wife responds dutifully: "I see all that. I never understood so well before" (Welter 1966:172). Holding up a belief in separate spheres as an ideal, this essay reiterates that a woman's proper place is in the home and man's proper place is in the public realm. Suffrage is an unnecessary evil because women's needs are met through their husband's vote.

SOURCES: Welter (1966) and Wetherell (1851).

A Woman's Place Today: The Continuing Power of Ideology

Political philosophy reflected and shaped prevailing ideas about women's nature and place throughout history. But cultural arguments against women's participation in politics continue to powerfully affect women's chances of attaining political power through the present. In a recent worldwide survey of female politicians, 76% of those interviewed claimed that prevailing values about gender roles limit the participation of women in politics (Inter-Parliamentary Union 2000). As a female politician from Central America states, "the patriarchal ideology prevailing in our society is the biggest stumbling block we have to face" (Inter-Parliamentary Union 2000:61).

Cultural ideas about women can affect their levels of representation throughout the political process, from individual women's decisions to enter politics to parties' selection of candidates to the decisions on election day made by the electorate (Giele and Smock 1977; Kohn 1980; Newland 1979). Consider an Australian female politician's views: "social values that it is a women's role to be wives and mothers are still strong in Australia. This creates psychological and emotional barriers to women participating in formal politics" (Inter-Parliamentary Union 2000:25). Even if women feel comfortable running for political office, voters are influenced by social views on women and may be more or less willing to elect them based on views about their competence. And, even after women have gained office, cultural norms can limit their effectiveness when dealing with their male counterparts. For example, harassment of women was commonplace in Uganda's parliament (Tamale 1999), and in Bangladesh Islamic fundamentalists turn their backs during speeches by female political leaders (Commonwealth Secretariat 1999:35).

What cultural features of a society matter for women in politics? Research has focused on three. First, as discussed in Chapter 3, broad-based regional differences in the percentage of women in parliaments can be at least partially attributed to ideological differences. Scandinavian countries, which are considered to have a pervasive ethic of equality, were among the first countries to grant women the right to vote and experienced higher numbers of women in parliament at earlier times than most other countries of the world (Bystydzienski 1995; Rule 1987). Studies that break countries into regions find more women in power in some regions across many different time periods (Kenworthy and Malami 1999; Paxton 1997). (These regional differences in women's participation in politics are discussed in greater detail in Chapter 8.) Consider also the evidence on women's suffrage from Chapter 2—western states in the United States, which had a frontier ideology of equality, were the first in the world to grant women the right to vote. But regional differences are broad and incorporate much more than ideology. So researchers also consider more specific cultural differences across countries.

Religion is an important source of cultural messages in most countries. The ideological influence of religion on women in politics can range from subtle suggestions that women should stay at home to overt use of particular interpretations of religious texts to maintain male domination of politics. Arguments about women's inferiority to men are present across all dominant religions, and religion has long been used to exclude women from aspects of social, political, or religious life across the world. Susan Moller Okin (1999:11) described how across myths and religious stories, women's importance is undermined or denied:

> The founding myths of Greek and Roman antiquity, and of Judaism, Christianity, and Islam . . . consist of a combination of denials of women's role in reproduction, appropriations by men of the power to reproduce themselves, characterizations of women as overly emotional, untrustworthy, evil, or sexually dangerous, and refusals to acknowledge mothers' rights over the disposition of their children.

When religion is used to justify male power, the ideological message is particularly powerful because it makes women's subordination appear divinely approved.

Religious doctrine or practice may be used to argue that women's political exclusion or lower status is the will of God. Indeed, in 1895 Elizabeth Cady Stanton wrote the *Women's Bible* because she saw the Bible as a central text used to prevent women from achieving equality. Here are just a few examples of religious text and practice that are used to assert women's inferiority, lower status, or rightful exclusion from public life. In Christianity, Apostle Paul in I Timothy 2:11–15 states that women should keep silent because they were created second and sinned first. The *Manusmriti*, a guidebook for human conduct and social and religious behavior in ancient Hindu society, states that "a woman is never fit for independence" (*Manusmriti* 9.3). In traditional Judaism, women are not counted in the *minyan*, a quorum required for public prayer, suggesting that they are indeed not a part of the public. And at the time of Buddha, a woman was believed unable to go to heaven through her own merits. She could not worship by herself, and it was believed that she could only reach heaven through unquestioning obedience to her husband, even if he happened to be a wicked person. The most recent examples of the direct use of religious doctrine to oppose women's political power took place in both Kuwait and Saudi Arabia, where antisuffragists used the *Shari'a*, the Islamic law or code of conduct, to combat women's agitation for political rights.

Of course, it is important to recognize that dominant religions have many branches or sects that disagree over women's status under God. The same passage can be interpreted quite differently by proponents and opponents of women's rights. For example, in Islam, Qur'an (also spelled Koran) 2:228 states, "And women shall have rights similar to the rights against them, according to what is equitable; but men have a degree (of advantage) over them." Although the first part of the passage ascribes rights to women, the second asserts women's lower status compared with men. Many Muslim women hear and read sacred texts as egalitarian (Ahmed 1992:66). And many modern Islamic scholars view the Qur'an as extending political equality to women. In fact, during the time of Prophet Muhammad, women actively participated in the equivalent of voting, known as *baya,* a way of endorsing political leadership.

Unfortunately, despite the possibility of alternative interpretations, religion is often used as a tool of those in power to justify or maintain the status quo. The Qur'an and Hadith, the main sources of Islam, have mainly been interpreted by men. Indeed, although women were important contributors to the early (verbal) texts of Islam, male censoring of the Hadith appears to have begun even as men wrote down the sayings and philosophy of Muhammad as articulated by his wives and daughter (Ahmed 1992:47–57). When women are prevented from learning to read or write, as was the case in Afghanistan under the Taliban, they are unable to challenge patriarchical interpretations of religious texts (Afghani 2005; Sorush 2005).

Similarly, the exclusion of women from most positions of power and authority in the Catholic Church meant that the major interpretations of the Bible were from a male perspective. In recent years, feminist scholars have also criticized the Apostle Paul's passages in the New Testament, arguing that Jesus originally taught an egalitarian view of gender relations. They argue that it was Paul who imposed a patriarchal interpretation of Christianity that taught that women are inferior, primarily culpable for sin and the fall of humanity and excluded from the ordained ministry. Early church fathers continued to cement a patriarchal, even misogynistic, view of women. Tertullian writes:

> *You* are the Devil's gateway. *You* are the unsealer of the forbidden tree. *You* are the first deserter of the divine Law. *You* are she who persuaded him whom the Devil was not valiant enough to attack. *You* destroyed so easily God's image, man. On account of *your* desert, that is death, even the Son of God had to die. (quoted in Reuther 1974:157)

Perhaps not surprisingly, across many religions, passages that promote women's equality have not received as much attention as passages that can be interpreted as justifying male superiority (Burn 2005:205–7).

It is important to note that some religious doctrines are explicitly grounded in ideas of egalitarianism. For example, the Quakers, a religious community founded in England in the 17th century, follow the teachings of Christ and believe in spiritual equality between the sexes. They grant men and women equal authority to speak in meetings for worship. The Quakers were influential in early suffrage movements in both the United Kingdom and the United States. Sikhism, a religion that emerged in the Punjab region of India in the 15th century, employs religious texts that explicitly call for the equal treatment of women (Burn 2005). When 140 apostles were trained to manage the expansion of the religion in the 1500s, 52 of them were women.

Despite that women are typically subordinated in all religions, the major religions of the world are differentially conservative or patriarchal in their views about the place of women, both in the church hierarchy and in society. Scholars expect Muslim and Catholic countries to have fewer women in power because those countries are likely to hold more conservative gender ideologies. Countries with many Islamic adherents may resist women's acquisition of political power because Islamic law is typically interpreted in a manner that constrains the activities of women (Ahmed 1992; Caldwell 1986:175–6; Glaser and Possony 1979). As explained by the 2003 Nobel Laureate Shirin Ebadi, "many people use Islam to justify the unequal position of women" (Associated Press 2004). Scholars also expect Catholic countries, especially Orthodox Catholic countries, to have fewer women in power than Protestant countries because women have traditionally been denied positions of power within the Catholic Church hierarchy. In contrast, scholars have highlighted how predominantly Protestant countries facilitate the education of women, stress individual (men and women) interaction with religious texts, promote nonhierarchical religious practices, and more readily accept women as religious leaders.

Researchers looking at women in politics have compared the percent of women in politics across countries with different dominant religions (e.g., Paxton 1997; Paxton and Kunovich 2003; Reynolds 1999). These statistical studies of women's participation in national legislatures have consistently found an impact of religion, across many countries and time periods. These studies show that predominantly Muslim and Catholic countries have lower levels of women in parliament than countries that are predominantly Protestant.

You can see evidence of the power of religion in Table 4.1, which presents the percentage of women in parliament across countries with different dominant religions. Table 4.1 shows that, especially in the most recent time periods, majority Protestant countries do have higher percentages of women in parliament than majority Catholic countries do. And both Protestant and Catholic countries have more women in parliament than

Orthodox or Muslim countries do. For Orthodox countries, this only occurs in 1990 and 2000. For the earlier time periods, that many Orthodox countries were in Eastern Europe, and therefore subject to the political ideology of communism, resulted in higher percentages of women in politics. Again, that women's participation in politics dropped dramatically in many of the countries after the fall of the Soviet Union suggests that a negative cultural ideology regarding women's place reasserted itself once the political ideology of communism was removed.

Table 4.1   Average Percentage of Women in Parliament, by Country's Dominant Religion

	1970	1980	1990	2000
Protestant	5	9	12	17
Catholic	4	9	9	13
Orthodox	11	18	5	8
Muslim	4	6	5	5
Mixed	3	6	10	16

NOTE: A country is coded as mixed if no one religion is dominant, that is, if at least 50% of its population does not adhere to a single religion. The table does not include countries classified as having indigenous or other religions such as Judaism, Hinduism, or Buddhism.

In all time periods, Muslim countries have the fewest number of women in their parliaments. This is not entirely surprising considering that historical and contemporary interpretations of Islamic texts emphasize women's place in the private sphere. Although more liberal interpretations of these texts exist (Afghani 2005), they are not often visible in public discussion. Finally, countries with mixed religions (no dominant religion) fall in the middle. The absence of substantial trends in Table 4.1 suggests that religion continues to play an important role in the culture of many countries today.

Box 4.2   Women and Religious Fundamentalism

Over the last 200 years, women have begun to influence the interpretation of religious texts and challenge traditional patriarchal readings. But an important countertrend is the rise of fundamentalist movements in many of the world's major religions (Almond, Appleby, and Sivan 2003). Fundamentalist movements are typically exemplified by a rigid adherence to religious tradition and the literal interpretation of sacred texts, which have important consequences for women. Fundamentalists see an assault on the religious foundation of the social order from a secular modern world (Gerami and Lehnerer 2001; Zubaida 1987). The increasingly secular world is seen as responsible for society's moral degradation. Thus, an affirmation of religious authority and tradition is the appropriate, indeed essential, response. In America, Protestant fundamentalists want to correct modern deviations from a stronger Christian past. In non-Western countries and among Islamic fundamentalists, this rejection of the modern world is often linked to an explicit rejection of the West.

Recent fundamentalist movements have also worked to reiterate women's subordinate place (French 1992). Part of the modern world rejected by fundamentalists is the gains made by women in the public sphere. Fundamentalist movements have opposed women in positions of power in church—as ordained ministers, for example—because they fear that the natural order would be upset if women were given authority over men. Similarly, fundamentalist movements typically reaffirm a family power structure where women are subordinate. Fundamentalist movements see the family as a critical locale where morality is sheltered and safeguarded for the next generation. Moral decay in the family can quickly spread to other social institutions and result in universal moral ruin (Gerami 1996:31). Thus, keeping women private and protected in the family, with males as gatekeepers to the rest of the world, is essential to the protection of religious and moral values, not only for one's own family but also for the entire society.

Consider the following principles from the Coalition on Revival (COR; 1999), a network of Christian evangelical leaders. The statements and affirmations of the COR speak to the place of women in the home and preclude women's economic activity outside the home.

> We affirm that an able-bodied man must make every reasonable effort to support his family continuously (1 Timothy 5:8; Genesis 3:17–19); that the wife may augment the family's income through effective management of resources or, with the husband's consent, by home business (Proverbs 31:10–31); and that in cases of family financial crisis, the wife may, with her husband's approval, accept temporary outside employment, but that the family should view this as bondage, strive to liberate itself, and petition God for liberation. (1 Corinthians 7:21–23)

> We affirm that a mother's primary duty is to nurture her minor children; that the wife's responsibility is to manage the home and make it a center of ministry (1 Timothy 5:10,14; Titus 2:3–5; Proverbs 31:10–31); that Christian media therefore should not glamorize outside careers for mothers with minor children; and that the Church ought to commend godly wives and mothers who work at home as role models.

(Continued)

(Continued)

> We deny that married mothers of minor children should seek male
> economic provider roles; that Christian wives should put the world's
> idea of self-fulfillment through careers before the calling of God
> (Matthew 16:24–26; Mark 8:34,35; Luke 9:23–26); that following
> God's commands in this area exploits women. . . .

An independent identity for women in the public sphere seriously disrupts the
fundamentalist view of a hierarchical arrangement in the family—God, Man,
Woman (Gerami 1996:49). Using Ephesians, Romans, and I Peter, COR states:

> We affirm that the husband has final say in any family dispute . . . that
> a husband's headship is irrevocable . . . that a man's authority as head
> of his wife is delegated to him by God. . . . We deny that a husband
> must earn the right of headship . . . that he may be deposed by his
> wife . . . that wives ought to use Biblical limits on husbands' authority
> as opportunities to quibble and undermine their husbands' authority.

The divinely ordained headship of men in the family implies a headship
throughout society. Jerry Falwell, for example, described man as the decision
maker and the leader (1980:130). The implications for women as political
leaders follow.

Fundamentalist Islam also sees control of women as the bulwark against
societal moral decay. For example, fundamentalist Islamic scholars in Saudi
Arabia have issued religious edicts that women driving cars is sinful. As
explained by Sheikh Ayed Al-Qarni, an Islamic scholar, "I do not see women
driving cars in our country because of the consequences that would spring
from it such as the spread of corruption, women uncovering their hair and
faces, mingling between the sexes, men being alone with women and the
destruction of the family and society in whole" (Qusti 2004).

But do societies really differ in their attitudes about women? Yes. The
World Values Survey (World Values Survey Association 2000) surveyed
attitudes toward women in politics in a large number of countries. A random sample of individuals was drawn in each country, and each person was
asked how much he or she agreed with the following six statements:

1. On the whole, men make better political leaders than women do.

2. A university education is more important for a boy than for a girl.

3. When jobs are scarce, men should have more right to a job than women.

4. If a woman earns more money than her husband, it's almost certain to cause
   problems.

5. Do you think that a woman has to have children in order to be fulfilled?

6. If you were to have only one child, would you rather have it be a boy or a girl?

Table 4.2 presents the average answer to each question across 36 countries. The first column gives the average answer to a direct question asking individuals whether they thought men made better political leaders than women. Looking down the table, it is apparent that there are differences in the average number of people in each country agreeing that men are better leaders. As would be expected, the Scandinavian countries, with their long tradition of egalitarianism, score lower than other countries. The average answer in Scandinavia is between strongly disagreeing and disagreeing with that statement. In other Western countries, the average answer tends to be just "disagree." But looking at some of the countries in Eastern Europe, Latin America, Asia, and Africa, average answers are higher, suggesting that a larger percent of people agree with the statement that men make better leaders. Take Armenia and Nigeria as the most extreme cases: The average answer in those countries is between "agree" and "strongly agree" (although it is closer to "agree"). The first column of Table 4.2 therefore demonstrates that countries differ in their cultural values about women in politics. The other columns ask different questions about gender ideology but produce similar conclusions.

Women can hold negative attitudes about women as well as men. A pervasive cultural ideology suggesting women are inferior is exactly that—pervasive. For example, a UN Population Fund (2005) report found that in Egypt 94% of women thought it was acceptable to be beaten, as did 91% in Zambia. But the women surveyed in the World Values Survey hold slightly more positive attitudes about women than men. For example, on average, across all countries, women's average response to "men are better in politics" was 2.5, whereas men's was 2.7 (remember higher numbers indicate more negative attitudes about women). Men are also more likely to say that men have more right than women to a job (average of 2.1 vs. 1.8) and that a university education is more important for boys (men = 2.2, women = 2.0). Individual countries show big differences across men and women as well. In Pakistan, men's average answer to men as better in politics is 3.3, indicating agreement. Women in the country differ, giving an average answer of 2.6, between agree and disagree.

There is one additional item of particular interest in Table 4.2—the United States value in the fifth column, whether respondents would prefer a boy if they could have only one child, called **son preference**. In fact, almost 60% of people in the United States would prefer a male to a female

Table 4.2 World Values Survey Questions on a Women's Place

	Averages (Higher Values = More Negative Ideology)					
	Men Are Better Political Leaders[1]	University Education More Imp. for Boys[1]	Men Have More Right to a Job[1]	Women Need Children to Be Fullfilled[2]	If Only to Have One Child, Prefer a Boy[2]	Woman Earns More Causes Problems[1]
Western Industrialized Countries						
Australia	2.10	1.87	1.59	0.20	0.22	2.45
Britain	—	—	1.57	0.18	—	—
Spain	2.11	1.96	1.70	0.45	0.18	2.42
Switzerland	—	—	1.75	0.42	0.15	—
USA	2.24	1.93	1.54	0.18	0.59	2.38
W Germany	1.77	1.68	1.59	0.27	0.20	2.47
Finland	1.80	1.55	1.36	0.18	0.22	2.10
Norway	1.59	1.40	1.35	0.19	0.16	1.92
Sweden	1.67	1.34	1.15	0.17	0.14	1.96
Eastern Europe						
Bulgaria	2.80	1.97	1.95	0.71	0.31	2.42
Croatia	2.56	1.84	1.91	0.53	0.26	2.12
E Germany	1.97	1.79	1.58	0.57	0.24	2.39
Poland	2.79	2.28	2.03	0.70	0.18	2.36
Armenia	3.17	2.45	2.29	0.83	0.50	2.78
Azerbaijan	2.99	2.33	2.36	0.61	0.36	2.88
Estonia	2.92	2.17	1.79	0.80	0.31	2.56
Lithuania	2.69	2.11	1.84	0.76	0.28	2.67
Russia	2.77	2.37	2.10	0.83	0.34	2.54
Ukraine	2.82	2.34	1.92	0.80	0.30	2.51

Averages (Higher Values = More Negative Ideology)

	Men Are Better Political Leaders[1]	University Education More Imp. for Boys[1]	Men Have More Right to a Job[1]	Women Need Children to Be Fullfilled[2]	If Only to Have One Child, Prefer a Boy[2]	Woman Earns More Causes Problems[1]
Latin America & the Carribean						
Argentina	2.30	1.98	1.58	0.55	0.29	2.47
Brazil	2.42	1.74	2.34	0.53	0.39	2.78
Chile	2.40	1.94	1.85	0.61	0.37	2.68
Colombia	2.28	1.89	1.60	0.56	0.33	2.61
Mexico	2.45	2.20	2.21	0.44	0.33	2.68
Peru	2.27	2.27	1.64	0.51	0.32	2.54
Venezuela	2.32	1.92	1.79	0.60	0.49	2.70
Asia & the Middle East						
Bangladesh	2.70	2.46	2.33	0.97	0.38	2.71
China	2.60	2.10	2.06	0.82	0.40	2.30
India	2.53	2.16	2.10	0.84	0.45	2.61
Japan	2.65	2.36	2.14	0.71	0.32	2.53
Pakistan	2.96	2.33	2.55	—	—	2.70
Philippines	2.64	2.30	2.28	0.87	0.29	2.37
S Korea	2.73	2.32	2.19	0.67	—	2.58
Turkey	2.73	2.07	2.23	0.73	0.28	2.77
Africa						
Nigeria	3.13	2.27	2.16	0.82	0.46	2.99
S Africa	2.61	1.81	1.86	0.55	—	2.71

1. Questions could be answered on a 1 through 4 scale indicating strong disagreement, disagreement, agreement, and strong agreement.
2. Questions are answered yes or no. Numbers can be interpreted as the proportion of respondents that agree with the question. For all questions, higher numbers indicate more negative attitudes about women. Thus, they reflect negative gender attitudes.

SOURCE: From Pamela Paxton and Sheri Kunovich, "Women's Political Representation: The Importance of Ideology." *Social Forces*, copyright © 2003 The University of North Carolina Press. Used by permission of the publisher.

child, the highest percentage of any country surveyed. To understand the significance of son preference, see Box 4.3.

Box 4.3   Son Preference Around the World

In many regions of the world, families prefer male children. According to the United Nations, countries in South Asia, the Middle East, and South Africa are most likely to have high levels of son preference. For example, in northeast Kenya the Turkana people celebrate the birth of a boy with great feasting, whereas the birth of a female baby is followed by no such celebration (Burn 2005). But what does son preference indicate?

Shawn Meghan Burn (2005) explained that in some cases, son preference means that daughters receive less of the family's resources. In extreme cases, son preference may even lead families to the killing of female children, either intentionally or through neglect, called **femicide**. According to the United Nations, approximately 250,000 girls die due to their disadvantage relative to male children, specifically, discrimination in the feeding, health care, and support of female infants and young girls. In some countries, son preference also leads to sex-selective abortion, in which parents use ultrasounds to determine the sex of the fetus, and, when female, the parents abort the baby. This has been extremely common in China, where families are limited to a single child. After China's one-child policy was enacted in 1979, female infant mortality almost doubled, increasing from 38 per 1,000 to 67 per 1,000 (Sen 1990).

Femicide and sex-selective abortion can significantly decrease the number of girls who reach adulthood. In fact, the United Nations estimates that more than 100 million female children are "missing" due to son preference and the response by families (Sen 1990). In some cases, sex-selective abortion, infanticide, and neglect of girl babies have led to extremely distorted sex ratios. For example, in India, there are slightly more than 9 females for every 10 males. In the Indian region of Punjab, the sex ratio is even more abnormal—for every 1,000 boys, there are only 793 girls (Dugger 2001). Although one might expect that a shortage of females may lead to greater value placed on females simply due to scarcity, this has not yet been this case. One reason may be that in many societies, gender is tied to property and lineage. Whereas men stay in the family, providing for parents in old age, daughters are expected to leave the family on marriage. In fact, in some cultures daughters are viewed as "wasted investments." As one Indian proverb says "Raising a daughter is like watering a shady tree in someone else's courtyard" (Burn 2005:21).

As we see in the World Values Survey, 60% of families in the United States would prefer a male child if they could have only one. And, if families have more than two children, they often prefer more boys. In countries such as the

United States, son preference may not lead to femicide or a reduction in the female population. But recent newspaper advertisements tout new sperm-sorting techniques for sex selection. And in countries such as the United States, son preference may still have important repercussions for women. Research suggests that resources may still be unequally distributed, favoring male children, and son preference may negatively affect female self-esteem. Consider the following statement by American boxer Muhammad Ali when asked how many children he had fathered: "One boy and seven mistakes."

SOURCES: Atwood (2001), United Nations (1998), United Nations High Commissioner for Human Rights (2003), UN Population Fund (2003) cited in Burn (2005), Sen (1990), Sohoni (1995), and Dugger (2001).

But do these differences in ideology really matter for women's political power? Yes. Some research has explicitly considered how attitudes about women affect women's political power. For example, in a study of women's representation in U.S. state legislatures, Arceneaux (2001) found evidence that U.S. states with more accepting attitudes toward women in politics have more female representatives. Until recently there were few **cross-national** surveys of attitudes about women, so researchers relied entirely on region and religion to look for the effects of ideology on women's political participation. But the recent worldwide survey of individuals' attitudes about women in politics shows whether countries do differ in their cultural attitudes about women.

Pam Paxton and Sheri Kunovich (2003) used the questions discussed earlier to predict women's levels of participation in national legislatures. Their article demonstrated that national culture, when measured with direct questions, mattered more than other explanations, such as women's labor force participation, in predicting differences in women's political representation. Ideological beliefs were by far the strongest predictor of women's political power and were stable across many statistical models. Figure 4.2 reproduces a central figure from that article. The figure is a type of scatterplot that plots a country's percentage of women in parliament against its average agreement with the item "men are better in politics." (The scatterplot also statistically accounts for [controls] other explanations of women's political power.) The plot demonstrates a clear, strong, negative relationship between "men are better in politics" and the percentage of women in parliament. As negative attitudes about women increase, the percentage of women in parliaments decreases.

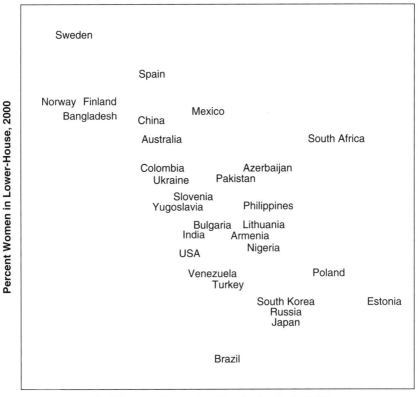

% of Country Answering Men Are Better in Politics

Figure 4.2   Relationship Between Attitudes About Women in Politics and Percentage of Women in National Legislatures

SOURCE: From Pamela Paxton and Sheri Kunovich, "Women's Political Representation: The Importance of Ideology." *Social Forces*, copyright © 2003 The University of North Carolina Press. Used by permission of the publisher.

To summarize, individuals, groups, and entire societies hold particular views about women's abilities and their place in society. These ideas matter for women's acquisition of political power. Cultural beliefs may influence women's decision to run for political office, regardless of their careers or level of education. As discussed in Chapter 1, three-dimensional power is exerted by influencing the beliefs or wants of others, even without their knowledge (Lukes 1974). If cultural values and traditions imply that men, not women, are political actors, women may come to assume that their political participation is not appropriate. Culture is therefore one important way to explain a lack of supply of females in the political process.

But Who Will Run? Social Structure

It is clear from the previous discussion that ideas, beliefs, and attitudes toward women in politics may constrain the number of women who run for public office. However, it is also important to consider how a country's **social structure** affects supply. It seems logical that when the structures of a society treat men and women more equally, women will be more able to compete against men for power. Further, a good deal of research on women in politics finds that when women do run, they win just as often as men. For example, U.S. research from the 1970s found that once women decided to seek nomination, they were elected to state legislatures and the U.S. Congress at rates equal to those of men (Darcy and Schramm 1977; Diamond 1977; Kirkpatrick 1974). Similar conclusions were made by political scientists studying Western industrialized countries (Norris 1997; Norris and Lovenduski 1995). It is natural, therefore, that we turn to structural reasons why women are not running for office in equal numbers as men.

According to structural perspectives, the family, education system, labor force, and other societal structures are configured in ways that prevent women from gaining the skills necessary to participate in politics or compete against men for public office. Social structures that privilege men in education and work result in too few qualified women to run for political office. Thus, instead of focusing on why men or women may not want women to run for political office, structural arguments often center on why women cannot run for political office.

In women-in-politics research, several theoretical traditions have contributed to structural arguments about the supply of women. One variant of the structural perspective, developed in political science, is the **resource model of political participation**. The resource model argues that differences in men's and women's political participation are the result of individual-level inequalities in certain prerequisites to participation, such as money, free time, and civic skills (Schlozman, Burns, and Verba 1994). A second group of theorists, elite theorists, link these factors explicitly to political decision-making positions, noting that political elites are often well connected and highly educated and hold professional jobs in certain fields, such as law (Putnam 1976). The elite perspective also compares and contrasts the paths to office by male and female politicians to evaluate which factors can help or hinder women's political participation. A third group, gender stratification theorists, focuses on societal-level inequalities in male and female economic power. This standpoint holds that greater female economic control must come before female political influence. We discuss each of these perspectives in this section, focusing on six structural factors that are thought to influence the supply of female candidates: money, time, civic skills and community participation, education, work, and economic power.

Money

When it comes to politics, it should be no surprise that money matters. As Herbert E. Alexander aptly summarizes, "people, not dollars, vote. But money helps to shape both voter behaviour [sic] and governmental decisions" (2001:198). And in recent years, politics has become a more expensive endeavor. Driven by a decline in loyalty to political parties around the globe, campaign ideologies are shifting to the political center, resulting in "expensive, personality-driven television and direct-mail campaigns" (Bussey 2000:77). Many countries, especially in the West, do not have any limits on private political donations, advantaging the wealthy and well connected (Casas-Zamora 2005). In the United States, for example, there is no shortage of examples of wealthy businessmen who have bankrolled their own multimillion-dollar campaigns. And in central and Eastern Europe, powerful business interests even form their own political party systems (Walecki 2005). Overall, one study of campaign finance regulations in 104 countries found that 59% of countries had no limits on campaign spending, and 72% had no limits on financial contributions by individuals, groups, or businesses (Pinto-Duschinsky 2002). With rising campaign costs and no caps on spending or contributions, money has become an ever more important political commodity.

In a world where money matters, women have less of it. On average, women are less likely to work full-time than their male counterparts, and even when they do women earn less money than men. In the United States, women working full-time, year-round make 76 cents on the male dollar (Burk 2005). And female British workers earn 27% less than their male colleagues (BBC News 2005b). Adriana Munoz, a Chilean parliamentarian, explains the problem of money:

> Being a candidate is difficult for a woman because you need to have a lot of money. We have little help economically. Men have access to circles or networks where money is lent—they are friends with bank managers. But we are

not supported this way. For us, it's pretty complicated, this arena of power and money. (quoted in Franceschet 2001:216)

In sum, women may be less able than men to contribute to campaigns, finance their own candidacy, or take on temporary or poorly paid positions in local or regional governments.

However, there are sources of hope for women office-seekers. In some countries such as Spain, a larger role is played by public financing of elections (Pinto-Duschinsky and Postnikov 1999). More than 80 countries offer candidates free political broadcasts, and more than 60 provide direct public subsidies for political campaigns (Pinto-Duschinsky 2002). And in some countries, women's political organizations have emerged that focus explicitly on financing women's political efforts. For example, EMILY's List, founded in 1985 in the United States, is a political network dedicated to providing early financial support to progressive female candidates. In the 1990s, the organization spread to Australia and the United Kingdom, aiding the successful election of more than 100 women to parliament in those nations (EMILY's List Australia 2005). At the end of 2004, the group was the largest single source of donations to candidates in the United States, directing nearly $11 million to pro-abortion-rights female candidates (Cillizza 2005). Perhaps because of such efforts, recent research has found that in the United States, men and women are equally well funded in political campaigns, with even a slight advantage for women (Hogan 2001).

Time

Another important political resource is time. As Schlozman et al. (1994) explain, "Most forms of political involvement—working in a campaign, taking part in a community activity, attending a protest—require an investment of at least some time" (p. 974). But women's responsibility for the overwhelming share of child care and housework may deprive them of the free time required to participate in politics (Phillips 1991:99–100). Even women who participate in the labor force still perform the lion's share of domestic tasks, such as cooking and cleaning, a phenomenon sociologist Arlie Hochschild coined the **second shift** (Hochschild 1989; Calasanti and Bailey 1991; Shelton 1990). Furthermore, running for and serving in public office is extremely demanding in terms of both time and energy. Women may fear that if they pursue political careers, they must do so at the expense of their families (Kirkpatrick 1974). Golda Meir, prime minister of Israel from 1969 to 1974, articulated this fear: "At work, you think of the children you've left at home. At home, you think of the work you've left unfinished. Such a struggle is unleashed within yourself, your heart is rent."

Research on women in political elites indicates that women tend to begin their political careers at an older age than men do (Dubeck 1976), and female elites are more likely to be widowed, divorced, or never to have been married (Sapiro 1982). Therefore, the combination of women's family or domestic roles and the substantial time required to campaign for and to serve in public office may place substantial limitations on the pool of female candidates.

It is also important to recognize that there are substantial differences in the amount of free time that women have in the industrialized West compared with women in the economic South. As we discuss later, development frees up time for individuals to pursue additional activities, including political activities. To illustrate the substantial constraints on time faced by women in developing societies, let's consider the free time of a woman living in a developing country—Sierra Leone (Box 4.4).

Box 4.4   A Typical Day's Work for a Woman in Sierra Leone

4:00 a.m. to 5:30 a.m.	Fish in local pond.
6:00 a.m. to 8:00 a.m.	Heat water, make breakfast, wash dishes, sweep floors.
8:00 a.m. to 11:00 a.m.	Work in rice fields while watching 4-year-old son and carrying baby on back.
11:00 a.m. to 12:00 p.m.	Gather berries and fuel for the fire while hauling water from a distant well.
12:00 p.m. to 2:00 p.m.	Process and prepare food, make lunch, wash dishes.
2:00 p.m. to 3:00 p.m.	Wash clothes, clean and smoke fish.
3:00 p.m. to 5:00 p.m.	Work in local gardens.
5:00 p.m. to 6:00 p.m.	Fish in local pond.
6:00 p.m. to 8:00 p.m.	Process and prepare food, make dinner.
8:00 p.m. to 9:00 p.m.	Wash dishes, care for children.
9:00 p.m. to 11:00 p.m.	Chat around the fire while making fishnets.
11:00 p.m. to 4:00 a.m.	Sleep.

SOURCE: Food and Agriculture Organization (2003), cited in Burn (2005).

This example makes it clear that the average woman in Sierra Leone would find it difficult to begin a life in politics. Even when women do have spare time, cultural norms may require them to spend that time in nonpolitical activities (Yarr 1996). Across democratic countries, research indicates that levels of women's political representation have been consistently higher in the industrialized world (Matland 1998).

Civic Skills and Community Participation

Participating in the political realm and running for office also require civic skills. Civic skills are the "communications and organizational abilities that allow citizens to use time and money effectively in political life" (Schlozman et al. 1994:974). Civic skills include the ability to speak in public, run a meeting, read a budget, or navigate through parliamentary procedure. These skills can be developed during the formative years through the family and educational systems but are solidified later in life through employment and activity in nonpolitical organizations and churches.

Women worldwide have fewer civic skills than men do. Women are less educated, and on average men are more likely to hold more highly skilled jobs (see later discussion). Research indicates that women also have less political knowledge. For example, in one study in the United States, men scored higher on objective tests of political knowledge than did women, a gain by men "roughly equivalent to that acquired from an additional 2¾ years of schooling" (Verba, Burns, and Schlozman 1997:1054).

Because women may have less access to civic skills in the workplace, their voluntary association memberships (e.g., in church or a bird-watching group) may be particularly important. Research in the United States supports this idea, finding that although men and women are equally likely to be affiliated with a voluntary nonpolitical organization, it affects men and women differently. Organizational activity does not affect men's political participation, but it significantly increases women's participation in politics (Schlozman et al. 1994).

Community action provides women with the motivation, connections, and civic skills to run for office. In her classic study of female legislators in the United States, Kirkpatrick (1974) argued that the motives that lead a woman to volunteer in her community are often the same motives that lead her to run for office. For example, one female state legislator recounted, "After years of working with the Urban League and civil rights groups, I just knew something more had to be done" (p. 62). Participation in voluntary associations may also foster networking and impart the civic skills necessary for political success. Legislators are often drawn from careers that foster connections to the public, and membership or leadership in community affairs may also cultivate these connections. Further, "a woman active in a civic organization learns how to run a meeting, how to plan one, how to develop an agenda and recruit support for a position. She learns how to operate in a public context . . . " (p. 64).

Although the nature and form of women's community participation differs across countries and regions of the world, research suggests that the value of organizational activity to women is widespread. In Canada, 64% of female members of the House of Commons in 1993 were members of women's associations. And in interviews with minority female members of parliament in Canada, Jerome Black (2000) found that many voiced that their extensive experience with volunteer organizations had made them more well-known to constituents. The impact of women's civic participation is also well documented across southern Africa. For example, Longman (2006) found that in Rwanda since the 1980s, women's growing participation in civil society has provided them with a route to politics. In fact, some Rwandans complain that the best women in civil society keep being drawn into government, named to commissions or ministries or the parliament (Longman 2006:138). In Tanzania and Uganda, women's organizations impart valuable skills to women, prepare them for office, and actively lobby for women's incorporation (Tripp 1994). And in her research on South Africa, Britton (2005:97) identified many women who pursued political careers after years of community activism.

Although community activism may currently provide an important path to power for women across the world, scholars suggest that in some national legislatures, this path may become less traveled. In Australia, Mexico, and South Africa, the professionalization of politics has decreased the number of women with community backgrounds who run for national office (Britton 2005; Camp 1998; Sawer 2000). The professionalization of politics means that party activities take precedence over other types of associations, so individuals with backgrounds in law and paid party work are more likely to populate parliaments (Sawer 2000). (See Chapter 9 for a discussion of professionalization in the United States.)

Education

Elite theorists point out that political elites are often highly educated (Putnam 1976). Thus, in countries where women have access to educational opportunities, one expects that they will be more likely to participate in politics. Basic education may be an especially important resource because it bestows political knowledge that may be essential for participation in the political realm (Verba et al. 1997). However, in Western industrialized nations, researchers often focus on graduate or professional education.

Education at elite institutions may also provide individuals with important connections or access to elite networks.

In the developing world, education means basic skills like literacy or language. International development organizations share the consensus that education is crucial to improving the quality of women's citizenship and leadership (Knight 2004). It is therefore encouraging that significant progress in female education has been made in recent years. For example, although education for women was outlawed under the Taliban in Afghanistan, since the 2001 U.S. invasion, the new government has opened hundreds of schools for women and girls. Unfortunately, however, women and girls are still less educated and more likely to be illiterate than men in many countries (UNESCO 2005). Across the developing world, 83% of men are literate compared with only 69% of women. As a specific example, in China, 95% of men are literate compared with 87% of women. In Pakistan, fewer people are literate, but gender differences remain strong—53% of men and 29% of women are literate (UNESCO 2005).

A more critical perspective argues that in developing countries, women's presence in schools can actually be "economically dysfunctional" (Robertson 1986:92). Because education encourages women's removal from the labor force, it may promote their dependence on men, reinforcing their subordinate roles. In sum, instead of presenting women with a path to greater autonomy and power, in the developing context education may actually function "as an instrument of oppression" (Robertson 1986: 92).

However, few researchers or policy makers agree with this position. They argue that in some situations education may provide a path to political power for women when other resources (such as wealth) are unavailable to them. In Uganda, for example, a woman was elected to the position of vice-chairperson in part because she had been through 7 years of schooling and could speak English. On the other hand, the chairman of the same council, a wealthy businessman in the village, did not have any formal education or English-language skills (Johnson et al. 2003).

Work

Just as elites are often highly educated, they are also usually successful businesspersons or come from professional occupations, such as law (Putnam 1976). Thus, the argument follows that where women are barred from obtaining prestigious or highly skilled positions in the labor force they will fail to be represented politically. Kira Sanbonmatsu (2002c) found that in the United States a greater percentage of women working in a state (including women executives and women in the legal field) increases the number of women in the state legislature. But while women's overall participation in the labor force is increasing worldwide, women are still concentrated in low-paying and low prestige jobs (Bielby and Baron 1986; England, Chassie, and McCormack 1982; Reskin and Hartmann 1986; Reskin and Roos 1993; Wright, Baxter, and Birkelund 1995). Furthermore, women still face limited economic rights and unchecked economic discrimination in several countries of the world (see Box 4.5).

Box 4.5   Women's Economic Rights Around the World

In 2004, human rights researchers David Cingranelli and David Richards developed a scheme for classifying countries into four ranked categories according to the economic rights they afforded women. Economic rights include equal pay for equal work, choice of employment without a male relative's consent, freedom from sexual harassment, and the right to work at night. A country in the highest category not only guarantees women's economic rights in law, but the government fully and vigorously enforces the law. In 2003, only eight countries achieved this feat, including Australia, Belgium, Canada, Iceland, Netherlands, the Republic of Moldova, Sweden, and Tunisia. In these countries, the government tolerates no or almost no discrimination against women.

Countries in the middle-high category also grant some economic rights for women under law, and the government enforces the laws effectively, but there is a degree of tolerance for low levels of discrimination against women. Inequalities tend to persist in pay and other areas. In 2003, 49 countries achieved this ranking, including Austria, Cambodia, Costa Rica, Fiji, France, Greece, Hungary, Israel, Italy, Libya, Lithuania, New Zealand, Norway, Peru, Portugal, Rwanda, South Korea, Switzerland, Thailand, Turkey, the United Arab Emirates, the United Kingdom, and the United States.

In the middle-low category, governments do not enforce the laws protecting women's economic rights effectively and tolerate a moderate level of discrimination against women. "Women are rarely compensated equally with men, are more likely than men to be laid off, and frequently hold lower paying, low-status jobs" (Cingranelli and Richards (2004a:37). This is the most common classification for countries in 2003. In fact, more countries are in this category than the other three combined. Although most countries in this group are still developing economically (e.g., Ethiopia, India, Mexico, North Korea), this category also includes industrialized countries, such as Japan, South Africa, and Spain.

Finally, in 2003, 12 countries fell into the lowest group, where there are no economic rights for women under law. In fact, systematic discrimination based on sex may be built into the law. "Employers often openly discriminate against women (e.g. pregnancy and marriage bars, discriminatory hiring practices, pay differentials, etc. . . .) and the government tolerates these practices. The Civil and Penal Codes contain discriminatory regulations against women, such as law allowing the husband to oppose his wife's right to work or to own a business" Cingranelli and Richards (2004a:37). Countries in this category are located in Asia (Afghanistan and Pakistan), Africa (Cameroon, Central African Republic, Chad, Guinea-Bissau, Lesotho, Liberia, and Togo), and the Middle East (Saudi Arabia and Yemen). Surprisingly, however, Cingranelli and Richards also placed the Russian Federation in this category.

SOURCE: Cingranelli and Richards (2004b).

Talking about women's labor force participation in general does not capture how certain jobs are conduits to political power. Without information on the types of jobs in which women work, it is unclear whether women are gaining politically relevant human capital from their job, or whether they are simply working too many hours to find the time to participate politically. But obtaining accurate information about women's share of professional or managerial occupations is a difficult task. The general lack of quality data on a worldwide basis has prevented important questions about the connections between women's professional and political lives from being answered. Labor force arguments about the supply of female politicians are further complicated by research that demonstrates that women may follow different career paths to politics. Women may pursue political office after careers in fields such as education (Jalalzai 2004:99). Therefore, women's occupational resources may be different from those of men. Critics of the labor force supply argument also contend that models based on female labor force statistics or women's share of positions in the professional occupations are based on Western models of women's incorporation into politics (Hughes 2004; Staudt 1986).

Economic Power

In most societies, women's work has long been overlooked or underestimated. Although many often think that throughout human history men have been the workers while women have been the mothers and wives, anthropological research indicates that among early civilizations women were the primary labor force in the vast majority of gathering and cultivating societies (Murdock 1967; cited from Blumberg 1984). Even today, statistics on labor tend to ignore the work of poor rural women (Donahoe 1999). Therefore, it is clear that women's labor alone is not sufficient to give them economic power. Specifically, economic power is based in control over the means of production and control over the allocation of surplus. It is control over surplus (in money, goods, land, or the labor of others) that leads individuals to have the resources to pursue and acquire political power. So though women's level of labor force participation or income may be important, gender stratification theorists argue that it is control over labor or income that matters (Blumberg 1984; Chafetz 1984). For example, Staudt (1986) explained that although women in Africa have control over money within their households, they cannot own land, putting them at a serious economic disadvantage compared with men in that society.

Although economic power does not guarantee that women will gain formal political power, gender stratification researchers argue strongly that women's economic power must precede political power. For example, according to Rae Lesser Blumberg (1984), a power hierarchy exists—political power rests at the top, and other types of power, such as economic power, appear below. Achievement of power at the lower levels of power, such as in the labor force, must occur before power can be reached at the next highest level (cited from Paxton 1997). In an ethnographic analysis of 61 preindustrial societies, Blumberg (1984) found only one instance in which women had significant political input without autonomous economic power. (The exceptional example was the Mende of Liberia. Although the women did not do much of the productive labor, they were organized in a secret society and used their clout to influence the political sphere.)

Structural Arguments: The Evidence

Arguments about the importance of a supply of qualified women eligible to run for public office are compelling. We begin evaluating their usefulness by comparing countries at different levels of development. As mentioned earlier, developed countries have industrialized and gained wealth over time, providing their female citizens with resources like free time, which should allow them to participate more extensively in politics. In Figure 4.3, we classify countries by level of development using the 2004 Human Development Index and show women's parliamentary representation from 1970 to 2005 (United Nations 2004). The Human Development Index is a composite measure of indicators of development including education, life expectancy, and gross domestic product (GDP). As Figure 4.3 demonstrates, women have higher average levels of representation in more developed countries.

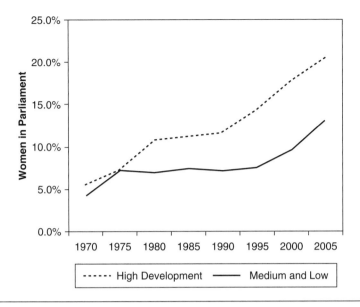

Figure 4.3   Percentage of Women in Parliament in 173 Countries by Level of Development, 1970–2005

SOURCES: Inter-Parliamentary Union (1995, 2005a) and United Nations Population Fund (2005).

But empirical research looking at the components of social structure has found, at best, mixed support for these supply-side effects on women in politics. For example, in a study of 12 states in the Midwestern United States, Susan Welch (1978) found that women's representation in the legislature was only one third of what would be predicted by the pool of women with the appropriate education, occupational experience, and associational memberships to qualify them to run for office. So structural supply does not fully explain women's low access to power.

Research also suggests that in some contexts, resource differences may not be as great or as important as previously thought. For example, in their investigation of the resource model of political participation in the United States, Schlozman et al. (1994) found only a slight gap between men and women in terms of political participation, and differences in political resources failed to fully explain the gap. Women and men were found to have roughly similar amounts of free time, and once women were politically active, they contributed more hours to political activities than men (Schlozman et al. 1994). This research took place in a Western, developed country, however, where one would expect women to have the greatest amount of free time.

But in statistical analyses performed in many countries around the world, measures of social structure are inconsistent predictors of women's representation in national politics. Generally, the most support has been found for the effects of women's labor force participation (Matland 1998; Moore and Shackman 1996; Paxton and Kunovich 2003; Rule 1981, 1987) or share of professional jobs (Kenworthy and Malami 1999). Still, a few studies contradict this trend, finding no real differences in female parliamentary representation when comparing countries in which women make up a greater part of the labor force to countries in which most women stay at home, once other theoretically important factors were taken into account (Kenworthy and Malami 1999; Paxton 1997).

When considering education, the opposite is true. Most research finds that women's higher educational attainment does not matter for their representation in national political bodies (Kenworthy and Malami 1999; Matland 1998; Moore and Shackman 1996; Norris 1985; Paxton 1997; Paxton and Kunovich 2003). Some researchers have suggested that this is a problem of development (Hughes 2004). What counts as significant education in one country may be taken for granted for another. For example, in the case of Uganda discussed earlier, 7 years of education was significant enough to allow a woman to gain leadership in a local village council. Yet in many countries education far beyond 7 years is compulsory for both men and women.

Although evidence for structural arguments is mixed, researchers often point out that this may be due to the limitations of current data. Information on women's position in the social structure, such as their participation in education and the labor force, is often difficult to collect, especially in less developed countries. Specific statistics, such as the percentage of women in professional or managerial occupations, is often only available in a few countries. In addition, as we noted earlier, what matters for women's access to politics in one country may be different from what matters in another. So it remains unclear whether, overall, structural factors are insignificant for women's political participation. What is clear is that, for women to be represented in politics, women must be willing and able to run for office. Political careers require time, money, and skills, and when it comes to these important resources women are structurally disadvantaged.

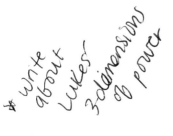

5

Explaining the Political Representation of Women—Politics

J ust as there is a supply side of women, created by cultural traditions and social structure, there is a demand side. Political parties may have different levels of demand for female candidates and voters may or may not support those female candidates. In this section, we discuss various political factors that affect the demand for women as candidates and legislators.

Recall the political recruitment process discussed at the beginning of Chapter 4. Explanations focusing on political demand are concerned with the latter portion of Figure 4.1. Once women decide that they would like to run for office, they must also pass the two barriers at the end of the process: They must be selected as candidates by gatekeepers and elected to office by voters.

The political recruitment process highlights that gatekeepers decide who among political aspirants gets to run as a candidate. Who are these gatekeepers? They are **political parties**. In most countries, the recruitment and selection of political elites occur entirely within political parties (Gallagher and Marsh 1988; Norris 1993). For an individual, man or woman, to run for political office, he or she must be selected and supported by a political party. As explained by Pesonen (1968:348), "The nomination stage eliminates 99.96% of all the eligible people; the voters choose from only .04%."

Understanding the role of political parties is therefore critical to understanding how women can gain access to politics. And to understand how political parties make their decisions about candidates, one must understand the electoral system under which they operate. A country's electoral system determines how the votes cast in an election get translated into seats won by parties and candidates (Reynolds, Reilly, and Ellis 2005:5). You can think of a country's electoral system as shaping the rules of the game played by various parties as they try to win political power. Electoral systems vary dramatically from country to country. So, although the rules of the game in one country may favor women, the rules of the game in another country may hinder women. Because political parties want to obtain political power, they need to put forward candidates who can win; therefore they are substantially influenced by their electoral system.

And of course parties operate in political systems that may be more or less democratic. Democratic systems, with clear, well-detailed, and consistent rules, make it easier for parties and candidates to follow the rules of the game. Nondemocratic systems, in contrast, might be based on the charisma of an individual leader or held via military force, leading to intermittent elections, changing rules, and difficulties in determining how political power can actually be attained. Also, the meaning of *candidate* or *legislator* differs depending on whether a country is a democracy or not. In some countries, women run as candidates in corrupted elections, and in others they are placed into legislatures that act purely as rubber stamps for the policies of a president-for-life.

In this chapter, we begin our discussion of the political demand for women at the broadest level by distinguishing democratic from nondemocratic political systems. We then turn to electoral systems and to a detailed discussion of how political parties make a difference for women. Finally, we address an important new source of demand for women in some countries—gender quotas requiring that a certain percentage of candidates or legislators be women.

Democracy

One of the most basic ways to classify countries' political systems is to determine whether a country operates under a **democracy**, a **semidemocracy**, or an **authoritarian regime**. Whether countries are democratic or not can influence whether women can attain, and how they attain, political power. It also influences how effective women are once they have obtained some power. One can begin by asking whether, theoretically, women should do better in democratic systems or in nondemocratic systems. Because women's political equality is often justified on grounds of democratic justice, it may seem logical that women would be more adequately represented in countries where democratic processes are more firmly entrenched. And in democracies, the rules of the political game should be clear and consistent, helping women to see how they can work within the system to attain power. But in nondemocracies, in the absence of true elections, women can be placed into power, even when citizens do not support them.

Large, cross-national statistical studies have shown that more democratic countries have no more women in parliament than less democratic countries (Kenworthy and Malami 1999; Paxton and Kunovich 2003; Reynolds 1999). In fact, some research has even found that women are less represented in democratic systems (Paxton 1997). One reason for this finding is that communist countries, such as Cuba and China, have high numbers of women in politics due to the continued use of affirmative action strategies by communist party elites (Norris and Inglehart 2001). This suggests that some nondemocracies are indeed placing women into power. Yet even excluding communist countries, level of democracy and the number of women in parliament appear to be unrelated.

A negative relationship between democracy and women's political power is seen if one looks at transitions to democracy rather than level of democracy. Countries that are newly democratizing often experience a decline in women's representation. For example, Yoon (2001) investigated the effects of transitions to multiparty democratic elections on women's representation in 31 countries in sub-Saharan Africa during the 1990s. Similar to patterns in Eastern Europe, some new democracies in sub-Saharan Africa experienced initial declines in female political representation. But the second set of democratic elections produced gains (see also Lindberg 2004). Even if women are very active in pushing for the transition to democracy, as they were in Latin America, once democracy is established and political parties are formed, women may be pushed aside (Franceschet 2001; Friedman 1998).

A positive effect of democracy appears when one considers female leaders. Female leaders are always elected through "regular" channels (Paxton and Goemans 2006). This means that they do not take power through irregular means, such as military coups. This is certainly reasonable because women are rarely the military leaders who would be placed into power through a coup. But it also suggests that female leaders are more successful in democratic systems.

It is also important to ask whether women's representation in ineffective national legislatures that serve under the thumb of a dictator should be treated the same as women's representation in an elected body that checks the power of the head of state. If the legislature has no real power, and instead serves as a "rubber stamp," does women's political representation still matter?

In some ways, women's presence matters regardless of the political system. The position of parliamentarian is visible and carries prestige, having important symbolic effects that may improve women's status in society. Watershed moments, such as the election of the first woman to parliament, were likely just as significant to women in Syria or Kenya as to women in the United States or the United Kingdom. Furthermore, as women's numbers in parliament increase, perceptions of women may change (Norris 1993). When only a few women are present in politics, people perceive that women's political roles are exceptional. But as countries move beyond token membership, it changes perceptions about how a parliamentarian looks and acts.

Yet, in very real ways, women's representation in nondemocratic systems limits their ability to influence legislation or otherwise make an impact. Even if women successfully pass legislation in parliament, a powerful president may simply dispose of the parliamentary reforms. Unlike democratic systems with executive controls, the legislature in an authoritarian state likely has no way to dispute or oppose the president's intervention. For example, in Goetz and Hassim's (2003) study of Uganda and South Africa, women's ability to change the law (not just propose legislation) depended on whether they were in a democracy or a semidemocracy (see also Box 7.1 in Chapter 7). Of course, when the powerful leader overriding a legislature is a woman (remember Indira Gandhi), that individual can have substantial political power.

Because women in authoritarian or semidemocratic systems have limited power, some researchers talk about women in politics solely in democratic regimes (e.g., Matland 1998). Others, feeling that women's symbolic power is important to acknowledge, discuss nondemocracies (e.g., Paxton and Kunovich 2003). Regardless, it is always important to ask whether one is talking about a country where women were elected under fully democratic procedures and have full political power or a country where they have only partial or symbolic power.

Electoral Systems

All countries that hold elections have an electoral system that determines the rules of the game. Electoral systems can be complicated, but they are very important for understanding the political demand for women. Electoral systems are typically divided into three broad families: plurality/majority systems, proportional representation systems, and mixed systems (Reynolds et al. 2005:28). **Plurality/majority systems** ask voters to vote for just a single person to represent them. Voters go to the polls, see a slate of candidates (one from every party), and choose just one person. The United States has a plurality/majority electoral system, as does the United Kingdom.

Proportional representation (PR) systems are different. PR systems typically ask voters to vote for a list of candidates to represent them. Voters go to the polls, see a slate of parties (each of which has a list of candidates), and choose a party to represent them. Voters therefore vote for parties rather than specific candidates. PR systems directly relate the number of seats won by a political party to the number of votes cast for that party. So, if a party wins 30% of the votes, the party receives 30% of the parliamentary seats. Legislators are selected by moving down the party's list, in order, until the party's 30% of seats are filled. A key feature of most PR systems is therefore that they have **multimember districts**, where multiple people represent the voters of a particular electoral district. Put another way, more than one candidate can be elected from a particular district in PR systems. In contrast, plurality/majority systems typically have single-member districts, where the voters in an electoral district have only one person representing them in the legislature.

Mixed systems combine both PR voting and plurality/majority voting, typically running side-by-side. Under a mixed electoral system, part of the legislature is elected through proportional representation and part through plurality/majority. (Note: This discussion of electoral systems is general and simplified. There are variants on each of these three types of electoral systems that are more complicated than presented here. But 70% of the world's electoral systems fall into the three types as described in this section. *Electoral System Design: The New IDEA Handbook*, http://www.idea.int/publications/esd/new_en.cfm, is an excellent source for more extensive detail on the types of electoral systems around the world.)

It is generally accepted that women do better in gaining political office under PR electoral systems (Kenworthy and Malami 1999; Matland 1998; Norris 1985; Paxton 1997; Rule 1987). For example, Paxton (1997) looked at 108 countries and found that, even controlling for other factors, such as

Table 5.1 Women's Representation in Plurality/Majority Versus PR Systems

	1945	1950	1960	1970	1980	1990	2000	2005
Plurality/Majority (single member)	3.1	2.1	2.5	2.2	3.4	8.2	15.7	18.6
PR (multimember)	2.9	4.7	5.5	5.9	11.9	18.1	25.8	27.8

Plurality/Majority Systems:

Australia, Canada, France (from 1960), Japan, New Zealand (1945–1990), United Kingdom, United States

PR Systems:

Austria, Belgium, Denmark, Finland, France, Greece, Iceland, Ireland, Israel, Italy, Japan (2000–), Luxembourg, Netherlands, New Zealand (2000–), Norway, Portugal, Spain, Sweden, Switzerland, West Germany/Germany

SOURCES: Adapted from Matland 2002 (1945–1990). Data for later years collected by the authors, 2000–2005.

democracy and level of development, PR systems have 3.5% more women in their national legislature. Richard Matland produced a table that succinctly demonstrates the difference in women's levels of representation between PR and plurality/majority systems in 24 national legislatures (2002:6). We provide an updated version of his table as Table 5.1.

Mixed systems are particularly interesting places to see the impact of electoral system. Countries with mixed electoral systems elect part of their legislature using plurality/majority methods and part using proportional representation. In countries with both systems, women are elected at much higher rates under the PR system than the alternative plurality/majority system (Henig and Henig 2001; Norris 1993:313; Rule 1987). For example after Germany's 1990 election, women won 28% of the PR seats and only 12% of the plurality/majority seats. In Australia's 1990 election, women won 25% of PR seats but only 7% of the plurality/majority districts. Similarly, in New Zealand's 2005 election, women won 43% of PR party-list seats but only 20% of the plurality/majority districts.

Why Are Proportional Representation Systems Good for Women?

Why do women do better under proportional representation systems? The key reason is **district magnitude**—how many representatives an electoral district sends to the national legislature. Remember the difference between multimember and single-member electoral districts? Single-member districts have a district magnitude of 1—only one person represents an electoral district. Other countries have much higher district magnitudes, sending 2, 20, or 50 representatives to a legislature. Sometimes the electoral district is the entire country, and individual voters are therefore simultaneously represented by hundreds of legislators.

Higher district magnitudes are better for women because they can get on a party's ballot without displacing a male. In a single-member district, getting on the ballot is a zero-sum process. If one person gets on the ballot, it means another person is not on the ballot. In single-member districts, therefore, parties must make a choice between male and female candidates, rather than placing both on the ticket. As relative newcomers to politics, when women compete head-to-head against men to be candidates, the women are disadvantaged. Men have been in politics longer, are entrenched in positions of power, and do not want to give up that power. Further, if women are seen as worse candidates then men, perhaps due to long-standing cultural traditions against women in politics, it is not in the party's interest to run women. The party elite wants candidates who they believe can win.

In contrast, proportional representation systems have multimember districts where voters vote for parties with published lists of candidates. When a party needs to produce a list of candidates, it is under pressure to **balance** its ticket across interest groups in society: "Rather than having to look for a single candidate who can appeal to a broad range of voters, party gatekeepers think in terms of different candidates appealing to specific subsectors of voters" (Matland 2002:6). So a party in a PR system wants to have some women on its list of candidates, so it can attract female voters. As a female legislator from Asia explains, "There has been recognition over the last 10 years (1988–98) that it is essential for the credibility of any political party to be seen to be preselecting and electing women to parliament" (Inter-Parliamentary Union 2000:57).

Running multiple candidates in the same district also allows parties in proportional representation systems to appease internal party factions more easily. Like interest groups in the general population, there are interest groups in parties. Balancing can be used by party gatekeepers to resolve internal party disputes through compromise (Gallagher and Marsh 1988; Matland 2002). If women in the party demand to be included as candidates, it is easier for a party operating in a proportional representation system to accommodate them. The cost is lower because men do not have to step aside to accommodate women. Instead, men and women can run side-by-side on the same party list.

Types of PR Systems

But not all PR systems are created equal (for women). There are important differences across PR systems that can also make a big difference for women getting nominated as candidates. First, even though PR systems typically have multimember districts, there is variation in actual district magnitude across countries. Countries may have a district magnitude of 3, or it may be 20 or higher. The higher the district magnitude, the better for women (Rule 1987, 1994).

Why? Remember that in PR systems parties get a share of seats in the legislature based on how many votes they got. Legislators are selected by moving down the party's list in order. So where are women on the party's list? Are they in a **safe position**, guaranteed to win a seat in the legislature based on the party's expected share of the vote? Or are they in a risky list position or even a hopeless list position? Parties can certainly present the appearance of balance between the genders but have men at the top of the list and women at the bottom (Kunovich 2003). Indeed, the party leaders (typically male) always hold the top spots on party lists. When women are not at the top of the list, parties have to go further down their list (by winning a higher percentage of the vote) for the women to become legislators. Wilma Rule (1994:18) puts some hard numbers on what is needed: "It is usually essential that the number of representatives per district be five or more for the election of women in meaningful numbers. Ten or fifteen members would enhance greatly the number of women candidates elected. . . . "

A similar way for women to benefit is when parties have high party magnitude. Like district magnitude, party magnitude is the number of seats a party tends to win in an electoral district. Parties in systems with high party magnitude go further down their lists and are therefore likely to pick up more women. Indeed, party magnitude is likely more important than district magnitude because it directly, rather than indirectly, determines how far down a list a party has to go.

Another important difference is between **closed** and **open party lists**. Under a closed list PR system, parties produce an ordered list of candidates that cannot be changed by voters. In open list systems, voters can influence the order of the candidates. Whether open or closed lists are better for women is disputable. It depends who is more likely to advance women on lists—party gatekeepers or voters (Matland 2002). In closed list systems, it is necessary to convince party gatekeepers to put women in winnable list positions. In open list systems, it is necessary to convince voters not to move men ahead of women on the party's suggested list.

Of course, why couldn't women use open lists to promote women on the list to winnable seats? If women can organize, this is certainly a possibility. But Richard Matland (2002:70) tells an interesting story of how such a strategy ultimately backfired in Norway:

> Norway does not have an open list voting system for the national parliament, but it does for local elections at the municipality level. In the early 1970s, women were able to organize a remarkably effective campaign to promote women. In the 1971 local elections women's representation in several large Norwegian cities rose from being approximately 15–20 per cent of the city council to majorities on the council. This "women's coup" became a source of great surprise and pride at women's abilities to take advantage of the electoral structure. It should be noted, however, that there was a reaction in the following election, when many men who felt that striking male candidates simply because they were men was unfair, went out of their way to strike women candidates. In the following local election and in every local election since, the number of women elected in local elections in Norway has probably been less than it would have been had there been no personal vote.

Intersectionality

Political parties creating lists face pressure to appeal to all sorts of voter constituencies. And that means including not only women, but minority groups as well. Therefore, PR-list systems are also beneficial to the representation of minority women, who face multiple forms of discrimination due to intersectionality (discussed in Chapter 1). After New Zealand transferred to their mixed system, the representation of Asians, Pacific Islanders, and Maori increased from 8% to 17%. Furthermore, even though 57% of the seats were elected by plurality/majority (including seven reserved seats for Maori) in the 2005 election, 56% of minority men and 70% of minority women in the legislature were elected from the PR portion of the electoral system. In her opening statement to the New Zealand House of Representatives, Asian female representative Patsy Wong (1997) attributed her election to the new mixed system, which enabled her to capitalize on support from "Chinese, Korean, and other ethnic communities throughout the country."

Certainly, electoral system doesn't explain everything. There have also been exceptional cases where White, rural constituencies elected minority women under the plurality/majority system. In 1999, for example, one such district in New Zealand elected the world's first transsexual parliamentarian, Georgina Beyer (2005). Beyer is Maori minority, who lived as a sex worker before undergoing a full sex change in 1984. Before being elected to parliament, Beyer worked as an actress, a broadcaster, an educator, an author, a justice of the peace, and a mayor. A documentary of her life, *Georgie Girl,* was released internationally in 2002.

Characteristics of Political Parties

Parties play a critical gatekeeping role in political systems and are a critical mediator between women and political power (Caul 1999; Kunovich 2003; Kunovich and Paxton 2005; Sanbonmatsu 2002a). Political parties make decisions about which candidates to field and how much support to give them (through, e.g., placement on party lists). As succinctly explained by a female legislator from Central America, "In order for women to be elected to Parliament, the political parties have the responsibility of trusting in women, encouraging them, and putting them forward in constituencies where they can be certain of electoral success" (Inter-Parliamentary Union 2000:97).

So how do political parties go about picking candidates? Unlike the primary system in the United States, candidate selection is not open for public inspection and participation in most other nations. Instead, in most countries, candidate selection is the purview of a small set of party elites (Gallagher and Marsh 1988:2). For example, both the Conservative and Liberal Democratic parties in Britain generate a list of centrally approved candidates that local constituency members use in selecting candidates (British Broadcasting Corporation 2001).

Generally, parties of all stripes look for certain features in their political candidates. First, parties want to field candidates who show a proven track record of winning. Thus, **incumbents** are much more attractive than challengers, evidenced by an extremely high rate of incumbent renomination (Matland 2002). Other experience with the party—a history of activism and party participation—is also important, especially for new candidates. Yet lacking high visibility in the party may be overlooked if a candidate has been highly visible in his or her community as a leader of a business or other organization. Because incumbents and community leaders are more often men, women may be less attractive to political parties as potential candidates (Matland 2002).

Political parties may all have the same goal—to attain political power. But parties vary substantially in the number of women they send to parliament (Caul 1999). Consider Table 5.2, which shows the percentage of female legislators in 1975 and 1985 by party for five different countries. Note that these are differences across parties within the same electoral system.

Why do some political parties do better than others in promoting women? The first explanation is the political ideology of the party itself—is it a party with a left agenda, or is it more to the right of the political spectrum? Parties that are further left in their political leanings tend to espouse egalitarian ideals and are more likely to put forward female candidates. Parties on the left may also better see the need to promote traditionally underrepresented groups, such as women (Caul 1999). Research on parties supports the idea that left parties do better in promoting women. For example, Richard Matland (1993) found that it was leftist parties that began sending women to parliament in Norway in the 1980s. Similarly, in a study of 68 political parties across 12 countries, Miki Caul (1999) found that parties on the left sent more women to parliament.

Another important distinction across parties is the composition of their leadership. The attitudes and values of candidate selectors (typically the party elite) matter for who is selected. So, if women are present in the party elite, they may advocate for a greater number of female candidates (Caul 1999; Kunovich and Paxton 2005). As a female legislator from Western Europe states, "It was the women in the party who encouraged me to get more deeply involved and to register on a list for the elections" (Inter-Parliamentary Union 2000:75). And women may be better able to see what

Table 5.2   Female Legislators by Political Party, 1975 and 1985

| | Percentage of Female Legislators | |
Country and Party	1975	1985
Belgium		
Christian People's (CVP)	12	18
Socialist (Flemish) (BSP)	3	6
Liberty (Flemish) (PVV)	0	5
People's Union (VU)	9	6
Ecology (Flemish) (AGA)	—	50
Germany		
Social Democratic (SPD)	5	10
Christian Democratic (CDU)	8	7
Christian Social Union (CSU)	2	6
Free Democratic (FDP)	10	9
Greens (G)	—	20
Norway		
Socialist People's (SV)	19	50
Labour Party (DNA)	19	42
Center Party (SP)	14	17
Christian People's (KRF)	5	25
Liberals (V)	0	—
Conservatives (H)	17	30
Progress (FRP)	0	0
UK		
Labour (LAB)	5	5
Liberal/Liberal Democrats (LIB/SDL)	0	0
Conservatives (CON)	3	3
USA		
Democrats (DEM)	6	5
Republicans (REP)	2	6

SOURCE: Caul (1999). Reprinted with permission of Sage Publications Ltd.

must be done to recruit female candidates in the first place. In Australia, a current female party leader made it possible for a former female party leader to return to politics (and ultimately be elected) by promising to make all the necessary flexible arrangements so that she could juggle the demands of a new baby (Commonwealth Secretariat 1999:20).

It is not only female party elites who make a difference. Miki Caul (1999) found that women in midlevel positions in parties (as delegates to national conferences and women working as local activists) can help create higher levels of female office holders. They do this partly by influencing party rules targeting certain percentages of women as candidates. Women in party leadership positions may also advocate the adoption of quotas for women (Caul 2001). Overall, 78% of women responding to an Inter-Parliamentary Union (2000) survey believed that the presence of women had brought about a change in their party's priorities.

Finally, like entire countries, parties can vary in the extent to which they have clear, consistent, and understandable rules. When candidate selection is transparent and institutionalized, anyone can understand what he or she needs to do to be selected as a candidate. In contrast, if selection rules and processes are unclear, the selection of candidates may seem capricious and based on random criteria. Political outsiders, such as women, should have an easier time breaking in when party rules are clear and transparent (Czudnowski 1975). Indeed, Miki Caul, in her work on 68 parties in 12 democracies, found that parties with clear rules are more likely to elect women to office.

Women's Parties

Form v. Context

Some countries have women's parties that run only female candidates. Throughout history, women feeling marginalized by existing political parties have formed their own parties. For example, in the United Kingdom in 1917, when Christabel and Emmeline Pankhurst dissolved the Women's Social and Political Union (see Chapter 2), they formed the Women's Party. The party focused on enlisting women for the war effort, and in the 1918 election Christabel ran for office but was unsuccessful, and the party dissolved in 1919. Women-only party lists have existed in Israel since 1918, when the Women's Society was elected to the first Representative Assembly (Simmons Levin 1999).

Women's parties have formed in a number of countries since the 1990s, including *Josei-tō*, a feminist party in Japan, and the Hellenic Women's Party in Greece. In 1996, the Northern Ireland Women's Coalition was founded, strongly opposed to violence in the region. Although two women from the party were represented in the Northern Ireland Assembly in 1998 and 2001, both women lost their seats in 2003.

Women's parties have also been formed in many postcommunist countries, including Armenia, Belarus, Bulgaria, Georgia, Kyrgystan, Lithuania, Moldova, Russia, and Ukraine. But though these parties may all seek to represent women, they are often quite different, attracting different kinds of supporters. For example, the Women of Russia, founded by elites with links to the past Soviet Bureaucracy, is more traditional in its ideology, whereas the Shamiram Women's Party in Armenia was more successful attracting younger, educated women and received support from feminists (Ishiyama 2003).

Although these parties may have different ideologies, they often share at least one thing—limited electoral success. Several women's parties have failed to ever win any seats in parliament, including the Democratic Women's Union in Bulgaria, the Women's Party of Georgia, and the Association of Women in Moldova. Moser (2003) argued that the very existence of a women's party can indicate that the women's movement is weak, unable to influence major parties to address women's issues. Further, the presence of women's parties can prevent other parties from believing they can effectively solicit the female vote, leading them not to field female candidates (Moser 2003). So even if a women's party is successful in one election, if it ever fails to win seats in parliament, women's overall representation may decline dramatically. This was the case with the Women of Russia, which obtained 23 seats in 1993 but only 3 seats in 1995 (Ishiyama 2003). Women's overall representation in the legislature simultaneously dropped from 13% to 10%. A similar drop occurred with the Shamiram Women's Party in Armenia, which received 16.9% of the vote in 1995 but failed to claim a single seat in 1999 (Ishiyama 2003). The overall representation of women in parliament in Armenia thus fell from 6% to 3%.

Yet women's parties have had some successes. In Lithuania, the formation of a woman's party encouraged other parties to expand women's participation in the party elite (Krupavičius and Matonytė 2003). In addition, female Prime Minister Kazimiera Prunskienė argued that it was the formation of the women's party and the ensuing pressure that led to the adoption of gender quotas, something that would have been unthinkable just years before. However, Prunskienė is not impartial: She was instrumental in the formation of the party after being pushed out of her own party over her foreign policy stance on dealing with Russia (Krupavičius and Matonytė 2003). And overall, Matland and Montgomery (2003) argued that where women's parties have arisen in the postcommunist world they have been more hurtful to women's representation than helpful.

Although many women's parties have dissolved, for example in Australia and Iceland, other countries are forming new women's parties. For example, in 2003, women formed the first all-woman party in India, called the Womanist Party of India, or WPI. The party is calling for an increase in reserved seats for women to 50% and inclusion of women's names in land ownership deeds, as well as reserving for women 50% of seats on boards of cooperative banks, state corporations, and other institutions (Telegraph 2004). And in Sweden, a new feminist party plans to contest the 2006 elections, threatening the dominance of the ruling Social Democratic Party.

According to *The Economist* (2005), the driving force behind the party is Gudrun Schyman, "former leader of the Left Party, who once accused Swedish men of being no better than the Taliban."

From Candidate to Legislator

Much of the discussion so far has focused on how women move from being aspirants to candidates. But what happens to those female candidates? Are they always elected? No.

Table 5.3 shows that countries send different percentages of their female candidates to political office (Kunovich and Paxton 2005). The table begins by recording the percent female candidates in 76 countries, then the percentage of female members of the national legislature, and finally the ratio of the two. Values of 1 for the ratio indicate a one-to-one relationship between percentage of candidates and percentage of female representatives. Looking at Table 5.3, one can see that the yield of female representatives ranges from values of considerably less than 1 (e.g., 0.3 in Morocco) to values greater than 1 (e.g., 1.22 in the Netherlands). Thus, though the "return" on female candidates is very low in Morocco, 3% female elected officials for every 10% female candidates, the return is greater than expected in the Netherlands. Sheri Kunovich and Pamela Paxton (2005) worked with these numbers and showed that the overall return on female candidates is lower than one-to-one. Across all of the countries, a 1% increase in the number of female candidates results in only a 0.67% increase in female legislators.

Or consider it another way. With the exception of four countries (the Netherlands, Mexico, Grenada, and Seychelles), the percentage of women in the national legislature is never more than 5% higher than the percentage of female candidates. On the other hand, there are numerous examples where the percentage of women in the legislature is substantially lower than the percentage of female candidates. For example, in Iceland, women are 50% of candidates and 25% of representatives.

What determines whether female candidates actually get elected? Obviously, voters are important. Especially in countries with a very negative culture against women in politics, voters may simply not vote for female candidates. But here again political parties play a large role. Political parties are the major source of support for candidates in their bid for public office. Parties in PR systems can support candidates by placing them in favorable list positions, whereas parties in plurality/majority systems can improve a candidate's chances of election by providing additional financial and institutional resources for campaigning.

Table 5.3   Percentage of Female Candidates and Women in National Legislatures

	Percent of Female:				Percent of Female:		
	Candidates	Parliament	Ratio		Candidates	Parliament	Ratio
Western Industrialized				**Asia**			
Australia	27.9	15.5	0.55	Cambodia	4.8	5.8	1.21
Austria	39.3	26.8	0.68	India	4.2	7.2	1.71
Canada	22.1	18.0	0.81	Japan	7.3	4.6	1.59
France	19.2	6.4	0.33	Kiribati	1.5	0.0	0
Germany	29.5	26.2	0.88	North Korea	20.1	20.1	1
Ireland	18.9	13.9	0.74	South Korea	2.2	3.0	1.36
Italy	12.7	11.1	0.87	Laos	10.4	9.4	0.9
Monaco	12.0	5.6	0.47	Mongolia	8.6	7.9	0.92
Netherlands	25.5	31.3	1.22	Nepal	6.0	3.4	0.57
Spain	32.5	24.6	0.76	Philippines	8.5	10.8	1.27
Switzerland	34.8	21.0	0.60	Samoa	4.9	4.1	0.84
United Kingdom	19.4	9.5	0.49	Singapore	3.2	2.5	0.78
				Sri Lanka	2.7	5.3	1.96
Scandinavia				Viet Nam	30.3	26.0	0.86
Denmark	30.0	33.0	1.1	**Central and South America**			
Iceland	50.4	25.4	0.5	Argentina	30.0	25.3	0.84
Sweden	43.6	40.4	0.92	Bolivia	16.6	6.9	0.42
				Brazil	5.7	6.6	1.16
Eastern Europe				Chile	11.5	7.5	0.65
Armenia	2.5	6.3	2.52	Colombia	8.5	11.7	1.38
Czech Republic	20.2	15.0	0.74				

	Percent of Female:		
	Candidates	Parliament	Ratio
Georgia	26.8	6.8	0.25
Kazakhstan	11.2	13.4	1.2
Latvia	23.0	9.0	0.39
Lithuania	20.6	17.5	0.85
Moldova	11.3	4.8	0.42
Poland	13.1	13.0	0.99
Romania	11.1	7.0	0.63
Slovakia	14.6	14.7	1.01
Slovenia	22.9	7.8	0.34
Tajikstan	5.1	2.8	0.55
Ukraine	9.3	3.8	0.41
Middle East and Northern Africa			
Algeria	2.4	6.6	2.75
Cyprus	9.9	5.4	0.55
Egypt	2.0	2.0	1
Iran	10.0	4.0	0.4
Jordan	0.6	1.3	2.17
Morocco	2.0	0.6	0.3
Tunisia	6.0	6.7	1.12
Yemen	0.8	0.7	0.88

	Percent of Female:		
	Candidates	Parliament	Ratio
Costa Rica	22.6	15.8	0.7
Cuba	22.8	22.8	1
Ecuador	10.4	3.7	0.36
Grenada	9.8	20.0	2.04
Guyana	16.7	20.0	1.2
Jamaica	9.3	11.7	1.26
Mexico	8.9	14.2	1.6
Nicaragua	26.4	10.8	0.41
Africa			
Benin	3.3	7.2	2.18
Burkina Faso	3.6	3.7	1.03
Kenya	2.5	3.0	1.2
Malawi	7.2	5.6	0.78
Mali	1.9	2.3	1.21
Namibia	13.8	18.1	1.31
Sao Tome & Principe	9.1	7.3	0.8
Seychelles	21.2	27.3	1.29
South Africa	41.2	25.0	0.61
Zimbabwe	12.6	14.7	1.17

SOURCE: From Kunovich, S., & Paxton, P., "Pathways to power: The role of political parties in woman's national political representation," in *American Journal of Sociology, 111*(2), copyright © 2005. Reprinted with permission of the University of Chicago Press.

So, if female party elites influence how many women appear as candidates, those same elites should also positively affect the ratio of representatives to candidates. Female party elites may try to support female candidates in their bids for election by influencing list placement or party contributions to candidate war chests. Consider this West African legislators comment: "Women asked me to stand in the legislative elections and they supported my candidacy in the one-party state system" (Inter-Parliamentary Union 2000:82).

Sheri Kunovich and Pamela Paxton (2005) found that female party elites indeed influence the number of women who run on the party ticket. But the situation is complicated by electoral system. Women's position in party elites translates into gains for women as candidates only under PR systems. In contrast, women's position in party elites increases the likelihood that female candidates will be elected only in plurality/majority systems.

This finding makes sense if you consider the difference between PR and plurality/majority systems. Remember that candidate selectors in PR systems feel pressure to balance their party's list between men and women. Thus, it should be relatively easy for female party elites in PR systems to convince the party to field female candidates. But those female elites may be less successful in getting them placed in safe positions on lists. Consider the complaint of a West African legislator: "Women actively participate in the same way as men, but they don't manage to move upwards, always holding subordinated positions in political organizations and on electoral lists" (Inter-Parliamentary Union 2000:60).

Contrast this to the situation of female leaders in plurality/majority systems. Once the battle for who will be a candidate is over, each party has the incentive to fully support their candidate, whether male or female. And female party leaders are in a position to provide additional support to their female candidates in the form of campaign money or better institutional resources for campaigning. In the United States, organizations such as EMILY's List raise money and provide additional training and institutional support for female candidates in their bid for office (see Chapter 9). Female party leaders can tap into these external resources to help women gain a legislative seat once they are nominated as a candidate.

Ultimately, therefore, we see that female elites can help women move from aspirant to candidate in PR systems but not in plurality/majority systems. But female elites can help women move from candidate to legislator in plurality/majority systems and not PR systems.

As for the voters, Kunovich and Paxton (2005) found that once the decisions made by party elites were accounted for, a country's culture did not matter for how many women were elected. This suggests that parties may be overly sensitive to perceived hostility to women as candidates, when in fact women are acceptable as candidates to voters all over the world.

Quotas

I'd give up my seat for you if it wasn't for the fact that I'm sitting in it myself.

—Groucho Marx (quoted in Baldez 2004:231)

On January 4, 2004, the grand council in Afghanistan adopted a new constitution to govern the war-ridden nation. The new constitution included **gender quotas** for both the upper and lower houses of the country's future parliament. Specifically, at least 2 women must be elected to the lower house from each province, guaranteeing a minimum of 65 women. Among the 10 seats set aside for Kuchis, a disadvantaged nomadic people in Afghanistan, three are reserved for women, bringing the quota to 27%. For the upper house, the president appoints one third of the members, and 50% of these appointees must be women, assuring women 17 of the 102 seats. But how did Afghanistan, a country formerly governed by one of the most repressive regimes toward women in modern history—the Taliban—adopt constitutional provisions that benefit women's parliamentary representation? To answer that question, one must first understand the broader context in which Afghanistan chose to adopt quotas.

Affirmative action strategies to increase women's representation have been around for decades. In the 1950s, Eva Peron lobbied for the use of quotas by the Peronist Party in Argentina, resulting in the election of 15% women to the national Chamber of Deputies in 1952 and 22% in 1955 (Jones 1998). At the time, Argentina had the fourth highest percentage of women in parliament, trailing only the communist systems of East Germany, the Soviet Union, and Mongolia (Jones 1998). Although communist countries often do not have explicit quota systems, many researchers note that they operate under informal quota systems, whereby communist party leaders select women to fill seats, guaranteeing their inclusion (Matland and Montgomery 2003; Siemienska 2004). Several Asian countries have a history of quotas. Taiwan, for example, reserved roughly 10% of seats for women beginning in 1953 (Chou and Clark 1994). Upon independence in 1971, Bangladesh reserved 15 of 315 seats in its parliament for women, who were chosen by the 300 parliamentarians elected to the general seats (Chowdhury 2002). And in 1978, a presidential proclamation doubled this number, increasing women's representation to 9.9%. During the 1970s, a small number of political parties in Western industrialized countries also adopted quotas. Reserved seats also appeared in North Africa during the 1970s: In Egypt in 1979, a presidential decree was passed reserving a seat in 30 districts for women, establishing a quota of 8.3% (Abou-Zeid 2003).

Since the 1990s, however, the pace of quota adoption has increased dramatically. National-level quotas spread throughout Latin America after 1990, and after 1995 many African countries followed suit with reserved seats and party-level quotas (Ballington 2004; Tripp 2003). During the 1990s, 22 countries adopted national electoral law quotas that required between 20% and 50% of candidates for legislative office to be women (Baldez 2004). In other countries, scores of political parties voluntarily adopted gender quotas to attract female candidates or voters. In some predominantly Muslim African countries, "the women's quota became part of an effort to contain the growing influence of Islamists" (Tripp 2003:1). Moving into the 21st century, governments and political parties in many additional countries adopted gender quotas, including Australia, Bosnia and Herzegovina, Burkina Faso, Iraq, Niger, and Tanzania, to name a few. In Southeast Asia, the people even speak of a sweeping "quota fever" (International Institute for Democracy and Electoral Assistance 2006). By the end of 2005, more than 100 countries had adopted some form of gender quota, and many more are still debating the issue. Gender quotas are therefore a new but important political factor for understanding women's representation in politics.

At a basic level, gender quotas simply require that women must make up a certain percentage of a candidate list, a parliamentary assembly, a committee, or a government (Dahlerup 2002). As affirmative action policies, gender quotas are designed to help women overcome obstacles to their election such as less political experience, cultural stereotypes, or incumbency. Most governments and political parties adopting quotas are attempting to move beyond token representation to reach at least a critical minority of 20%, 30%, or 40% women in parliament (International Institute for Democracy and Electoral Assistance 2006). And as noted in Chapter 3, many of the largest absolute and relative jumps in the history of women's political representation followed the implementation of gender quotas, allowing countries to move from making slow or incremental gains to running on the "fast track" (Dahlerup 2002; Dahlerup and Freidenvall 2005). Indeed, Aili Mari Tripp and Alice Kang (2006) found that quotas were a very powerful predictor of women's political representation across 149 countries.

Yet gender quotas exhibit a great deal of variation in how they are developed, implemented, and regulated and in how successfully they increase women's representation. As researcher Mona Krook (2003:1) accurately stated, "Not all quotas are created equal." Some quotas have proved wholly ineffective in increasing women's representation, whereas others have produced substantial gains. In some cases, the same quota legislation has produced completely different outcomes in societies operating under different electoral systems (Krook 2003, 2004a; Schmidt and Saunders 2004). Furthermore, one has to recognize that quotas raise serious questions about women's representation, and, in some cases, quotas meet strong resistance.

Evaluating Gender Quotas: Which Quotas Are Better?

Gender quotas differ in a number of important ways. First, some quotas explicitly regulate women's seats, whereas others are posed in gender-neutral terms. For instance, in 1988, the Social Democratic Party of Denmark required that 40% of each gender be represented in elections at both the local and regional levels (International Institute for Democracy and Electoral Assistance 2006). Gender-neutral quotas are especially common in Latin America and are framed neutrally to combat arguments that quotas are discriminatory (Ballington 2004). Although gender quotas are almost always adopted to address women's long-standing underrepresentation in politics, gender-neutral quotas do, in some rare circumstances, benefit men (Dahlerup 1988; Freidenvall 2003).

Although there are countless ways to classify the vast array of quota regulations, we focus here on four dimensions that are most important for determining how effectively quotas improve the status of women:

1. How regulations are put in place

2. Whether candidates, nominees, or elected members are regulated

3. The threshold for representation

4. Whether there are sanctions for failing to meet quota obligations

How Regulations Are Put in Place: Constitutions, Election Laws, and Political Parties

The International Institute for Democracy and Electoral Assistance (IDEA) in Stockholm, Sweden, is one of the main sources of data and research on gender quotas. IDEA classifies quotas based on the type of document, law, or rule that requires the quota be met. There are constitutional quotas, election law quotas, and political party quotas. Although most countries rely on only one type of quota, 23 countries have adopted quotas regulated in two forms, and 3 countries (Argentina, France, and the Philippines) have quotas regulated in all three ways (International Institute for Democracy and Electoral Assistance 2006).

The least common form of quota, called **constitutional quotas**, is mandated by a country's constitution. For example, Iraq's new constitution mandates that at least 25% of the elected legislature be female. Only 13 countries have constitutional quotas, and of those only Bangladesh and Guyana do not pair this form with another kind of quota. Table 5.4 reports the countries that have this type of quota, along with the percentage of women in parliament in the country as of April 2005. Countries with constitutional quotas have, on average, 21.3% women in parliament—about 5% higher than the world average of 16.1% (Inter-Parliamentary Union 2005a). (Bangladesh did not hold elections before April and after constitutional quotas were put in place, so the percentage of women in parliament is not reported.) In some countries, constitutional quotas do not suggest a certain percentage of candidates or parliamentarians who should or must be female. Instead, these quotas enshrine gender equality as a goal, and often they dictate that quotas be pursued through election law or by political parties. In France, for example, the parity reform was added to the constitution in 1999 stating that "the law favors the equal access of women and men to electoral mandates and elective functions" and that political parties were responsible for facilitating equal access (International Institute for Democracy and Electoral Assistance 2006).

Table 5.4　Constitutional Quotas

Country	Required % of Women	% Women, 2005
Afghanistan	25.6% elected (2 women per province)	17.7%[1]
Argentina	n/a	33.7%
Bangladesh	13% elected	n/a
France	n/a	12.2%
Guyana	33% of party electoral lists	30.8%
Iraq	25% elected	31.6%[1]
Kenya	2.7% appointed	7.1%
Nepal	5% of candidates per party	5.9%
Philippines	20% elected[2]	15.3%
Rwanda	30% elected	48.0%
Taiwan	n/a	22.2%
Tanzania	20–30% reserved seats	21.4%
Uganda	18.3% elected	23.9%
Average % Women		21.7%
Average for Countries With Only This Type		30.8%

1. Percentages given are for provisional assemblies.

2. Seats are shared with other marginalized groups.

Because constitutions are often the supreme law of the land, it would be logical to expect that constitutional quotas may have more force than quotas regulated by electoral laws or political parties, making them more effective. Yet research has demonstrated that this is not necessarily the case. The success of gender quotas more frequently depends on sanctions for noncompliance and the general context in which quotas are implemented (Dahlerup and Nordlund 2004), which we discuss in more detail later.

The second form of quota, the **political party quota**, is a set of rules or targets mandating that a certain percentage of party candidates be women. Political party quotas are regulated through the internal rules of political parties and are enforced by party leadership. Table 5.5 lists the countries that have political party quotas, the number of parties that have adopted a gender quota, and the percentage of parliamentary seats held by those parties (Election World 2005; International Institute for Democracy and Electoral Assistance 2006). Because the adoption of gender quotas by political parties may be in addition to or apart from quotas required under a country's constitution or national election laws, countries with only political party quotas are italicized. Overall, by 2005, 129 political parties in 69 countries had adopted gender quotas.

By the average numbers, political party quotas appear to be less successful than constitutional quotas. On average, countries with political party quotas have approximately 18.2% women in their parliaments, only slightly higher than the world average of 16.1% (Inter-Parliamentary Union 2005a). And, countries that only have political party quotas without other quota types are about the same, 19% on average. But what is evident from Table 5.5 is that political party quotas only affect women's representation if that political party can gain seats in parliament. For example, Armenia may have an all-women's party as well as a party with a 20% quota for women, but because neither party holds a single seat in parliament, the percentage of women remains low at 5.3% (Election World 2005; International Institute for Democracy and Electoral Assistance 2006). On the other hand, when parties with quotas hold 70% to 90% of seats, there are usually at least 30% women in parliament, such as in Argentina, Austria, Costa Rica, Germany, and South Africa. Still, there are no guarantees, and some party quotas are simply ineffective.

Electoral law quotas, the third way to regulate quotas, are adopted in the form of national legislation. Unlike party quotas, electoral law quotas apply to all political parties in a country and are therefore regulated by bureaucracies or judiciaries, rather than the political party leadership (Jones 1998). Electoral law quotas are legislated by parliaments, however, and are not enshrined in constitutions, like constitutional quotas.

Table 5.5 Political Party Quotas

Country	# Parties	Seats Won	Quota Level	% Women	Country	# Parties	Seats Won	Quota Level	% Women
Algeria[1]	2	52%	20–40%	6.2%	Luxembourg	1	35%	33–50%	23.3%
Argentina	10	82%	30–35%	33.7%	Macedonia	1	36%	30%	19.2%
Armenia[2]	2	0%	20%	5.3%	Malawi[3]	2	56%	25–33%	13.6%
Australia	1	40%	40%	24.7%	Mali	1	28%	30%	10.2%
Austria	3	90%	33–50%	33.9%	Malta	1	46%	20%	9.2%
Belgium	3	35%	20–25%	34.7%	Mexico	2	64%	30–50%	24.2%
Bolivia	1	0%	50%	19.2%	Moldova	1	0%	50%	21.8%
Bosnia & Herzegovina	1	10%	30%	16.7%	Morocco	1	15%	20%	10.8%
Botswana	2	23%	30%	11.1%	Mozambique	1	64%	30%	34.8%
Brazil	1	18%	30%	8.6%	Namibia[3]	2	77%	50%	15.8%
Burkina Faso	2	67%	25%	n/a	Netherlands	2	33%	?–50%	36.7%
Cameroon	1	83%	25–30%	8.9%	Nicaragua	1	48%	30%	20.7%
Canada[3]	2	50%	25–50%	21.1%	Niger	1	42%	5 seats	12.4%
Chile	3	45%	20–40%	12.5%	Norway	5	55%	40%	38.2%
Costa Rica	3	88%	40–50%	35.1%	Paraguay	4	46%	20–30%	10.0%
Cote d'Ivoire[4]	1	43%	30%	8.5%	Philippines	1	1%	25%	15.3%
Cyprus	1	7%	25%	16.1%	Poland	3	47%	30%	20.2%
Czech Republic	1	35%	25%	17.0%	Portugal	1	53%	25%	21.3%
Dominican Republic	1	49%	25%	17.3%	Romania	1	34%	25%	11.2%
Ecuador	5	34%	2.5–50%	16.0%	Senegal	1	8%	33%	19.2%
El Salvador	1	37%	35%	10.7%	Slovakia	1	0%	20%	16.7%
Equatorial Guinea	1	3%	?	18.0%	Slovenia	1	47%	33%	12.2%

Country	# Parties	Seats Won	Quota Level	% Women	Country	# Parties	Seats Won	Quota Level	% Women
France	1	24%	50%	12.2%	South Africa	1	70%	33%	32.8%
Germany	4	88%	33–50%	32.8%	South Korea	1	53%	30%	13.0%
Greece	1	39%	20%	14.0%	Spain	1	47%	40%	36.0%
Haiti	1	0%	25%	3.6%	Sweden	3	55%	50%	45.3%
Hungary	1	46%	20%	9.1%	Switzerland	1	26%	40%	25.0%
Iceland	2	32%	40%	30.2%	Taiwan	2	75%	25%	22.2%
India	2	27%	15–35%	8.3%	Thailand[3]	1	22%	30%	10.6%
Ireland	4	35%	20–40%	13.3%	Tunisia	1	80%	25%	22.8%
Israel	4	37%	10–30%	15.0%	United Kingdom[4,5]	2	72%	33–50%	18.1%
Italy	5	32%	20–50%	11.5%	Uruguay	2	6%	30–36%	11.1%
Kenya	1	17%	33%	7.1%	Venezuela	2	30%	30%	9.7%
Kyrgyzstan[2]	1	3%	100%	3.2%	Zimbabwe	1	56%	30 seats	16.7%
Lithuania	1	14%	33%	22.0%					
	Total Parties	**129**					**Average % Women**		**18.2%**
	Average Seats Won by Parties With Quotas		**39%**			*Average for Countries With Only This Type*			**19.0%**

1. For one of the parties, quotas are subnational, and the party is not used when calculating seats in parliament.
2. Includes an all-women's party.
3. Quotas are only targets.
4. Unsure if election took place after quotas were put in place.
5. Quotas were outlawed, so party "ring-fenced" 50% of winnable seats for all-women shortlists.

SOURCES: Data from Election World (2005) and Inter-Parliamentary Union (2005a).

Table 5.6 presents the countries with electoral law quotas, again with the country's percentage of women in parliament and countries in italics depicting those with only electoral law quotas.

In 1990, Argentina became the first country in the world to adopt an electoral law quota, called the *Ley de Cupos* or "Law of Quotas" (Bonder and Nari 1995; Gray 2003; Jones 1998). Following the implementation of the Ley de Cupos, the percentage of women in the Chamber of Deputies jumped from 4% to 21%. After this success, the vast majority of Argentina's provinces implemented similar quota regulations for provincial and municipal elections (Jones 1998). Countries throughout Latin America also followed the Argentinean example and established electoral law quotas, including Bolivia, Brazil, Colombia, Costa Rica, the Dominican Republic, Ecuador, Mexico, Panama, Paraguay, Peru, and Venezuela (International Institute for Democracy and Electoral Assistance 2006; Schmidt and Saunders 2004; Squires 2004). But electoral law quotas did not prove as successful in all countries. To understand why, one must turn to other features of quota systems.

Regulating Candidates, Nominees, or Elected Members

A second major difference among gender quotas is whether they place regulations on the pool of potential candidates, the actual nominees, or elected parliamentarians (Dahlerup 2003). The first type of quota, which attempts to influence the pool of potential candidates, is infrequent. But some quota systems are designed with this goal in mind. In the United Kingdom, for example, women's shortlists were introduced by the Labour Party, requiring that women-only shortlists be used in 50% of winnable districts (Squires 2005). Dahlerup (2003) argued that the main goal of these lists has been to broaden the pool of women from which the party selection committee or primary may choose.

On the other hand, most gender quotas regulate party nominees (Dahlerup 2003). But if the quota only stipulates that a party must field a certain percentage of female candidates, there is still no guarantee that the party will support its female candidates or that in the end the women will be elected. For instance, Brazil has a national-level quota of 30% for female candidates. However, the law also states that a political party can put forth candidates up to 150% of the number of seats up for grabs in an election. So hypothetically, if 100 seats are being contested, a party may put forth 150 candidates. If 30% of the party's candidates are women, there can still be up to 110 male candidates available to fill 100 seats. Therefore, if Brazilian parties and voters want to avoid electing female parliamentarians,

Table 5.6   Election Law Quotas, 2005

Country	Required % of Women, Lower House or Unicameral	% Women
Afghanistan	Electoral law states that "the most voted female candidates in each constituency shall be awarded seats"	17.7%
Argentina	30% of party electoral lists; additional election requirements based on available seats	33.7%
Armenia	5% of party electoral lists; applies to only 57% of seats	5.3%
Belgium	33% of party electoral lists; top three spots on list must be of different sex	34.7%
Bolivia	33% of candidates	19.2%
Bosnia and Herzegovina	33% of party electoral lists; a woman must be one of top two on list; 2 among first 5 candidates; and 3 among top 8	16.7%
Brazil	30% elected	8.6%
Costa Rica	40% of party electoral lists and 40% of electable seats	35.1%
Djibouti	10% elected	10.8%
Dominican Republic	25% elected	17.3%
Ecuador	20% elected; 30% candidates for each district, increasing 5% each election until parity is reached	16.0%
France	50% of candidates	12.2%
Honduras	30% elected	5.5%
Indonesia	30% of candidates	11.3%
Iraq	1 out of first 3 on party electoral lists, 2 out of top six, etc.	31.6%
Jordan	5.5% reserved seats	5.5%
Macedonia	30% of party electoral lists	19.2%
Mexico	30% of candidates, excluding 300 districts that use primaries	24.2%
Morocco	9.2% of seats are filled from women-only lists	10.8%
Nepal	5% of candidates from any party	5.9%
North Korea	20% elected	20.1%
Pakistan	17% of seats are filled from women-only lists	21.3%
Panama	30% for party primary elections	16.7%

(Continued)

Table 5.6 (Continued)

Country	Required % of Women, Lower House or Unicameral	% Women
Paraguay	20% for party primary elections	10.0%
Peru	30% elected	18.3%
Philippines	20% elected, women must be included on all party electoral lists	15.3%
Rwanda	30% of seats, 2 women from each province, are filled using a women-only ballot	48.8%
Serbia and Montenegro	30% of party candidate lists in Serbia, no gender quota in Montenegro	7.9%
South Korea	50% of party electoral lists, 30% of candidates for single-member districts	13.0%
Sudan	9.7% reserved seats	9.7%
Tanzania	16.3% reserved seats	21.4%
Uganda	18.4% reserved seats	23.9%
Uzbekistan	30% of candidates	17.5%
Venezuela	30% elected to seats from closed lists	9.7%
	Average % Women	**17.5%**
	Average for Countries With Only This Type	**13.4%**

they can do so and still be in compliance with the gender quota. It should therefore come as no surprise that Brazil has only 8.6% women in its national legislature.

To deal with this problem, several governments and parties have adopted what can be termed *double quotas,* which combine a traditional quota with rules about the order of male and female candidates on electoral lists, called **placement mandates** (Dahlerup and Nordlund 2004). For example, in Bosnia and Herzegovina, not only must women hold 33% of the positions on electoral lists, but woman also must be one of the top two candidates on the list, two of the first five candidates, and three of the first eight candidates. Another example is the zipper system used by the Social Democratic Party in Sweden. The party nomination committee proposes two candidate lists, one for each gender, and these are combined like a zipper, alternating men and women (Dahlerup and Freidenvall 2005). In the United Kingdom, the Labour Party developed a similar strategy for plurality/majority systems, called twinning. In Scotland and Wales, constituencies are paired according to geography and probability of victory, and one male and one female candidate are selected for each (Squires 2005). Other placement mandates are less specific about candidate order but still require that women must be placed in "electable" positions. Although innovative quota regulations such as twinning can foster women's participation in plurality/majority systems, PR systems are often more effective when paired with quotas (Jones and Navia 1999). In 1999, the Supreme Electoral Tribunal of Costa Rica ruled that the quota law requires women to have 40% of candidate positions on party lists and also 40% of electable positions. Electable positions are determined using results from the prior election (Jones 2004; Quesada 2003). Some of the other countries with placement mandates at the national or party level are Algeria, Bangladesh, Belgium, Bolivia, Dominican Republic, Ecuador, Iraq, Mexico, Moldova, and Paraguay (International Institute for Democracy and Electoral Assistance 2006; Jones 2004).

Whereas quotas regulating candidates or nominees do not ensure women's representation, a third type of quota mandates that a certain percentage of women are elected. Countries often meet this requirement by setting aside seats in the parliament for women, called **reserved seats**. Under these systems, certain parliamentary seats may be filled only by women, regardless of the number of female candidates or nominees. Therefore, although women may still compete for unreserved seats, a minimum percentage of women in parliament are guaranteed. Countries with reserved seat systems include Afghanistan, Bangladesh, Eritrea, Jordan, Morocco, Rwanda, Somalia, Sudan, Taiwan, Tanzania, and Uganda. Because reserved seats are often criticized as antidemocratic, these quota systems are more commonly found in nondemocratic and semidemocratic countries (Dahlerup and Nordlund 2004).

Like other quota legislation, reserved seat systems vary widely. First, the level of competition for seats differs. In Kenya, for example, women are appointed by the president to 3% of seats, whereas in Jordan and Morocco women compete for reserved seats in elections (Dahlerup and Nordlund 2004; International Institute for Democracy and Electoral Assistance 2006). Across countries where women run in elections, some quota systems use an electoral college designed to elect women from each district. In Uganda, for example, a special electorate of men and women in each of the country's 56 districts elects two women to parliament (IDEA 2006). Alternatively, some countries use a women-only list in which women compete nationwide for a set of reserved seats regardless of their districts. This type of system is in place in Tanzania, where a quota for women is allocated to parties based on the number of seats won in the election, and parties use women-only lists to fill seats. Still, in other cases, such as in Morocco and Somalia, women compete against each other for reserved seats regardless of district or political affiliation (Tripp 2003).

Many researchers are especially critical of reserved seat systems. For example, Najma Chowdhury (2002) argues that "Instead of contributing to women's political agency and autonomy," the reserved seat system in Bangladesh "accentuated their dependence in politics and reinforced their marginality (p. 1). Though the framers of the Bangladesh constitution envisioned that the reserved-seat system would only be necessary for 10 years, a sufficient time to allow women to gain the skills and resources necessary to compete against men on equal footing, this has far from been the case. Instead, the reserved seats served as an extra block of votes for the party in power, the party usually responsible for filling the seats. Though a few women who entered politics through the quota system grew to become active participants in national politics, many more served as placeholders. Often, the party in power elected wives or daughters of deceased members of parliament or women who had close blood or marriage ties to the political leadership (Chowdhury 2002).

Threshold for Representation

One clear and simple difference between quotas is the level at which representation is required. Nepal, for example, has a quota of 5%, whereas Costa Rica has set the bar at 40% women in parliament, and France aims for equality between the sexes—50%. Many countries, however, choose a number around 30%. One reason for the popularity of this threshold is that the United Nations identified 30% as the level of representation necessary for women to affect the operation and output of parliamentary bodies.

Quota thresholds in some countries have increased over time. For example, the Socialist Party of Chile initially introduced a 20% quota, raising it to 30% for the 1997 and 1998 elections and again changing it in 1999 to a 40–60% gender-neutral quota. Some threshold increases are also built into quota legislation. For example, in 1997, a 20% quota was introduced in Ecuador for the Chamber of Deputies, and the percentage is to be increased with each subsequent election until 50% is reached (International Institute for Democracy and Electoral Assistance 2006).

Sanctions for Noncompliance

Regardless of the type of quota being implemented, we have seen that in some cases, quotas are ineffective. As scholar Drude Dahlerup states, many quota laws are merely "window dressing" and are not enforced in practice (Ballington 2004:14; Dahlerup 2002). Therefore, one important consideration when evaluating quota systems is whether there are **sanctions for** noncompliance. The lack of enforcement mechanisms explains many of the quota conundrums apparent in the earlier tables. For example, in 2000, Honduras instituted a 30% quota requirement with the aim of reaching gender parity across political parties, the National Parliament, the Central American Parliament, mayors, deputy mayors, and regional leaders. But no sanctions for noncompliance were introduced to enforce the new legislation. And in 2001 the first national elections following the adoption of the quota failed to register any gains for women. Another such example is occurring in Chile, where there is no national-level quota, but three major parties have quotas ranging from 20% to 40%. Although these parties hold almost half of the seats in parliament, none of them strongly enforce their quota provision (International Institute for Democracy and Electoral Assistance 2006).

Even among countries that have sanctions, some are also easier to circumvent or simply accept. According to Dahlerup and Freidenvall (2005), the most effective sanctions require that the electoral commission reject electoral lists that fail to comply with quota regulations, whereas monetary sanctions are often less successful at motivating compliance. Quotas in France demonstrate this point. In 2000, a new French election law mandated that a parity reform requiring 50% of each sex, called *parite,* would apply to all elections with a proportional ballot as well as to the overall balance among male and female candidates for each party in national legislative elections, which are determined by plurality/majority vote. Yet the sanctions for noncompliance were different for municipal and national-level elections. At the municipal level, lists were rejected that failed to comply with the quota. Thus, in districts where the quota applied, female representation often doubled (Dahlerup and Freidenvall 2005). On the other hand, at the national level where only financial sanctions were used, parties simply accepted the fines for not fielding 50% women. And the percentage of women in parliament remained far from parity at 12.2%.

The Adoption of Gender Quotas

How do countries or parties decide to use a quota, and why do they choose a particular type? Interestingly, countries within the same region are likely to adopt similar types of quotas, suggesting that countries look to their neighbors as examples. Researchers call this phenomenon **diffusion**. Even within the same country, one political party may also adopt a quota rule first formulated by another party to avoid losing women's votes, called a **contagion effect** (see Matland and Studlar 1996).

In addition to diffusion and contagion effects, there are a number of other explanations used by researchers to account for the adoption of candidate gender quotas in countries around the world. One important explanation is women's activism. In some countries, quota measures are debated extensively, suffer defeats in the legislature, and succeed only after extensive lobbying by indigenous women's groups. For example, in Argentina, women "demonstrated notable solidarity and collective action in the struggle for the quota law. . . . Some women also made intense individual efforts to ensure the implementation of the law, often at great personal costs" (Gray 2003). Yet in other countries, quotas are approved without great debate or controversy. In Brazil, for instance, a national electoral-law quota passed with little fanfare (Araújo 2003). And in Belgium, gender quotas were rather easily accepted as simply one more quota that fit into a normative framework accepted there, the "politics of presence" (Meier 2000).

Researchers also highlight the importance of international conferences and country ratification of the Convention on the Elimination of All Forms of Discrimination Against Women (CEDAW) on women's subsequent successes in quota adoption (Baldez 2004; Htun and Jones 2002; Jones 2004). See Chapter 6 for a discussion of the importance of international influences on women in politics.

By the 1995 Fourth World Conference on Women in Beijing, positive discrimination policies had reached a prominent position on the agenda of the international women's movement (Jones 2004; United Nations 1995). Researchers stress the importance of Beijing for raising consciousness about women's political underrepresentation, providing transnational activists with the tools necessary to pressure for quotas on a country-by-country basis and increasing the attractiveness of quota proposals to national parliaments (Araújo 2003; Htun and Jones 2002). Further, though Beijing may not have set the process in motion, "international conferences help explain why certain countries moved from party-level to national quota laws" (Baldez 2003:8).

Regime change can also affect quota adoption or cancellation. For example, the assassination of President Sadat in Egypt only 2 years after the quota came into effect resulted in a change in government. The new regime took a more conservative stance regarding women, responding to arguments from candidates that the quota law was unconstitutional and canceling the quota in 1986 (Abou-Zeid 2003).

Challenges to Quota Adoption

The adoption of quotas often faces opposition on a number of grounds. First, quotas are often criticized as antidemocratic (Gray 2003): Voters should be able to decide who is elected, but quotas mandate that women be elected (Dahlerup 2002). Quotas may also face legal challenges based on gender equality laws. For example, in the United Kingdom, in January 1996 the Industrial Tribunal overturned the Labour Party's all-female shortlists on the grounds that they violated the Sex Discrimination Act of 1975. The British Parliament had to pass an additional law in 2001, the Sex Discrimination Elected Candidates Act, to allow political parties to use affirmative action measures to increase women's share of elected positions.

Quota opponents often argue that there are not enough qualified women to fill the quota (Gray 2003). And including underqualified women may hurt rather than help women's future efforts at representation. For example, as one Lithuanian member of parliament notes, "quotas for women in the Soviet legislature, which existed and which were preserved at any price, spurred a social prejudice that women are incompetent on political matters" (Paliokienė 1999, cited in Krupavičius and Matonytė 2003:94). Further, many women do not want to be elected simply because they are women. For instance, when asked about quotas, one Lithuanian member of parliament made the following response:

> We have enough women working in important positions because of their professional qualities, not because they are women. We don't have women sitting on the working group on NATO enlargement because of a gentlemanly attitude towards including women. It happens because of a pure appreciation of our competence. (cited from Krupavičius and Matonytė 2003:95)

Finally, women's groups argue that quotas may become a ceiling rather than a floor. Because women's presence is guaranteed at a certain level, parties or governments may not pursue strategies to include women in greater numbers. Some opponents argue that quotas are superficial and will not alter the structural and cultural factors that create women's underrepresentation (Squires 1996). Instead, broader political reforms, such as altering the electoral system, are preferable to gender quotas. Quotas alone are no magic fix to women's underrepresentation. Birgitta Dahl, the Swedish speaker of parliament, stated:

> One cannot deal with the problem of female representation by a quota system alone. Political parties, the education system, non-governmental organizations (NGOs), trade unions, churches must all take responsibility within their own organizations to systematically promote women's participation from the bottom up. This will take time. It will not happen overnight, or in one year or five years; it will take one or two generations to realize significant change. (Dahlerup 2002:2)

Therefore, although quotas are one of the most powerful ways of influencing the political demand for women, they may create an artificial demand. They are a way to bypass low party or voter demand for women. But ultimately all of the factors discussed in this and the previous chapter must work together for substantial and sustainable gains for women in politics. In the next chapter, we turn to examples of how all three explanations—culture, structure, and politics—can interact to affect women in politics.

6

Explaining the Political Representation of Women— Overarching Factors

I n the previous two chapters, we distinguished two sets of factors that affect women's levels of political representation around the world. Supply factors increase the pool of women with the skills to run for political office, and demand factors make it more or less likely that women will be pulled into office from the supply of willing candidates.

But many explanations of women's representation in politics affect both supply and demand. For example, cultural factors simultaneously influence both the supply of and demand for women. On the supply side, cultural beliefs may influence women's decision to run for political office, regardless of their careers or level of education. For instance, a female politician from Australia explains, "Social values that it is a women's role to be wives and mothers are still strong in Australia. This creates psychological and emotional barriers to women participating in formal politics" (Inter-Parliamentary Union 2000:25). On the demand side, cultural beliefs may influence the likelihood that voters will accept women as their elected politicians and influence the likelihood that party elites will select and support female candidates (Gallagher and Marsh 1988).

In this chapter, we discuss two overarching explanations that affect both the supply of and demand for women in politics. Returning to the political recruitment process discussed at the beginning of Chapter 4, we provide explanations in this chapter that affect the entire process depicted in Figure 4.1. We begin with a look at armed conflict and women in politics. Armed conflict extracts a terrible toll on men, women, children, and societies. Yet armed conflict provides some opportunities for women in politics because it changes both supply and demand. We then turn to international influences on women in politics, explaining how international actors such as the United Nations can increase the supply of women while simultaneously influencing states to increase their demand for women. The two theories discussed in this chapter are also newer theories that are designed partly to help explain women's representation in places and countries where the traditional explanations from Chapters 4 and 5 are less helpful (see also Chapter 8 for a discussion of regions and regional theories).

Armed Conflict: Devastation yet Hope?

When we think about the supply of female candidates for positions of political influence, we often first think about political candidacy like it were any other job. Women need to be qualified, which often comes about through access to leadership roles and certain types of education, such as law school. However, increasing the supply of female candidates does not always come about by steady gains in women's education or labor force participation. In some instances, women's participation outside of the home and their greater role in society may change much more rapidly due to terrible and violent circumstances, such as war, revolution, and genocide. Although such events are devastating to the makeup of society and often leave thousands or even millions of individuals scarred by loss, these crises may also create opportunities for women to gain political representation (Goetz 1995; Hughes 2004; Lipman-Blumen 1973; Putnam 1976).

In the history of any nation, wars serve as defining moments, turning points, and catalysts for change. Armed conflict often alters the very fabric of society, shifting the ideas, beliefs, and social positions of its members. Specifically, with regard to women in politics, revolutionary movements or armed conflict may increase women's subsequent political representation for a number of reasons: increased supply of female candidates, influence of cultural beliefs about women's participation in ways favorable to their election, or alteration of the political opportunity structure to facilitate women's entry into the halls of power.

Increasing the Supply of Female Candidates

War has historically allowed women to operate outside of the constraints of traditional gender norms and to gain access to roles that were previously closed to them (Geisler 1995; Waylen 1994). As men are pulled into combat and away from their jobs, women enter the labor force to fill the vacancies. One familiar example of this phenomenon is the influx of women into the labor force during and after World War II. Although women's participation may have been taboo prior to the war, women are able to gain a foothold in the public realm. And, once conflict has subsided, it may be difficult to reinstitute sharp boundaries between public and private spheres. As discussed in Chapter 4, participation in the workforce may provide women experience that allows them to run for public office.

Yet during wars women's participation is not limited to serving as placeholders for men or even playing other supportive roles, such as nursing the dying or wounded. Women in conflict situations also serve as armed combatants. Although the image of a soldier is usually male, women have fought in battles throughout history and around the world. For example, during the 18th and 19th centuries in the Dahomey Kingdom in West Africa, an all-female combat unit numbering in the thousands fought for the King (Goldstein 2001).

Women have disguised themselves as men to serve as soldiers (Binkin and Bach 1977; Holm 1982), but women have also held visible combatant roles in the revolutionary movements of Algeria, China, Nicaragua, Northern Ireland, Rhodesia, Russia, Sri Lanka, Vietnam, and Yugoslavia (De Pauw 1981; Denich 1981; Geisler 1995; Goldman 1982; Isaksson 1988; Randall 1981; Segal, Segal, and Li 1992). For instance, during the Ethiopian civil war of the 1980s, roughly one third of the rebel fighters were women (Bloomfield, Barnes, and Huyse 2003). And even today, more than 30% of the fighters of the Revolutionary Armed Forces of Colombia (FARC) are women (Susskind 2004). Wartime heroism is one important channel through which women can rise to positions of power (Denich 1981). Furthermore, serving in combat may make female candidates better able to compete with men by providing them experience with matters of state defense or security.

In addition to providing women with access to the labor force and the military, conflict situations may also cause women to enter the public realm through participation in social movements. (See Chapter 8 for a discussion of women's social movement participation in Latin America.) In conflict situations, women create campaigns and demonstrations, institute human rights reporting, lobby for cease-fires, and build networks to care for refugees and support victims of war (Rehn and Sirleaf 2002). At national, regional, and international levels, women organize to end the use of land mines, enforce treaties, end sexual violence, and recognize specific acts of violence against women (Bop 2001). And national peace movements are often led by women, who "are committed to finding alternatives to violence" (Kelly 2000:51). For example, in the Yugoslav civil war of the 1990s, women were both the majority of peace activists and the first to lead protests against the war (Morokvasic 1998). Women active in social movements may pursue formal political careers once conflict has subsided. For example, many South African women who were active in the antiapartheid and women's movements were later incorporated into the government (Kumar 2001).

Increased organizational activity during periods of reconstruction may also provide women with a route to political influence. Faced with the aftermath of violence, women have learned to unite and organize. For instance, after the war and genocide subsided in Rwanda, "women's organizations, both new and old, took a leading role in efforts to help women reconstruct their lives" (Longman 2006:138). And many women moved through these organizations into political office. In sum, through their experiences serving as armed combatants, activists, organizational members, and movement leaders during and after conflicts, women may gain the skills necessary to compete with men for political power.

Changing Culture

In addition to affecting the pool of qualified female candidates, wars and revolutions provide important moments for reshaping beliefs and ideas about gender and women's proper role. As Sambanis (2002) suggests, civil war is "a disruption of social norms that is unparalleled in domestic politics" (p. 217). And case studies have demonstrated that under conditions of change that undermine tradition, women in developing countries may rise to political leadership positions (Chaney 1973). Groups struggling for independence or to overthrow the current regime often put forth an alternative vision of society, and women's activism may ensure that expanded women's rights become part of that vision. For example, during the mid-19th century, the Taiping Peasant Rebellion in China included demands for sexual equality, and where the rebels won control, **foot-binding** was banned, and women were given governmental positions (Chafetz and Dworkin 1986:137). Similarly, as we discuss in Chapter 8, the revolutionary ideas in the Nicaraguan insurrection changed perceptions about women's participation in public life and ultimately led to more women-friendly public policies (see Box 8.2).

But not all wars and revolutions advance ideas favorable to women. Indeed, international feminist scholars point out that state military organizations have historically and cross-culturally depended on maleness (Enloe 1987). And during struggles for liberation, movement leaders may draw on ideas of the nation as a family, casting women as symbols of the nation and voicing support for women's "traditional" roles (Yuval-Davis 1997). Acknowledging variation in the ideas put forth by different movements, Moghadam (1997) categorizes two types of revolutions: patriarchal and modernizing. **Patriarchal revolutions** connect national liberation to discourse about women in traditional familial roles. Women are cast as mothers of the revolution rather than actual revolutionaries. **Modernizing revolutions**, on the other hand, advance models that serve to emancipate women.

Even for modernizing revolutions, the postwar context often leaves revolutionary promises about gender unfulfilled. Some researchers argue that to date no revolution has ever successfully maintained "an emancipating atmosphere for women" after the war subsided and the honeymoon period ended (Hale 2001:123). But although the promises of change may remain unfulfilled, the ideas developed and spread by modernizing revolutions may still inspire feminist consciousness (Moghadam 1997; Shayne 2004). One former woman fighter in Eritrea described this tension:

> [Our families] were happy at first that we came back alive. But after a year it changed. We have very different ideas from the rest of society. Women must stay at home and take care of their children, not go out and talk with men. We do not accept these traditional ideas of our parents, but it is difficult to change them. It is very hard for us because we were used to equality in the field. (Hale 2001:127)

Thus, though the entire society may not welcome women into politics following a war or revolution, armed conflict may still alter the beliefs and attitudes of individual women.

Changing Politics

It is also important to consider how armed conflict may produce openings in the **political opportunity structure**. Even if the pool of female candidates and ideology toward women remain stable, wars and revolutions may create windows of opportunity where it is easier for women to succeed in elections. One reason is that the male candidate pool may be significantly depleted due to the death or imprisonment of large numbers of men. Following the Rwandan genocide, for example, women and girls significantly outnumbered in the country's population, and an estimated 90,000 men were imprisoned (Powley 2003; Remmert 2003). Women may therefore be encouraged to fill the gap in candidates simply out of necessity. And certainly, after conflict has subsided, women may serve as powerful symbols of healing and rebirth, making them attractive candidates for political office.

Another political opportunity explanation for women's rise in post-conflict situations is that the former regime is often replaced. Research indicates that incumbency effects often hinder the access of women and minority groups (Darcy and Choike 1986; Putnam 1976). Therefore, when governments are toppled and incumbent politicians are pushed out of office, space is created for new candidates. In support of this view, Hughes (2004) found that across developing countries only civil wars that challenged the central government led to increases in female parliamentary representation in subsequent years. On the other hand, wars fought over territory that failed to displace the regime did not increase women's political presence. Table 6.1 shows how the distinction between civil wars fought

Table 6.1   Civil Wars and Women's Political Gains

Challenging the Government		*Women in Parliament*		
Country	*Years*	*Pre-War*	*2000*	*Change*
Angola	1990–94	14.5	15.5	1.0
Ethiopia	1976–91	1.6	7.7	6.1
Mozambique	1981–92	12.4	30.0	17.6
Nicaragua	1983–88	21.6	9.7	−11.9
Rwanda	1991–92	17.1	25.7	8.6
Tajikistan	1992–93	3.0	12.7	9.7
Uganda	1981–89, 1991	0.8	17.8	17.0
Average		*10.1*	*15.9*	*6.9*
Territorial Civil Wars		*Women in Parliament*		
Country	*Years*	*Pre-War*	*2000*	*Change*
Azerbaijan	1994	2.0	10.5	8.5
Ethiopia	1974–91	1.6	7.7	6.1
Georgia	1993	6.3	7.2	0.9
India	1989–93	7.8	9.0	1.2
Indonesia	1990	12.4	8.0	−4.4
Sudan	1983–92	8.5	9.7	1.2
Average		*6.4*	*8.7*	*2.3*

SOURCE: Data from Hughes (2004).

against the central government and civil wars fought over territory produce different political gains for women.

Not only are incumbent politicians often displaced following armed conflict and revolutions, but also new constitutions are often written, altering existing political structures. Further, especially if governments are reorganizing during recent time periods, they must contend with pressure from the international women's movement. As we discuss later, international nongovernmental organizations (INGOs) and bodies such as the United Nations may pressure countries to adopt political structures or electoral systems that are more favorable to women. Therefore, new governments may include features such as gender quotas, guaranteeing women access to political representation.

Not All Wars Are Created Equal

Overall, conflict situations may alter the supply of women, attitudes about women's roles, and the political opportunity structure in combinations of ways that subsequently increase female representation. During the 1990s in sub-Saharan Africa, women were able to emerge from conflict situations with greater political representation. Perhaps the most notable example of postconflict gains occurred in Rwanda (see Box 6.1), but many researchers have also pointed to the National Resistance Movement's (NRM) guerrilla war as a key factor that thrust a generation of Ugandan women into politics (Boyd 1989; Byanyima 1992; Goetz 1995; Pankhurst 2002; Tripp 1994; Wakoko and Labao 1996). Women also made real gains following the revolution in Mozambique (Urdang 1989), and Bauer (2004) attributed the significant number of women in Namibian politics (currently around 27%) in part to women's participation in the country's violent struggle for independence. Pankhurst (2002:124) argued that gains in the region are a result of both the rise to power of regimes with a previously stated commitment to gender inequality and the adoption of new democratic forms.

**Box 6.1   Almost 50/50: Women's Political
             Representation in Postconflict Rwanda**

In 2003, the central African country of Rwanda ousted Sweden from its long-standing position as the world leader in female parliamentary representation. Women were elected to 48.8% of the seats in the lower house of Rwanda's national legislature, bringing it the closest to gender parity of any national

(Continued)

(Continued)

parliament in the history of the world. Independent from Belgium in 1962, Rwanda had been ravaged by political and economic upheaval and civil war, and the 2003 election established the first national parliament following a horrific ethnic genocide that had taken place 9 years earlier. What follows is a brief overview of the events surrounding the ethnic genocide, the involvement of female actors in the conflict and reconstruction, and the mechanisms that were developed to incorporate women into the new government.

Rwanda is a country roughly the size of Maryland with more than 8 million people. Its population is predominantly Christian (56.5% Roman Catholic and 26% Protestant), and there are two primary ethnic groups, the Hutus—the majority—and the Tutsis—the largest minority group. Under Belgian rule, the Tutsis were a privileged ethnicity, but 3 years before the country's 1962 independence, the Hutus deposed the ruling Tutsi king. In the conflict that followed, thousands of Tutsis were killed, and approximately 150,000 were driven to surrounding countries. In 1985, the children of the exiled Tutsis formed a rebel group called the Rwandan Patriotic Front (RPF). In October 1990, the RPF launched a civil war from Uganda, which aggravated ethnic tensions. The situation came to a head in April 1994 when the plane of Rwanda's president, Juvénal Habyarimana, was shot down near Kigali airport. The RPF was immediately blamed for the crash, and "on April 7th, all Tutsis—men, women, children, including new-born babies and the very old—became targets. They were murdered in their homes and on the street; they were hunted down in the bushes and forests and they died *en masse* in the churches, schools and hospitals where they had sought refuge" (Women for Women International 2004:9). Within 100 days, roughly 800,000 Tutsis and moderate Hutus were murdered. Ultimately, the Tutsi rebels defeated the Hutu regime, ending the killing in July 1994.

Although many individual women risked their lives to save others, women were far from blameless in the genocide. Some women aided the killers by identifying Tutsis or leading them to hideouts, and "female teachers, nurses, civil servants, and even some nuns joined the killers" (Women for Women International 2004:10). Women in the political system were also involved. Alongside their male counterparts, female councilors helped incite the population to commit acts of genocide, and the two women in government at the time both played leading roles in the events. Pauline Nyiramusuhuko, the minister of the family and the promotion of women, is accused of complicity in rape and is currently being held by the International Criminal Tribunal. The minister of justice at the time, Agnés Ntamabyariro, is the highest level official held at present by the Rwandan government and is awaiting trial for charges of genocide.

Although women participated in the genocide as perpetrators and accomplices, women overall make up only about 2% of genocide suspects. Men were killed and imprisoned in much higher numbers than women were. After the genocide, women and girls outnumbered men in Rwanda's population. This gender imbalance likely left room for women to enter politics. But women's actions also convinced men in the transitional government that women were capable of taking leadership roles. As parliamentarian Berthe Mukamusoni stated, "Men and women both took part in the fight against the genocide, even at the front. When the men saw how tough the women were, healing the sick and cooking the food, as well as their presence at the front, they saw what women were capable of and the value of collaborating with them" (Women for Women International 2004:12). Women also took the lead in postgenocide reconstruction and reconciliation efforts, further justifying their incorporation into politics.

When the postgenocide transitional government was formed, it viewed women's incorporation into political decision-making positions as essential for sustainable peace. The body developed innovative mechanisms to ensure women's participation in political leadership at all levels of government. First, women's councils and elections where only women participate were established to guarantee female representation down to the grass-roots level. Second, a triple balloting system was put in place to ensure women a certain share of seats at the sector and district levels. Third, the transitional government established the Ministry for Gender and Women in Development as well as gender posts in all other government and ministerial bodies. These posts are charged with ensuring that policies are sensitive to women's special needs. Finally, the new constitution mandated that women fill 30% of all policy-making posts in Rwanda. Initiatives to ensure women's incorporation into the political realm were successful. In 2003, women were elected to 48.8% of seats in the lower house and appointed to 30% of seats in the upper house of the national legislature.

Although Rwanda is an authoritarian state, women's participation in parliament has led to legislation that serves women's interests. For example, Timothy Longman (2006) reported, "The Forum of Women Parliamentarians was key in pushing through revisions to the inheritance laws, a law banning discrimination against women, and a strengthening of rape laws" (p. 149). Women's inclusion has also served to alter perceptions about female office holders. Some argue that, "women in government are now perceived by Rwandans as more approachable and trustworthy politicians than their male counterparts" (Remmert 2003:25). Evidence also suggests that Rwandan women in government (specifically the Forum of Women Parliamentarians) have developed successful models for working across party and ethnic lines.

(Continued)

(Continued)

Still, skeptics argue that the focus on women diverts attention from the absence of ethnic diversity within government.

Overall, it is clear that things have changed. As Suzanne Fafin, an employee of the UN Development Programme, highlights, "I was here before the genocide, between 1982–1984, and at that time when we received [Rwandan] colleagues at home, women never talked—never—and I [wondered], 'but why?' But now it is not the same, there [has been] a big change" (Powley 2003:30).

SOURCES: Central Intelligence Agency (2004), Gabiro (2000), Longman (2006), Powley (2003), Remmert (2003), and Women for Women International (2004).

But not all war situations lead to women's inclusion in politics after peace is negotiated. The documented cases of women's successes are often found only in recent years. One reason is that although gender differences may be suspended during times of conflict, men may attempt to reinforce the status quo afterward (Geisler 1995; Pankhurst 2002; Waylen 1994). And in the past, in most cases, women left the military and returned to more traditional roles following a conflict's resolution (Denich 1981; De Pauw 1981; Enloe 1980; Geisler 1995; Goldman 1982). Women also have difficulty in converting wartime activity to peacetime gains because they have historically been denied access to peace negotiation processes. For example, despite that more than 30% of the fighters of the Revolutionary Armed Forces of Colombia (FARC) are women, FARC included only one woman among its representatives to official negotiations with the Colombian government (Bloomfield et al. 2003). Therefore, after conflict has subsided, women's organizing efforts, as well as their roles as combatants and political leaders in national liberation movements, are sometimes ignored.

Finally, though conflict situations may in some cases increase women's political representation, we must be careful not to glorify war. Armed conflict between or within countries is a horrible and disastrous occurrence. Therefore, although war may be a force for change, we must first acknowledge the tremendous suffering that is involved, particularly for women. Whereas men more often die on the battlefield, women disproportionately suffer crimes such as mass rape, forced prostitution, torture, and other atrocities. Rape is employed systematically by armed forces to undermine social stability or even as a form of ethnic cleansing (Meznaric

1994; Sideris 2001). And these instances are not few and far between. From 1990 to 2002, Jennifer Green (2004) identified 30 cases of mass rape, overwhelmingly perpetrated by members of the state military or police forces. Further, women in postconflict situations are more often displaced, as widows struggle to hold onto property in societies that do not recognize their rights. Still, it is somewhat comforting to realize that in some circumstances hope for change may rise out of the most devastating of circumstances.

International Influences

The second overarching influence on women in politics is literally overarching. When talking about the role that international agents such as the international women's movement or the United Nations play in women's political representation, one has to think beyond the level of individual countries. In contrast to explanations within countries, theories of international influence suggest that individual nations do not stand apart from the international arena (Berkovitch 1999; Meyer et al. 1997; Ramirez et al. 1997). Instead, the connectedness of the world means that nations must pay attention to each other and to the international bodies that write treaties, mediate international disputes, and dispense aid. The connectedness of the world is economic, through trade ties between nations or international economic agreements. Connectedness is also cultural because countries import and export cultural products, such as movies, television shows, and books. Finally, there are political connections between countries because countries exchange diplomats, sign international accords, and create mechanisms for international governance, such as the United Nations.

In this section we demonstrate that this international connectedness can be used by female activists to influence women's political representation (and women's status generally) worldwide. First, we discuss the international women's movement and its goals for women in politics. Then, we discuss how international bodies, especially the United Nations, have adopted this vision for women's political representation. The next section gives examples of how international bodies can affect both the supply of and demand for women in politics. The chapter closes by discussing the Convention on the Elimination of All Forms of Discrimination Against Women (CEDAW), possibly the most important international treaty related to women to date.

The International Women's Movement

The international women's movement grew substantially over time (D'Itri 1999; Rupp and Taylor 1999). From just a few organizations in Western nations in the late 1800s, the international women's movement ultimately grew to encompass more than 40,000 women and men from more than 180 countries, coming together in Beijing for the Fourth Global Conference on Women. As discussed briefly in Chapter 2, unlike women's movements at the national level, which vary in size and strength, the international women's movement has been steadily increasing in size and strength (Berkovitch 1999).

One way to consider the growth of the international women's movement is to chart how many women's international nongovernmental organizations (WINGOs) are founded each year. Figure 6.1 shows that WINGOs were founded steadily from 1885 to 1970 except in breaks during wartime periods. Early WINGOs included the World's Woman's Christian Temperance Union (1884), the International Council of Women (1888), and the International Woman Suffrage Alliance (1904). In the 1970s, foundings of WINGOs increased, changing from steady, almost linear growth over time to almost exponential growth.

International women's groups do not all work directly for women's incorporation in politics. But women's political incorporation is often one important goal. Female suffrage was central to the aims of many early WINGOs. In fact, many of the first groups were founded with women's suffrage in mind. For example, the International Woman Suffrage Alliance's

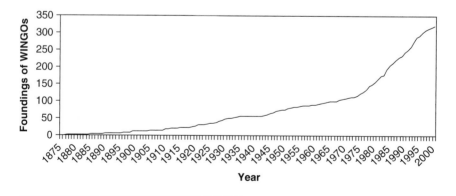

Figure 6.1   Growth in Women's International Nongovernmental
             Organizations

SOURCE: Berkovitch (1995, 1875–1985 data).

founding principles state, "Women should be vested with all political rights and privileges of electors" (International Alliance of Women 2005).

The importance of women's political participation to many WINGOs continues today, although the aims of the movement are different. Today, WINGOs are more likely to call for 30%, or even 50%, representation in legislatures. For example, in June 2000, the Women's Environment and Development Organization (WEDO), an international organization that advocates for women's equality in global policy, launched the 50/50 campaign. The campaign's goal is to increase the percentage of women in local and national politics worldwide to 50%, and since its inception the campaign has been adopted by 154 organizations in 45 countries.

A Brief History of Women's Activism in the United Nations (UN)

The international women's movement does not work alone in trying to influence states to increase women's political representation. Instead, women work with the international bodies that connect the world to make sure women's interests are served. Although women and women's movements were active prior to the formation of the UN, its creation gave women a place to focus their efforts on influencing large numbers of countries. Therefore, women and women's groups have targeted the UN from its inception as a place to work on gender equality. For example, during the UN's formation, suffragette Alice Paul and her World Women's Party lobbied for inclusion of the phrase "the equal rights of men and women" in the UN Charter Preamble. Ultimately, the UN General Assembly recommended during its first session in 1946 that all member states fulfill the aims of its charter, "granting to women the same political rights as men" (resolution 56 (I)). Throughout the rest of the UN's history, international feminists worked to keep women, and women's political rights, on the agenda. For example, 18% of all organizations officially allowed to consult with the UN during its first decade were women's organizations (Berkovitch 1999:107–8).

The 1970s were especially important for women's global organizing at the UN. Motivated by the demands of the Women's International Democratic Federation, the UN declared 1975 International Women's Year (Chen 1995). The primary event of the women's year was the first UN World Conference on Women in Mexico City, attended by 133 national delegations. In the same year, the UN General Assembly declared the Decade for Women (1975–1985). The events that followed, including the second and third World Conferences in Copenhagen (1980) and Nairobi (1985), brought worldwide attention to the women's movement.

The international women's movement was an integral part of the planning for these conferences and in participation. In fact, official NGO forums were held alongside planned conference events to encourage greater participation by a wide range of women's groups. Ultimately, in addition to the thousands of women who participated in these conferences, "tens of thousands were mobilized by the process in countries around the world" (Tinker and Jaquette 1987:419).

During the 1990s and beyond, the international women's movement and women's organizations continued to place women on the international agenda. In addition to participating in the Fourth World Conference on Women in Beijing (1995), international women's organizations successfully drew attention to women's issues at conferences dedicated to a wide range of other issues, including the environment (1992), human rights (1993), population and development (1994), social development (1995), food security, settlements (1996), and food security (1997) (Antrobus 2000; Friedman 2003). Another key success was the incorporation of women's rights into conceptions of human rights (Berkovitch 1999; Joachim 2003; Ruppert 2002).

As we discussed in Chapter 2, early women's movements across the world were dominated by White, upper-class women from Western countries (Chafetz and Dworkin 1986). In the United States, although women of color, such as Sojourner Truth, played significant historical roles in expanding notions of women's rights to include women of all racial, ethnic, and socioeconomic backgrounds, not all women felt equally a part of the women's movement. The same divisions have been present in the international arena. Indeed, the first UN global women's conferences were sites of significant conflict between women of the global north and south. But scholars argue that during the 1990s the international women's movement truly became global, integrating women from the global south and giving them a greater voice. See Box 6.2 for a brief summary of women of the north and south in the international women's movement.

Box 6.2   The Globalization of the International Women's Movement

In the international arena, the divide between women of the global north and south was a significant stumbling block throughout most of the 20th century. During the first wave of women's organizing, women of the global north sought to incorporate women of color into their suffrage organizations. But the predominance of White, Western women in early organizing led nationalists in developing countries to discredit women's movements as bourgeoisie or imperialist.

As women's suffrage was attained and the goals of the international women's movement shifted, the rift between women of the global north and south remained. By the second wave of women's organizing, women of the global south were determined to form their own groups that addressed issues of greatest importance to their lives. As women came together in the global conferences, women of the global south accused Western feminists of ignoring their regional concerns, and conflict over the agenda stalled progress. Women also lined up on different sides of the fence on particular issues. For instance, the Second World Conference in Copenhagen was almost torn apart by the Israel–Palestinian conflict, where women of the global north supported Israel, and women from developing countries supported the Arabs or Palestinians.

Despite these challenges, the 1985 World Conference in Nairobi showed that the world's women could cooperate across all types of boundaries—national, racial, and economic. Researchers note that by the end of the decade for women, there had been a tremendous increase in the number and types of women's organizations across the world as well as networks and alliances to bridge the gaps between. And during the 1990s, groups such as Development Alternatives with Women for a New Era (DAWN), Women Living Under Muslim Law (WLUML), and the Sisterhood is Global Institute (SIGI) "transcended the earlier political and ideological differences" to build a common agenda (Moghadam 2005:9). The integration of global north and global south visions during the 1990s led scholars to argue that women's movements had moved from being international to truly being global.

SOURCES: Antrobus (2000), Chen (1995), Friedman (2003), Margolis (1993), Moghadam (2005), and Zinsser (1990).

Throughout all time periods, WINGOs and the rest of the international women's movement kept the political rights of women on the agenda of the UN and its conferences. For example, 1 of 34 resolutions adopted at the First World Conference in Mexico in 1975 called on governments to "pay special attention to political rights of women" (United Nations 2000a). At the outset of the second conference in Copenhagen, conference delegates suggested that one of the obstacles preventing attainment of goals set out in Mexico was that too few women held decision-making positions. And at the 1985 NGO forum in Nairobi, the most heavily attended workshop was "If Women Ruled the World," where 18 female parliamentarians from around the world discussed women's contributions as political leaders and the struggle to gain support, even from female voters, for women's political representation (United Nations 2000a).

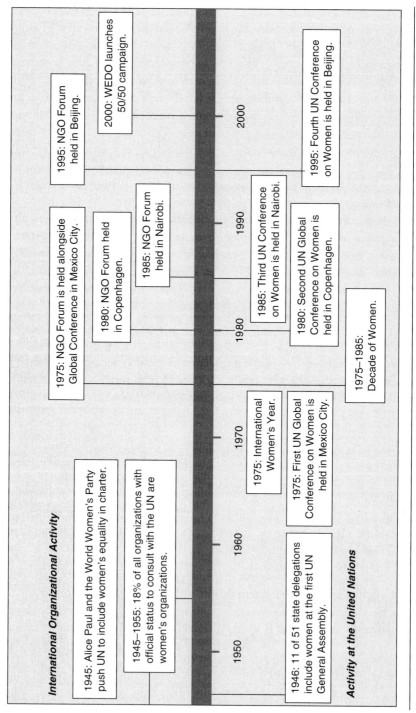

Figure 6.2 Significant Events for the International Women's Movement and the UN

To summarize, Figure 6.2 presents a timeline of major events related to the international women's movement and the UN.

Does It Make a Difference?

To this point, we have discussed women's activity in the international arena, both in international organizations and at the UN. Is there any evidence that this activity has made a difference to women in formal politics? Yes. There are a number of pieces of evidence suggesting women's international organizing influenced individual countries. Further, recent research looked at many countries and found an effect of women's international organizing (Paxton et al. 2006a; Ramirez et al. 1997).

To begin, international activity can increase the supply of women interested in and able to compete for political office. For example, the international conferences that are so central to women's international organizing inspire and train local women's movements. Participants learn social movement tactics that have been successful in other parts of the world. Women exchange arguments against the enduring cultural beliefs that work against women's participation in politics. Women swap ideas to develop new strategies for action and unite with other women from their home countries to seek common goals. As Elizabeth Jane Prichard, an activist from New Zealand, stated, "Attending the Beijing Conference on Women provided for me a much fuller perspective of what can be achieved by any woman who is prepared to participate fully in the work of the conference and then return to address key issues in her own country" (United Nations 2000a). Similarly, activists from Namibia and Uganda have described how UN conferences on women encouraged domestic women's organizations as they sought to influence their governments to adopt national gender policies (Bauer 2006; Tripp 2006).

International bodies may also work directly to increase the supply of women. For example, the United Nations Development Programme (UNDP) provided training to 144 female candidates in Vietnam. And the UNDP claims that their efforts contributed to a rise in women's representation in Vietnam's national legislature from 18% to 26% (United Nations Development Programme 2000:97). More indirectly, the UN, the International Labor Organization, the World Bank, and a wide range of international nongovernmental organizations all provide money, personnel, and training to promote women's empowerment throughout the world. For example, the International Labor Organization (ILO) provides training in employment and skills development. And, in a workshop titled "Rural Women and Land," the UN Food and Agriculture Organization (FAO) brought rural women together from across Senegal to address their access to land and natural resources. Empowering women by helping them get employment training, education, or access to valuable resources such as land can help create the supply of women with the knowledge, skills, and interest to run for political office.

Women's international activity can also increase the demand for female politicians. Most directly, international organizations have pressured states to adopt gender quotas (Childs and Krook 2005; Krook 2004b; Towns 2004). For example, in 1997 the male-dominated legislature of Peru approved gender quotas, "without prior pressure from domestic women's organizations and with minimal debate, presumably because then-president Alberto Fujimori had sensed the advantages of such a measure" (Towns 2004:214). What would be the advantage to male political leaders of instituting gender quotas? One advantage could be money. International bodies grant the loans and provide the foreign aid that poor countries so desperately need. When taking money from an international organization, a country may be more willing to listen to suggestions for changes to laws, such as quota laws. For example, the funding of a $4 million governance program by the United Nations Development Programme in Bangladesh allegedly led the country not only to extend lapsed quota legislation for women in parliament but also to increase the percentage of women required from 7% to 30% (United Nations Development Programme 2000:97).

National and local women's organizations may also join with international forces to increase demand for women in politics. Domestic actors search out international allies to bring pressure to bear for their cause. By taking advantage of links to international actors, domestic women's groups can gain leverage, information, money, and other resources that would otherwise be out of reach. Keck and Sikkink (1998) call this process—seeking international support to pressure governments to act—the boomerang effect. One active example of this process is underway in Namibia, where women pressing for 50% women in parliament have linked to the WEDO's global 50/50 campaign, lending greater resources and legitimacy to their efforts (Bauer 2006).

Whereas domestic actors may sometimes call on international forces for assistance, actors and forces external to nations may also initiate change. International influence is perhaps most apparent in the two recent constitutional transitions in Iraq and Afghanistan. Arguably, neither of these countries had either a strong internal demand or supply of women for political office. But outside agents were central in the formation of their new, post-war constitutions that both include substantial gender quotas. Though

Nordlund (2004) finds no evidence that the UN actively promoted the adoption of a gender quota in Afghanistan, it did strongly advocate increases in women's parliamentary representation. In fact, the UN actively worked to get the issue included on the agenda. Further, the international community pressured for women to be represented at the table during constitution building. Women's inclusion during this stage, and a lack of other options for increasing women's representation, may have been influential in the choice to adopt gender quotas (Dahlerup and Nordlund 2004).

Finally, a recent study statistically tested the impact of women's international organizing on women's acquisition of suffrage, and 10%, 20%, and 30% women in parliament. Paxton et al. (2006a) looked at data from more than 100 countries from 1893 to 2003. They found that the combination of women's organizing in the form of WINGOs and UN activity had a powerful impact on women's parliamentary representation over time. To give an example of how powerful an effect, at the beginning of the period, a country had a 2.5% chance of attaining suffrage. As international organizing increased, by 1948, the chance of suffrage had increased to 71%.

The Convention on the Elimination of All Forms of Discrimination Against Women (CEDAW)

The UN has many documents that promote equality of men and women's rights, including the UN Charter, the Universal Declaration of Human Rights, and a number of specialized agency resolutions, declarations, and recommendations (Cook 1994). Arguably the most important international treaty for women's rights, however, is CEDAW. CEDAW is also known as the Women's Convention and is sometimes described as the international bill of rights for women. Because it is so important, it is worth discussing CEDAW and its impact in some depth.

CEDAW tries to confront the social causes of women's inequality by addressing "all forms" of discrimination against women, including discrimination in the areas of education, employment, finance, health care, law, marriage and family relations, and politics. Although the UN has crafted several international treaties that address women's rights, CEDAW goes further than other treaties in demanding that *states change their laws* to help women. For example, countries that sign the treaty are urged to introduce measures of affirmative action that promote gender equality. Through **ratification** of CEDAW, countries declare a common goal of gender equality, and they also pledge to pursue policies and practices to reach that goal. Domestic actors may then seek help from the international arena to ensure that states comply with the goals enshrined in the treaty, producing a boomerang effect.

Ratification of CEDAW has increased strikingly over time since the treaty's adoption by the UN General Assembly in 1979. As of March 2005, 180 countries had ratified the treaty, making it one of the most widely accepted treaties in UN history. Although President Jimmy Carter signed CEDAW on behalf of the United States in 1980, the United States has never ratified the treaty and is the only Western country not to do so (see Box 6.3). Other nonratifying countries are located in the Middle East (Iran, Oman, and Qatar), the Pacific region in Asia (Brunei Darussalam, Marshall Islands, Nauru, Palau, and Tonga), and sub-Saharan Africa (Somalia and Sudan).

Has CEDAW made a difference in the status of women across the world? Advocates credit the treaty with encouraging a number of positive developments, including the expansion of women's citizenship rights in Botswana and Japan, inheritance rights in Tanzania, property rights in Georgia, and political participation in Costa Rica (Hadassah 2004). After CEDAW ratification, twenty-two countries instituted equal employment policies, and a number of countries, such as Guatemala, the Philippines, Poland, and Spain, improved maternity leave and child care for working women (Hadassah 2004). Some researchers also argue that the treaty has been important for securing gains in women's political representation, often through the implementation of gender quotas in various forms.

Despite these favorable arguments by CEDAW's proponents, some research has pointed out that ratification of the treaty is a highly political decision that may have little to do with general attitudes about women (Paxton and Kunovich 2003). Although a nation may succeed in ratifying CEDAW, implementing and fulfilling the provisions of the convention at the domestic level may prove to be a much more difficult task (Holt 1991). Evidence of this difficulty abounds: Though many nations have ratified CEDAW, women still experience oppression around the world and remain strikingly underrepresented in many of the world's parliaments.

Some governments may simply be responding to international pressure and have no real intentions to alter the status quo regarding women's status after ratifying the treaty. A few examples illustrate this point. Kuwait ratified the treaty more than a decade before allowing women to vote, and Saudi Arabia, which still denies women the vote, ratified CEDAW in 2000. The Taliban government of Afghanistan was one of CEDAW's original signatories; yet clearly the Taliban was not committed to advancing women's political equality. In addition to these notable examples, several empirical studies have investigated the relationship between ratification of CEDAW and the percentage of women in parliament across a large number of countries. Most of this research fails to find that CEDAW has any appreciable effect (e.g., Hughes 2004; Paxton and Kunovich 2003).

It is important to recognize, however, that one of the main obstacles to CEDAW's success early on was a lack of enforcement mechanisms or ways to hold governments accountable. The **Optional Protocol** was developed to overcome this barrier. In 1999, the UN put forth this supplemental treaty to CEDAW. If a country ratifies the Optional Protocol, women are better able to hold governments accountable for their obligations under CEDAW. And the Optional Protocol enables the international CEDAW committee to conduct inquiries into systematic violations of women's rights. As of January 2005, 71 countries had already ratified the Optional Protocol (United Nations Population Fund 2005). But because it has so recently been adopted, researchers do not yet know its effect.

As one way to demonstrate the relationship between CEDAW and women's political status around the world, we use data on women's political equality for 123 countries from 1981 to 2003, available from the Cingranelli-Richards Human Rights Dataset (Cingranelli and Richards 2004b). We separate the 123 countries into two groups: ratifying and nonratifying. Figure 6.3 presents the average political equality scores

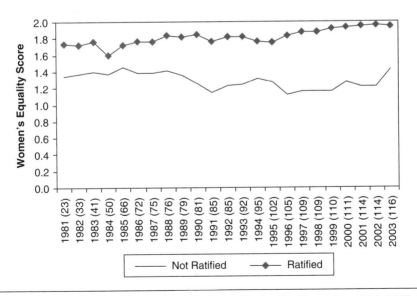

Figure 6.3   Women's Average Political Equality in 123 Countries, 1981–2003

for these two groups. Because the number of countries who have signed the treaty changes over time, the number of countries in the ratifying group appears in parentheses next to the year on the *x*-axis. This graph makes it clear that over time countries that ratify CEDAW minimize political inequality between men and women more so than countries that refuse ratification. Although again this does not prove that CEDAW is the cause of women's improving political situation, CEDAW may at least generally indicate a shared commitment to women's political equality.

Box 6.3   CEDAW Ratification in the United States

I ask you to think about this convention [CEDAW] and its impact. It has a proven record of helping women around the world to combat violence, gain economic opportunity, [and] strike against discriminatory laws. Its provisions are consistent with United States law, which already provides strong protections for women. It offers a means for reviewing and encouraging other nations' compliance. . . . When you look ahead to this new century and new millennium and you ask yourselves what you would like the story of the next 100 years to be, surely all of us want one big chapter to be about how, finally, in all nations of the world, people of all races and ethnic groups, of many different religious persuasions and cultural practices came together to guarantee that every young girl got a chance to grow up to live up to the fullest of her abilities and to live out her dreams.

—President Clinton (The White House 1998)

Today, arguments against the ratification of CEDAW in the United States are made on a number of grounds. Opponents of U.S. ratification stress that, although they support the treaty's goals, they are not sure if CEDAW is the best way to achieve them. Some fear that ratifying the treaty would threaten United States sovereignty, imposing an unnecessary UN bureaucracy to oversee the United States. Many opponents have little belief in the treaty's ability to cause real change, arguing that the pact has no enforcement power.

Other opponents maintain that CEDAW could be used by women's groups to impose an objectionable reproductive rights agenda in both the United States and abroad. For example, Senator Jesse Helms of North Carolina, the ranking Republican on the Foreign Relations Committee during the last vote to send CEDAW to the full Senate for ratification, stated in a letter to other committee members, "There can be no doubt that CEDAW supporters are attempting to use this treaty to advance a radical abortion agenda." Along these lines, many

Republicans argue that ratification of the treaty would undermine "traditional" moral and social values, including marriage, motherhood, family structure, and even Mother's Day. (The CEDAW Committee criticized Belarus for making the celebration of Mother's Day their only response to the problem of discrimination against women.) The treaty's harshest critics attack CEDAW as a "toxic" document that tries to impose "radical feminism" around the world.

CEDAW proponents counter that the treaty takes no position on abortion and that the document is not antifamily. The document calls on ratifying countries to recognize the "common responsibility of men and women in the upbringing and development of their children" and states that "the parents' common responsibility [is] to promote what is in the best interest of the child" (United Nations 1979). Many human rights and women's organizations have placed considerable pressure on the United States to ratify the treaty, arguing that failure to ratify hinders the ability of the United States to exercise political or moral leadership in the human rights field. Furthermore, they contend that by refusing to ratify CEDAW, the United States relinquishes the opportunity to influence further development of women's human rights. They ask how the United States can demand, for example, that India and Pakistan increase efforts to protect women from honor killing when the United States has not even ratified the treaty. Furthermore, by refusing ratification, the United States is barred from appointing a member to the CEDAW committee, leaving the United States unable to influence the body from within.

In 1993, 68 senators signed a letter asking President Clinton to support ratification of CEDAW, and the Senate Foreign Relations Committee has twice voted to send CEDAW to the full Senate for ratification (in 1994 and 2002). However, in neither instance did the measure actually come before the full Senate. In 2002, Scott McClellan, spokesman for the Bush administration, explained, "For 22 years now, Republican- and Democratic-controlled Senates alike have declined to ratify because of issues it raises. We too believe there are issues that must be addressed before considering ratification" (Dao 2002:A3).

Though the measure has failed at the national level, several state and local governments have passed resolutions in support of CEDAW. In April 1998, San Francisco became the first city in the United States to implement the principles of CEDAW locally. A task force now coordinates efforts to identify and combat discrimination against women. The CEDAW framework encourages public policy that explicitly considers the experiences of women, for example, adding streetlights to make neighborhoods safer for women (Hadassah 2004). Other state and local governments that have passed similar measures include Palo Alto and Los Angeles, California; the Connecticut State Senate; Hawaii; the Illinois House of Representatives; Iowa; Maine; Massachusetts; New Hampshire; New York City; North Carolina; and South Dakota.

SOURCES: Center for Reproductive Rights (2004), Dao (2002), and Hadassah (2004).

In sum, large, overarching factors, such as armed conflict and women's activity in the international arena, can make a difference to women's political representation around the world. These factors influence both the supply of women available for political office and the demand of political actors for women. And it is finally worth pointing out that, though this chapter focused on the international women's movement and international organizations as an explanation for women's political representation across countries, these same forces for change are also examples of women's political activity.

7

Do Women Make a Difference?

In previous chapters, we discussed women's fight for representation and what factors explain women's differential success in gaining power around the world. But a final question remains to be answered—what difference do women make anyway? Put another way, does having women in positions of power change anything? Have women changed the style of politics? Have they influenced public policy? If you viewed the past three chapters as addressing how women gain descriptive representation (see Chapter 1), then this chapter addresses women's substantive representation.

Even if women act and legislate exactly the same way as men, justice arguments imply that, as half the population, women should appear in politics. But arguments for women's representation are even more powerful if women bring to office interests and priorities that are different from those of men (Carroll and Dodson 1991). The difference is whether women are passive representatives, representing women just by being in office, or active representatives, working for women and their interests (Reingold 1992).

Determining whether women make a difference to politics is not easy. To begin, there are any number of questions to be asked and answered:

- Are female politicians, as opposed to male politicians, more likely to see women as a group as important constituents? Do female politicians "see" their female constituents better than male politicians do?
- Do men and women differ in their attitudes and policy priorities? Do women prioritize political issues differently than men do?

- Do male and female legislators have different voting records? Do female legislators vote more often in favor of "women's issue" bills, such as curbing domestic violence?
- Are women writing bills on issues of interest to women? Are they taking the initiative to act for women?
- Are women able to get women's issue bills, or any bills, passed once they are initiated? Are women powerful enough to support and shepherd their bills through the legislative process?
- Do women have a different legislative style than men? Do they act through regular and traditional channels of power, or are women changing the rules of the political game?
- Are women better able to sponsor and pass bills related to women, or to support a different legislative style, when there are more of them in office?
- Can women have an effect outside of legislative bodies?

Addressing each of these questions has its own specific problems, and researchers have done a better job answering some than in answering others. Generally, several ongoing limitations in this area of research constrain researchers' ability to make definitive statements about what is "known" of women's impact. For example, most of the research in this chapter focuses on the United States and a few other Western countries. At the present time, researchers simply do not have many studies of women's impact in non-Western countries. In fact, the way current research discusses women's impact is often Western—defining women's issues as Western feminist issues and assuming democratic channels of power. Also, throughout this chapter, we try to make it clear just how difficult it is to distinguish women's impact from the surrounding **context**, including the political party women belong to or the amount of power women hold. These caveats aside, in this chapter, we review the current state of knowledge about women's impact on politics.

Thinking Differently: Women's Views on Women and Their Policy Priorities

We can begin by asking female politicians whether they think they represent women and their concerns. Remember the argument in Chapter 1 that, due to different socialization and life experiences, women may simply be different from men (Phillips 1991; but see Molyneux 1985b). So are female legislators more likely than male legislators to see women as a group of special constituents? Beth Reingold (1992) talked to male and female state legislators from Arizona and California. Thirty-four percent of the women she interviewed spontaneously mentioned women as an important constituency. In contrast, only 6% of male senators mentioned anything about women (i.e., 3 male legislators out of 49). When directly asked whether they thought female legislators were better able to represent women's special concerns, almost 80% of female legislators said yes, whereas only 30% of men said yes. Combining these results suggests that, although male legislators tend to view themselves as capable of representing women's interests, they do not spontaneously mention women as an important constituency. Women seem to do a better job instinctively seeing the special needs or interests of women.

Similarly, Sarah Childs (2002) interviewed female British members of parliament (MPs), nearly half of whom spoke directly about trying to articulate women's concerns. As one female MP explained, "I've become increasingly aware that there are issues that affect women disproportionately and that unless women pursue them nobody else will" (Childs 2002:144). About a third of the women interviewed also said they felt their female constituents were more comfortable talking to them about women's issues. As one MP explained, "Some women actually do say 'Oh I wouldn't have gone to see a man about that; I would never have sat down and told a man that'" (Childs 2002:149).

If female legislators see specific issues affecting women, does it affect the kinds of bills they prioritize? Research suggests that female legislators prioritize different political issues than men do. For example, looking at U.S. state representatives, researchers found that, compared to men, women are more likely to prioritize bills related to children, family, and women (Thomas 1991; Thomas and Welch 1991) and health care and social services (Little, Dunn, and Deen 2001). And, in Sweden, female members of parliament are more likely than men to give high priority to issues such as family policy, elder care, and health care (vs. other priorities, e.g., jobs, the environment, taxes) (Wangnerud 2000; see also Skjeie 1991, 2002; Solheim 2000).

Similarly, in Latin America, male and female legislators articulate different legislative priorities (Schwindt-Bayer 2006). In a survey of 292 MPs from Argentina, Colombia, and Costa Rica, 65% of female legislators stated "women's equality" is a very high priority, compared with only 25% of male legislators. And 43% of female legislators felt children's and family issues are a very high priority, compared with 28% of men (Schwindt-Bayer 2006). In contrast, male legislators were more likely than female legislators to prioritize agriculture and employment issues.

Apart from different views on so-called women's issues, female legislators may view all issues differently than men do. Lyn Kathlene (1995) looked at legislators in the Colorado House of Representatives and found that women and men saw both the origins of, and solutions to, crime very differently. Female legislators viewed criminals as connected to others and society and as victims of circumstance as well as perpetrators of crimes.

Women viewed crime as the result of life-long issues stemming from early childhood, poor education, and lack of adult opportunities. In contrast, men viewed criminals as independent individuals who are individually responsible for their actions. Men focused more on the crime, rather than the fact that it was committed by a person.

Their different views of the people involved led the men and women of the Colorado House to have different policy recommendations. Female legislators were more concerned with prevention (e.g., early childhood education, youth diversion programs, increased job opportunities), whereas men were more reactive in their response (e.g., stricter sentencing, longer prison terms). The women were also more likely to talk about the possibility of rehabilitation than were the men.

Acting Differently: Women's Voting Patterns and Bill Sponsorship

But do their different views and priorities lead women to act differently than men do? For example, do individual female legislators vote differently simply because they are women? There are two difficulties in trying to demonstrate that female politicians "act differently" or even "act for women" in their voting behavior. The first is that one has to separate women's interests as women from the interest of their party. Women run as candidates and are elected as members of parties—parties that differ widely on public policy. To take a U.S. example, just as male Republicans differ from male Democrats, female Republicans differ from female Democrats (Carroll 1984). The problem is that, because the Democratic Party is generally more politically left than the Republican Party, Democratic candidates and politicians are more likely to espouse and vote for politically left policies that also get defined as "of interest to women." For example, Democrats in general are likely to vote for bills extending family and medical leaves. But family and medical leaves could also be classified as a woman's issue.

A similar issue is how to separate a female politician acting for women from her actions in support of her constituents. Nancy Pelosi represents San Francisco in the U.S. House of Representatives. When she votes to support a bill of interest to women (e.g., increasing funding to the U.S. Department of Education), is she voting to represent women or just to represent her largely liberal constituents? Whether San Francisco's politician is male or female, he or she will vote to support funding increases if it is what the voters want. And if liberal constituencies are more likely to elect women, then a critic might argue that female politicians aren't acting for women at all but are only faithfully representing their liberal constituents.

Michele Swers worked to separate the impact of female politicians in the 103rd Congress (1993 to 1994) from both their party and their constituencies (Swers 1998). She looked at how congressmen and congresswomen voted on bills concerning women's issues. The 14 bills she considered women's issue bills included the Family and Medical Leave Act, the Family Planning Amendments Act of 1993, and the Elementary and Secondary Education Act. After accounting for party (Republican or Democrat) and district characteristics (urban vs. rural, constituent income, and percentage of Black constituents), she found that a congressperson's gender made a difference in voting for these bills. Congresswomen were more likely to vote for women's issue bills than their male colleagues were. And this was especially true when she considered the bills most directly related to women, such as reproductive issues or women's health. But party was still important. Democrats, both male and female, tended to vote for these women's issue bills. So it was the defections of Republican women from the way the rest of their party voted that created the gender difference.

A similar pattern of defection occurs in other countries. For example, in New Zealand during early debates on parental leave, conservative women crossed party lines to support parental leave (Grey 2002). And women act for women in Britain as well. Sarah Childs and Julie Withey considered who signed early day motions, which are nonbinding policy statements on a variety of topics that allow members of parliament to put their views on record. (Although the researchers did not deal with constituency effects, they did deal with party effects by only considering women in the Labour Party.) They found that female MPs were more likely to sign "feminist" early day motions, especially those related to abortion and women's health (Childs and Withey 2004).

An unusual but potent example of women working for women's interests was in the early day motion, initiated by Christine McCafferty and signed by many, that stated female sanitary products should be exempt from the VAT (a European tax) along with other essential items. Childs and Withey (2004) explained that despite constituting only 15% of the Commons, women accounted for 22% of the 249 MPs who signed EDM 89 (99/00):

> That this House believes that sanitary products should be classed in the category of essential to the family budget, just as food, children's clothing and books already are, and that, like such products, they should be classed as VAT-free under EC sixth Directive. (p. 553)

But even if women want to defect from their party or their constituents and act "as women," there are additional constraints that may prevent them from doing so. Female legislators are subject to the same institutional and party constraints that any legislator feels. And a very important factor is whether a female legislator is in a party that is in power or in an opposition party. Women in governing parties have more opportunities to generate legislation but simultaneously have more opportunities to anger party leadership with defection (Swers 2002a:17). Similarly, women in governing parties have more opportunities for leadership positions on committees but are thus concurrently more susceptible to threats of removal upon defection from the party agenda. The importance of institutional context is apparent if one considers what happened to the defections of Republican women from their party in the 104th Congress (1995 to 1996), which followed the 103rd.

At the end of her article on women's impact in the 103rd Congress, Michele Swers warned that a distinct women's impact might be harder to find in the next, 104th Congress (1995 to 1996). A number of changes in the legislature led to this prediction. Campaigning on the "Contract with America" platform, Republicans had taken over control of the legislature, leading to the most conservative Congress in decades. As part of this change, the newly elected Republican women were also more conservative than their predecessors. Indeed, a number of female Republican freshmen presented Rush Limbaugh (a conservative talk-radio host) with a plaque declaring that none was a "Femi-Nazi" (Hawkesworth, Casey, Jenkins, and Kleeman 2001).

Mary Hawkesworth and colleagues interviewed congresswomen in both the 103rd and 104th Congresses. They concluded that the change in leadership and general conservative turn of Congress had "severe repercussions for bipartisan efforts to develop and promote a women's legislative agenda" (Hawkesworth et al. 2001:17). The new Republican leadership, headed by Newt Gingrich, consolidated power and demanded greater party discipline and adherence to party-line policy stances. Defectors from the party line were threatened with party-endorsed primary opponents if they failed to support the leadership on key votes. Their interviews with congressional staffers suggested that moderate Republican women felt a new caution in focusing on women's issues. "One Congresswoman who had participated in the CAWP research about the 103rd Congress refused an interview after the 104th, with her apologetic staffer explaining that she had to be careful about 'things such as this' (i.e., women) now" (Hawkesworth et al. 2001:17).

The change in power and in climate had an impact. In a later investigation of the 104th Congress, Swers (2002a:117–9) found that Democratic women continued to vote for women's issue bills (on average 13.5 of the 15 during the 104th Congress), but Republican women reduced their votes by almost 50% (to only 3.9 of the 15 possible). Although Republican women continued to defect from their party at times, it was at a lower rate (Swers 2002a:113–25). Further, although Republican congresswomen had sponsored "feminist" bills during the 103rd Congress, they shifted focus to general social welfare bills in the 104th (Swers 2002b:276). With their party in power and new penalties against defection in place, the moderate Republican legislators who might have defected on women's issues in the past now worried about supporting issues like family planning and child care. They felt it was dangerous to be "perceived as an advocate for Democratic interest groups" (Swers 2002b:277).

Similarly, Sandra Grey found that party mattered in New Zealand for women's support of parental leave policy. Despite reaching over 29% women in the legislature by 1998, the country's parental leave policy did not substantially change from earlier incarnations. Much of the opposition to broader legislation came from the party to the political right (the party in power), which was concerned about loss of free-market principles. Thus, "in discussions of the 1998 Paid Parental Leave Bill, four women politicians expressed opposition to the proposed provisions, all from the right of the political spectrum" (Grey 2002:26).

In sum, female politicians work within institutions, institutions that can have a substantial impact on their ability to act for women. Whether or not Republican women wanted to defect in the 104th Congress, or women on the right in New Zealand wanted to support Paid Parental Leave, institutional and party forces made it difficult for them to do so.

Besides voting for bills, are women initiating bills related to their policy preferences? That is, on an individual basis, female legislators at times defect from their party or sign particular motions simply because they are women. But do women propose bills that are different from the bills of men? And do they propose bills of special interest to women?

Women do propose bills on women. Bratton and Haynie (1999) found that women in the U.S. Congress are more likely than congressmen to introduce women's interest bills to reduce gender discrimination or to improve the economic status of women (controlling for party and district characteristics) (see also Swers 2002a:32–56). Women are more likely to introduce bills on women's rights in Honduras (Taylor-Robinson and Heath 2003) and initiate 11% more women's issues bills than men do in Argentina, Colombia, and Costa Rica (Schwindt-Bayer 2006).

Women are also more likely to sponsor bills on topics related to women. In Latin America (Argentina, Colombia, and Costa Rica), women are more likely to introduce bills related to children and the family, education, and health (Schwindt-Bayer 2006). (But in the Honduran legislature, women are no more likely than men to initiate bills on children or families; Taylor-Robinson and Heath 2003.) In the United States, women are also more likely to sponsor bills related to education, health care, children's issues, and welfare policy (Bratton and Haynie 1999; see also Thomas 1991).

Again, context, in the form of the distribution of committee assignments across men and women, matters to bill introduction. Legislative committees are expected to produce bills on particular topics. Members of a health and social welfare committee, for example, are expected to produce bills on health and social welfare (Heath et al. 2005; Schwindt-Bayer 2006). Thus, because women often sit on committees relevant to women's interests, they can use their committee assignments to either propose women's interest legislation or block legislation perceived as harmful to women (Berkman and O'Connor 1993).

Returning to the women of the Colorado statehouse, one can ask whether their different views of crime led them to initiate different types of legislation. Lyn Kathlene's research demonstrates that the attitudinal differences she documented between men and women in their views of crime translated into the kinds of crime and prison bills they proposed. In general, women's solutions were "contextual, multifaceted, and long-term," whereas men rarely "addressed crime from a long-term perspective; rather, they sponsored legislation that responded directly to the crime event" (Kathlene 1995:721).

Table 7.1 reproduces a table from Kathlene's article. Two of the eight bills sponsored by women addressed prevention, compared with none of the bills sponsored by men. (Remember that women were more likely to talk about crime in terms of prevention.) Similarly, only women talked about the victims of crime in their interviews, and the only victim rights bill was sponsored by a woman. In contrast, the bills on crime sponsored by men tended to focus on expanding laws to include new crimes or increasing the penalties of existing laws.

Acting Successfully: Women's Legislative Effectiveness

But what about legislative effectiveness? Are women effective in actually getting their bills passed? This question has two parts. First, women may be generally less effective in the political process than men are. Because males have controlled legislatures, a male legislating style has dominated throughout most of history. A male-gendered institution may reward "male" qualities, such as

Table 7.1 Crime Bills Introduced in 1989 Session, Colorado State House, by Sex of Sponsor

Female-Sponsored Bills (n = 8)				Male-Sponsored Bills (n = 12)			
Bill #	Title	Purpose	Outcome	Bill #	Title	Purpose	Outcome
1027	Release of Records Pertaining to Juvenile Offenders	Intervention	Postponed Indefinitely	1091	Concerning Criminal Procedures	Legal procedures	LAW
1072	Crime Prevention Resources Center	Prevention/ Intervention	Postponed Indefinitely	1197	Dismissals of Actions	Legal procedures	LAW
1302	Strengthen Crime Victim Compensation Act	Victim help	LAW	1162	Concerning Crimes	Legal procedures	VETOED
1099	Financing Judicial Facilities	New financing for increased court expenses	Postponed Indefinitely	1231	Discovery in Criminal Proceedings	Legal procedures	LAW
1226	Concerning Court Actions	New financing for police to fight drugs	Postponed Indefinitely	1054	Obstruction of Peace Officer's Animal	Expands law	Postponed Indefinitely

(Continued)

Table 7.1 (Continued)

Female-Sponsored Bills (n = 8)				Male-Sponsored Bills (n = 12)			
Bill #	Title	Purpose	Outcome	Bill #	Title	Purpose	Outcome
1205	Criminal Penalities for Animal Owners	Stricter sentencing	Postponed Indefinitely	1245	Safety on Educ. Institution Premises	Expands law	LAW
1111	Driving Privileges of Minors	Stricter sentencing	LAW	1259	Expand Crime of Equity Skimming	Expands law	LAW
1289	Alcohol Related Vehicular Offenses	Expands law, stricter law, stricter sentencing	LAW	1028	Maintenance of Juvenile Records	Stricter sentencing	LAW
				1075	Crime of Sexual Abuse	Stricter sentencing	LAW
				1335	Gang-Related Crimes	Stricter sentencing	LAW
				1166	Driver's License Revocation for Drugs	Stricter sentencing	LAW
				1124	Crimes Involving Acts of Domestic Violence	Rehabilitation	LAW

SOURCE: From Kathlene, L., "Alternative views of crime: Legislative policymaking in gendered terms," in *Journal of Politics*, 57, copyright © 1995. Reprinted with permission of Blackwell Publishing Ltd.

competitiveness, rather than "female" qualities, such as collaboration (Eagly and Johnson 1990; Jeydel and Taylor 2003; Rosenthal 1998a). Therefore, women may not be effective legislators because they have the "wrong skills." Of course, to preserve their own power, men may also directly work to undermine the power of female newcomers (Heath et al. 2005).

Second, women may be less effective in getting bills passed that specifically deal with women's issues or that take a woman's perspective. If women have a different outlook on defined social problems, such as crime (Kathlene 1995), or even see new social problems, such as gender discrimination (Bratton and Haynie 1999), then their legislation may be seen as, at best, innovative and, at worst, inappropriate, in ways that make it difficult for women to successfully find support for their proposals.

Despite these gloomy predictions, research suggests that women can be as effective as men in getting their bills turned into law. In U.S. state legislatures, women are more successful than men in getting bills directly related to women, children, and families passed (Thomas 1991). Women in state legislatures are also as good as men at passing bills on topics of broad interest to women (education, health care, etc.) (Bratton and Haynie 1999). And, in the U.S. Congress, women are as successful as men in shepherding all types of bills into law (Jeydel and Taylor 2003). Men are also no more likely than women are to successfully amend other laws, influence domestic spending, or channel money to their home districts. This research suggests, therefore, that women can be effective legislators, both on issues related to women and, more broadly, on all issues.

But when we look more closely at the bills that get passed by women, the answer to women's effectiveness is more complex. Kathlene (1995) found that female legislators in Colorado were only partially successful in getting their crime-related bills (see Table 7.1) passed. Only the female-sponsored crime bills that addressed crime in "male" terms became law. Women's more innovative bills, addressing crime with a long-term perspective, were not successful. So women were able to pass their bills when they legislated like men.

But it is worth noting a different pattern for female-sponsored prison bills. These had a much higher success rate, and bills with a "female flavor" were passed by the legislature. The difference may have been that prison overcrowding and tight budgets led all lawmakers to consider nontraditional solutions to the problem. In an environment of crisis, the new perspectives brought by female legislators were accepted.

Also, even if women have equal success, it does not mean the process is equal. Female politicians are political newcomers with less institutional (and social) power than their male colleagues. This means they have less power in face-to-face interactions, such as in the committee meetings where bills are first discussed and debated. Looking at these committee meetings demonstrates a pattern of male domination:

> Regardless of whether the chair [of the committee] or the sponsor [of the bill] is a man or a woman or the hearing is on a family issue, female committee members engage later, speak significantly fewer words, take significantly fewer turns, and make and receive fewer interruptions than their male counterparts. (Kathlene 1994:569)

Further, women-sponsored bills receive more scrutiny, debate, and hostile testimony than male-sponsored bills do (Kathlene, Clarke, and Fox 1991). And male power is still evident in the treatment of male and female expert witnesses. Consider what Lyn Kathlene saw in committee hearings in the Colorado state legislature:

> A woman who testified was usually addressed by her first name by male chairs, whether she was an unknown expert, citizen, familiar lobbyist, or bureaucrat; but a witness who was a man received a title in front of his name, both at the time of introduction and at the conclusion of his remarks. Female chairs used titles with both men and women who were unknown to them and reserved first names for witnesses of both sexes with whom they were familiar. The most egregious example of the sexist treatment occurred in a hearing on a health issue, in which several doctors testified. Although the woman witness clearly stated her title and name as "Dr. Elisa Jones," the male chair addressed her repeatedly as "Elisa" and finally thanked "Mrs. Jones" for her testimony. Needless to say, perhaps, none of the male doctors were referred to as anything but "Dr. ___." (Kathlene 1994:572)

The effectiveness of female legislators in getting legislation passed is also highly dependent on context. For example, Swers (2002b) explained that Democratic women were able to influence the legislative agenda when theirs was the party in power during 1993–1994 but were substantially limited in their ability to influence the agenda when their party was out of power in the subsequent congress. Similarly, nondemocratic systems limit women's ability to influence legislation or otherwise make an impact. Even if women successfully pass legislation in parliament, a powerful president may simply dispose of the parliamentary reforms. Box 7.1 provides such an example, cataloging women's failed attempts to influence land tenure reform in semi-democratic Uganda in the late 1990s.

Box 7.1   The Limitations of Semidemocracies: Land Tenure Reform in Uganda

Uganda is a tropical, land-locked country located in East Africa. English is the official language, and most of the country's 27 million inhabitants are Roman Catholic or Protestant. Independent from the United Kingdom since 1962, the parliament of Uganda was dissolved several times following military over-throws. For years, the country was ruled by a series of regimes that had among the world's worst human rights records. But on January 26th, 1986, the National Resistance Movement (NRM) seized the capital and removed the military ruler. Lieutenant General Yoweri Kaguta Museveni became president and established a "no-party" democracy governed by the NRM, now called "The Movement."

Under President Museveni, the government initiated substantial political liberalization, general press freedom, and broad economic reforms. Affirmative action policies were instituted at both the national and local levels to ensure participation by women. Women now hold 74 seats in the national legislature, 25% of the 295 seats, and affirmative action policies have also resulted in women receiving high-profile appointments to senior civil service positions. Despite that women are freed from competing with men and that they have made significant political gains, women in Uganda have no way to assert their rights to run as candidates in open elections. The government is often classi-fied as a semidemocracy or "benevolent autocracy."

Like many countries in Africa, women in Uganda have limited ownership rights over land. Even where women have the funds to purchase their own land, they often register it in a man's name, giving women limited rights over what the land produces. Thus, in 1997, when the Ugandan government proposed to regularize titling and tenure systems, a coalition of women's groups entered the reform debate to secure land control rights for women. Specifically, the groups proposed a clause granting women ownership rights in spousal homestead property. Although the clause was eventually approved in parliament, when the Land Act was published a few days later, the clause granting women land rights had been removed. In the end, President Museveni admitted that he had personally intervened to delete the amend-ment. In this case, the benevolent autocrat had not been so generous. In the country's semidemocratic system, women had no way to fight back, and women's groups in Uganda continue to fight for land reform.

SOURCES: Central Intelligence Agency (2005), Goetz (2003), Goetz and Hassim (2003), Kawamara-Mishambi and Ovonji-Odida (2003), Norris (1993:329), U.S. Department of State (2005), and Women of Uganda Network (2005).

Considering the difficulties women have being heard in committee meetings, the belittling of women's authority as expert witnesses, and the hostility they face in shepherding their bills through the policy process, their equal bill passage rates are actually quite impressive. Women know they have to fight to get their bills passed in the face of opposition on multiple fronts. And women do fight, taking a long-term view to passing legislation and trying multiple times to get bills passed (Kathlene et al. 1991)

Legislating Differently: Women's Legislative Style

What about legislative style? Women may not only change the products of legislatures through different policy priorities and innovative legislation, but they may also change the process of legislating or the procedures of the legislature. Asked as a question, do women change the way business is done in legislatures? Already we explained that women view social problems differently than men do, which leads women to propose different types of legislation. But research suggests that women have a different style of legislating as well. Recall the discussion of political leaders in Chapter 3—women tend to be more democratic and participatory in their leadership style than men are (Eagly and Johnson 1990). Female legislators also tend to be more collaborative in their leadership styles than men are, answering more positively when asked whether they "try hard to find a fair combination of gains and losses for all sides," "pull people together," and "share power with others" (Rosenthal 1998a:855). For example, Sue Thomas (1994) interviewed state legislators from California, Georgia, Mississippi, Nebraska, Pennsylvania, and Washington. These female legislators saw women as advocating a different style of politics—one that is more consensus and compromise oriented.

Differences in legislative style may arise from a different view of power (Kanter 1977:166; Thomas 1994). Feminist theory and studies of female legislators both suggest that women view power as a way to get things done, rather than as a way to control or influence other people. Consider the female legislator interviewed by Cantor, Bernay, and Stoess (1992:40), who explained that "power is basically that sense of strength and understanding about how to pull together resources to get your agendas done." Or consider what Iowa's Lieutenant Governor Jo Ann Zimmerman had to say: "I didn't think about having power myself. There are just things to do, and you get them done" (Cantor et al. 1992:48).

Women may have a different style of doing politics, but does it make a difference to the whole legislature? Has it affected the way business is conducted? A 2001 survey of United States state legislators found that a majority of both men and women say that the increased presence of women has made a difference to the "way legislators conduct themselves on the floor of the legislature" (Center for American Women and Politics 2001:11). These numbers suggest some spillover from female legislators to their colleagues, at least in the United States. Further, women's presence appears to highlight the needs of other traditionally disadvantaged groups. The same survey found that a majority of male and female legislators agreed that women have made a difference in "the extent to which the legislature is sympathetic to the concerns of racial and ethnic minority groups," and "the extent to which the economically disadvantaged have access to the legislature" (Center for American Women and Politics 2001:1). Thus, women may increase awareness not only of "women's issues" but also of issues related to other disadvantaged groups. Consider what Congresswoman Patsy Mink (Democrat for Hawaii) had to say:

> I think basically that poor women are the ones that have no representation in Congress, other than from congresswomen who feel a sense of commitment to represent their causes. It's the poor women who are left out in much of this debate, certainly the legal immigrant women and legal immigrant children . . . and to some extent elderly women who are also poor and on Medicare, and so forth . . . these are the types of bills that I press on. (quoted in Hawkesworth et al. 2001:10)

Of course, simply asking male and female legislators whether women make a difference to politics cannot directly show whether the legislature objectively changes when women are present. But Bratton and Haynie (1999) found that women are more likely to introduce bills of interest to African Americans (e.g., school integration and funding of sickle cell anemia research). And Black legislators are more likely to introduce bills of interest to women.

And of course, realistically, politics continues to involve zero-sum, win-lose decisions, and women who may naturally have a different legislative style feel pressure to adapt to that environment, at least at times. As explained by state legislator Jean Marie Brough, "I don't like the process, but in order to make a change, you have to get power, and in order to get power you have to play the system" (quoted in Thomas 1994:122). Or consider the views of Maria Rozas, a Chilean parliamentarian: "In order that they do listen to you, women have to shout or swear, but that means adopting masculine behaviour, and it should not be like that" (quoted in Franceschet 2001:215). Generally, the problem is well described by Joni Lovenduski: "A great dilemma for the second wave of feminism has been whether women will change institutions before institutions change women" (1993:6).

In choosing between incremental change and large-scale systematic change, women face serious potential drawbacks to any decision (Thomas 1994:122–7). Do women fight within the system, making small changes but perhaps remaining dissatisfied? Or do women fight to change the entire system, risking marginalization and derision? Box 7.2 outlines the choice one women's party in Iceland faced and their ultimate decision.

Box 7.2   Iceland's Women's Alliance Party: Adapt or Stay Out?

In 1987, the *Kvennalistinn* party (known in English as the Women's Alliance) won six seats in Iceland's election. This was a high enough percentage of seats to make the Kvennalistinn a political player, and the party was asked to join a coalition government. Being a part of the coalition government would increase the party's power and influence substantially. But for the Women's Alliance, this was a tough decision. Should the party agree to join the coalition but compromise some of its primary goals, or should it decline the offer and stand fast to its principles?

To understand why the decision was difficult for the Women's Alliance, it is important to understand the party's policies and goals. The Kvennalistinn believed in power sharing and active democracy and therefore had no chairwoman or even leaders in a conventional sense. Decisions were made through consensus and without voting. Furthermore, all decisions were made at national conventions that could be attended by women from all over the country (Olafsdottir Bjornsson 2001).

Considering the name of the party, it should come as no surprise that women were central to the objectives of the Kvennalistinn. As stated in the party's platform it had a goal: "to make women's perspectives, experience and culture a no less important policy-making force in our society than that of men. The Women's Alliance wants to nurture and develop that which is positive in women's outlook on the world and to harness it for the betterment of society as a whole" (Kvennalistinn 1987). Thomas (1994:28) explained:

> The kinds of political products that members of the Kvennalistinn advocate include women's issues such as childcare, sex education, and fair salaries. Despite a special dedication to these issues, however, members of the alliance insist there is a need for a women's point of view on all domestic and foreign issues. Its platform addresses each issue based on the economic model of a housewife on a limited budget.

In sum, the Kvennalistinn hoped to change the political system in Iceland by incorporating women and women's perspectives. And in 1987 they were given the choice to be part of the coalition government. But joining the coalition would mean giving up some of their top policy demands, such as a minimum wage proposal.

Ultimately, the party decided against joining the coalition. As explained by one party member, "We were ready to take part in the government, but only if it would really matter. We didn't want to be flowers to make the government look good to the world" (quoted in Thomas 1994:28). The women of the Kvennalistinn decided it was more important to hold fast to their principles and remain on the outside than to compromise those principles to gain additional power.

Did the Kvennalistinn disappear when they wouldn't play politics as usual? No. In fact, in 1988, the Kvennalistinn was the most popular party of Iceland's six major parties, with support from 31.3% of the population. The party lost ground over time, partly because other parties expanded their numbers of female candidates. But the message of the Women's Alliance continued to resonate over time. It contested and won seats and polled in second place among parties in 1994 (Koester 1995). In 1997 the members of the party split on joining a new coalition, and the party was dissolved.

SOURCES: Koester (1995), Olafsdottir Bjornsson (2001), and Thomas (1994).

Do Numbers Matter?
Critical Mass and Women's Impact

A final question relates to whether the number of women present in a legislature makes a difference for women's impact. That is, are women better able to make a difference when there are a lot of them in office? To understand the question, think about the difference between one or two women struggling for survival in a traditionally male environment and a group of women supporting each other as they bring new ideas to the legislative table. Women may be better able to leave a distinctive imprint on the policy process when there are more of them in place.

Women in politics scholars use the term **critical mass** to suggest that when women reach a certain percentage of a legislature, they will be better able to pursue their policy priorities and legislative styles. The term has its origins in Rosabeth Moss Kanter's (1977) work on women in an American corporation. Although she did not use the term *critical mass*, Kanter made a distinction between four different types of groups:

- Uniform groups have only one type of person (e.g., 100% men, 0% women).
- Skewed groups have mostly one type of person (e.g., 85% men, 15% women).
- Tilted groups are moving toward balance (e.g., 65% men, 35% women).
- Balanced groups have nearly equal numbers (e.g., 50% men, 50% women).

Women in a skewed group are **tokens** and were found by Kanter (1977) to be more visible than men, suffer from stereotyping, and feel compelled to conform to dominant (male) norms. Because token women feel pressure to blend into the male culture, they may find it difficult to form alliances with other token women to further their interests. Although she only studied a skewed group, Kanter suggested that changes in women's behavior and to the culture of a group were possible if a group moved from skewed status to tilted or balanced status.

The theoretical link to women in politics is clear—if the only women in politics are token women, they may not be able to make a difference to policies or legislative style (Dahlerup 1988). But if women reach a critical mass and move out of token status, the increased influence of women and a feminization of the political agenda will be seen.

What exactly constitutes a critical mass? Common use of the term cites 30% women in parliament as the critical cutoff. Indeed, the United Nations used this cutoff when it argued that women need to make up 30% of national elites to exert meaningful influence on politics (United Nations Development Programme 1995). Research has often used 15%, to signify movement out of Kanter's skewed group category.

There is anecdotal evidence for the importance of critical mass. For example, a female politician from Southern Europe discussed legislative style as follows: "If . . . the number of women politicians is small as in the case of my country, politics may change women because, in order to survive politically, women may copy the men in their methods and behavior" (Inter-Parliamentary Union 2000:23). Especially in highly visible positions, women may also need to be cognizant of sanctions for being seen to act in the interests of women. Relating the experience of Labour MPs in Great Britain, Childs (2002:151) explained:

> The most common perception is that women who seek to act for women act only for women. This results in a tension between a woman MP's parliamentary career and acting for women. If an MP desires promotion, she cannot afford to be regarded as acting for women too often or too forcefully.

When women make up only a small portion of a political party, they are, according to an East African female politician, vulnerable: "The few who are determined to confront the male politicians within the party end up being called all sorts of names—insolent, would-be men, etc.—and they are often ignored and pushed to one side" (Inter-Parliamentary Union 2000:56).

But anecdotal evidence aside, it has been difficult to demonstrate that reaching a critical mass matters for women in politics. In searching for an effect, research has either looked over time at a legislature to see whether something changes when women hit 15% of a legislature (e.g., Grey 2002; Saint-Germain 1989), or research has compared U.S. states with different percentages of women to see if they sponsor more women's issue bills (e.g., Bratton 2005; Thomas 1991). This research provides only a little bit of evidence of critical mass effects. For example, in New Zealand, female politicians verbally represent themselves as women more often as they reach 15% of a legislature (Grey 2002). And Michelle Saint-Germain (1989), looking at the Arizona state legislature, found gender differences in the sponsorship of women's interest bills only after women reached 15% of the legislature. But women were not more successful at passing legislation as their numbers rose. In fact, women did better when their numbers were smaller.

In research on critical mass, just like research on women's impact in general, the problem of distinguishing women's impact from the impact of party or district characteristics exists. For example, in 1988, the two states with the lowest percentage of women in their legislature, Mississippi and Pennsylvania, also had the fewest legislators prioritizing bills dealing with women or with children and families (Thomas 1991). But a skeptic might argue that those states might have been more politically conservative than the others, which led to both fewer women appearing in politics and in less legislation related to women and children being sponsored. Kathleen Bratton (2005) looked at the concept of critical mass on women's sponsorship of bills and in their success at passing those bills. She accounted for party and district characteristics in the legislatures of California, Illinois, and Maryland from 1969 to 1999. Women in all three legislatures consistently sponsored more women's interest bills than did men, regardless of the percentage of the legislature they held—suggesting no effect of critical mass. In fact, Bratton found that as the percentage of women in the legislatures of these states rose from around 5% to around 27%, gender differences in bill sponsorship actually diminished. Even more striking, Bratton found that women were better able to pass the legislation they proposed when they were a smaller percentage of the legislature. In discussing her results, Bratton points out that, in contrast to women in a corporation, women in politics may never feel that it is a disadvantage to focus on women's issues. Furthermore, when women appear in only small numbers, they may feel an especial need to act for women, resulting in overachievement on sponsoring and passing women's issues.

As for legislative style, in New Zealand women became more aggressive (making personal attacks and interrupting other MPs) as their numbers rose in the legislature (Grey 2002). Generally, women still made fewer personal attacks than men did. In fact, "male MPs' share of personal attacks was higher than their share of the debates on child care and parental leave in 11 of the 25 years" (Grey 2002:23). But women seem to have adopted more masculine behavior over time, concomitantly with their rise in numbers.

In understanding whether having high numbers of women, a critical mass, makes a difference to women's impact, it is important to recognize that power is not evenly distributed in legislatures. As discussed earlier, being a part of the party in power is important for whether women can influence policy. The party, or parties, in power have a much greater chance than opposition parties of getting their agenda passed. Remember that women in the U.S. Democratic Party had more influence in the 103rd Congress when their party was in power. But Democratic women's ability to pass laws related to women and women's interests declined after Republicans took power in 1994 (Swers 2002a). Similarly, in New Zealand between 1988 and 1990, many discussions of child care and parental leave took place. During this period, women comprised 19.3% of the Labour Party and the Labour Party was in office. But "from late 1990, when women made up only 11.9% of the National group and National was in office, there was a drop in the incidences of debate of the two 'women's issues'" (Grey 2002:22).

Legislators who chair powerful committees or fill cabinet posts also have greater influence on public policy than the regular rank-and-file. Seniority matters in many legislatures, giving long-standing members of parliament the headships of committees and important cabinet positions. Thus, even if women reach 15% or 30% of a legislature, if they are newcomers, they will still be disadvantaged in positional power. This suggests that though greater numbers may help women develop a voice, it could take more time for women to truly affect policy outcomes (Grey 2002).

It is also important to note theory and evidence that increasing numbers of women can have a *negative* effect on outcomes for women. Kanter's (1977) analysis of proportions is only one way of thinking about how minority groups interact with majority groups. In contrast, sociologist Peter Blau (1977) focused on the social networks possible between minority and majority group members. When minority members are only a small part of a group, they must have more contact with and connections to majority group members (e.g., the only Black kid in a high school is likely to have many White friends). The social connections between the minority group member and majority members may increase the support from the dominant group. When numbers of minority members increase, they can have more connections with each other and consequently fewer with majority members. Fewer connections between the majority and minority groups could decrease support from the dominant group and potentially increase discrimination against the minority group.

Further, as women's numbers rise, women become a more threatening minority, and a backlash may result. Janice Yoder's (1991) theory of intrusiveness suggests that when women are a small minority, they can use their token status to draw attention to women's concerns. But when women increase in numbers, they start to threaten the power and privilege of men, leading to competition, hostility, and discrimination. "Numerical surges threaten the majority, who react with heightened levels of discriminatory behaviour in order to limit the power gains of the growing lower-status minority" (Yoder 1991:184).

There is some evidence to support this alternative perspective. In the New Zealand legislature, personal attacks against women rose as women's numbers rose. Just when women reached approximately 15% of the legislature, there was a "rise in hostility toward women politicians" (Grey 2002:25). Female legislators in Colombia are reluctant to address gender because it "threatens men" (Schwindt-Bayer 2006:573). In the United States, Cindy Simon Rosenthal (1998b:88–93) compared men and women's behavior in legislative committee meetings where women held few leadership positions and many leadership positions. She found that women in the committees were more likely to be inclusive, collaborative, and accommodating as the percentage of women in leadership positions increased. But men were less likely to be inclusive, collaborative, or accommodating as the number of women increased in leadership power.

Rosenthal's finding suggests that both Kanter and Yoder may be correct. Women feel more comfortable using a "female" legislative style when there are more of them in power. But men appear to be threatened by female power and subsequently reduce their tendency to compromise or accommodate. Both sides are apparent in a quote from one of Rosenthal's chairwomen:

We're at the point where we have enough women in leadership, a critical mass, that we try to caucus and inform one another about our bills. . . . And I don't see anymore the situation when a woman gets up and blows it, that she's treated as a woman who blew it as opposed to a legislator who blew it. . . . We also have a women's conference committee, it's not for real, we only do it to irritate the men. We just go back in a room by ourselves and talk about something . . . and then they're dying to know what we're doing. (Rosenthal 1998b:92)

The increase in women has reduced women's token representation of all women (being treated as a woman who blew it rather than a legislator who blew it) in this Texas legislature. But the increase in women is also likely threatening to the men who are "dying to know" what the women are doing.

Ultimately, it may be the critical acts of women, rather than their critical mass, that matters for policy influence (Childs and Krook 2005; Dahlerup 1988). Indeed, many female politicians feel that that the quality of female leaders is as important as numbers: "Just one courageous woman can be a vehicle for profound change where 30% may be of little effect" (Pacific politician, cited in Inter-Parliamentary Union 2000:68).

Women's Movements and Women's Policy Machinery as Alternative Sources of Influence

Our discussion of critical mass suggests that even after women achieve a significant number of parliamentary seats, governments may still refuse to address women's concerns. Thus, S. Laurel Weldon (2002a) pointed out that one should also think "beyond bodies" in legislatures. Even in countries and regions where women are woefully underrepresented in political office, women can achieve substantive representation through their participation in women's movements or women's groups. Women's movements "pursue women's gender interests . . . [and] make claims on cultural and political systems on the basis of women's historically ascribed gender roles" (Alvarez 1990:23; see also Beckwith 2005). They are therefore a place outside the government where women can speak for women as everyday citizens and activists.

When the voices of female legislators are being pushed to the sidelines, women's movements may push women's interests back into play. For instance, women's groups in Mozambique were critical to getting the New Family Law Act, which allowed women to work without their husband's permission, passed in 2003. Even after elected women held 30% of Mozambique's parliament in 1999, the draft bill was stalled in parliament. Parliamentarians made excuses, did not debate the bill, and generally treated it as a low priority. But in November 2003, more than 1,000 women marched to the National Assembly building and demanded that the New Family Law be debated in parliament. Just 1 month after the march, the bill was passed (Disney 2006:43).

Women's movements may have an impact even when governmental structures work against women. Indeed, in Chapter 2, we discussed how without female legislators, women's movements can be a powerful force.

But women's movements need not always be oppositional. When women hold legislative seats, they may provide a sympathetic ear and allow women's groups to help set the agenda. And countries and political parties may also establish structures that help bridge the gap between women's movements and government.

An alternative place for women to make a difference is within the **machinery of government**. Governments have various agencies, departments, and ministries that develop and implement policy. Although feminists have traditionally been leery of governments, viewing them as sites of oppression, many now see the benefits to engaging directly with the state to advocate women's rights. Acting within government bureaucracy allows "the development and implementation of gender-sensitive national policy, as well as representation of women's interests within the state" (Friedman 2000:48). And individual women can influence policy in gender-sensitive ways, not just in their position as legislators but also in their position as bureaucrats, or "femocrats" (Sawer 1990).

Today, most national governments have some form of **women's policy machinery**, or government body devoted to promoting the status of women (Staudt 1998; Stetson 1995; Weldon 2002b). Government-level women's policy machinery can take the form of a national women's agency, a women's commission, or a women's ministry. Having a designated space for women within a government promotes women's interests in a number of ways. First, women's policy machinery can coordinate and consolidate the development and implementation of policy (Stetson 1995; Stetson and Mazur 1995; Weldon 2002a). Without a single site for the creation of gender-sensitive national policy, a government response to gender inequality is likely to be spread across multiple agencies or departments.

> Government response to violence against women . . . requires action in areas as diverse as criminal justice, education, and income assistance policy. But these areas are usually the responsibility of a variety of different agencies, posing considerable coordination problems. (Weldon 2002a:1159)

In contrast, a response to domestic violence can be better designed and more effectively promoted under a single women's agency.

Further, an institutionalized women's policy machinery produces a single, direct route to government cooperation with agents, such as women's movements, who traditionally act outside the state (Friedman 2000; Stetson and Mazur 1995; Weldon 2002a, 2002b). Women's movements may critique or comment on existing agency proposals, assist with policy formation, and help represent the different bases for inequality across women, such as race, ethnicity, or sexuality. Indeed, Weldon (2002a) found that across 36 democratic countries, a strong women's movement acting in conjunction with an effective women's agency predicted the extent of government commitment to domestic violence.

In Summary: What Do We Know?

On the surface, demonstrating women's impact on politics and policy might seem a simple task. Indeed, we argued that women have a shared experience that results in common interests that are different from men's interests. And advocates for women assert that a critical mass of women changes both the process and outcomes of legislative bodies. But, ultimately, we must caution that right now, when asking if and how women influence politics and policy making, we have few answers. What we do not yet know about women's political impact is far greater than what we know. Not only must researchers continue to grapple with the difficulties of separating the effect of gender from the effect of political party and constituency, but future research must also consider what women's impact means outside of the Western industrialized world.

Another important issue is that we know very little about the impact that minority women can make. As discussed earlier, women's presence appears to highlight the needs of other traditionally disadvantaged groups. But that does not mean that disadvantaged women are having their needs addressed. Remember the discussion in Chapter 1—researchers need to ask whether female politicians are making policy that represents all women. Women are not just women—they are women of a particular race, ethnicity, religion, class, or sexual orientation.

Feminists have argued that laws are designed and implemented in exclusive ways if women are not at the table. For example, when politicians discuss the rights of cultural minorities, if women are absent, then women's rights may be taken away. And if only male members of an indigenous group are present to articulate the group's beliefs, traditions, or interests, women's interests are likely to be pushed aside (Okin 1999). One example of this occurred in Peru in 1991, when a national assembly of 112 men and 8 women passed legislation to protect codefendants in gang rape from prosecution if one of the perpetrators agreed to marry the victim (Inter-Parliamentary Union 1995; Okin 1999). The law seeks to alleviate the disgrace brought on the family of the rape victim, who is left with a tainted, unmarriageable young woman (Associated Press 1997). Female legislators lobbied against the law, arguing that rape is not an honor crime against families but an assault on women. But their arguments were countered by indigenous congressmen, who held that the laws were based in indigenous custom. Without the voice of indigenous women, the law was upheld.

The flipside suggests that, even if women are present, laws are likely to be designed and implemented in exclusive ways if minorities are not at the table (Eisenstein 1993; Hill Collins 2000). Women from majority groups may draw on their own experiences when crafting legislation, and they simply may not be aware of certain obstacles faced by minority or low-income women (Crenshaw 1994). For example, do the bills on domestic violence proposed by women in countries such as Namibia or the United States fully address racial, ethnic, class, or other differences among women? Women of lower classes may require help accessing domestic violence resources—is that addressed in the bill? Does the bill address same-sex domestic violence? Consider bills on sexual or reproductive rights. These too may be meaningless for the poorest women if they do not include provisions to help women access resources and facilities (Yuval-Davis 1997:18). Do equal-opportunity employment policies address those women who have trouble entering the labor force? Do they address disabled women? In the United States today, all 14 female senators are White women. Whose voice is represented? How might this affect the bills they initiate and pass?

We pose these questions to remind readers that women differ from each other in a number of important ways. But, realistically, we may not be able to elect a woman to represent the unique interests of women at the intersections of every social category. How can people ensure that the voices of all women are represented? Weldon (2002a) may provide a solution to this problem. She argued that the women's movement, as a site of interaction and debate, can help create a group perspective and a set of priorities that is the product of multiple voices. So even if all the female legislators in a country are from the dominant ethnic group, or are all from the upper class, women's movements can be a place where alternative views are articulated.

But how can women's movements represent all women? Consider Weldon's (2002a) puzzle analogy:

> Group perspective can be thought of as a puzzle of which each member of the group has a piece. The more pieces of the puzzle, the better picture we have. When additional pieces are very similar to existing pieces (the same color or texture) we learn little about other areas or features of the puzzle. The greater the diversity in pieces, the better idea we have about the different areas and parts of the puzzle. Moreover, when members of the group come together, they can compare their puzzle pieces, and each person gains a greater understanding of the larger puzzle to which she or he holds a piece. (p. 1156)

Of course, the ultimate picture revealed by the puzzle may still be debated. Like a work of art, one individual may interpret the picture in one way while another interprets it in an entirely different way. But the picture is still more complete when more pieces of the puzzle have been added. When trying to understand women's impact on politics, it may therefore be important to consider both the efforts of women in political office and the contribution of women in organizations and movements.

Overall, it is likely that the ultimate answers about women's impact on politics will be nuanced rather than straightforward. Research by both Lyn Kathlene and Michele Swers showing the importance of context (including issue area, outside crises, party in power, and committee processes) provides a hint to the types of conclusions researchers are likely to reach about the impact of women in the future. Still, at present we can say that, whether in the majority of legislators or only a small minority, many women feel a commitment to furthering women's interests, and many will act to do so.

8

All Regions Are Not Created Equal

I n previous chapters, we identified a number of factors and general processes that influence women's political power across the world. But though it is important to understand the big picture, one must also recognize that there is substantial regional variation in both the nature of the obstacles faced by women and the avenues open to women to pursue political inclusion. In parts of the Middle East, women continue to struggle for the most basic social and political rights, whereas in Scandinavia women are close to closing the gender gap in political power. Although we cannot delve deeply into the specifics of women's political situations in every country, in this chapter we identify some of the key issues and trends common to particular regions of the world.

The Geography of Women in Politics

To begin, we divide the globe into six regions: Western industrialized countries, Eastern Europe and Central Asia, Latin America and the Caribbean, sub-Saharan Africa, Asia and the Pacific Islands, and the Middle East and North Africa. Countries in each of these categories are fairly geographically concentrated, with the exception of the West, which includes Canada and the United States, Northern and Western Europe, Australia, and

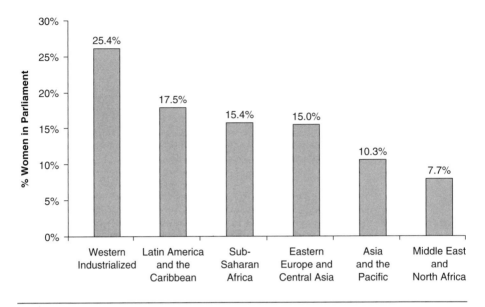

Figure 8.1   Women's Parliamentary Representation for 187 Countries by Region, 2006

SOURCE: Data from Inter-Parliamentary Union (2006b).

New Zealand. Figures 8.1 and 8.2 present an overall picture of the variation in women's political representation and leadership across these six regions.

When focusing on national legislatures, Western industrialized countries lead the world, averaging 25% women. Latin America, sub-Saharan Africa, and Eastern Europe fall in the middle range with 15% to 18%. Asia and the Middle East have the fewest women, where women hold an average of only 8% to 10% of seats. When looking at national leadership, however, the regional picture of women's political power changes somewhat. Women in Asia and Latin America perform better than those in the West in attaining primary national leadership positions, whereas in Africa, Eastern Europe, and the Middle East, women lag behind (see Chapter 3 for a discussion of the different categories of political leadership).

In the following sections, we examine each region in turn. Overall, we cover a number of topics related to culture, including Scandinavian political culture, *marianismo*, Catholicism, nationalism, and women in Confucian thought. We also address political and structural matters such as gender quotas at the local level in Southeast Asia and the family law system in the Middle East and North Africa. Similar to the theories outlined in Chapter 6 that influence women's political outcomes in myriad ways, we also discuss the

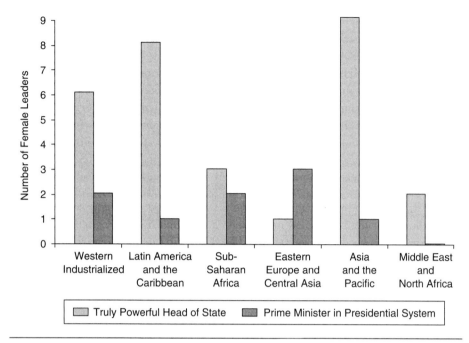

Figure 8.2   Total Number of Women Ever Serving as a Truly Powerful Head of State or Prime Minister in a Presidential System, by Region

complex and contradictory impact of colonialism. This chapter also identifies inroads to the political realm that are more commonplace in particular regions, such as women's politicization in democratic movements in Latin America or the family route to political leadership in Asia.

Western Industrialized Countries

> *"Daddy, on television today they said that a man was prime minister.*
> *Is it possible that a man can be prime minister?"*
>
> —Reportedly asked by the child of a news correspondent after Gro Brundtland, Norway's former female prime minister, was ousted from office (Solheim 2000:75)

In no Western industrialized country are women fully excluded from political representation in national politics. In recent years, no head of state in the region has appointed an all-male cabinet, and by 2006 women held a minimum of 9% of parliamentary seats in all countries (Central Intelligence Agency 2006b; Inter-Parliamentary Union 2006a). However, across the West, substantial differences in women's political representation and leadership remain. As depicted in Map 8.1, one country, Sweden, has more than 40% women in its parliament, nine countries have reached at least 30% women, and eight countries have more than 20% women. But several countries—France, Greece, Ireland, Italy, Malta, San Marino, the United States, and the United Kingdom—also have less than 20% women in their national legislatures. Even among these lower performers, there is variation in the histories of female political leadership: The United Kingdom elected a truly powerful female head of government, France elected a female prime minister in its presidential system (a position with moderate power), and Ireland elected two women to a largely symbolic national leadership position. Alternatively, Greece, Italy, San Marino, and the United States have not been led by a woman throughout their entire histories. We further explore women in U.S. politics in Chapter 9.

Although women's political representation has increased significantly in a number of Western countries in recent years, it is important to note that since the 1970s, Scandinavia has led the world (see Figure 8.3). Scandinavia is a region of northern Europe that includes Denmark, Finland, Iceland, Norway, and Sweden. With slightly more than 20 million people, Scandinavia comprises "small, homogenous societies with relatively high standards of living, a fairly common historical tradition and culture, and emphasis on Protestantism, democracy, and social welfare" (Solheim 2000:29). During the 1970s, increasing education, declining birth rates, and a higher cost of living pushed many women into the workforce. But unlike other Western countries, women's political progress in Scandinavia proceeded faster than improvements within the family or the workforce (Solheim 2000).

As of 2006, Nordic countries held four of the top five positions in the world rankings of women's parliamentary representation. Ranging from a low of 33.3% in Iceland to a high of 45.3% in Sweden, the average percentage of women in parliament in Scandinavia is more than 15% higher than the rest of the West (Inter-Parliamentary Union 2006b). This pattern is also evident in the executive branch of government, where by the early 1990s, 37% of cabinet members in Scandinavia were women, whereas the average figure in Western Europe was 9% (Karvonen and Selle 1995). Another impressive political accomplishment of women in Scandinavia is that they have been able to break out of the areas traditionally staffed by women, such as education and family policy, holding cabinet positions in industry, energy, defense, environmental affairs, and justice (Karvonen and Selle 1995).

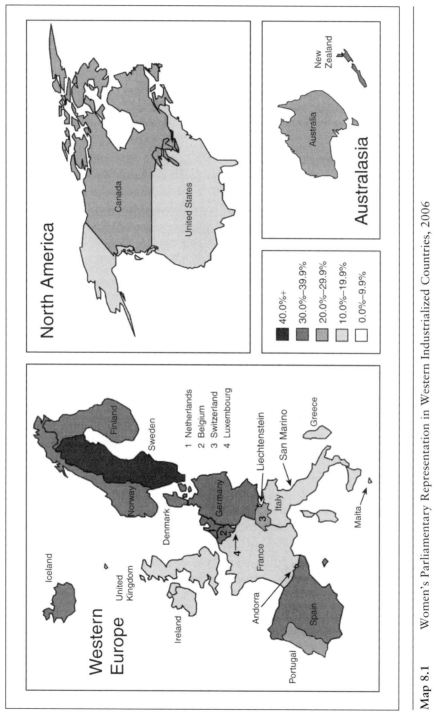

Map 8.1 Women's Parliamentary Representation in Western Industrialized Countries, 2006

SOURCE: Data from Inter-Parliamentary Union (2006a).

North America

Australasia

New Zealand

Australia

Canada

United States

40.0%+
30.0%–39.9%
20.0%–29.9%
10.0%–19.9%
0.0%–9.9%

Western
Europe

Iceland

United
Kingdom

Ireland

Norway

Sweden

Finland

Denmark

1 Netherlands
2 Belgium
3 Switzerland
4 Luxembourg

Germany

Liechtenstein

San Marino

Italy

Greece

Malta

France

Andorra

Portugal

Spain

221

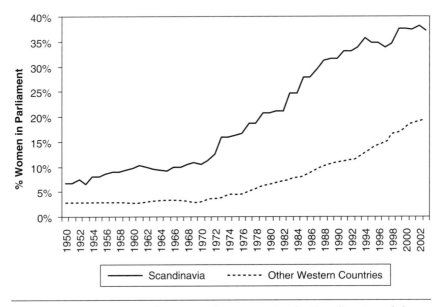

Figure 8.3   Women's Parliamentary Representation for Scandinavia and the
West, 1950–2003

SOURCE: Data from Paxton, Hughes, and Green (2006b).

So why are the Nordic countries so different? A number of explanations
have been put forth to justify women's exceptional political involvement in
Scandinavia, and many of them are discussed in previous chapters:
Protestantism, a high level of education and labor force participation for
women, the dominance of leftist parties, a proportional representation electoral system, and a well-organized women's movement (Bystydzienski
1995; Haavio-Mannila and Skard 1985; Matland 1993; Norris 1985;
Solheim 2000). But scholars also argue that **political culture** in Scandinavia
is different from the political culture in other parts of the world.
Scandinavians value equity, consensus, and integration, making politics an
arena of accommodation and deference (Solheim 2000). Following **social
democratic** principles, Scandinavians emphasize the collective good, not
individual rights or privileges. And since the early 1970s, the new feminist
movement in Nordic countries has argued for women's political representation in terms of the collective good (Skjeie 2002). Therefore, the notion
of electing women in substantial numbers became integrated with existing
ideas about the collective good, democracy, and fair governance.

Not only is the political culture conducive to including women, but also the tradition and culture of the region places value on the feminine. For example, anthropologist David Koester (1995) noted that compared with the Hebrew, Greek, and Roman traditions that serve as the foundation for many modern European societies, women are more highly regarded in Icelandic literature. Although women in Icelandic sagas were not equal to men, they were given "relatively authoritative and influential positions" (Koester 1995:574). Furthermore, even in medieval times in Scandinavia, women owned property, ruled households, and had the right to divorce their husbands (Koester 1995).

Although Scandinavian countries currently lead the world in the realm of women in politics, one must be careful not to overglorify women's position in the Nordic countries. Even in Scandinavia, women face obstacles and setbacks. For example, in 1993 elections in Norway, all three major political parties were led by women, but just 4 years later all parties were led by men, and women's parliamentary representation dropped 3%. Further, women still face a number of barriers in other areas of life. Across Scandinavia, women still perform the bulk of unpaid labor, are concentrated in the service sector, and are underrepresented in management in the private sector (Solheim 2000).

Eastern Europe and Central Asia

Ideologies favorable to women's political participation are also a part of the history of the former communist world. As we introduced in Chapter 3, social equality for women was a central tenet of communist ideology. In 1920, Vladimir Lenin stated:

> In law there is naturally complete equality of rights for men and women. And everywhere there is evidence of a sincere wish to put this equality into practice. We are bringing the women into the social economy, into legislation and government. All educational institutions are open to them, so that they can increase their professional and social capacities. . . . In short, we are seriously carrying out the demand in our programme for the transference of the economic and educational functions of the separate household to society. That will mean freedom for the woman from the old household drudgery and dependence on man. That enables her to exercise to the full her talents and her inclinations. (Zetkin 1920)

Thus, across all domains, including the political, women were to be treated as equals to men.

Influenced by this ideology of gender inclusiveness, many public policies and practices during communist times were beneficial to women. For example, East Germany (GDR) passed a decree on equal pay for equal work in 1946, which was some of the earliest legislation targeted to benefit women in world history (Einhorn 1991). And several countries in Eastern Europe provided abortions for free within the first trimester.

Across the Eastern bloc, women's numbers in politics were also boosted by gender quotas that set mandatory levels for women's participation. Gender quotas ensured that, compared to women in the West, women in most communist countries experienced relatively high levels of political representation. In the former Soviet Union, for example, women held 17% of seats in the national legislature in 1946, the highest level of female representation at the national level in the world at the time. In 1967, East Germany became the first country to reach 30% women in parliament, followed by the former Soviet Union in 1970 and Romania in 1980. Alternatively, a democratic country did not achieve this feat until 1985, when Sweden elected 31.5% women to parliament. In some countries, such as Poland, women held an even larger share of political offices at the regional and local levels (Shaul 1982).

The Fall of the Soviet Union: Women Fall Too?

Transitions to democracy in Eastern Europe in the early 1990s raised fundamental questions about the resilience of women's political power. In short, would women's past roles in government allow them to compete against men for positions in newly democratic countries? The simple answer to this question is no. During the 1990s, women's political representation in former communist countries plummeted, often dropping from levels around 30% to less than 10%, and sometimes less than 5% (Matland and Montgomery 2003; Saxonberg 2000). Now, more than a decade later, the level of representation in Eastern Europe and Central Asia averages only 15%, a full 10% lower than the average in 1988 (Inter-Parliamentary Union 2006a; Paxton, Hughes, and Green 2006b).

Looking back, it is now clear that "women were ill prepared to influence the State and the newly active political parties during the very rapid collapse of the old order" (Waylen 1994:347). First, the women chosen to serve in communist parliaments were not likely to pursue politics once countries transitioned to democracy. Describing the communist situation in Bulgaria, Kostova (1998) stated:

> Many of the women . . . were weavers, seamstresses, heroes of socialist labor, and women with low-status jobs. The fact that these women did not have experience to be taken seriously in important decision-making was exactly the reason they were chosen. (p. 211)

But this pattern was not unique to Bulgaria. Across the communist world, women's representation was acknowledged as token, and women were known as "milkmaid" politicians (Waylen 1994).

Furthermore, as we noted in Chapter 3, women's representation in the legislatures of communist countries did not mean they had genuine power. Under communism, the real power is held in the central committee or **politburo**—the executive body that governs the communist party—whereas legislatures serve only as "rubber stamps" (Matland and Montgomery 2003:6). And though Lenin argued that a "woman communist is a member of the Party just as a man communist, with equal rights and duties" (Zetkin 1920), men held the positions of power in the politburos (Einhorn 1991; Montgomery 2003). For example, in East Germany (GDR), not a single woman entered the politburo during its history (Einhorn 1992, cited in Waylen 1994). Women's party participation and share of leadership positions were greatest during the period before and immediately after the communist revolution but declined as communism was consolidated (Wolchik 1981, 1994).

Women were further marginalized during the politics of transition. As elites negotiated the forms that new social, political, and economic institutions would take, women were swept aside. As Einhorn (1991:17) described, "In all those cases where past dissidents formed or were important in the first democratically elected governments—in pre-unification GDR, in Slovenia, in Czechoslovakia, in Poland—it is men ... who became government ministers." For example, during the transition period in Czechoslovakia, of the 21 positions of ministerial rank in the interim government, there was only one woman (Wolchik 1994). Women "were present at the big demonstrations, on the happy streets, but disappeared from the negotiating tables" (Kiss 1991:51).

One explanation for women's exclusion is that during the process of transition there was little to no activity by women's movements. In part, this is a legacy of communist policy. Lenin argued that the communist women's movement should be a part of the greater revolution against capitalism, so women should not form special organizations (Zetkin 1920). "No independent women's organizations were tolerated, and those women's organizations that did exist were essentially part of the Communist Party apparatus" (Waylen 1994:345). Although these restrictions on organizing were lifted once communist dominance ended, it is not so easy to create a vibrant **civil society** with active citizen participation (Putnam 1994). Instead of motivating them to action, women's loss of position in their new democratic system created a sense of shock that perpetuated women's inactivity (Einhorn 1991). Overall, with no underlying structure of activism to push for women's incorporation, women's individual demands could simply be ignored.

But there are also reasons why women retreated from the public realm. Regional experts often note that though communism espoused an ideal of gender equality, the revolution was incomplete. Women living under communism were still marginalized by the patriarchal system (Fodor 2002; Gal and Kligman 2000). The policies establishing women's equality were part of a "revolution from above" that left the everyday structures of life and the relations between men and women at the most basic levels relatively unchanged. In addition to their workplace roles, women continued to shoulder the overwhelming majority of domestic work and child care. This double burden of work and family roles was further extended into a **triple burden**—participation in politics. Therefore, once the requirements on women's work and political participation were removed, it was not difficult to push women back into traditional patterns (Einhorn 1991; Kiss 1991).

Since the transition to democracy and market economics, women in some former communist countries have been more politically successful than others. For example, women now hold only 5.3% of seats in Armenia and Ukraine, whereas Bulgaria has even surpassed its high point of women's legislative representation under communism, electing 26.2% women in 2001. What explains why some countries were able to rebound and others were not? What are the barriers to women's political incorporation today? To answer these questions, one must consider the cultural, economic, and political circumstances faced by women throughout Eastern Europe and Central Asia since the fall of the Soviet Union.

Explaining Women's Political Power
Since 1990: Culture, Structure, and Politics

Like in other parts of the world, women seeking political office across Eastern Europe and Central Asia must now contend with traditional beliefs about women's proper roles as well as negative stereotypes about women in politics. Across the region, there has been "an explicit rebirth of the ideology of women's primary role as wife and mother, tender of the domestic hearth" (Einhorn 1991:18). And because women held token positions under communism, male politicians often do not take female politicians seriously. For example, Ekaterina Lakhova, former head of the Presidential Commission on Women, Families, and Demography in Russia, states, "Men see us as women, but not as deputies. You're explaining something to him about infant mortality, and he says that it doesn't become you to talk about such serious things; that you have to be a woman" (cited from Sperling 1998:159).

One significant problem for women seeking to organize for change is the prevalence of antifeminist attitudes. Across the region, feminism carries negative associations because of both its connections to the West and its association with the communist period. In fact, "'gender equality' is a term that most politicians, male and female alike, hesitate to use" (Rueschemeyer 1994:233). The discrediting of feminism limits both the abilities of women to successfully organize and the ability of female politicians to represent women's interests (Goven 1993; Jaquette and Wolchik 1998; Matland and Montgomery 2003; Rueschemeyer 1994). A female candidate speaking about equal wages risks accusations that she is a communist. Therefore, female politicians may be more likely to toe the party line to acquire or hold on to power. Birch (2003:149) states, "Female politicians in Ukraine are clearly using the institution of the political party to their advantage; the question remains as to whether they are using it to the advantage of Ukrainian women."

But although traditional beliefs about women's gender roles and antifeminism are quite common across the region, there is also significant variation in cultural support for women in politics both across and within Eastern European countries. According to data from the World Values Survey (discussed in Chapter 5), support for women as political leaders is lowest in Georgia and Armenia and highest in Slovenia and Macedonia (Wilcox, Stark, and Thomas 2003). And across the region, older, less educated, politically conservative, and Muslim citizens were less supportive of women in politics than their younger, more educated, more liberal, and Christian counterparts (Wilcox, Stark, and Thomas 2003).

Some stereotypes about women have even served them well politically. For example, across Eastern Europe, women have been marketed as especially good candidates for fighting corruption. "With an image as an outsider, women can be seen with brooms sweeping out the corruption that still exists in the halls of power" (Matland 2003:329). One particularly interesting example of the relationship between gender and corruption is Yulia Tymoshenko, former prime minister of Ukraine. During Ukraine's transition to democracy, Tymoshenko was accused of selling abroad enormous quantities of stolen Russian gas, earning her the nickname "gas princess" (Zarakhovich 2005). But Yulia later cast herself as an economic reformer in the political realm. She said. "I want to say to people, 'Forget about paying bribes. Pay taxes'" (Tymoshenko 2005).

Women have also had trouble translating their high levels of education and employment, encouraged during the communist period, into political gains in the postcommunist period. Under communism, approximately 92% of working-age women in the Soviet Union either participated in the labor force or were furthering their education (Wejnert 1996). But since democratization, women make up the majority of the unemployed. In Ukraine, for example, women make up 70% of the unemployed population, even though two thirds of these women have higher education (Birch 2003). Women's exit from the workforce matters for the usual structural reasons. But to combat negative stereotypes about female politicians' lack of qualifications holding over from the communist era, women today may even need to be overqualified. In Poland, for example, female parliamentarians hold more university-level degrees than their male counterparts and often have longer records of party and trade union service (Siemienska 2003).

In terms of political factors, many of the patterns established in research on the West hold for Eastern Europe: Proportional representation systems tend to favor women, leftist parties also more consistently field a larger number of female candidates, and high party magnitudes can ensure that women, who are often placed lower on party lists, will gain seats (Kunovich 2003; Matland and Montgomery 2003). Of course, there are exceptions. In Russia's mixed system, for example, women have fared better competing in the plurality half of the system than in the party-list system (Moser 2003). In Lithuania, the conservative Homeland Union Party included just as many women as other parties with more leftist ideologies (Krupavičius and Matonytė 2003; Matland 2003).

In conclusion, we should not romanticize the high number of women in communist governments. The drop in women's legislative representation associated with the transition to democracy may be striking, but there are also increasing opportunities for women to gain true political power in the new democracies of this region. As Lithuanian scholars Krupavičius and Matonytė describe, "While the number of women in formal positions of power has dropped precipitously from the Soviet period, the women who are active in politics have been able to carve out more authentic places for themselves, with meaningful power" (2003:103). Competing in elections may present new obstacles for women, and change may be slow, but the benefits are real.

Latin America and the Caribbean

> *Who would have said, 10, 15 years ago, that a woman would be elected president?*
>
> —Michelle Bachelet, female president of Chile, 2006

In January 2006, women held approximately 18% of the seats in the national legislatures of Latin America and the Caribbean. Although 18% is still far from equality, women have clearly made gains in the region in recent years. Only four countries have less than 10% women in their lower house

Table 8.1   Women in Parliament, Women Ministerial Appointments, and
Female National Leaders in Latin America and the Caribbean, 2006

South America

Country	% Women Parliament	% Women Ministers	Current or Former Female Chief Executive
Argentina	36.2%	20.0%	
Guyana	30.8%	21.1%	Janet Jagan
Venezuela	29.9%	11.1%	
Suriname	25.5%	11.8%	
Peru	18.3%	6.7%	
Bolivia	16.9%	14.3%	Lydia Gueiler Tejada[1]
Ecuador	16.0%	13.3%	
Chile	15.0%	50.0%	Michelle Bachelet
Colombia	12.1%	38.5%	
Uruguay	11.1%	16.7%	
Paraguay	10.0%	30.0%	
Brazil	8.6%	4.3%	
Average	19.2%	19.8%	

Central America

Country	% Women Parliament	% Women Ministers	Current or Former Female Chief Executive
Costa Rica	35.1%	16.7%	
Mexico	24.2%	5.6%	
Honduras	23.4%	6.7%	
Nicaragua	20.7%	23.1%	Violeta Chamorro
Panama	16.7%	8.3%	Mireya Moscoso de Arias
El Salvador	10.7%	7.7%	
Guatemala	8.2%	15.4%	
Belize	6.7%	6.3%	
Average	18.2%	11.2%	

Caribbean

Country	% Women Parliament	% Women Ministers	Current or Former Female Chief Executive
Cuba	36.0%	19.2%	
Grenada	26.7%	15.0%	
Bahamas	20.0%	25.0%	
Trinidad & Tobago	19.4%	21.7%	
Saint Vincent & the Grenadines	18.2%	22.2%	

(Continued)

Table 8.1 (Continued)

Country	% Women Parliament	% Women Ministers	Current or Former Female Chief Executive
Caribbean			
Dominican Republic	17.3%	16.7%	
Barbados	13.3%	31.3%	
Dominica	12.9%	10.0%	Eugenia Charles
Jamaica	11.7%	17.6%	Portia Simpson-Miller
Saint Lucia	11.1%	9.1%	
Antigua & Barbuda	10.5%	0.0%	
Haiti	3.6%	16.7%	Ertha Pascal-Trouillot[1]
Saint Kitts & Nevis	0.0%	0.0%	Claudette Werleigh[2]
Average	15.4%	15.7%	

1. Interim or acting leader.

2. Prime minister in mixed system.

SOURCES: Data from Central Intelligence Agency (2006a) and Inter-Parliamentary Union (2006b).

NOTE: Ministers include only cabinet members who hold the formal title of "Minister" or "Secretary of State"; data are for most recent time point available.

of parliament—Brazil, Belize, Guatemala, and Haiti—while four countries have more than 30%—Argentina, Costa Rica, Cuba, and Guyana (see Table 8.1). In fact, the regional average for South America, 19.2%, even slightly exceeds the average level of female representation in Europe, 19.0% (Inter-Parliamentary Union 2006b).

One example of women's success in the region is the election of Michelle Bachelet, who won a run-off election in 2006 to become the first female president of Chile. As a separated mother of three and a self-described agnostic, Michelle Bachelet does not conform to conventional ideas about womanhood in her conservative and Catholic homeland. Yet, as we discuss later, like many women across Latin America, she was politicized by the struggle for democracy and liberation from brutal military rule. Her election has already affected women's political power in Chile—fulfilling a campaign promise, she appointed women to 50% of the seats in her cabinet (Chilean Government 2006).

Another example of marked improvement in recent years is in Costa Rica (see Figure 8.4). Costa Rica is exceptional in the region of Latin America for its governmental stability, suffering only two brief periods of war in its long democratic history (Central Intelligence Agency 2006c). Prior to the 1990s, women's political representation increased only slowly and inconsistently (Quesada 2003). But in 1996 the adoption of a 40% quota for women on party lists accelerated women's involvement, increasing representation at the national level from 15.8% to 19.3%. Once placement mandates were added to the law in 2002, women's parliamentary representation jumped even further. Female parliamentarians have also had significant legislative success. Studies have shown that laws submitted by female deputies have been approved 81% of the time, whereas for men the statistic is only 48% (de Figueres 2002).

Women's political advancement in Chile and Costa Rica suggests at least two forces for women's political progress across Latin America. First, women's participation in revolutionary struggles has sometimes changed ideas about women's proper roles. Political transitions have fostered women's integration into newly ruling parties, furthered public policy that benefits women, and catapulted women like Michelle Bachelet into political leadership. Second, the wave of national quota legislation that has washed over the region since the 1990s has also fostered real improvements in women's political situations in some countries (Bonder and Nari 1995; Htun and Jones 2002; Jones 1998, 2004; Quesada 2003; Schmidt and Saunders 2004). For example, Argentina, the first country in the world to adopt a national quota law, now leads the region with 36.1% women in its lower house.

Despite these advances, it is important to remember that the overall picture of women in Latin American politics is one of mixed success. Women have historically faced a number of obstacles to their political empowerment,

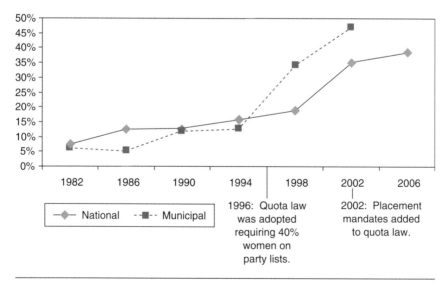

Figure 8.4   Women's Political Milestones and Representation at the National and Municipal Levels in Costa Rica, 1982–2006

SOURCES: Data from de Figueres (2002) and Jones (2004).

including the Catholic Church, machismo and *marianismo*, and repressive exclusionary governments. Women's participation in democratic movements does not guarantee gains in women's formal political roles after a regime has been toppled, for example, in Brazil and Guatemala. And where women have entered formal politics, they continue to be hindered by restrictive gender cultures.

Cultural Barriers to Women in Politics in Latin America

As in countries across the world, gender roles in Latin America have been constructed to exclude women from the public realm. The ideal woman does not work outside the home but focuses on her responsibilities as mother and housewife. Mothering and nurturing are considered women's natural roles. Even in recent times, while women are increasingly participating in paid labor, women still view motherhood as their primary identity (Craske 1999). Traditional gender roles and the ideal of motherhood are reinforced by the Catholic Church, which has remained a powerful force across the region. As Mair (1991) states, "Catholic patriarchal dogmas have been the major element in glorifying women as mothers, and thereby confining them to domesticity" (p. 159). Central to Catholicism is the symbol of the Virgin Mary, which reinforces a female ideal of selfless motherhood (Craske 1999).

Cultural attitudes about appropriate behavior for men and women are summarized in the extremes of machismo and *marianismo*. The male ideal, machismo, not only calls for arrogance and sexual aggression in the relations between men and women, but also cultural standards such as having a large family and women staying home are linked to male virility (Craske 1999). The female counterpart, *marianismo*, depicts the female ideal as the selfless mother—morally superior and spiritually strong but submissive to men and therefore dependent, timid, and conformist (Craske 1999). In politics, this refers to "an extremely aggressive or competitive style of speech and a condescending or patronizing attitude towards women" (Franceschet 2001:215). Many people across Latin America believe that to a greater or lesser extent these ideals reflect the biological nature of man and woman (Seitz 1991).

Gender roles and the feminine ideal have structured both women's political exclusion and the forms of their participation. Because politics is viewed as a corrupt arena, women should not participate unless to influence social issues. And when women enter the halls of power, cultural attitudes are not left at the door. For example, in her 1960s study of women in politics in Chile and Peru, Elsa Chaney (1973) found that female politicians often see themselves as *supermadres*, or supermothers, who must manage a particularly large family in the large "house" that is their municipality or country. Chaney (1973) also demonstrated that women were segregated into women's wings within political parties and marshaled into areas that dealt with "appropriate" issues for women, such as education, health, and the general social welfare. More than 40 years later, women have expanded their view of their political role (Furlong and Riggs 1996; Schwindt-Bayer 2006), but the practice of assigning women to committees dealing with social issues continues (de Figueres 2002; Heath et al. 2005).

Democratization and Women's Political Empowerment

With the exception of Cuba and Haiti, citizens across Latin America are currently living under democratic or semidemocratic administrations (Freedom House 2006). But for much of the region's history, this was not the case. In countries where democracy existed, it was often interrupted by military interventions and rule by brutal authoritarian regimes. Because such regimes place significant limitations on political activism of all types, women seeking political recognition of any type faced substantial barriers (Craske 1999). As Nikki Craske aptly stated, "Women's growing participation has to be understood in the context of a generalized exclusion which has characterized the region's political systems and the long-term struggle for democracy" (p. 3).

Across Latin America, transitions from **military authoritarianism** to democracy did not proceed smoothly but were fueled by popular protest, guerrilla warfare, and revolution. And in each of these forms of struggle, women played key roles. By the late 1970s, across the region, "women of all social classes defied their historical exclusion from things political and joined the opposition in unprecedented numbers" (Sternbach, Navarro-Aranguren, Chuchryk, and Alvarez 1992). For example, following the 1973 military takeover of Chile and the murder of as many as 30,000 people within the first few months, women were the first to mobilize against the repression (Chuchryk 1991; Noonan 1995).

But Chile is far from an isolated case. In Argentina, a group of women who came to be known as Las Madres de la Plaza de Mayo marched weekly, wearing white headscarves that were embroidered with the names of missing relatives (Craske 1999:119). Also in military-ruled Brazil and Uruguay, women were internationally known for their participation in human rights struggles (Alvarez 1994; Sternbach et al. 1992). For an example of women's revolutionary participation, see Box 8.2, which discusses women's roles and hardships in the overthrow of Nicaragua's brutal Samoza regime.

Paradoxically, it was women's confinement to the singular role of motherhood that often empowered them to organize against the human rights violations of authoritarian governments. "After all, they were only being 'good' wives and mothers searching for the thousands of beloved family members who disappeared" (Noonan 1995:95). As an identity that crosses ethnicity and class, the ideal of motherhood allowed women to unite against oppression (Craske 1999). To describe this pattern, Alvarez (1990, 1994) coined the term *militant motherhood*.

The very notion that women were apolitical also allowed them to undermine authoritarian regimes. As Chuchryk (1991:156) stated, "It was precisely women's traditional public invisibility which allowed them to become political actors during a time when it was extremely dangerous for anyone to do so." In places where public meetings were banned, women could meet in groups because their interaction was perceived as "harmless gossiping" (Craske 1999:119).

Furthermore, the Catholic Church, which has served to restrict women to traditional gender roles, legitimized their participation in social and political struggles (Mair 1991). Throughout Latin America during the 1960s and 1970s, sectors of the Church aligned against the military regimes and supported women's organizing (Jaquette 1994). Women's participation was in line with a Christian ideal of womanhood, which called for a focus on improving family welfare or defending life. And, as Craske (1999:126) noted, "it was difficult for partners, parents and the authorities to criticize women for participating in something endorsed by the Church."

This space for women's resistance within authoritarian regimes and the backing of their struggle by the Catholic Church do not mean that women were safe from regime persecution. Women participated in resistance movements often to their own peril. Women were taken as political prisoners, raped, tortured in front of their own children, and murdered (Jaquette 1994). In one example, Rogelia Cruz, named Miss Guatemala in 1963 and a delegate to the Miss Universe pageant in 1959, was captured by the army and tortured for her participation in the resistance movement—her breast was cut off, and she was beaten severely with a rifle. In some instances, babies born to female prisoners were even taken away and given to couples with close ties to the military elite (Jaquette 1994).

In sum, the factors that have excluded women from politics in Latin America—the Catholic Church, the ideal of motherhood, and authoritarian regimes—have been the very same factors that have enabled their political participation. So what are the ultimate consequences of these political contradictions? On one hand, there are increasing numbers of female politicians who challenge traditional ideas about women's political participation. For example, Beatriz Paredes in Mexico and Julia Alsogaray in Argentina have not married and become mothers but pursue a political career full time. But stereotypes about women in politics persist. For example, Argentinian Senator Graciela Fernandez Meijide stated that many male politicians "still saw her as 'Mrs. Mop,' there to clean up politics" (Craske 1999:13).

For the Catholic Church, there remain clear boundaries of appropriate involvement for women. So though women are making their way into the political arena,

> this has not implied an erosion of gender roles as such; rather it has required a redefinition of women's place within society as a whole, one which has added on to, rather than eliminated their traditional gender responsibilities, while leaving men's largely untransformed. (Molyneaux 1998:222, footnote 7)

Like in Eastern Europe, for many women, political participation simply means a triple burden that follows productive and domestic tasks (Craske 1999).

Over the last few decades, countries across both Eastern Europe and Latin America have experienced massive political change. Yet women seeking formal political representation in the new democracies of Latin America have enjoyed greater success than women in Eastern Europe, where in most countries, women continue to struggle to make appreciable gains. Why were democratic transitions in Latin America more favorable for women's political incorporation than transitions in Eastern Europe and Central Asia? One explanation is simply women's mobilization. Whereas women across Latin America marched, demonstrated, and fought in guerrilla movements to topple authoritarian regimes (Craske 1999), women across Eastern Europe were not an organized force (Waylen 1994). Therefore, not only were women politicized in the democratic transitions in Latin America, but also, once regimes toppled and democratic institutions began to form, women were better positioned to press for their inclusion.

Gender quotas are another important piece of women's political advancement in the Latin American region. As discussed in Chapter 5, Argentina was the first country in the world to adopt an electoral law quota (Jones 1998). Remember that electoral law quotas apply to all political parties in a country, rather than just select political parties. Countries throughout Latin America followed the Argentinean example and established electoral law quotas, including Bolivia, Brazil, Colombia, Costa Rica, the Dominican Republic, Ecuador, Mexico, Panama, Paraguay, Peru, and Venezuela (International Institute for Democracy and Electoral Assistance 2006). Although electoral law quotas can be found around the world, they are most concentrated in Latin America.

Box 8.1   Daughters of the Revolution:
Women in Politics in Nicaragua

Nicaragua is the largest country in Central America, located between Honduras and Costa Rica. Colonized by Spain in 1524, the country became a sovereign republic in 1838, but then a U.S. protectorate in 1911. Many were opposed to the American presence and sought to expel U.S. forces through guerrilla tactics. But in 1934, General Somoza, the U.S.-trained leader of the Nicaraguan National Guard, had the leader of the guerrilla movement killed and was elected president in fraudulent elections. The Somoza family dynasty ruled Nicaragua for the next 42 years, controlling as much as 40% of the economy and impoverishing the people.

Nicaragua's poor economic situation had severe implications for poor and working-class women. Faced with the inability to support their families, many fathers and husbands abandoned their families. Responsible for the survival of themselves and their children, mothers entered the labor force in large numbers. Nicaraguan women made up a large proportion of the country's agricultural field workers, making them the first to be affected by unemployment, inflation, and shortages. When the Marxist Sandanista National Liberation Front (FSLN) began its first campaign against the Somoza regime in 1974, working-class women were motivated by their economic circumstances to participate in the resistance. But as opposition grew and the Somoza regime became even more oppressive, women of all classes responded to this repression by joining the revolution.

Women were involved in every facet of the opposition movement. They demonstrated on the streets, participated in strikes, fought on the front lines, participated in support tasks, worked undercover in government offices, and helped to hide undercover soldiers and weaponry. By the final offensive in 1979, women made up 30% of the revolutionary army and held important leadership oppositions, commanding everything from small units to full battalions. As revolutionary Amada Pineda recounts, women were also repressed and victimized by Somoza's regime:

> They took us away—seven men and me. I was the only woman. They locked us all together in the same room, in a house they had nearby. . . . They used different kinds of approaches. Sometimes they used torture—they would beat me. Sometimes it was soft talk. When they came to rape me, after a while it was just . . . unbearable. [They] raped me seventeen times. . . . Toward the end, they said they were going to take me up in a helicopter and drop me from the sky. . . . But they didn't. Instead, they took the other prisoners and tortured them in front of me. They beat them. They burned them. They half-buried them in ant hills. After six or seven days of that, they let me go. . . . It was

terribly traumatic. I felt like I smelled bad, and I couldn't get rid of the smell. . . . There are many women in Nicaragua who can tell of the barbarities they've suffered. And many others who didn't live through the nightmares. . . . (Randall 1981:86–90)

The revolution had profound implications on gender relations and women's rights in Nicaragua. The 1987 Nicaraguan constitution was one of the most advanced in Latin America in its recognition of the rights of women, and the Sandinista government granted women increased access to both health care and education. Women's formal political roles also improved—the percentage of women in parliament in 1980 jumped from 11.4% to 21.6%, and, by 1987, 31% of the executive positions in the Sandinista government were held by women.

Still, researchers and country experts agree that the revolution toward gender equality was incomplete. Generally, the continued attempts by the United States to topple the Marxist government hindered its ability to make sweeping changes. And direct opposition by the Catholic Church, failed attempts to organize women in the labor force, and the persistence of traditional attitudes about appropriate male and female behaviors created obstacles to institutionalizing women's equality.

SOURCES: Central Intelligence Agency (2006c), Giriazzo (2004), Inter-Parliamentary Union (1995), Luciak (2001), Randall (1981), and Seitz (1991).

Sub-Saharan Africa

In the past, researchers' depiction of women's political situation in Africa has been grim. Naomi Chazan (1989) summarized:

The female experience in African politics during the past century is . . . one of exclusion, inequality, neglect, and subsequent female consolidation and reaction. Women have neither played a significant part in the creation of the modern state system on the continent, nor have they been able to establish regular channels of access to decisionmakers. (p. 186)

Experts on the region have noted that for many women in Africa, women's political participation has been "little more than an extension of their submissive domestic role" (Geisler 1995:547). Women who attained seats in national parliaments often did so through the women's wings of political parties, which left women marginalized and alienated from the policy formation process. Furthermore, the conservative culture of women's wings often meant that women were expected to reinforce the very traditions that subjugated them. For example, during the 1970s and 1980s, female leaders of the Women's League of the United Independence Party (UNIP) in Zambia worked to assure men that women's participation in the political realm was, in fact, not a challenge to male authority and that they still sought to serve their husbands. This pattern meant that young professional women seeking empowerment often rejected formal political membership and instead joined or formed civic associations (Geisler 1995).

In recent decades, however, this picture has been changing. Since 1960, no region has experienced a rate of increase in women's political representation higher than in sub-Saharan Africa, which jumped from 1% in 1960 to 14.3% in 2003 (Tripp 2003). Rwanda now leads the world in women's parliamentary representation, and 4 other countries in the region are among the top 20 (Inter-Parliamentary Union 2006a). This change is fueled in large part by gender quotas (see Chapter 5). Approximately 20 countries across sub-Saharan Africa have adopted gender quotas, and most take the form of reserved seats (International Institute for Democracy and Electoral Assistance 2005; Tripp 2003). Only a few political parties in the region have voluntarily adopted quotas; exceptions include the African National Congress (ANC) in South Africa and Front for the Liberation of Mozambique (FRELIMO) in Mozambique, both of which emerged from struggles for national liberation (Ballington 2004). Map 8.2 displays women's representation across the countries of sub-Saharan Africa.

As women's political representation in countries in sub-Saharan Africa increases, researchers can both test theories developed for Western Europe in the African context and explore new topics or paths to political power. Recent research on gender and politics in Africa has focused on a range of matters, such as armed conflict, civic participation and activism, colonial history, democratization, development, electoral systems, ethnicity and intersectionality, gender quotas, and the impact of women's political representation on government policy (Ballington 2004; Bauer 2004; Britton 2001, 2003; Fallon 2003; Goetz and Hassim 2003; Hassim 2004; Hughes 2004, 2005; Johnson et al. 2003; Lindeke and Wanzala 1994; Pankhurst 2002; Tripp 2001, 2003; Waylen 1996; Yoon 2001). Although we do not explore all of these topics in detail—we limit our discussion to the lasting effects of colonialism and issues of ethnicity, nationalism, and intersectionality—it is clear that research on women in politics in Africa is burgeoning.

No discussion of the political situation in Africa today can occur without first acknowledging the enormous effects of European intervention in the region through colonialism. By the late 1800s, the "scramble for Africa" was underway as European powers, such as England, France, Spain, and Portugal, sought to conquer and rule indigenous societies across the African continent. European governments imposed foreign political and legal

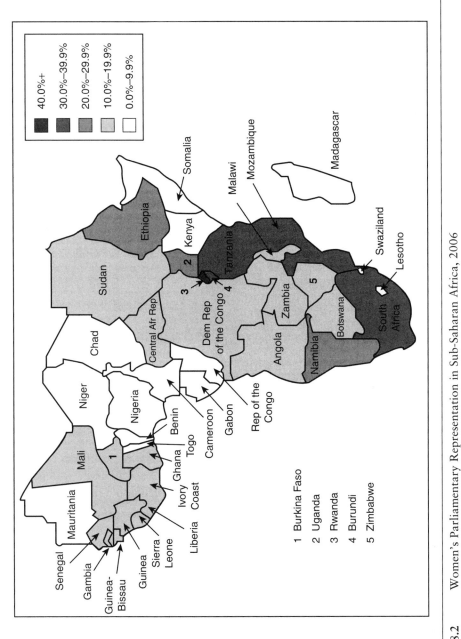

Map 8.2   Women's Parliamentary Representation in Sub-Saharan Africa, 2006

SOURCE: Data from Inter-Parliamentary Union (2006a).

Legend:
- 40.0%+
- 30.0%–39.9%
- 20.0%–29.9%
- 10.0%–19.9%
- 0.0%–9.9%

1 Burkina Faso
2 Uganda
3 Rwanda
4 Burundi
5 Zimbabwe

structures, drew arbitrary territorial boundaries, extracted valuable resources, spread disease, and enslaved, slaughtered, evangelized, and attempted to "civilize" indigenous populations. But colonialism was far from uniform across Africa. European powers brought their own distinct ideas about how indigenous cultures should be governed or assimilated, colonies were populated and governed differently, and colonial governments faced varying levels and types of indigenous resistance over time and place. It makes sense, therefore, that colonialism's impact has been both complex and contradictory.

Colonialism undermined women's power and status in Africa relative to their position in precolonial times. In many traditional societies, men and women were not equal, but gender relations were characterized by interdependence—men and women had different but complementary roles (Waylen 1996:50). For example, among the Baule in what is now the Ivory Coast, subsistence was traditionally based on the production of yams and cloth. Although men and women both took part in the production of these items, men initiated the production of yams and controlled their distribution, while women initiated the production of cloth and therefore took responsibility for it (Etienne 1980; Waylen 1996).

But when colonial governments came to power, they fostered export-oriented economies that interfered with the economic interdependence of men and women (Waylen 1996). Not only did European powers limit the extension of important resources such as credit and training in new technologies to men only, but women's workloads also increased as men withdrew from subsistence agriculture to focus on cash crops. Because men became the sole wage earners, women became dependent on men to pay the tax demanded by colonial governments.

Colonialism also brought important legal changes that affected women's power, such as changes in **land tenure**. Property rights were individualized, and women lost their rights to customary land, transforming women from economic partners to the status of laborers in men's fields (Etienne 1980; Waylen 1996). Colonial governments also codified male power over women through separate "customary" legal systems. Men sought to maximize power by exaggerating their authority in traditional arrangements to male colonial administrators, who were willing to assist African men with controlling their women (Barnes 1992:602). Thus, as Martin Channock (1982) strongly emphasized, the customary laws put in place during colonialism are not based on African practices surviving from precolonial times but instead are a product of the colonial imposition.

Women's political roles in traditional societies also often disappeared with the advent of colonialism. For example, in precolonial Ghana, there was a female counterpart to the male "king" called the *omanhemaa*, or queen mother. Not only was the conduct and welfare of the girls and women in the state her direct responsibility, but, "as the authority on kinship relations, she determined the legitimacy of an aspirant to the royal stoolship, or throne, and had the prerogative of nominating the *omanhene* (king), subject to the ratification by a council of elders" (Okonjo 1994:288). Furthermore, if the king had to leave his throne to lead his soldiers into battle, the queen mother ruled the state until his return. When the British took control of the region, however, authorities instituted political structures that defined governance as a male domain. Formal contact between the indigenous states and the Europeans was between Black and White males, isolating women from the state establishment (Okonjo 1994).

African women did not accept their changing circumstances passively. The colonial state was a site of gender struggle, and "some women attempted to use the limited spaces which had opened up to their advantage" (Waylen 1996:68). For example, in the early colonial period, young Swazi women used the colonial courts to bring charges of assault and rape against men (Booth 1992). And in some areas, women benefited somewhat politically. For example, women in colonial Sierra Leone were elected as paramount chiefs in areas where women had never served in positions of formal executive authority (Day 1994). But Day (1994) also argued that this transition to formal chiefship was grounded in women's authority as lineage heads, founders of towns, and secret society officials prior to colonial times, which left them well situated to move into chief positions. For example, in Baoma, the town founder, war champion, and head of the village's prominent people was Madam Nenge. Recognized as chief by the British, her descendants have claimed the right to rule, and her daughter as well as two of her granddaughters held office after her death (Day 1994:489). But overall, this research indicates that women's political position was undermined by the colonial project.

Colonialism may continue to have effects on women's empowerment today through structures established during colonial times. For example, in Zimbabwe, the current school curriculum is modeled on the colonial British education system, which educated girls for domesticity (Gordon 1998). Although the formal curriculum appears gender neutral, girls are expected to focus their education on religion, fashion, fabric, and nutrition, while boys are taught science, geography, history, and mechanical skills. Textbooks are rife with traditional gender stereotypes. In a recent study of textbooks by Brickhill, Hoppers, and Pehrsson (1996), women were represented as "housewives who cook and clean and nag their children and husbands," whereas "the father is the provider and makes important decisions" (quoted from Gordon 1998:55). Thus, decades after reaching independence, the socialization of children is still influenced by colonial history.

Indeed, recent research supports that cultural links between colonies and European powers continue to affect women's political representation to this day. Specifically, Hughes (2005) found that former colonies tend to mirror their former colonial rulers in their current levels of women's parliamentary representation. For example, among the European imperial powers, France has a very low rate of female parliamentary representation at the national level—12%. Former French colonies tend to mirror these low levels—for example, Benin (7.2%), Djibouti (10.8%), and the Ivory Coast (8.5%)—and have lower percentages of women in parliament on average than former Spanish or Belgian colonies (Inter-Parliamentary Union 2006a). Thus, though the era of colonialism has now passed, its impact has extended far past its historical decline.

Although countries in Africa share many features, women in Africa are far from a monolithic group. Christianity and Islam coexist alongside a diverse array of indigenous beliefs. And, across the continent, hundreds of ethnic groups speak distinct languages. Each of these groups has its own relationship to state power, influenced by group resources (including ties to other groups in the region), precolonial and colonial relations, the road to independence, and strategies used by government actors to balance or usurp power. Thus, a woman's religion or ethnicity may exclude her from power even more so than her gender. And the resources and political access of peasant women are clearly different from the resources and access of the privileged women of the urban bourgeoisie. For these reasons, countries in Africa serve as particularly important cases for the study of intersectionality.

It is impossible to discuss ethnic and race relations in Africa without returning to colonialism. European powers often negotiated their borders, drawing country boundaries without regard to the homelands of distinct populations. This meant that single tribal groups were often divided among two or more countries or that traditional enemies were forced to live alongside each other with no buffer between them. Furthermore, European powers often sought to dominate indigenous populations by privileging one group or class over another. Different ethnic groups received different levels of education, training, and employment, and they were often allotted different political roles. This practice fostered hatred and mistrust between ethnic groups that was not present prior to colonization. Perhaps the most devastating example of this practice occurred in Burundi and Rwanda, where ethnic tensions between Tutsis and Hutus nourished under German and Belgian colonialism eventually gave rise to the ethnic genocide of 1994 (see Box 6.1 in Chapter 6).

As the women and men in colonial societies fought for independence, group identities were formed that continue to influence racial and ethnic relations in Africa today. Specifically, the struggle of a people to define themselves and fight for self-rule generates **nationalism**. Nationalism is a political belief that groups bound by common ethnicity, language, or values have the right to self-govern within an independent territory. The relationship between women and nationalism is quite controversial (Jayawardena 1986; Moghadam 1994). On the one hand, Bystydzienski (1992:209) argued that nationalism has "empowered millions of women . . . created pride in indigenous cultures, a demystification of innate superiority of foreign oppressors, and a recognition of community." Yet, on the other hand, in nationalist struggle women are often constructed as the symbolic form of the nation, whereas men are represented as the nation's chief agents (Pettman 1996). This means that when statehood is achieved, men emerge as the major beneficiaries (Wilford 1998). There is no acknowledgment of women's greater economic and political roles prior to the colonial imposition, nor of their role in the independence struggle. Women face an uphill battle to be recognized as political actors, and "male politicians who had consciously mobilized women in the struggle, push them back into their 'accustomed place'" (Jayawardena 1986:259; Pankhurst 2002).

On the other hand, as we discussed in Chapter 6, when ethnic conflict becomes armed conflict and topples governments, women's political representation may subsequently increase. Women are often perceived as consensus builders and capable of crossing ethnic divides. The use of representative legislative bodies in postconflict situations to further reconciliation and prevent future outbreaks of ethnic violence may also benefit minority women in particular. One such example occurred in Burundi (see Box 8.2).

Box 8.2   Gender, Ethnicity, and Intersectionality in Burundi's National Assembly

A former Belgian colony, Burundi achieved independence in 1962. Similar to Rwanda, Burundi has three major ethnic groups—Hutu, Tutsi, and Twa—which have been in conflict with one another since independence. As part of the peace process to resolve the long-running civil war, a power-sharing quota system was put in place in the national legislature and the cabinet to ensure that the three ethnic groups each have political representation. The majority Hutus are allotted 60% of seats in the lower house, the minority Tutsi are allocated 40% of the seats, and three seats are reserved for Twa representatives.

But because there is also a national-level quota requiring 30% women, Burundi must balance both the ethnic and gender composition of its national legislature simultaneously. To ensure the proper breakdown by ethnicity and gender, all candidates compete on equal footing for 101 seats, but additional

(Continued)

(Continued)

seats are added to produce the right numbers. Following the 2005 election, 18 seats were added to balance the numbers of women and minorities.

Because Tutsi or Twa (minority) women can meet both the ethnic and gender requirement while filling only a single seat, the combination of ethnic and gender quotas has increased their political numbers. In fact, of the female members of Burundi's National Assembly, 57% are minorities (Tutsi or Twa), and of the 18 added positions, more than half are minority women. But the greater participation of Tutsi and Twa women has meant that Hutu women are underrepresented. Hutu women make up more than 40% of the population, but they only hold 14% of the seats in the assembly.

The case of Burundi challenges the assumption that when women enter national politics, they are likely to be of the dominant racial, ethnic, or religious group. If majority group men are attempting to hold on to power, the ability of minority women to improve the statistics for both women's and minority representation simultaneously makes them attractive candidates. In sum, where both gender and ethnic quotas exist together, women from minority groups may benefit politically.

SOURCES: Burundi Parliamentary (2006), Central Intelligence Agency (2006a), and Inter-Parliamentary Union (2006a).

Ultimately, women's governance or political power may be especially important in countries across Africa. To begin, "discriminatory statutory, customary, and religious laws still pose significant obstacles to women" in this region (Yoon 2001:170). But further, the region faces a range of other problems—civil war, escalating debt, ethnic genocide, government repression, HIV/AIDS, infant mortality, poverty, and starvation, to name just a few. Therefore, not only are women's voices necessary to deal with discriminatory legislation against women, but also increasing female representation may allow women to join the ongoing effort to solve these intractable issues.

Asia and the Pacific Islands

Addressing women's political experiences in Asia and the Pacific is an important task if only because of sheer numbers. As of 2003, more than three billion people occupied the region—roughly half the world's population—and 5 of the 10 most populous cities in the world were located in China, India, Pakistan, and South Korea (United Nations 2004). China, India, and Japan also have the second-, third- and fourth-largest economies in the world today, and they continue to grow rapidly.

Countries in Asia and the Pacific have, on average, one of the worst records for women's parliamentary representation, better only than the Middle East and North Africa. As of 1998, women held only 5.9% and 3.9% of cabinet positions in Asia and the Pacific, respectively (Reynolds 1999). And even where women turn out to vote in elections in high numbers, they may refuse to vote for female candidates. For example, Quirina Tablo, a 65-year-old mother of nine from the Philippines, "has seldom missed voting in an election. But her candidates of preference have always been men because she believes that 'politics is not for women'" (Mission 1998).

But women have made gains politically in recent years. In 1997, women's share of seats in the National Assembly of Laos rose from 9.4% to 22.4%, and during the 1990s women's parliamentary representation in Mongolia more than doubled (Paxton, Hughes, and Green 2006a). Perhaps the most obvious change has been in Afghanistan, where, prior to 2005, women peaked at 3.7% of parliamentary seats but now hold the highest percentage of seats in the region—27.3%. Furthermore, although women's parliamentary representation in Asia and the Pacific is generally low, there is still a good deal of variation across countries. As of February 2006, Afghanistan, Vietnam, and East Timor each crossed the barrier of 25% women, whereas Nauru, Palau, Micronesia, Solomon Islands, and Tuvalu had elected not even one female parliamentarian.

Women seeking to ascend the political ladder in Asia face many barriers. Similar to other regions of the world, women's exclusion from the public realm is justified by a number of ideas about culture, tradition, and "natural" gender roles. Women's subordination is further deemed necessary to privilege Asian or Confucian values and reject the individualistic feminism imported from the West. Women also face a range of structural barriers that contribute to their disadvantaged status and marginalization:

- In Afghanistan, violations of women's human rights remain widespread. Women face forced marriage, domestic abuse, abduction and rape, honor killings, and "daily discrimination from all segments of society as well as by state officials" (Amnesty International 2005).
- Women in Fiji and Samoa have the highest suicide rate in the world. Suicide, usually by ethnic-Indian women, has become Fiji's biggest killer (UNIFEM 2005). Forty-one percent of the suicides reported in 1992 were related to domestic violence (Dutton 1992).
- Although women in Japan comprise about 34% of nonmanagerial positions in the workforce, they hold only 3% of director positions and 5% of section manager positions (Japanese Ministry of Health, Labour, and Welfare 2005).
- In Bangladesh, the average age at first marriage for women is 14 years (Haub and Cornelius 2000).

- In Vietnam, the practice of *Doi moi* means that women's spare time must be dedicated to income generation, not involvement in public life. Women's political participation is therefore effectively hampered not by any specific government policy prohibiting their involvement, but by their lack of time (Yarr 1996).

With these obstacles to women's equality, it is not surprising that women across the region struggle to obtain positions of political power.

Although we speak of Asia and the Pacific as a single region, the 36 countries we discuss are quite different, incorporating both religious and secular societies, highly industrialized states and poor agricultural nations, a diverse array of political systems, and multiple distinct civilizations. Thus, unlike the other regions, we cannot present a unified theme explaining women's political representation across Asia and the Pacific. Instead, we introduce cultural, structural, and political factors that affect some, but not all, of the countries in the region.

To begin, we might expect that women's representation in national legislatures and their presence in positions of national leadership, such as president or prime minister, would go hand-in-hand. Asia belies such a conclusion. In Asia, women have low numbers in national legislatures and government ministries, but multiple women from political families have reached positions of national leadership. In fact, as pictured in Figure 8.2, the region has the largest number of countries in which women have served in national leadership. As we noted in Chapter 3, Sri Lanka was the first country to elect a female head of government in 1960. Since then, Bangladesh, India, and Pakistan have elected female prime ministers, and Indonesia, the Philippines, and Sri Lanka have elected female presidents. Three of these countries have even been led by more than one female leader.

Remember, however, that many female leaders act as a surrogate for their politically powerful husband or father. Although this phenomenon is not unique to Asia, the importance of family connections for women's political empowerment is particularly prevalent. Of the region's nine powerful heads of government to date, three were wives and six were daughters of politically powerful men. For example, Gloria Macapagal-Arroyo, current president of the Philippines, is the daughter of former Philippine President Diosdado Macapagal. She has stated that her role model is her father, and her living role model is Corazon Aquino, former president of the Philippines, who was the wife of assassinated opposition leader Benigno Aquino, Jr.

And, although ascension to national leadership but lack of substantial political representation is a pattern that is common across Asia and the Pacific, it does not hold for all countries. For example, in China the pattern is inverted. Although 36% of Chinese officials are women and women hold 22% of seats in the National People's Congress, few women hold positions of senior leadership. There is only a single Politburo member and one female state councilor (United Nations Development Programme 2004b). Wu Yi, a female member of the Central Committee of China's Communist Party and Minister of Health from 2003, was identified as the second most powerful woman in the world in *Forbes* in 2005. Overall, the pattern of women in politics in China more closely resembles Eastern Europe prior to the 1990s than most Asian countries today.

But unlike in Eastern Europe, women in China and other Asian countries are affected by the philosophy of Confucianism. Although sometimes thought of as a religion, Confucianism is an ethical and philosophical system developed from the Chinese sage Confucius. The Confucian tradition has had tremendous influence on the history of the Chinese civilization and therefore a number of countries in Asia, including China, Japan, the Koreas, Vietnam, and Singapore.

Under Confucianism, women at every level are to occupy a position lower than men. The following statements are popular sayings (see Women in World History 2006), quotes from Confucian philosophers, and remarks attributed to Confucius himself:

- "A woman ruler is like a hen crowing."
- "Women are to be led and to follow others."
- "The woman with no talent is the one who has merit."
- "Disorder is not sent down by Heaven, it is produced by women."
- "Man is honored for strength; a woman is beautiful on account of her gentleness."
- "Women's nature is passive."
- "A woman should look on her husband as if he were Heaven itself, and never weary of thinking how she may yield to him."

The Confucian *Book of Rites* presents an ideal model that women were supposed to follow in traditional China: "The woman follows (and obeys) the man: in her youth, she follows her father and elder brother; when married, she follows her husband; when her husband is dead, she follows her son" ("The Single Victim at the Border Sacrifices" 1885).

As we discussed in Chapter 4, when a culture dictates that women are subordinate to men and should follow the opinions of their husbands and fathers, they are less likely to be politically active. Simultaneously, in culturally hostile environments, the few women who are politically active are not taken seriously by political leaders or regular citizens. Therefore, Confucian ideals can suppress women's political participation and representation.

Another feature of a number of Asian countries is their rapid and recent **modernization**. As discussed briefly in Chapter 4, theorists have long asserted that the forces of economic modernization would inevitably liberate women. As societies transition from "traditional" to "modern," standards of living rise, giving women more free time, and individuals move to the cities, undermining traditional extended kinship systems that oppress women. Further, increased access to education and labor force participation provide women with more individual resources and autonomy.

Yet Asia helps one understand that economic modernization and industrialization are not sufficient for women's political power. Across a range of newly industrializing countries, such as those in Asia, as women entered the labor force they were often relegated to low status and unskilled positions, and new agricultural techniques were dominated by men, marginalizing women in agricultural production as well (Boserup 1970; Horton 1995; Ward 1984). Thus, we must make a distinction between jobs that provide skills and resources to women and jobs that exploit women for the low cost of their labor. Can women translate their labor force participation into political capital? Are women simply working too many hours to find the time to participate politically? Women's factory labor across Asia may boost women's labor force participation rates, but such work roles are unlikely to supply women experience or skills that will benefit them politically (Kunovich and Paxton 2005).

As the most economically developed country in the region, Japan demonstrates that national wealth and economic power do not necessarily foster women's political participation. Japan has one of the lowest levels of women in parliament, arguably the worst in the developed world. As of February 2006, only 28 of 164 countries surveyed had lower levels of women's representation than Japan. So in this truly industrialized and modernized country, what explains women's poor political performance? It is likely a combination of both cultural and political factors (see Box 8.3).

Box 8.3   How Organizations Matter: The Impact of *Kōenkai* on Women's Political Underrepresentation in Japan

Women all over the world face the same difficulties, the same hurdles. But especially in Japan. Women are not supposed to be outspoken in front of the public. Male members of the labor organization told me, "Please, just stand in front of the audience. If you open your mouth, you are very very radical. But just stand and smile."

—Mariko Mitsui, Alliance of Feminist Representatives in Japan

So why is women's political representation so low in Japan? Researchers have advanced a number of explanations. Some assert that the highly patriarchal culture of Japan prevents women from competing successfully against men. Others cite incumbent advantage, the political dominance of the conservative party, and a lack of female candidates. But recent research has also highlighted a unique combination of characteristics of the political system in Japan that contribute to women's political underrepresentation—namely, strict campaign regulations and strong personal support networks.

In Japan, door-to-door campaigning is prohibited, media advertising is strictly limited, fundraising activities and campaign spending are highly regulated, and even the number of posters and pamphlets that may be distributed is controlled. But organizations provide a loophole through which candidates can interact with the electorate:

> A candidate or election worker may not canvas door-to-door in Japan, but the same worker may go door-to-door visiting members of an organization. The number of campaign mailings is strictly limited, but an organization may provide information on its endorsements to all of its members without state oversight or regulation. (Christensen 2000:31)

Because of this loophole, political candidates invest their time and energy developing personal support organizations, called *kōenkai*. A combination of existing organizations and a candidate's personal contacts, *kōenkai* are the core of political campaigns.

Kōenkai is difficult to develop, but there are a number of ways that an aspiring politician can gain a *kōenkai*, such as inheritance through a politician in the family. But most ways of gaining *kōenkai* exclude women. For example, male politicians often only pass down their *kōenkai* to their sons or sons-in-law, not their daughters or daughters-in-law. Further, it is easier to build a *kōenkai* as a member of a cohesive minority group. Yet in Japan, women as a group are not unified or cohesive. They are divided by other identities, such as social class, religion, and ethnicity. These ideas suggest that women's underrepresentation in politics is a function of both the political environment, which makes personal support networks so important, and the larger cultural context, which makes it difficult for women to build or inherit them.

SOURCES: Christensen (2000), Darcy and Nixon (1996), Inter-Parliamentary Union (2006a), and Public Broadcasting System (2002).

Finally, although much of past research about women in politics has focused on female leaders or grassroots movements, recent developments in Asia have increased attention to local-level governance in the region as well. Whereas women have rarely made inroads at the national level, gender quotas have provided women access to political positions at the local level—for example, in city and village councils (Raman 2002; United Nations 2000b). Gender quotas at the local level have been implemented in India, Bangladesh, and Nepal. For more about the local gender quota adopted for village elections in India, see Box 8.4.

Box 8.4   Women in the *Panchayat*:
Representative Politics at the Local Level in India

Like many societies across the world, Indian culture and tradition dictate that politics is a man's world. Men often tell their wives how to vote, and although a small number of elite women from political families have ascended to political leadership, women's political representation at the national level remains among the lowest in Asia. When parties field female candidates, it is often in "losing" constituencies, where the party does not expect to win the contest and therefore does not wish to "waste" a male candidate. Of those few women who have successfully won seats at the national level, most are women from privileged backgrounds, leaving poorer women from lower castes without representation.

Despite these obstacles at the national level, women of all backgrounds have made inroads at the local level of government. In 1992, India amended its constitution to revitalize the village government system, or *Panchayat Raj*. The new system requires that marginalized castes and tribes be represented in proportion to their population and that one third of seats must be reserved for women. The 30% gender quota applies to seats for both dominant and marginalized groups, to all three tiers of the new local government structure—the village cluster, block, and district—and to both member and chairperson positions (Raman 2002). In the first elections after the new legislation came into effect, nearly one million women entered local political institutions, shattering the myth that Indian women are fundamentally disinterested in the political process (Raman 2002). Since then, women in some regions have even achieved numbers beyond what is required by law, such as in Karnataka, where women hold 43.6% of *panchayat* seats, and in Manipur, where women comprise a full 50% of the chairperson positions in the *Zilla Panchayats*.

Research suggests that women's entrance in significant numbers to these bodies have allowed them to challenge men and alter the political agenda (Raman 2002; United Nations 2000b). Women's priorities have included issues such as alcohol abuse, domestic violence, education, health, and water. The *panchayat* system is also credited with affecting women and society in positive ways beyond the policy-making arena, including improvements in women's self-esteem and small but significant changes in gender roles. Women's incorporation into local government has also empowered women from different sectors of Indian society. Although chairperson positions continue to be occupied by women from more well-to-do sectors of society, approximately 40% of women in *panchayats* are from marginalized communities or groups.

Despite these advances, we should not gloss over the continued barriers faced by women seeking political power in India. Men have refused to work with female *panchayat* members, and when women oppose men, they may be subject to physical violence. Female members of lower castes may also face opposition by upper caste women. Furthermore, although national politicians recognized that a democratic mechanism was necessary to give a voice to rural and poor women, extending a gender quota to the national level is a topic of fierce debate. An amendment to establish a 33% quota at the national level was put forth in 1995, but in successive legislative meetings the measure has failed to pass. One often-lodged criticism of the amendment, which is called the Women's Reservation Bill, is that it does not guarantee representation to marginalized minority groups or castes. Thus, critics assert that power would remain in the hands of elites, and female members of parliament would simply be relatives of those already in power. Still, the bill has almost unanimous support from national women's organizations, which continue to exert pressure on male legislators.

Figure 8.5   Women Protest for Passage of Women's Reservation Bill in India, 2005

Photo: From the Press Trust of India Photo Library. Copyright © 2005 by the Press Trust of India. Reprinted by permission of the publisher.

SOURCES: Mathew (2000), Rai (2002), Raman (2002), Shvedova (2002), Stepen (2001), Sumbul (2004), Szyber (2005), United Nations (2000b), and www.feministing.com.

Middle East and North Africa

I do not even think it is necessary for us to talk about being in politics as women, we must do our work and do it well—showing our strength through our work and thereby saying here we are, reckon with us.

—Farkhanda Hassan, member of the ruling
National Democratic Party in Egypt (Karam 1999)

Across the Middle East and North Africa, women are still struggling for the most basic of rights. In Saudi Arabia, women cannot drive, and in Lebanon proof of education is required for a woman to vote. Women have won battles to extend their rights in recent years, such as in Kuwait, where women were finally granted suffrage in 2005 (see Chapter 2, Box 2.5). Generally, however, women's political situation in the region is grim. Women hold only approximately 6% of parliamentary seats (Inter-Parliamentary Union 2006b) and less than 3% of ministerial positions (Reynolds 1999), and only one woman has led her country as the head of government, Golda Meir of Israel. Viewed pictorially and especially in contrast to Western Europe (Map 8.1), the low levels of women's parliamentary representation in the Middle East and North Africa are striking (Map 8.3).

In the minds of many people in the West, Arab culture and Islamic fundamentalism dominate the Middle East and North Africa. And both are conceived as oppressive to women. But there are several populations that live in this region that are not Arab either by ethnic or linguistic definition. Examples include the Berbers of North Africa and the Kurds of Iraq, Syria, and Turkey. There are also three countries in the region that are not predominantly Arab: Israel, Iran, and Turkey. In addition, Islam is not a singular cultural force. There are two major schools of thought in Islam, Sunni and Shi'a, and there are more than 150 distinct sects. Major divisions include the Wahhabis or Salafis (mostly in Saudi Arabia), the Ibadhi (mostly in Oman), and the *ijtihadists,* or liberals. There are also religions linked to Islam, such as the Druze and the Alawites (mostly in Syria). Furthermore, a number of other religious beliefs persist in the region, most notably Judaism and Christianity.

As discussed in Chapter 4, these other religions are not necessarily helpful to women's quest to attain political power. For example, from the early 1980s until recently, there were no women Knesset members representing religious parties. And, after a national law requiring 25% women in the Knesset was defeated in 1999, the minister of justice explained that it would

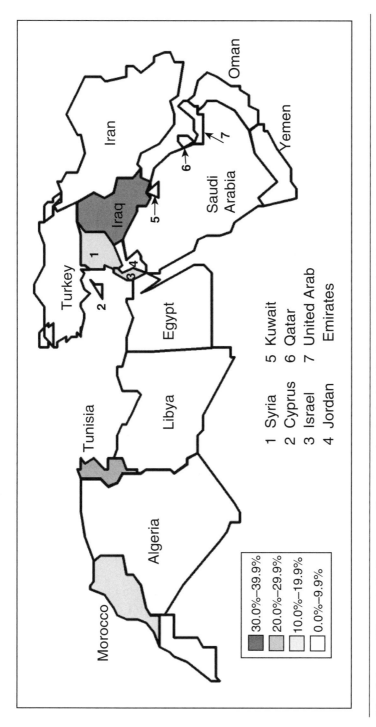

Map 8.3   Women's Parliamentary Representation in the Middle East and North Africa, 2006

SOURCE: Data from Inter-Parliamentary Union (2006a).

be "an impossible requirement, in light of the entirely male constituency of the religious parties in the Knesset" (Halperin-Kaddari 2004:142).

In sum, the peoples, religions, and cultures of the Middle East and North Africa are diverse, and one should resist overgeneralizing about the region and its women. As Karam (1999:5-6) effectively puts it:

> In much of western popular imagination, the Arab world is frequently associated with veiled women, men with long beards, religious fundamentalism (inevitably Islamic), terrorism, war, and hostage-taking. . . . All together, both the region and its women remain interesting objects of (mis)information. The available statistics reinforce the above images of women's exclusion. And yet, Arab women outnumber men in some countries, and historically, have a long legacy of activism—politically, economic, and culturally.

Many researchers who focus on the Middle East and North Africa stress that, although women have been excluded from formal politics, women have participated in critical ways in a range of informal political activities. First, women are active in **civil society**. Experts estimate that there are thousands of organizations across the Arab world that deal with women's issues. "Assessments of their role in promoting women's political participation differ, but there is overall consensus that . . . they are filling in a vacuum and performing a useful function in mobilizing public opinion and making visible women's issues" (Karam 1999:14). Women have also wielded power in other ways. Judith Tucker (1993) noted: "The political importance of marriage alliances, for example, given that marriage arrangements are often controlled by women, has accorded women considerable power in the sphere of informal politics" (p. xiii).

These caveats aside, women's formal participation in the Middle East and North Africa is the lowest in the world. Why is this the case? To begin, although women's informal activism has been an important force for change across the region, women's struggle for political incorporation has always been set aside in favor of other goals—freedom from colonial rule, the implementation of socialism and Arab nationalism, or democratization and human rights (Karam 1999). Although many feminists in the Arab world are now arguing that it is time to put women's rights first, scholar Azza Karam (1999) found that "there remains a general preference, from a strategic and moral point of view, not to divide the issues" (p. 10). Summarized in the words of a Palestinian legislator: "How are we going to argue for women's rights above all else, when our human right to exist and truly govern ourselves as a people, is denied us?" (Karam 1999:10).

More important, across the region, women's subordination is institutionalized in personal status, or **family laws**, that are often based on Shari'a, or Islamic law (Moghadam 2003; Molyneux 1985a; Shehadeh 1998). Family law regulates marriage, divorce, child custody, inheritance, and division of marital assets. Typically, family law in the Middle East and North Africa is linked to religious law and places women in a subordinate position to men. Valentine Moghadam (2003) explained that "religiously-based family laws reinforce the distinction between the public sphere of markets and governance—which are cast as the province of men—and the private sphere of the family, with which women are identified" (p. 70). Or alternatively, as human rights activist Asma Khadar (quoted in Charrad 2001:5) succinctly stated, "Family law is the key to the gate of freedom and human rights for women."

Although the family laws of the Middle East and North Africa are typically detrimental to women, laws vary across countries in their level of repressiveness. Mounira Charrad (2001) discussed family law and women's status in three countries in North Africa: Algeria, Morocco, and Tunisia. As these countries achieved independence, the relationship between the ascending political elite and tribal kin groupings affected the family laws that were ultimately put in place. Whereas Algeria and Morocco adopted legal systems that limited women's rights, the political elites of Tunisia, to undermine the power of traditional kin elites, established a family legal structure that expanded women's rights. Tunisia's liberal family laws created a climate where women could make political gains more easily. In fact, across all of the Middle East and North Africa, Tunisia is one of only two countries that has crossed the threshold of 20% women in politics.

In addition, the regimes that have held power in the Middle East and North Africa have generally resisted adopting significant quotas for women in parliament. When quotas are adopted, they are often a low level—around 5% to 9%. For example, from 1979 to 1986, a quota reserving 30 of the 360 parliamentary seats was implemented in Egypt; however, women were excluded from competing for the other seats, effectively creating a 92% quota for men. When the quota was revoked, one justification was that, while in office, the women did not affect Egyptian law or women's status. From 1984 to 1987, women only raised five political issues, and none submitted a single draft law (Abou-Zeid 2003). As of 2006, women in Egypt hold only 2% of parliamentary seats.

Tentative quotas have also been adopted in Morocco, where 30 national seats were reserved for women in the 2002 elections. Although this development had profound effects, increasing the percentage of women in the national legislature from 0.7% to 10.8%, the quota is not guaranteed in law. Prior to the elections, the political parties sought to appease the organized women's movement by setting aside the national seats for women (Tahri 2003). But after the elections, the legislature refused to institutionalize the quota in law on the grounds that it would violate the constitution. Furthermore, despite the gains that have been made, women in Morocco remain largely excluded from political power. At the national level, women are excluded from leadership positions—no woman chairs a parliamentary committee—and, at the local level, only 127 women were elected out of a total of 22,944 local council members, or 0.6% (Tahri 2003).

One exception to this pattern is in Iraq, where international influences led to the adoption of a 25% gender quota (Nordlund 2004). Another exception to the political patterns of the region is Israel, which is the region's longest-standing democracy. Four major political parties have adopted gender quotas for women, including the ruling Likud party. With 15% women in their parliament, Israel has one of the highest levels of women's parliamentary representation in the region, second only to Iraq and Tunisia.

Further, unlike other countries in the region in its ethnic and religious composition and culture, Israel presents a particularly interesting case to investigate intersectionality. As a multiparty parliamentary democracy that uses a proportional electoral system, the political system of Israel allows for the representation of minority groups. And in the Israeli parliament, called the Knesset, 11 of the 120 elected members of parliament are not Jewish but Christian, Muslim, and Druze (a distinct religion similar to Islam). Because all 11 current "minority" members are male, Israel seems to fit the pattern that when women gain representation, they tend to be from the dominant ethnic or religious group (Halperin-Kaddari 2004; IDEA 2006; Sharfman 1994). (But for a contrary example, see Box 8.3 on Burundi.)

Overall, across the Middle East and North Africa, there are examples where women are making gains in the formal political arena. However, compared with other regions of the world, these gains have been much smaller, slower, and more prone to reversals. Still, recent trends toward democratization in the region foster hope. Although we know that women's increased political representation under democratic institutions is far from guaranteed, such developments may allow women's organizations to turn their focus from the broader goal of democracy to the plight of women.

9

Middle of the Pack

Women and Politics in the United States

Because the United States leads the world in a number of ways—the largest economy, the most medals in the 2004 Summer Olympic games, and the world's largest foreign aid contributor—many people expect that America should lead the world in gender equality as well. But as we noted in Chapter 1, in terms of women in politics, the United States is far from dominant. In fact, with 15% women in parliament, the United States falls in the middle of the pack.

America's mediocrity is evident in Figure 9.1, which displays the distribution of women in parliaments across the world. The figure also includes examples of countries that have reached particular levels of women's incorporation. So, for example, there are 11 countries that have no women in parliament, and two examples are Kyrgyzstan and Saudi Arabia. Most countries in the world fit in the 10–14% range, and only Sweden and Rwanda have over 40% women. The United States falls in the 15–19% category along with Panama, Uzbekistan, and 30 other countries. The percentage of women in the U.S. Congress is below that of Liechtenstein, a country where women could not vote until 1984.

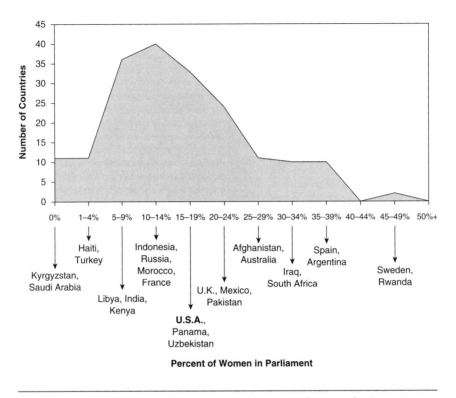

Figure 9.1   Distribution of Women in Parliament With Example Countries

SOURCE: Data from Inter-Parliamentary Union (2006a).

In this chapter, we first discuss women in positions of formal political power—women in the U.S. House of Representatives, and the Senate, women in state legislative bodies, female governors, and women in executive appointed or elected positions, such as members of the president's cabinet. But the vast majority of women in the United States participate in politics more informally. Thus, in the second half of the chapter, we turn to a discussion of women as citizens, voters, or activists, focusing on the gender gaps that exist between men and women.

Women in the U.S. Senate and House of Representatives: Growing Slowly

One place to start to understand women in U.S. politics is to look at how they have improved their representation in the U.S. House and Senate over time. Make no mistake, women are still terribly underrepresented—only

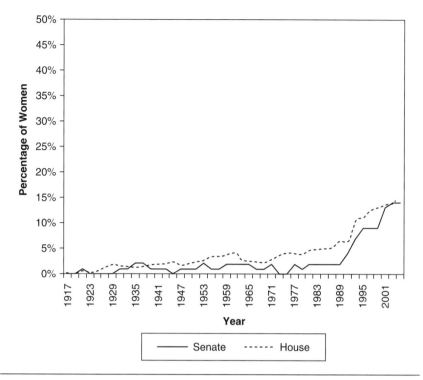

Figure 9.2   Percentage of Women in Congress, 1917–2005

14% of the Senate and 15% of the House today. But Figure 9.2 shows that these percentages are a marked improvement from even 20 years ago. And of course, Nancy Pelosi was recently elected Speaker of the House, a position that places her third in the line of succession to the presidency.

From the first woman elected to U.S. Congress, Jeannette Rankin in 1917, women slowly increased their numbers in the House until about 1990. By *slowly*, we mean that women did not hold even 5% of the House of Representatives until 1981. After 1981, women continued to slowly increase their numbers until the 103rd Congress (1993–1995), when their numbers increased dramatically, nearly doubling from 6% to 11%.

Before continuing with statistics on women's low numbers in the U.S. Congress, it is worth pointing out that it was not always smooth sailing for female representatives, especially when they were few in number. In 1972, Pat Schroeder was elected to represent the people of Denver in the House of Representatives. Soon after her arrival, she was appointed to the Armed Services Committee, along with a Black legislator, Ron Dellums. Their appointment occurred over the strong opposition (and attempted veto) of the committee's chairman, F. Edward Hebert. Despite their apparent appointment victory, Dellums and Schroeder arrived for their first House Armed Services Committee meeting to find a surprise. Pat Schroeder recounted:

> [Hebert] announced that while he might be unable to control the makeup of his committee, he could damn well control the number of chairs in his hearing room. . . . He said that women and blacks were worth only half of one "regular" member, so he added only one seat to the committee room and made Ron and me share it. Nobody else objected, and nobody offered to scrounge up another chair. (Schroeder 1998:40)

Rather than make a scene, the two sat together "cheek to cheek," and participated in the committee meeting.

Returning to impartial numbers, a similar pattern of slow growth in women's representation appears in the Senate. Between 1917 and 1991, women never held more than 2% of the Senate. Even as late as 1977, women were sometimes not represented in the Senate. But in 1992, women's numbers in the Senate doubled to four women, and in 1994 almost doubled again reaching seven. Women's percentage of seats in both the House and Senate continues to rise, although they continue to be far lower than women's percentage of the general population.

Why the sudden shift after 1992? Most observers explain it with two words—Anita Hill. As discussed in Chapter 1, on October 6, 1991, 2 days before the Senate was scheduled to vote on the nomination of Clarence Thomas to the Supreme Court, a distinguished law professor, Anita Hill, accused Thomas of sexually harassing her in 1981. During the televised Senate judiciary hearings that followed, Americans saw a panel of White men questioning the validity of a Black woman's claims. Angered by the hearings, unprecedented numbers of women were spurred to run for political office. As explained by Barbara Boxer: "America, and in particular, American women, were uncomfortable with the way the whole issue was handled, were uncomfortable with the way the Senate looked—and the Anita Hill incident became a catalyst for change" (Boxer 1994:39–40).

But though women are generally underrepresented, there are differences across states in the percentage of women they send as part of their **congressional delegation**. For example, in the 109th Congress (2005–2007), California sent 19 women, out of 53 delegates (36%), to the House of Representatives, and 2 women were elected to both of California's seats in the Senate. Michigan sent 2 women, out of 15 delegates, to the House (13%) and 1 woman, out of 2 delegates, to the Senate. None of Massachusetts's 12 delegates (10 to the House and 2 to the Senate) are women.

But Massachusetts is not alone. Overall, 19 states currently have no women as part of their delegation: Alabama (9), Arizona (10), Delaware (3),

Hawaii (4), Idaho (4), Iowa (7), Kansas (6), Massachusetts (12), Mississippi (6), Montana (3), Nebraska (5), New Hampshire (4), New Jersey (15), North Dakota (3), Oklahoma (7), Rhode Island (4), South Carolina (8), Utah (5), and Vermont (3).

The majority of these female national legislators has been White, but some women of color appear in Washington. Early pioneers began to take office in the 1960s. In 1968, Shirley Chisholm (Democrat from New York) was the first Black woman elected to the House of Representatives. And Patsy Mink, elected from Hawaii in 1964, was the first Asian American woman in Congress. Republican Ileana Ros-Lehtinen was the first Hispanic woman in Congress. She was elected in 1988 and continues to serve today. Carol Moseley Braun, a Democrat from Illinois (1993–1999), was the only woman of color to ever serve in the U.S. Senate.

In 2006, all Senate women were White. But a quarter of the women in the House of Representatives (20 total) were Black, Asian American, or Hispanic. The distribution of women of color across the two parties is uneven—of these 20 women of color in the House, 95% (19 of 20) are Democrats (Center for American Women in Politics 2006a). Ileana Ros-Lehtinen, mentioned earlier, was the only Republican woman of color in Congress in 2006.

Figure 9.3   Shirley Chisholm, the First Black Congresswoman

SOURCE: Courtesy of the Library of Congress, Prints and Photographs Division.

Before moving on, it is also important to understand that although there are only 20 Black, Asian American, and Hispanic women in the House of Representatives, women of color are more represented within their respective racial groups than are White women. For example, in the 108th Congress, only 12% of representatives in the U.S. House were female, but women were 33% of Black representatives, 29% of Hispanic representatives, and 29% of Asian representatives. And though this is a new area of study, limited evidence suggests that Black women are more likely to run for political office than are White women (Bedolla, Tate, and Wong 2005). One reason may be that Black women tend to have higher levels of political ambition than White women (Darcy and Hadley 1988).

Overall, though their numbers have been small, research suggests that women of color have had a significant impact on Congress. As Bedolla et al. (2005:153) reminded us, "Because of their minority status, blacks, Asian Americans, and Latinas bring to their elective office significantly different experiences from their white female, white male, and minority male counterparts." Although their small numbers make their impact difficult to measure, it is clear that their presence alone challenges stereotypes.

Women in the States

Going by numbers alone, it appears that women have a larger role in state government than at the national level. Compared to the 15% of seats women hold in the U.S. Congress, almost 23% of the state legislators are women. A similar pattern appears in committee leadership. In 2005, no woman chaired a standing committee in the U.S. House of Representatives, and two women chaired committees in the U.S. Senate, but women make up about 19% of committee chairs in state legislatures (Rosenthal 2005). And though no woman has ever served as the country's commander in chief, Nellie Tayloe Ross became the first female governor in 1925. Since Nellie Ross, 27 other women have served in the position of governor, and a woman has been elected to a statewide executive office in every U.S. state except for Maine (Center for American Women and Politics 2006c). Overall, women's political incorporation has proceeded faster at the state level of government.

Women in the State Legislature

There is considerable variation in women's representation across states. For example, in Delaware, Nevada, Vermont, and Washington, at least one third of state legislators are women (Center for American Women and

Politics 2006b). Women in these states have more than four times the share of seats held by women in South Carolina, where women hold only 8.2% of seats. Map 9.1 displays the different levels of women's numbers in state legislatures across the United States (darker shades indicate more women). Women have the highest levels of legislative representation in the West and the Northeast, whereas women are most underrepresented in the South. One surprise in Map 9.1 is Wyoming, which we stated in Chapter 2 is called the Equality State for its status as the first state in which women had the right to vote and hold public office. Wyoming also elected the first female governor, Nellie Ross. Yet women in Wyoming only hold 15.6% of state legislative seats, leaving Wyoming with a rank of 44 out of 50 states.

In addition to considering women's share of legislative seats, we can also look at women's placement in committees and their access to committee leadership positions. As at the national level, state legislatures divide their work into committees that solicit testimony from experts and citizens to prepare or review legislation in a particular area. Committee chairs are the "middle management of state legislatures" (Rosenthal 2005:199).

Where are women in the committee system? As we found internationally in Chapter 3, women in the United States are more likely than their male counterparts to serve on health, welfare, and human services committees (Diamond 1977; Thomas and Welch 1991). But though women continue to serve on these traditional committees, they are increasingly serving on or chairing committees, such as Appropriations, Industry and Commerce, Transportation, Agriculture, and the Judiciary (Darcy 1996; Ford and Dolan 1999). Overall, women hold about 19% of committee chair positions (Rosenthal 2005).

A final outcome to discuss is women's share of top state leadership positions, such as the House Speaker or Minority Leader. Women's representation in top leadership may be especially important because women holding top leadership may be given the responsibility for recruiting women as candidates (Moncrief, Squire, and Jewell 2001). Although women's gains in top leadership have lagged behind their gains in membership, women's portion of these positions is still growing. Women were less than 3% of top leadership two decades ago, and now their numbers are about 14% (Rosenthal 2005). State variation is evident for this outcome as well. Rosenthal (2005) summarized: "Not surprisingly, women leaders are most common in states with a significant number of female members and a higher number of women committee chairs" (p. 199).

Before leaving the topic of women's presence in state legislatures, we must also address the presence of women of color. Box 9.1 and Figure 9.4 provide a contemporary look at intersectionality in U.S. state houses.

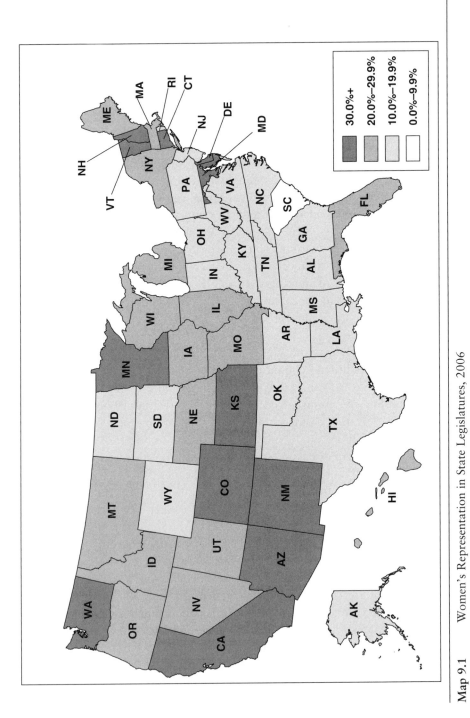

Map 9.1   Women's Representation in State Legislatures, 2006

SOURCE: Data from Center for American Women and Politics (2006b).

Legend:
- 30.0%+
- 20.0%–29.9%
- 10.0%–19.9%
- 0.0%–9.9%

Box 9.1   Intersectionality in State Legislatures

To understand the representation of women of color among female state legislators, we compare their percentage of legislators to their percentage of the population. This provides a way to assess whether women of color are being elected to state legislators in proportion to their numbers in the population. To begin, although Black women hold only 13.5% (see Figure 9.4) of all seats held by women in state legislatures, this percentage is actually slightly larger than the overall percentage of Blacks in the U.S. population—12.3% (Center for American Women and Politics 2006a; U.S. Census Bureau 2001). But the distribution across states is uneven, and in 11 states, there are no Black female state legislators at all. Similarly, the distribution across parties is uneven. Black women hold 226 seats in state legislatures—60 in state senates and 166 in state houses—and 222 (98%) of these women are Democrats.

Asian American women hold 25 seats in state legislatures, and 72% of them are Democrats. They hold seats in eight states with varied percentages of Asian population: Hawaii (where 42% of the state is Asian), California (where 11% is Asian), Washington (6%), Maryland (4%), Minnesota (3%), Texas (3%), Iowa (1%), and South Carolina (1%) (Center for American Women and Politics 2006a; U.S. Census Bureau 2001). Asians make up more than 4% of the population in Alaska, Nevada, New York, and New Jersey, but no Asian American women hold seats in these state legislatures.

There are 19 state senators and 51 state representatives of Hispanic origin, 89% of which are Democrats (Center for American Women and Politics 2006a). Latina state legislators are found in 17 states in all regions of the country. Latinas have representation in all states where Hispanics make up at least 10% of the population, but they are not represented in five Western states where they are a significant minority (more than 6%): Hawaii, Idaho, Oregon, Utah, and Wyoming.

Finally, Native Americans and Alaskans make up less than 1% of the U.S. population. However, they constitute a significant minority in a number of states: Alaska (16%), New Mexico (10%), Oklahoma (8%), South Dakota (8%), Montana (6%), Arizona (5%), and North Dakota (5%). Of these, Native American women are excluded from the state legislature in New Mexico and Arizona. Native American women are present in the Colorado state legislature, where Native Americans make up only 1% of the state population (Center for American Women and Politics 2006a).

Female Governors

We must also consider women's political representation in the executive branch of state government. Of particular importance is the highest executive

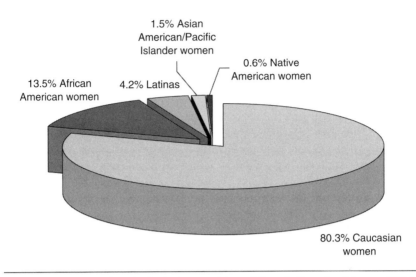

Figure 9.4   Racial and Ethnic Composition of Female State Legislators, 2006

SOURCE: Center for American Women and Politics (2006a).

position at the state level, the governor's office. Governors are key political players because in many states they are responsible for administering, "large annual budgets and major public programs like welfare" (Weir 1999:248). But even in states where the position does not wield much formal power, as in Texas, governors are highly visible, generating name recognition. And in recent decades, the governor's office has been a main route to the American presidency. Jimmy Carter, Ronald Reagan, Bill Clinton, and George W. Bush all were governors before they became presidents. If a woman is ever to become president, one route may be through the governor's mansion.

Women serving in the governor's office may also be important because they may appoint more women to the executive branch, facilitating the political careers of other women. For example, Christine Todd Whitman, a Republican governor from New Jersey, appointed many women to leadership positions, including attorney general, chief of staff, and the executive director of the New Jersey/New York Port Authority (Weir 1999:253).

Similarly, Ann Richards, the Democratic governor of Texas from 1991 to 1995, promised that state government would no longer be the domain of White men. Of her appointees, 20% were Hispanic, 15% were Black, 2% were Asian, and a full 46% were female (Weir 1999). But though female governors may appoint women of color to important positions in their administration, "no woman of color has served as governor of any state" (Center for American Women and Politics 2006a:2).

So what has been women's share of governorships? In 2006, eight states had female governors. Arizona, Delaware, Kansas, Louisiana, Michigan, and Washington elected Democratic female governors, and Hawaii elected a Republican female governor. In addition, M. Jodi Rell, a Republican, was elected Connecticut's lieutenant governor but was sworn in as governor when her predecessor resigned (Center for American Women and Politics 2006d). Table 9.1 provides information about the 28 female governors who have served in the United States throughout its history. Notice that, like the female leaders discussed in Chapter 3 who filled in as political surrogates for their husbands or fathers, the United States has had its share of female governors who succeeded their husbands to power. Women have also often entered the governor's mansion by moving up from lieutenant governor after a resignation.

Women and the American Presidency

Although women have not yet ascended to the presidency in the United States, women's role in the White House to date has instead been as first ladies. Some first ladies have taken active roles in their husband's presidency. For example, in addition to passionately advocating for civil rights, Eleanor Roosevelt worked hard to promote the New Deal for her husband, Franklin Delano Roosevelt. Sixty years later, Hillary Clinton took an even more active role, leading the fight for universal health care by heading a task force on reform and speaking out publicly to advance the cause. But active first ladies also face criticism. Many in Washington disliked Hillary Clinton's active policy role, and when the health care initiative failed, pundits questioned Bill Clinton's decision to place the first lady in such a prominent political role. In contrast to the active roles taken by some first ladies, others have stayed out of the limelight. For instance, Laura Bush has distanced herself from the hazards of policy making more than her predecessor. Laura Bush received press for suggesting that her husband should replace outgoing Supreme Court Justice Sandra Day O'Connor with a woman, but she has avoided any large policy role in George W. Bush's administration.

Scholars sometimes argue that the executive branch is the most masculine branch of government (e.g., Duerst-Lahti 1997). The executive branch is more closely connected to the military than to the other two branches of the government, and the executive branch is more hierarchical in its organization as well. The United States has never had a female president. But there is a general dearth of women in other national-level executive positions as well.

The presidential cabinet administers the branches of the executive and wields substantial power. Examples of cabinet officials include the secretary

Table 9.1   Female Governors Throughout History

Name	Party	State	Dates Served	Special Circumstances
Nellie Tayloe Ross	D	WY	1925–1927	Won special election to replace deceased husband
Miriam "Ma" Ferguson	D	TX	1925–1927, 1933–1935	Inaugurated 15 days after Ross; elected as surrogate for husband who could not succeed himself
Lurleen Wallace	D	AL	1967–1968	Elected as surrogate for husband who could not succeed himself
Ella Grasso	D	CT	1975–1980	First woman elected to governor in her own right
Dixy Lee Ray	D	WA	1977–1981	
Vesta Roy	R	NH	1982–1983	Elected to state senate and chosen as senate president; served as governor for seven days when incumbent died
Martha Layne Collins	D	KY	1984–1987	
Madeleine Kunin	D	VT	1985–1991	First woman to serve three terms as governor
Kay Orr	R	NE	1987–1991	First Republican woman governor and first woman to defeat another woman in a gubernatorial race
Rose Mofford	D	AZ	1988–1991	Elected as secretary of state, succeeded governor who was impeached and convicted
Joan Finney	D	KS	1991–1995	First woman to defeat an incumbent governor
Ann Richards	D	TX	1991–1995	
Barbara Roberts	D	OR	1991–1995	
Christine Todd Whitman	R	NJ	1994–2001	Resigned to take presidential appointment as commissioner of the EPA
Jeanne Shaheen	D	NH	1997–2003	
Jane Dee Hull	R	AZ	1997–2003	Elected as secretary of state, succeeded governor who resigned, later elected to a full term

Name	Party	State	Dates Served	Special Circumstances
Nancy Hollister	R	OH	1998–1999	Elected lieutenant governor; served as governor for 11 days when predecessor took U.S. Senate seat and successor had not yet been sworn in
Jane Swift	R	MA	2001–2003	Elected as lieutenant governor, succeeded governor who resigned for an ambassadorial appointment
Judy Martz	R	MT	2001–2005	
Olene Walker	R	UT	2003–2005	Elected as lieutenant governor, succeeded governor who resigned to take a federal appointment
Ruth Ann Minner	D	DE	2001–	
Jennifer M. Granholm	D	MI	2003–	
Linda Lingle	R	HI	2003–	
Janet Napolitano	D	AZ	2003–	First woman to succeed another woman as governor
Kathleen Sebelius	D	KS	2003–	Father was governor of Ohio
Kathleen Blanco	D	LA	2004–	
M. Jodi Rell	R	CT	2004–	Elected as lieutenant governor, succeeded governor who resigned
Christine Gregoire	D	WA	2004–	

SOURCE: Center for American Women and Politics (2006c). From Center for American Women and Politics (CAWP), *History of Women Governors*. Copyright © 2004 by CAWP. Reprinted by permission of the publisher.

of state, the attorney general, and the secretary of labor. Including Frances Perkins, who was appointed to be the secretary of labor in 1933 by President Franklin D. Roosevelt, 22 women have received 24 cabinet nominations to 11 departments over 8 presidential administrations (statistics updated from Borelli 2002). Over time, women's inclusion in the cabinet has been "characterized by advances, reversals, and hesitations" (Borelli 2002:21). This is evident in Figure 9.5, which shows the maximum percentage of women cabinet secretaries under each president since the Roosevelt administration. Though most presidents since Roosevelt have incorporated

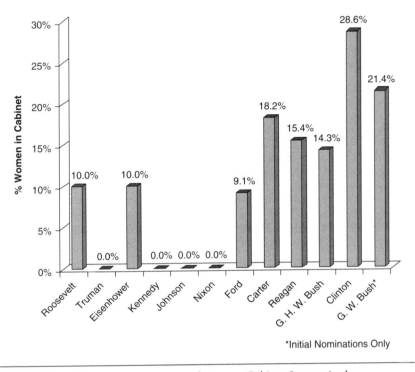

Figure 9.5   Maximum Percentage of Women Cabinet Secretaries by Administration

SOURCE: Data from Borelli (2002:27).

women into their cabinets, Presidents Truman, Kennedy, Johnson, and Nixon had male-only cabinets. On the other side of the spectrum, President Clinton had at one time 28.6% women among his cabinet appointees.

What affects numbers of women in the presidential cabinet? Ultimately, it comes down to the president—members of the cabinet are appointed by, and can be removed by, the president. Consider Richard Nixon, president of the United States from 1969 to 1974, who was captured on tape: "I'm not for women, frankly, in any job. I don't want any of them around. Thank God we don't have any in the Cabinet" (Lithwick 2001). As Nixon explained to his attorney general, "I don't think a woman should be in any government job whatever. I mean, I really don't. The reason why I do is mainly because they are erratic. And emotional" (Lithwick 2001).

Throughout recent American history, women in the U.S. cabinet have often served in positions related to social welfare, health, and education. For example, women were the first secretaries of the Health, Education, and Welfare Department (now Health and Human Services) and the Education Department (Borelli 2002). Some cabinet positions are so often filled with women that they are called the woman's slot (Borelli 2002; Duerst-Lahti 1997). For example, following in the footsteps of Frances Perkins, seven women have been nominated to the position of labor secretary.

But in recent administrations, the appointment of women such as Janet Reno, Madeleine Albright, and Condoleezza Rice to the prominent cabinet posts of attorney general and secretary of state has received a great deal of attention from pundits, the media, and scholars alike. But sometimes the attention is not to their management skills but to their style of dress. In February 2005, Rice received a great deal of press attention for wearing high-heeled boots, described as sexy, or even more boldly, as conjuring the image of a dominatrix (Givhan 2005). Overall, researchers note that women's cabinet nominations have both contradicted and reinforced traditional gender roles.

Scholars tend to agree, however, that as in other countries, women are more often given positions of lesser power. For example, MaryAnne Borelli (2002) argued that women have often served as the secretary of labor during Republican administrations. In those instances, "the nomination of a woman secretary-designate seemed designed more to buffer the president against an otherwise formidable interest than to offer women greater representation in executive policy-making circles" (Borelli 2002:9). Similarly, in the majority of cases, women have been nominated to cabinet positions in areas distant from the president's policy agenda (Borelli 2002:61).

Unlike women's appointment to the U.S. cabinet, women's share of other presidential appointments (e.g., undersecretaries, assistant undersecretaries, and regional directors of various agencies) has grown rather consistently over time (see Figure 9.6). But interestingly, as women's appointments have increased, so has the number of posts to fill, especially in the lower ranks. And women were more likely to take these "expanded positions" rather than higher level positions (Martin 1997:59). Thus, though the Carter and Reagan presidencies had fewer women as a percentage of their total appointees than the Bush or Clinton administration, these earlier presidents appointed more women to the highest level offices—secretary, deputy secretary, and undersecretary (Martin 1997).

A Woman as Commander in Chief?

In ABC's 2006 drama *Commander in Chief,* Geena Davis played MacKenzie Allen, the first female president of the United States. Geena Davis won a Golden Globe award for her performance, and the television show received high ratings from U.S. audiences. But the question remains: Will a woman president only rule on a Hollywood set, or will the United States see a female president in Washington in next 20 years? In the 1960s, feminist Betty Freidan remarked that the thought of a woman president in the United States was so inconceivable it was a joke. And in the following

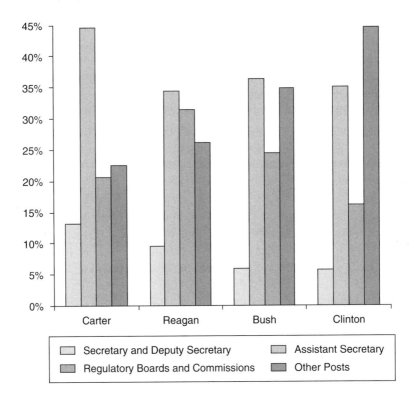

Figure 9.6   Percentage of Appointments Going to Women, 1961–1994

SOURCE: Data from Martin (1997).

decades, few women were true contenders for the position. No woman has ever received either major party's nomination for president of the United States, and only one woman has been nominated to run for vice president.

In the 1984 presidential election, Geraldine Ferraro was selected by the Democratic Party to run for the position of vice president along with presidential candidate Walter Mondale. The pair challenged the incumbents Ronald Reagan and George H. W. Bush, who were ahead in election polls from the start. Ferraro had served three terms in the U.S. House of Representatives before her nomination, but her credibility and her liberalism, rather than her experience, were the focus of greatest criticism. As a Catholic, Ferraro received criticism from the Church for her support of abortion rights, and then during the campaign she refused to release her husband's tax returns, generating controversy. Ultimately, the majority of voters, both male and female, voted against Mondale and Ferraro. Though Ferraro's nomination was a watershed moment for women in politics in the United States, her failure led some to question when a major party will once again be willing to risk supporting a woman.

In recent presidential races, women have sought their party's nomination for president. In 2000, Elizabeth Dole vied for the Republican Party nomination, and in 2004 Carol Moseley Braun, a Black woman, sought the support of the Democratic Party. Although neither of these women were ever front runners, analysts, journalists and pundits argue that women will likely play a much larger role in the 2008 presidential race. Hillary Clinton is considered a top contender, and some speculate that Condoleezza Rice may challenge her on the Republican side.

Women running for president of the United States today have additional support from women's groups. For example, the White House Project, founded in 1998, is a national nonpartisan nonprofit organization that works to elect a woman to the U.S. presidency. The Web site of the White House Project states:

> No one challenges the credibility of a man to run for president whether he is a magazine owner or an evangelist, but if a woman, no matter how well credentialed she is, appears in Iowa or New Hampshire she is questioned about her qualifications. The job of The White House Project is to make it normal for women to show up in Iowa and New Hampshire. Indeed the only way we will be able to select a woman based on her agenda rather than her gender is if we have many women candidates who take up the challenge.

Thus, though the idea of a female president may once have been a joke, the climate for women seeking presidential office in the United States may be changing. As Harriet Woods (2000:215) argued: "Today we're in a new era. We've had a woman secretary of state and a woman attorney general. The question no longer is whether there will be a woman president but who she will be, and the precise date of her inauguration."

Explanations

Why are women underrepresented in U.S. politics? And why have women succeeded in gaining political power in some cities or states and not in others? The explanations for women's political power in U.S. politics parallel those found in cross-national research (Chapters 4 and 5). Women-in-politics researchers postulate that cultural, structural, and political factors matter. Sometimes the explanations sound exactly the same as those used to explain differences across countries. But the United States also has some unique cultural, structural, and political features that influence women's access to power. In this section, we address each broad category of explanation in turn.

Culture

Cross-nationally, research has shown that what people think about women and a woman's place matters for women's ability to attain political power (Norris and Inglehart 2001; Paxton and Kunovich 2003). Similarly, in the United States, if women are considered too emotional or incompetent, they will not be taken seriously as contenders for power. In 1995, one chain of large retail stores pulled girls' T-shirts with the message "Some day a woman will be president" from shelves after a customer complained that the message "goes against family values" (Flynn 1995).

Does the United States have a culture that supports women in politics? Lawless and Theriault (2005), using data from a variety of polls, compiled attitudes about women in politics in the United States from 1937 to 2002. Figure 9.7 tracks two questions about women: "If your political party nominated a woman for president, would you be willing to vote for her if she were qualified for the job?" and "Tell me if you agree or disagree with this statement: Most men are better suited emotionally for politics than are most women."

Figure 9.7 shows that the percentage of Americans willing to vote for a woman for president has risen over time, from a low of 33% in 1937 to over 90% in most of the 1990s. Interestingly, the sharp drop in support for a female president in 2002 may be the result of the increase in true, viable female contenders for president in recent years, such as Hillary Clinton, Carol Moseley Braun, and Elizabeth Dole. It may be easier for Americans to pay lip service to the idea of a woman in the White House than to actually support the efforts of a real woman to get there.

Indeed when a different question is asked, whether the country is ready for a woman to lead the country, 38% of those polled said the country was not ready (CBS News 2006). Interestingly, men were more likely than women to believe the country is ready. Further,

> Younger Americans are also more likely to think America is ready for a woman commander-in-chief. Seniors are actually split on the question: 46 percent do not think the country is ready, while 44 percent say it is. When it comes to politics, 61 percent of Democrats think the country is ready for a woman president, compared to 48 percent of Republicans. Liberals are also more likely than conservatives and moderates to believe America is ready for a woman to be president. (CBS News 2006)

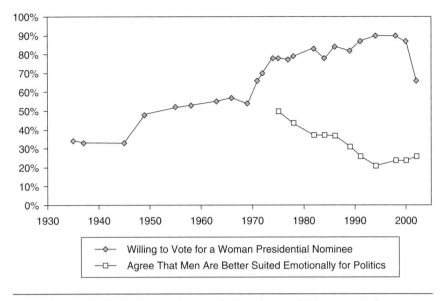

Figure 9.7   Attitudes Toward a Female President and Women in Politics, 1935–2002

SOURCES: Data from Mansbridge (1986) and Lawless and Theriault (2005).

Answers to the other question charted in Figure 9.7, on women's emotional unsuitability for politics, have halved over time, moving from 50% agreement to about 25%. Still, 25% of the population answers in 2002 that men are better suited emotionally to politics. Similarly, in another survey, taken in the late 1990s, 15% of Americans agreed with the statement that "women should take care of running their homes and leave running the country up to men" (Fox and Lawless 2004:270). Thus, though cultural attitudes about women in politics appear to have improved over time, there are still nontrivial numbers of Americans that do not believe women belong in politics—nontrivial numbers that could certainly make a difference in close elections.

Can culture explain differences across U.S. states in the percentage of women in their state legislatures? Researchers have measured cultural differences across U.S. states in a number of ways. The first distinguishes between states and regions with traditionalistic, individualistic, and moralistic political cultures (Elazar 1966). A traditionalistic political culture is believed to exist mainly in the South and stresses elite control of politics and maintenance of the existing social order. The individualistic political culture, found in various U.S. regions, emphasizes politics as a career and the adjudication of competing interests. Finally, a moralistic political culture emphasizes amateur participation in politics and the improvement of the public good. The moralistic political culture is found mainly in the Northwest and Northeast (Darcy, Welch, and Clark 1994:56; Rule 1990).

Women are expected to do worse in traditionalistic political cultures where they are political newcomers to an environment that stresses established elites (Diamond 1977). In contrast, women, with their perceived integrity and concern for public welfare, are expected to do better in moralistic political cultures (Arceneaux 2001:147). Indeed, when researchers compare traditionalistic, individualistic, and moralistic states, states with a "traditional" culture have fewer women in legislative office (Hill 1981; Nechemias 1987) or in executive office (Oxley and Fox 2004). In contrast, states with "moralistic" cultures have more women in legislative office (Arceneaux 2001; Hill 1981; Nechemias 1987).

But, labels aside, political culture measured in this way is really about U.S. regions. Traditional political culture especially is highly correlated with the Southern region. Indeed, when Sanbonmatsu (2002c) considered the impact of political culture and region on women's presence in state legislatures, neither a traditionalistic nor a moralistic culture helped explain women's political representation. In response, some researchers compare women's representation in politically conservative and liberal states. Generally, if the electorate is more conservative, then fewer women are found in state legislatures (Arceneaux 2001; Norrander and Wilcox 2005; Sanbonmatsu 2002c).

Just like comparing across countries, however, the best way to measure cultural differences across states is to directly ask people what they think about women in politics. Kevin Arceneaux ranked states on their citizens' positive views of women in politics using two of the questions discussed earlier: Do you agree that "women should take care of running their homes and leave running the country up to men" and that "most men are better suited emotionally for politics than are women" (Arceneaux 2001:148)?

Map 9.2 presents a map of attitudes toward women in politics, using Arceneaux's (2001:157) state rankings. Darker colors indicate more accepting views of women in politics. The darkest states have attitudes about women that are at least 1 **standard deviation** above the average for all states. The second darkest have attitudes between 0.5 and 1 standard deviation above the average. The lightest states have attitudes at least 1 standard deviation below the average of all states. (Georgia and South Carolina were the only two states with attitudes between 0.5 and 1 standard deviation below the average, so they are combined with the other "average" states.)

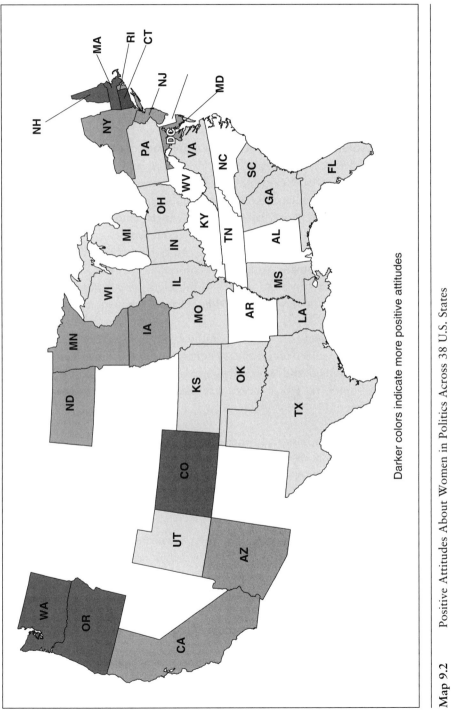

Darker colors indicate more positive attitudes

Map 9.2 Positive Attitudes About Women in Politics Across 38 U.S. States

Map 9.2 suggests that region makes a difference to women in politics. Southern states, those with a traditionalistic political culture, generally have less approving attitudes about women in politics than other regions. The Northwest and Northeast, home of moralistic values, tend toward more lenient attitudes. But even within regions with different political cultures, and across conservative and liberal states, specific attitudes about women in politics make a difference to women's numbers. Arceneaux (2001) found that a moralistic culture, a conservative ideology, and a direct measure of gender-role attitudes are all independently important in explaining the percentage of women in state houses.

Fifteen percent of Americans may say that women should leave running the country up to men. But, looking at male and female candidates, there is little evidence that voters are biased against female candidates in the present. Though there may be pervasive views about women in politics that prevent women from running or winning, most researchers demonstrate that women receive as many votes as men do (e.g., Darcy et al. 1994). In fact, gender does not appear to matter to men, but female voters seem to prefer women as candidates (Dolan 1998; Seltzer, Newman, and Leighton 1997; Smith and Fox 2001).

But stereotyping male and female candidates is still prevalent and can have a more subtle effect on elections. Remember that women tend to be seen as compassionate and honest, whereas men are seen as tough and aggressive (Chapter 3). This concept translates into political issues in the following manner:

> Male candidates are considered better able to deal with foreign policy, the economy, defense spending, arms control, foreign trade, and farm issues; female candidates are considered better able to deal with day care, poverty, education, health care, civil rights, drug abuse, and the environment. (Kahn 1996:9)

So, if voters think that women are better advocates of an issue such as poverty, and they care about that issue, then they tend to support female candidates (Sanbonmatsu 2002a). Further, women tend to select themselves out of running for offices that do not match their stereotypical strengths (Fox and Oxley 2003). And choosing to run in only certain races may be rational—female candidates do better in political races where the issues are stereotypically in their favor (Kahn 1996).

Finally, what about the role of the media? Gender differences in news coverage could exacerbate existing stereotypes about female candidates, or even create new ones. The media can certainly play a powerful role in politics by shaping what citizens know and even what they think is important. Kim Fridkin Kahn studied how the news media respond to male and female candidates for statewide offices. In both U.S. Senate campaigns and gubernatorial campaigns, the press was more responsive to the campaign messages of male candidates. Rather than simply relating the issues discussed by female candidates, the press instead focused either on women's negative chances in Senate races or on women's personality characteristics in races for governor. Kahn (1996:133) concluded, "the media's misrepresentation of women candidates' campaign messages limits the effectiveness of women's campaigns."

Of course, a media bias against female candidates can also be incredibly direct. Consider the following story related by Whitney (2000:53): "In 1990, when Dianne Feinstein and Pete Wilson were engaged in a hotly contested race for governor of California, they faced off in a televised debate. The next day, the *Los Angeles Times* declared the debate to be a virtual tie. However, the paper gave Wilson a slight edge because he 'looked' more like a governor." Something about Dianne Feinstein's appearance, despite her equal performance in the debate, made her seem the less viable candidate to the journalists at the *Los Angeles Times*. That editorial opinion was then transmitted to countless subscribers.

Structure (Social Eligibility)

Social eligibility is the U.S. counterpart to the social structural explanations discussed in Chapter 4. Recall that social structural arguments focus on men's greater money, time, and access to education and certain professions. In the United States, most legislators are more educated than the general public and come disproportionately from a few occupations. The most common occupation for a U.S. state legislator or congressperson is law— approximately 45% of the members of the U.S. House of Representatives are lawyers. Thus, getting women into elected office requires a pool of educated women and women's participation in political pipeline occupations, such as law. If few women have the requisite education and occupational qualifications, then there may be too few qualified women to run for political office.

Though today women outnumber men in law schools around the country, this is only a recent development. In the 1960s, women made up only 4% of law school students; in 1972, they made up 9%; and in 1978 the figure had risen to just 29%. In 1960, women obtained only 35% of all bachelor's degrees, and almost 40% of those degrees were in education (National Center for Education Statistics 2006). Harvard Law School first admitted women in 1953. And Yale University first admitted female under-graduates in 1969.

A pipeline analogy is apt—one has to remember that the pool of women available for office was likely educated 20 or more years prior to running for office. Thus, the extremely small numbers of women in law school in the 1960s were the women in the pipeline for office in the late 1970s and 1980s. The women available to run for office today were part of the only 29% of women in law school in the late 1970s.

Though many women were likely socialized against pursuing high levels of education or professional careers, the low percentages of women in the law profession were not simply a matter of choice. Women were overtly discrim-inated against in education and employment until the 1970s when a variety of anti-gender-discrimination laws were passed. And the first pioneering women in law experienced active discrimination. Consider the following story related by Pat Schroeder, U.S. congresswoman from 1973 to 1997:

> The best preparation for infiltrating the boys' club of Congress was the boys' club of Harvard Law School. In 1961 there were fifteen women in my first-year class, and the five hundred men acted as if we constituted estrogen cont-amination. I was stunned when several of them insisted on changing their assigned seats in the lecture halls, as if mere proximity to women could be haz-ardous. . . . Maybe *none* of them thought women belonged there!
>
> The dean certainly didn't. Erwin Griswold was . . . a member of the United States Civil Rights Commission, but the idea of gender equity had not pene-trated his comprehension. The first week of school, he invited the freshman women to his home and informed us that he was opposed to women attend-ing law school but that the board had outvoted him. He said that the admis-sions committee counted the number of women in the class and then admitted that many additional men, certain that the women would never use the degrees and the world might otherwise be deprived of enough Harvard lawyers. Then he . . . ordered each of us to state why we were there, occupying . . . no, wast-ing such sacred space.
>
> In stark terror, sitting uncomfortably on our chairs placed in a circle, each of us tried to sound profound and controlled in our answers. I said something trite and predictable like, "Oh, I am here to bolster my love of the law." But one of the women blithely said, "I'm here because I couldn't get into Yale." (Schroeder 1998:93–95)

Imagine trying to get an education under such hostility and pressure. These were the women in the pipeline for political office in the 1970s and 1980s.

Research across states shows that the pool of available women makes a difference to the number of women elected to state legislatures. Having more women in pipeline occupations such as law leads to more female state legislators (Arceneaux 2001; Norrander and Wilcox 2005) and state executives (Oxley and Fox 2004).

Now, certainly not all office holders are lawyers, or even highly educated. And women both in and out of the workforce participate in churches, school boards, and political parties, giving them valuable political experience (Burns, Schlozman, and Verba 2001). Women have successfully run for public office as homemakers. But attaining political office even among homemakers requires that the women have name recognition in the community. Thus, there must be women who have "held local office, who have been active in community affairs, and who have name recognition in the community, ties to important established political groups, or other resources that help win elected office" (Norrander and Wilcox 2005:182). As we discuss later, women's generally lower levels of participation in many types of political participation can prevent them from gaining these critical connections.

One last important difference in the pipeline of women compared with the pipeline of men is in political ambition. Richard Fox and Jennifer Lawless (2004) surveyed individuals who could run for political office. That is, they surveyed men and women in the four professions most likely to yield political candidates in the United States—law, business, education, and politics. Looking just at this group of men and women (who share the same professional credentials), women are much less likely to aspire to political office. And even when they do aspire to political office, they are less likely to actually run. As Figure 9.8 shows, when you begin with a 50/50 pool of men and women who could run for political office, 59% of the men will consider running for office compared with only 43% of the women. And, of those who consider running for office, 20% of men will actually run, compared with only 15% of women. But Figure 9.8 finally demonstrates that of those men and women who decide to run, there is no gender difference in who actually wins office.

Part of the explanation for the difference in aspiration was that the women did not view themselves as qualified to run. But women were also encouraged to run for office less often than men were. Only 43% of the men they surveyed, compared with 32% of the women, received encouragement to run for office from a party leader, elected official, or political activist (Fox and Lawless 2004). Unfortunately, this research suggests that even as more women enter the eligibility pool of qualified candidates, they are neither likely to see themselves as qualified for political office nor likely to be asked to run.

To combat low numbers of female candidates, a number of organizations have grown to support women's bids for public office. As mentioned in

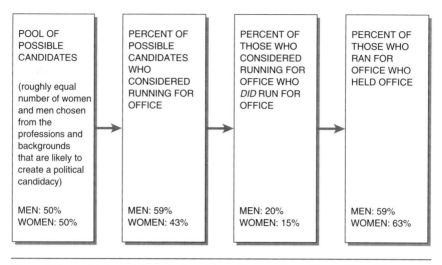

| POOL OF POSSIBLE CANDIDATES

(roughly equal number of women and men chosen from the professions and backgrounds that are likely to create a political candidacy) | PERCENT OF POSSIBLE CANDIDATES WHO CONSIDERED RUNNING FOR OFFICE | PERCENT OF THOSE WHO CONSIDERED RUNNING FOR OFFICE WHO *DID* RUN FOR OFFICE | PERCENT OF THOSE WHO RAN FOR OFFICE WHO HELD OFFICE |
| MEN: 50%
WOMEN: 50% | MEN: 59%
WOMEN: 43% | MEN: 20%
WOMEN: 15% | MEN: 59%
WOMEN: 63% |

Figure 9.8   Male and Female Candidates Emerge From Pool of Possible Candidates

SOURCE: From Fox, R. L., & Lawless, J. L., "Entering the arena? Gender and the decision to run for office," in *American Journal of Political Science*, 48(2), copyright © 2004. Reprinted with permission of Blackwell Publishing Ltd.

Chapter 4, one of the most successful women's political finance organizations in the United States is EMILY's List, a political action committee (PAC) that supports prochoice, Democratic women. EMILY is an acronym standing for "Early Money Is Like Yeast" because it helps the dough rise. The premise is that during campaigns, early financial support suggests to other potential donors that a candidate is viable, so more money is likely to follow, and early money also discourages potential challengers from entering the race. Thus, by providing money to female candidates early in their campaigns, EMILY's List seeks to improve women's political chances. Founded in 1985, EMILY's List was instrumental in the election of the female senator Barbara Mikulski in 1986. And since then, it has helped to elect 61 congresswomen, 11 senators, 8 governors, and 216 women to state and local office (EMILY's List 2006). Today, EMILY's List is the largest PAC in the United States, slightly larger than the National Rifle Association.

A Republican counterpart to EMILY's List, called WISH List (2006), was founded in 1992. The organization attracted 1,500 members and raised $250,000 in the first year of its operation, and, in 1994, WISH List distributed $370,000 to women candidates (Burrell 1998; Thomas 1998). Since its inception, WISH List has helped elect Republican congresswomen, such as Jennifer Dunn (WA) and Deborah Pryce (OH); governor Christine Todd Whitman; as well as U.S. Senator Susan Collins. But, like EMILY's List, the WISH List also supports prochoice candidates. To fill this gap, the Republican PAC Susan B. Anthony List was founded in 1994 to support prolife Republican women running for political office. And today, the Susan B. Anthony List has over 80,000 members (Susan B. Anthony List 2006).

Politics

Just as different countries have different levels of political demand for women, U.S. states can have differential demand for women. It is easy to understand that nations vary in their political systems, but the U.S. states are also actually 50 different institutions (Sanbonmatsu 2002c). States vary in their electoral systems, how many **open seats** are available, whether legislating is considered a full-time job, and how expensive it is to win political office. In explaining women's access to political power in the United States, researchers have therefore also turned to these political explanations. Some are unique to the United States, whereas others are similar to those we discussed in Chapter 5.

Political scientists have turned to incumbency as one important explanation for women's lack of representation in politics in the United States. In the United States, **incumbent** reelection rates are typically more than 90%. Candidates who currently hold public office are more likely to have higher name recognition, an effective campaign organization, and more money. High incumbency reelection rates are also due to political **gerrymandering** by both parties that ensures incumbents well over 60% of the vote. For example, in 2004, 99% of incumbents were reelected (Abramowitz, Alexander, and Gunning 2005). Any challenger, male or female, contesting a seat against an incumbent, faces serious opposition. For women, therefore, the logic is straightforward:

- Incumbents seek reelection 75% of the time.
- Incumbents typically win reelection (99% of them did in 2004).
- Most incumbents are male.

In the 2004 elections, only one woman who won a seat in the House of Representatives defeated an incumbent. The other seven women to win seats in the House did so in open seats or seats where the incumbent did not run for reelection (Ruthven 2005). Similarly, among candidates for governor, since 1970 women have won only about 32% of the races in which they have participated (Center for American Women and Politics 2006d). But 35% of the time they ran as challengers to male incumbents and only 12% of the time as incumbents.

When researchers focus on individual legislators, incumbency stands out as very important, especially at the national level. Mathematical analyses demonstrate that incumbency creates glacial pace of change in women's numbers over time (Darcy and Choike 1986; Darcy et al. 1994). Researchers also show that in special elections (with no incumbent) women do as well as men (Gaddie and Bullock 1997).

But trying to show the effects of incumbency across states has been more difficult. States vary in ways that make it harder or easier for incumbents to keep their seats. For example, some states have term limits that force long-term incumbents out of office. To try to measure the effect of incumbency at the state level, researchers have modeled turnover, or the number of seats that are contested in a given year. Based on what we know about incumbency, states with higher turnover rates should have higher numbers of female legislators. But turnover rates do not predict women's share of state legislatures (Arceneaux 2001; Norrander and Wilcox 2005) or only weakly predict it (Nechemias 1987). The lack of an effect of turnover across large numbers of legislators may be partly due to less-than-optimal numbers of women in the pipeline to run.

And what about **term limits**? Term limits cut off how long incumbents can stay in office and should increase turnover. Theoretically, fewer incumbents should benefit women because they can contest in open seats. But evidence for the benefits of term limits to women is not generally positive (e.g., Carey, Niemi, and Powell 1998; Carroll and Jenkins 2001). One study demonstrated that term limits increase numbers of women in upper houses but decrease them in lower houses. Norrander and Wilcox (2005:192) explained that of the 11 states that instituted term limits between 1994 and 2002, 7 had more women in the state senate but experienced a leveling-off or drop in women in the lower house.

Another political explanation in the United States is the professionalism of the legislature. Professional legislatures meet more often, pay more, and generally have larger staffs. Because professional legislatures are more prestigious and have more perks, getting elected to them is generally more desirable than getting elected to a less professional legislature (Diamond 1977). State legislatures vary in their degree of professionalism.

The argument goes that professionalism matters to women in politics because women face stronger competition for more desirable seats. When a political office is more desirable, more male candidates are likely to run for it.

More male candidates increase competition and make it more difficult for women to get the desirable seats. In less desirable races, women face less opposition from men and should gain seats in greater numbers.

There is some evidence that the attractiveness of the office partly explains women's representation. Research studies show that states where legislative salaries are higher have fewer women in state legislatures (Arceneaux 2001; Hill 1981) or that when the power of a state executive office (e.g., governor) is higher, fewer women hold it (Oxley and Fox 2004). Generally, states with weak executives or legislatures had a higher percentage of women holding office.

Also, consider differences between state congresses and senates. Senate seats are considered more valuable because there are significantly fewer of them, so a single senator holds more sway over the legislation passed than a single representative (Norrander and Wilcox 2005). Women hold a slightly higher percentage of seats in state houses than in state senates— 24% compared with 21% (Center for American Women and Politics 2006b). Therefore, women's lesser representation across the most prominent political positions is apparent.

But the explanation of the professional legislature is not only about the attractiveness or desirability, in terms of power and pay, of the office to men. It could also reflect the attractiveness of the office to women. There is wide variation in how often state legislatures meet. Nine states have full-time legislatures, the legislatures of six states meet once every other year, and the remaining meet annually for a limited time (Norrander and Wilcox 2005:183). Women traditionally make up a larger percentage of part-time legislatures (Norrander and Wilcox 2005). It may be that women are happy to have the flexibility afforded by part-time legislatures to pursue an occupation or to devote time to their family if they have spousal monetary support. Further, it could also be that greater weight is given to the education or profession of candidates in races for professional legislatures, and some women who run for office run as homemakers or have largely civic experience.

Finally, it may surprise you to find out that U.S. states differ in their electoral system and that some states have **multimember districts** where multiple people represent the voters of a particular electoral district (see Chapter 5). Thirteen states have at least some multimember districts (Norrander and Wilcox 2005). And just like in countries with multimember districts, party leaders feel some pressure to balance their ticket to appeal to important groups of voters, such as women.

Much like what we discussed across countries, multimember districts benefit women in the United States. Women do better in states with multimember districts compared to states with only single-member districts

(Arceneaux 2001; Sanbonmatsu 2002c). And within states that use both systems, women get elected at higher rates in the multimember races (Darcy et al. 1994:160–6; Matland and Brown 1992). Finally, in states that changed their electoral system and dropped multimember districts in the last 30 years, a drop in the number of female legislators has occurred (Darcy et al. 1994; King 2002).

Donkeys and Elephants:
The Influence of Political Parties

Women elected to national political office have represented both the Republican and Democratic parties. From 1917, when Jeannette Rankin became the first woman elected to Congress, more than 80 distinguished women have ascended to the U.S. House or Senate through the Republican Party. And more than 140 Democratic women have also achieved this feat.

Overall, the numbers listed suggest that women have greater success achieving national political office in the Democratic Party. In early 2006, the Republican Party controlled both the U.S. House and Senate, but 64% of the women in each of these bodies were Democrats. Historically, only 36% of women in the U.S. Congress have been Republicans. In the House of Representatives, from Jeannette Rankin's time to 1965, Democrats and Republicans traded prominence in female representation. But since then, Democratic women have outpaced Republican women. Further, the margins of difference between the parties in the House of Representatives grew larger during the 1990s, when Democratic began to outpace Republican women by 2 to 1.

The balance between Democratic and Republican women has been more even in the Senate. From 1917 to 2006, the number of Democratic and Republican women holding seats in the U.S. Senate was often the same (during 17 Congresses). Democratic women were more prevalent in the Senate during 16 Congresses, whereas Republican female senators outpaced Democratic female senators in 12 Congresses. But again, during the 1990s, women's representation in the Democratic Party grew more rapidly, and since 1991 Republican women have consistently fallen behind Democratic women in their numbers.

The Effects of Political Party in State Legislatures

When considering the relationship between women's legislative representation and party affiliation, we can examine at least two distinct issues.

First, we can look at the percentage of legislators within each party that are women. We find that of the 3,647 total state legislative seats held by Republicans in January 2006, 17% are women. In contrast, of the 3,664 seats held by Democrats 29% are women (Center for American Women and Politics 2006b). This 12-point gap provides evidence either that women may be more likely to run as Democrats or that the electorate favors Democratic women. However, women's greater share of Democratic seats is a relatively new phenomenon. Until 1991, Republican women held a slightly higher percentage of their party's seats in the legislature, 2% to 3% higher than that of Democrats (Sanbonmatsu 2002a:47).

A different question is whether women do better when their party is in or out of power—whether majority party status, or **party dominance**, helps or hinders women. Specifically, how do women's numbers differ when their party holds the majority of the legislative seats from when their party is not in power? Looking at the question in the broadest terms, as of 2006, in the 24 lower houses controlled by the Democratic Party, women held 28% of Democratic seats and 18% of Republican seats (Center for American Women and Politics 2006b). Alternatively, in the 25 state lower houses controlled by the Republican Party, women held 31% of Democratic seats and 17% of Republican seats (CAWP 2006b). Therefore, for both parties, women obtained a slightly higher share of seats when their party was not in the majority. And the benefit for Democratic women in Republican-majority legislatures is slightly higher.

But to make things more complicated, this pattern did not hold for state senates in 2006. Democratic women held 29% of Democratic seats in the 24 state senates where they were the majority, compared with 27% when they were the minority party. In the 24 state senates where Republicans were the majority, women held 13% of Republican seats, compared with 12% when they were the minority. So in 2006, women did better in state senates when they were in the majority party. Indeed, the relationship between party dominance and women's legislative representation is not simple.

Women-in-politics researchers have sometimes argued that it is not party dominance, but Democratic Party dominance, that reduces women's numbers (Rule 1999; Sanbonmatsu 2002c). For example, in her analysis of political parties and female state legislators from 1971 to 1999, Kira Sanbonmatsu (2002c) found that being in the majority has a negative effect on the recruitment of Democratic women, but she did not find the same pattern for the Republican Party. Sanbonmatsu (2002c) also found that in states where Democrats were in the majority, women were less likely to report that they received party support. Sanbonmatsu

(2002c) concluded, "There appears to be greater competition for seats within the Democratic party in Democratic majority legislatures, compared to competition within the Republican party in Republican majority legislatures" (p. 804).

But there is not consensus on this issue (Matland and Brown 1992). An alternative perspective is that it is party dominance more generally, not Democratic Party dominance per se, that depresses women's representation within party. And still other researchers have, in fact, found a positive effect of Democratic Party dominance. For example, in analyzing data at the district rather than the state level in New Hampshire, Matland and Brown (1992) found that by the late 1980s, women did distinctly better in districts dominated by the Democratic Party.

One factor to keep in mind is that, over time, there have been increasing numbers of Republicans in state legislatures. Now that Republicans are now more often dominating legislatures, one can better evaluate whether it is Democratic Party dominance that is problematic for women or simply party dominance. Figure 9.9 suggests that, in 2006, there is still a slight negative effect of Democratic Party dominance. For example, women's share of Democratic seats is greatest in Idaho, where Democrats have the smallest percentage of seats.

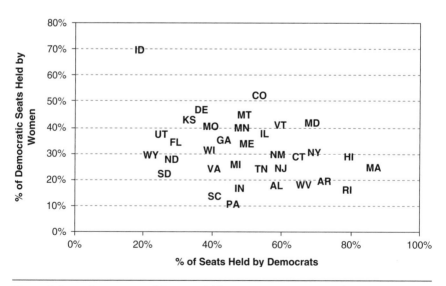

Figure 9.9   Percentage of Seats Held by Democrats Compared With Percentage of Democratic Seats Held by Women, 2006

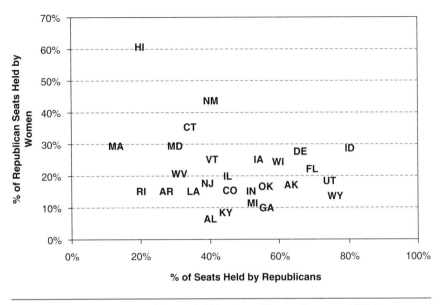

Figure 9.10   Percentage of Seats Held by Republicans Compared With
Percentage of Republican Seats Held by Women, 2006

But a negative effect of party dominance is also present for the
Republican Party (see Figure 9.10). Women's share of Republican seats is
largest in Hawaii, where Republicans have the second fewest seats.

Women and Parties in the Governor's Mansion

The numbers also suggest that Democratic women have a clear advantage when seeking the highest executive position in state government—
the governor's office. Not only are six out of the eight current female governors Democrats, but female governors have also been more likely to be
Democrats throughout history. Figure 9.11 shows the cumulative number
of female governors by political party since the mid-1970s. Though the
number of Republican female governors has increased in recent years,
Democratic women seeking the governorship are clearly at an advantage. In
fact, it was not until 1998 that the Republicans elected three female governors, a feat the Democrats reached in 1967, more than three decades prior.

It is also important to contrast how these women achieved office. Even
these recent gains for women in the position of governor may be deceiving.
Of the nine female Republican governors, only three were elected in their own
right. The rest were elevated to the position from another elected position

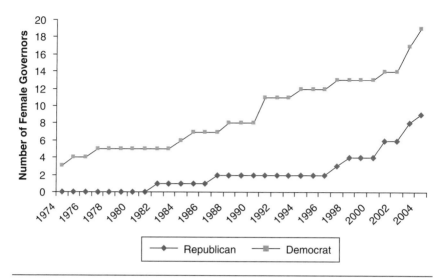

Figure 9.11   Cumulative Number of Female Governors by Political Party, 1974–2004

when the male governor resigned. Democrats are not exempt from this trend. The first three female Democratic governors were all surrogates for husbands who either died while in office or were barred from running for reelection (Center for American Women and Politics 2006c). And Rose Mofford, Democratic governor of Arizona from 1988 to 1991, filled the position after the male governor was impeached and convicted (CAWP 2006b).

Explaining Differences in Women's Success in the Two Parties

As we discussed, women in the Democratic Party generally fare better in terms of raw percentages. But a question remains: Are Republican women simply not running, or are they just not winning? Are Republican women being shut out at the primary stage by party members or do the voters simply reject the idea of a female Republican? We can look at governors to begin to answer this question. Data from the Center for American Women and Politics (CAWP) suggest that, overall, Democratic women are more successful than their Republican female counterparts when they run for governor (Center for American Women and Politics 2006d). From 1970 to 2004, Democratic women won 38% of the times they ran for governor, whereas Republican women won only 21% of their gubernatorial races. However, this is largely because Democratic women are more likely to contest open seats rather than challenge incumbents. Democratic women ran for an open seat 64% of the time, whereas for Republican women this figure is only 32%. Furthermore, the Democratic Party fields more female candidates than the Republican Party by almost a 2 to 1 margin (Center for American Women and Politics 2006d; see also Weir 1999).

But women in the Democratic and Republican parties may seek different types of political offices, leading to the differences discussed here. Or the two political parties may recruit or channel women into positions differently (Sanbonmatsu 2002a). For example, although Democratic women are more often legislators and governors than their Republican counterparts, Republican women hold more statewide elective executive offices overall, 52% Republican to 48% Democrat. Further, women in the two parties hold different types of elected positions in state government. Eighty-eight percent of female state treasurers, 71% of female state auditors, and both women elected corporation commissioner are Republicans, but all three women elected as state attorney general belong to the Democratic Party (Center for American Women and Politics 2006c). Sixty percent of female lieutenant governors are also Republican. (But only two of these female Republican lieutenant governors ran independently—the rest were part of a ticket with a male gubernatorial candidate.)

Some also argue that, in general, Democratic leaders have simply been more successful recruiting women. Ralph Wright, former Democratic minority leader in the Vermont House, stated:

> We recruited women. We didn't set out to do it, but it wasn't long before we realized there was a big political difference between the sexes. . . . Simply stated, women make better candidates than men. One reason was political, the other philosophic. They were candidates uncorrupted by the process. (Moncrief et al. 2001:102)

During Wright's term, the Democrats came to power in the Vermont House of Representatives in part because of the success of running women (Moncrief et al. 2001). And even after Wright left the legislature, his successors continued to actively recruit women candidates. But the success of Democrats does not mean that Republicans are not trying to enlist women. For example, Jo Ann Davidson, GOP leader in the Ohio House of Representatives, worked hard to recruit women (Moncrief et al. 2001).

The Rise and Fall of the Equal Rights Amendment

At the beginning of this chapter, we explained that we would divide our discussion into two parts. In the first half of the chapter, we discuss women's formal political participation, as legislators, governors, and so on. In the second half of the chapter, we discuss women as citizens and voters. At the nexus of these two halves is the fight for the **Equal Rights Amendment** (ERA). Individual women, organized women's movement groups, and female legislators all fought to pass this most important piece of legislation about women in U.S. history. In this section, we briefly review the history of the ERA.

"Equality of rights under the law shall not be denied or abridged by the United States or by any State on account of sex." First passed by Congress in 1972, these are the words of the ERA, language that at one time seemed on its way to becoming the 27th Amendment to the U.S. Constitution. Although it may be difficult at first glance to see why these words would be controversial, the ERA was in fact a subject of great debate among politicians, women's organizations, and individuals over the span of several decades. The amendment was ratified by 35 states but ultimately fell 3 states shy of becoming a part of the Constitution (Woods 2000).

Whereas the story of the ERA's ratification is largely a story of the 1970s and 1980s, the history of the Equal Rights Amendment dates back to the early decades of the 20th century, not long after women attained suffrage. First drafted by Alice Paul and submitted to Congress in 1923 by the nephew of Susan B. Anthony, the amendment was already a topic of fierce debate. Writing about the period, historian William H. Chafe summarized, "No issue divided women's organizations more than the Equal Rights Amendment to the Constitution" (McGlen, O'Connor, Assendelft, and Gunther-Canada 2002:41). One continuing concern was that the ERA would negate existing protective labor legislation for women and make future efforts to protect women as a group impossible (Brown, Emerson, Falk, and Freedman 1971; McGlen et al. 2002; Sanbonmatsu 2002a).

Though debate over the amendment among women's groups continued, some form of the ERA was introduced in at least one chamber of Congress during every legislative session between 1923 and 1971. In 1948, the House of Representatives held hearings on the proposed amendment, and the Senate actually passed the amendment in 1950 and 1953 (McGlen et al. 2002). But it was not until the 1970s, supported by a burgeoning second-wave women's movement and the pervading ethos of civil rights reform, that the bill passed both houses of Congress—350 to 15 in the House of Representatives and 84 to 8 in the Senate (McGlen et al. 2002; Woods 2000).

When the ERA first passed Congress, it had widespread support from politicians and the public at large. In fact, during the first year after Congress passed the ERA, 22 states ratified the amendment without any significant opposition (Woods 2000). The amendment also received support from both men and women. For example, in one 1977 survey, men and women reported very similar attitudes toward the ERA (Seltzer et al. 1997).

Furthermore, the ERA began to unify women's organizations. Woods (2000:70) explained, "The ratification effort politicized the traditional women's organizations that had been so fearful of taking up political issues, and it attracted thousands of new recruits to the new political organization, the National Organization for Women." The National Organization for Women (NOW) pushed strongly for the ERA, believing that passage of an amendment was the easiest way to guarantee equality. And because the courts and the Equal Employment Opportunity Commission began to strike down protective labor laws or extend women's protections to men, the divisiveness of the issue for women's organizations declined (Mansbridge 1986; Sanbonmatsu 2002a).

Despite initial optimism and enthusiasm, however, the momentum for ratification faded, the women's movement splintered, opposition grew, and male legislators remained unconvinced that the amendment was necessary (Elfin 1982; Mansbridge 1986; McGlen et al. 2002; Woods 2000). The time period for ratification was set to expire March 22, 1979, but was controversially extended for 3 years by the 95th Congress in 1978. But the extension of the deadline mattered little, and on June 30, 1982, the ERA was finally put to rest. In the end, 15 states refused to ratify the ERA, and another 4 states voted to rescind their original approval, including Idaho, Kentucky, Nebraska, and Tennessee (Mansbridge 1986).

So with all the initial support, why did the ERA ultimately fail to become part of the U.S. Constitution? Some suggest that it was in large part the lack of female legislators. After describing her experience in the Missouri Senate, where the ERA failed to pass by one vote, Harriet Woods (2000:69) noted:

> The legislative bodies that were deciding whether women would have equal treatment under the law were filled with men. . . . After it was all over, in the final count, three-fourths of women legislators across the country supported ratification compared to only 59 percent of men. In the fifteen states that never ratified, 79 percent of women legislators supported the amendment, compared to 39 percent of men.

Simply put, there were simply not enough women in politics during the early 1970s to carry the amendment through the state ratification process.

Many scholars link the fall of the ERA to the changing tide in American political culture and the struggle over women's proper roles in society (Gelb and Palley 1987; Mansbridge 1986; McGlen et al. 2002; Sanbonmatsu 2002a). Public opinion about the ERA was critical to its ratification across states (Soule and King 2006; Soule and Olzak 2004). By the mid-1970s, an opposition movement was spearheaded by fundamentalist religious groups and other conservative political organizations. Led by prominent Republican activist Phyllis Schlafly (see Box 9.2), the opposition framed the ERA as a fundamental threat to women's way of life (Critchlow 2005; McGlen et al. 2002). Opponents argued that the ERA would end men's obligation to support their wives, would require sending women into combat, and would mandate federal funding for abortion (Mansbridge 1986; McGlen et al. 2002; Sanbonmatsu 2002a). And once the battle became about women's proper roles and no longer about women's equal rights, the ERA movement was substantially crippled (Gelb and Palley 1987).

Box 9.2   Phyllis Schlafly and the Equal Rights Amendment

In the spring of 1973, in a debate with Phyllis Schlafly at Illinois State University, feminist icon Betty Friedan blurted out, "I'd like to burn you at the stake!" Why the animosity? Friedan was, in fact, showing a frustration commonly held by feminists across the country at the time, who held Phyllis Schlafly responsible for stalling the progress of the Equal Rights Amendment. Though the amendment had once been easily marching toward ratification, the future of the ERA was now in peril.

Attacking the ERA as "radical, unnecessary, and a threat to legal rights of women and the American family," Schlafly had already mobilized tens of thousands of women in the STOP ERA movement (Critchlow 2005:12). Schlafly's rallying cry against the ERA was published in a 1972 antifeminist manifesto titled "What's Wrong with 'Equal Rights' for Women?" In this article, Schlafly laid out the basic principles that would guide the anti-ERA movement over the next decade. She charged that the ERA would "abolish a woman's right to child support and alimony" and would "absolutely and positively make women subject to the draft" (Critchlow 2005:218). Though equal pay for equal work was desirable, such goals could be met with specific legislation. But Schlafly's attack was not only against the ERA but also against feminists as a group. She argued, "Women libbers view the home as a prison, and the wife and mother as a slave. . . . The women libbers don't understand that most women want to be a wife, mother, and homemaker—and are happy in that role" (Critchlow 2005:218).

Tapping into passionate anti-feminist and anti-ERA sentiments among women, and aligned with other conservatives who were critical of the way the government was being run, Phyllis Schlafly was quickly becoming a heroine to the Right. And by making Schlafly the sole target of their attacks, feminists inadvertently contributed to Schlafly's fame. Over the next few years, Schlafly emerged as the most well-known opponent of modern feminism as well as a major spokeswoman for the conservative movement, which would grow to culminate in the election of conservative Ronald Reagan to the U.S. presidency in 1980. Today, she is honored as the "conservative movement's founding mother" and given credit for a profamily movement that rallied millions of religious voters to vote for Reagan (Critchlow 2005:270).

Today, some feminists continue the fight. There are constitutional experts who argue that if three additional states ratify the amendment, it could still become law. And in some states, legislators continue to press for ratification. For example in October 2005, Arthenia Joiner filed the ERA ratification bill in the Florida House of Representatives. ERA supporters take solace in the fact that, generally, the public has always supported the amendment. Over the ERA's history, public support never fell below 53%, and after the ERA was defeated, more than 70% of women felt that another effort should be made for passage (Seltzer et al. 1997). But largely, the ERA is a story of the past. By the late 1970s, the legal status of women had significantly improved, and many of the problems the ERA was designed to address had been resolved (Mansbridge 1986). For most politicians today, the ERA is simply no longer on the agenda, and other women's issues, such as abortion, have taken over center stage.

Gender Gaps in American Politics

Although women's formal roles in politics have historically been limited, women in the United States have participated widely in the public realm since before the American Revolution. During revolutionary times, women organized public demonstrations, boycotted English tea, formed organizations, signed public petitions, raised money in the name of the revolution, and published their ideas (Burrell 2004). Thus, women have long participated in causes for the general good of the society in which they lived. This practice has continued into the modern era, when women have voted, petitioned, lobbied, demonstrated, and protested to affect public policies from gun control to nuclear proliferation (Burrell 2004).

Thus, women act politically not only as legislators or governors but as average citizens, voters, and activists. But women do not always act the same way as men. If female voters or citizens hold different political positions on issues or participate in different numbers than their male counterparts, there is said to be a **gender gap** in political orientation or in political participation (Conover 1988; Manza and Brooks 1998; Shapiro and Mahajan 1986). In this section, we consider the differences between men and women in their policy preferences, party affiliations, vote choices, and types of participation. We also explore why gender gaps may have developed in the first place and how the differences between men and women have changed over time.

Policy Attitudes

Across a number of policy issues, American men and women have quite different beliefs and attitudes. For example, in Figure 9.12, a few political issues of the mid-1990s are broken down by gender. Women are more supportive of a larger government role to address social problems such as poverty, racism, and lack of adequate child care. Women are also more likely to favor gun control legislation than men are. On the other hand, men are more likely than women to favor a smaller government and support the use of military force to settle international disputes.

But across a number of policy issues, there is no significant disagreement between men and women. For example, although abortion is said to be a women's issue, men and women hold much more similar attitudes toward laws on abortion from year to year than women or men hold as a group over time.

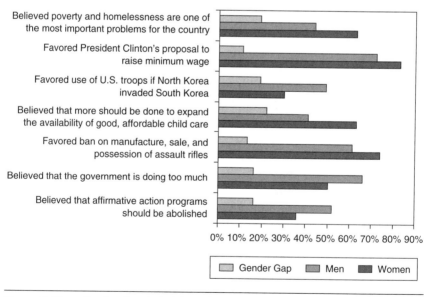

Figure 9.12   Gender Gap in Public Policy Attitudes, 1994–1996

SOURCE: Data from Center for American Women and Politics (1997).

The greatest difference between men and women appeared in 1996, when women were more polarized than men. Forty-three percent of women believed that abortion should always be a personal choice, compared with 36% of men, but women were also more likely than men were to believe that abortion should never be permitted by law, 14% and 12%, respectively.

So what explains the different positions held by men and women on certain issues? To begin, theory has pointed to differences in men's and women's political socialization. In childhood, girls are socialized differently from boys (Chodorow 1978), and as adults women may be strongly affected by their experience as mothers (Ruddick 1989). In theory, women's distinct upbringing and mothering experience make them more caring, nurturing, and compassionate, which then leads to different attitudes on public policy.

Some scholars have also turned to women's feminist attitudes to explain gender gaps in policy preferences (Conover 1988; Cook and Wilcox 1991). Feminism may change women's values and policy preferences by causing them to identify with the problems and interests of women as a group. For example, categorizing women as feminists, potential feminists, and nonfeminists, Conway, Steuernagel, and Ahern (1997:67) found that feminists are more supportive of increases in federal funding for child care, aid to the unemployed, environmental programs, welfare programs, the homeless problem, public schools, and urban assistance. And, if women are more likely to have a feminist identity than men, it would create gender differences among men and women on these attitudes (Conover 1988).

Party Affiliation

Historically, the Republican Party has been more supportive of women's rights than the Democratic Party (Freeman 1987). As the first major party to favor women's suffrage, the Republican Party played a leading role in securing women the right to vote. In fact, 26 of 36 state legislatures that voted to ratify the 19th Amendment granting women suffrage were under Republican control. Republicans were also the first major party to place the ERA on their party's platform in 1940. And, prior to the 1960s, women were more often Republicans (Inglehart and Norris 2000).

But beginning in the 1960s, and especially since the 1980s, women's attitudes and beliefs have more often aligned with the Democratic Party. Women are more likely to identify as Democrats, and women are also more likely to approve of the job performance of Democratic legislators. For example, women have been more likely than men to disapprove of the job performance of the past four Republican presidents (Center for American Women and Politics 2005a). Alternatively, Bill Clinton's approval ratings as president were higher among women (Center for American Women and Politics 2005a).

Of course, women's attitudes toward the political parties also translate into differences in voting behavior. For example, in the 2004 presidential election, 48% of women voted for George W. Bush, whereas 55% of men did so (Center for American Women and Politics 2004). This difference also held across all key segments of the population—Blacks, Whites, Hispanics, and Asians; those in the highest income and educational brackets and those in the lowest; and all age groups (Center for American Women and Politics 2004, 2005c).

But this gap is not unique to 2004. The difference between men and women in 2004 is smaller than in 2000, when only 43% of women compared with 53% of men voted for Bush (Center for American Women and Politics 2004). And looking over time, there has been a significant gender gap in presidential elections since 1980 (see Figure 9.13). Women have always voted more Democratic than men, and even when faced with an unfavorable Republican candidate, men have been more willing than women to vote for an outsider such as Ross Perot or Ralph Nader (Center for American Women and Politics 2005b).

These differences are not only evident in presidential elections but carry to other races as well. According to 1998 exit polls of 33 gubernatorial and 32 Senate races, there was at least a 4% gender gap in the vast majority of races (Center for American Women and Politics 1999). In 14 races, gender gaps were even greater than 10%. And in all but 3 of the 47 races with gender gaps, women favored Democratic candidates. In 13 races, a majority of women voted differently than did the majority of men—five Democrats owe their victories to women, whereas eight Republicans owe their victories to men. For instance, when Black Democrat Carol Moseley Braun lost her U.S. Senate seat in 1998, challenger Peter Fitzgerald received only 47% of the women's vote but 55% of votes from men (Center for American Women and Politics 1999).

Why the gender gap in party affiliation? Like the explanations for the gender gap in attitudes, scholars have discussed gender socialization and feminist consciousness (see Manza and Brooks 1998 for a review). If socialization causes women to have different policy preferences, then they would be more likely to vote for the party that exemplifies those preferences.

But men's and women's positions in the social structure have also changed over time, and that can help explain why the gender gap in voting has also changed over time. First, the dual trends of rising divorce rates and rising age at first marriage create more women who are economically and psychologically autonomous from men (Carroll 1988; Manza and Brooks 1998). In the absence of the common interests created by marriage, differences in party

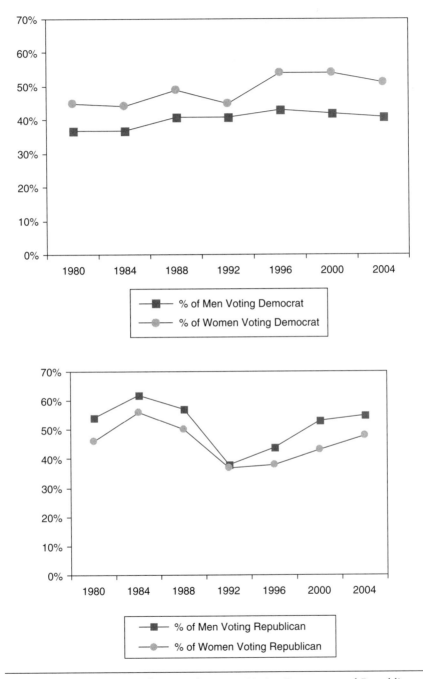

Figure 9.13   Percentage of Men and Women Voting Democrat and Republican in U.S. Presidential Elections, 1980–2004

SOURCE: Data from Center for American Women and Politics (2005b).

affiliation may appear. Similarly women's rising rates of labor force participation create women who are more autonomous, whether they are single or married. But women's labor force participation may also increase feminist consciousness, as women move away from traditional gender roles and experience gender inequality in the workforce (Gerson 1985; Klein 1984). A rising feminist consciousness from workforce participation could lead to different policy preferences and different party voting (Manza and Brooks 1998).

Voter Turnout

But how women affect an election is not just a function of their political attitudes but also their numbers. From when women gained the vote in 1920 throughout the 1970s, women cast their ballots less often than men did. But during the 1980s, women began to outnumber men at the polls, and in the 2004 presidential election 8.8 million more women voted than men (Center for American Women and Politics 2005c). As depicted in Figure 9.14, the key transition year was 1980, when President Ronald Reagan was elected. The same pattern holds in off-years, when there is not a presidential race; women began turning out in greater numbers in 1986 and have since voted more often than men (Center for American Women and Politics 2005c). And

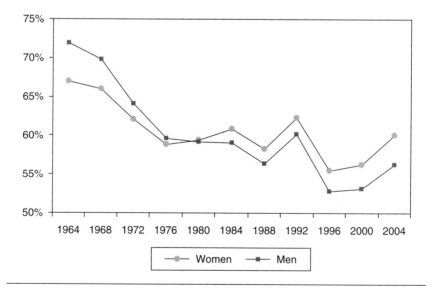

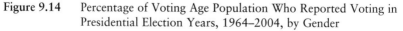

Figure 9.14   Percentage of Voting Age Population Who Reported Voting in Presidential Election Years, 1964–2004, by Gender

SOURCE: Data from Center for American Women and Politics (2005c).

predictably, women also outnumber men as registered voters since the 1980s (Center for American Women and Politics 2005c).

Of course, looking closely at Figure 9.14, it does not tell a story of women substantially increasing their percentage turnout. Instead, men are decreasing their turnout at a faster rate than women, and that has led to the transition.

One interesting question when looking at the gender gap in voting is how the gap differs by age. Age is a strong determinant of voting such that older citizens are more likely to vote. But older generations of women may fall into more traditional voting patterns and participate less. In fact, for the 1996, 2000, and 2004 presidential elections, this is exactly what we find (Center for American Women and Politics 2005c). While approximately 44.9% of women ages 18 to 24 years old reported voting in 2004, 63.9% of women age 75 years and older reported doing so. Among males, however, even fewer of the youngest age group voted, 38.8%, while men in the oldest age group outpaced women with 71% voting.

What affects women's rates of voting? As discussed in Chapter 4, time is an important resource (Schlozman et al. 1994). Because women are more often burdened with household and child-rearing activities, even when both partners are employed full-time (Calasanti and Bailey 1991; Hochschild 1989; Shelton 1990), women may have less free time to participate in politics. In fact, though the number of children in the household does not affect the voting patterns of men, women are less likely to vote as they have more children. For instance, in 1992, 80% of women with no children in their household reported voting, whereas this statistic was 76% for women with one child, 73% for two children, 71% for three children, and 57% for four or more children (Conway et al. 1997). It is important to note that a few recent studies do not find this effect (Burns, Schlozman, and Verba 2001). However, it is clear that women's family roles affect resources such as time that are valuable in the political context.

When Does the Gender Gap Matter?

In recent years, women have more often voted for Democrats and voted in higher numbers, so why aren't Democrats dominating the political arena? It is important to understand that the gender gap will not necessarily affect the outcome of an election. For instance, if 60% of men favor the Republican candidate, and 60% of women favor the Democratic candidate, their different preferences cancel each other out, but the Democratic candidate would win because more women vote. But, even if women turn out in higher numbers, if males have stronger preferences than women, it is men's votes that will determine the outcome. Indeed, this is what happened in 2004, when 51% of women favored John Kerry, but 55% of men favored George W. Bush. Even though eight million more women voted, men's stronger Republican leanings outweighed women's more marginal Democratic preference. But in other races, it is women who are thanked by the victor. For example, in 1992, the gender gap in female and male preferences resulted in the election of both Dianne Feinstein and Barbara Boxer to the U.S. Senate (Conway et al. 1997).

Campaign Activities

Voting is far from the only form of political activity. There are many other ways to influence an election. Surveys conducted by National Election Studies (NES) have asked Americans about their participation in five such activities since the 1950s: talking to others to try to influence their vote, attending rallies and other political meetings, displaying support for a candidate through buttons or bumper stickers, volunteering for a campaign, and contributing money. Overall, the most popular form of political participation is engaging in a discussion to try to influence someone's vote. Significantly fewer Americans attend a political meeting or volunteer for a campaign, and less than 5% of Americans report making a campaign donation.

How does women's participation in these activities compare to men's? In short, women's greater participation in voting does not appear to carry over to these other political activities. Burrell (2004:101) reported:

> Women have consistently reported lower levels of involvement, and the gap has not diminished over the course of the contemporary era. . . . With respect to the 2000 election, for instance, 48 percent of men and 39 percent of women reported having participated in at least one of these activities.

In general, over time, men have been consistently more likely to try to influence votes through debate. Differences across the genders for other political activities are much smaller. For instance, during the 2004 election, 51% of men and 45% of women reported talking to others to try to influence their vote—a 6-point gender gap—whereas 22% of men and 19% of women wore a campaign button or displayed a bumper sticker—only a 3-point gender gap. But again, beyond talking to others to try to influence their vote, very few men and women are likely to participate in campaign activities.

The rarest, but perhaps most influential, form of political participation is the campaign donation. Using data from the Federal Election Commission for the 2000 election, Burrell (2004) found that just 0.5% of men donated $200 or more to candidates for national office, and 0.2% of men donated $1,000 or more. Though this is quite a small fraction of the population, the percentage of women making contributions was less than half that of men, 0.2% at the $200 level and 0.09% donating $1,000 or more.

Women have tended to participate less in campaign activities. However, in 2004, women closed some of the gaps. Interestingly, for both men and women during the 2004 election, 3% volunteered, 7% attended a political meeting or rally, and 13% donated money.

Again, women's political participation is determined in large part by factors such as individual motivation, access to resources, time, social status, and the broader political and legal environment. As discussed in Chapter 4, the resource model of political participation suggests that access to resources such as education and outside employment are important factors for women's political participation (Burns et al. 2001; Schlozman et al. 1994). For example, women employed outside the home are more likely to participate in politics (Conway et al. 1997). Certain attitudes may also stimulate political involvement:

> A sense of moral obligation to participate in politics, an empowering sense of personal political efficacy, loyal commitment to a candidate or political party, concern about a policy issue or set of issues, and the social context (including pressures to participate that may exist in any social status group). (Conway et al. 1997:84)

Individuals may also be motivated externally by candidates, parties, interest groups, or social movements. But these "psychological orientations to politics—political interest, information, and efficacy" are powerful factors in explaining differences in men and women's participation (Burns et al. 2001:383).

Intersecting Gaps

Gender gaps are not the only gaps in U.S. politics. Indeed, race gaps in U.S. politics are much more pronounced than gender gaps. Returning to the idea of intersectionality, what do we know about gender/race gaps in American politics? Summing up a range of political activities, such as working in a campaign, contacting a government official, and attending a protest, Burns et al. (2001) found that, overall, within groups of Whites, Blacks, and Latinos, men are consistently more politically active than women. Considering differences across race and ethnicity, Whites are the most politically active, followed by Blacks, and Latinos are the least politically active. And at the intersection of these categories, Latina women are consistently the least politically active. For example, Latina women are less than half as likely as Black women and a little more than a third as likely as White men to be affiliated with a political organization. And whereas White women contribute an average of $51 to political campaigns, Latina women contribute an average of only $18. The gap between male and female political participation is smallest among Blacks. Indeed, although Black women are less likely than men to attend protests and contact a public official, Black men and women have comparable rates of other types of political action (Burns et al. 2001).

Like the discussion of gender gaps in political participation discussed earlier, the exception to women's lower rates of political action is voting (Center for American Women and Politics 2005c; Prestage 1991). For the last five presidential elections, Black, Hispanic, and White women have all voted in higher numbers than Black, Hispanic, and White men. The greatest gap in voter turnout is among Blacks, in which 59.8% of women voted in 2004 compared with 51.8% of men (Center for American Women and Politics 2005c). For Asians and Pacific Islanders, the first year in which data for both gender and race is 2000, and though men were found to have slightly higher turnout than women in that year, Asian and Pacific Islander women voted in slightly higher numbers than men in 2004 (Center for American Women and Politics 2005c).

But what about intersecting differences in party affiliation and policy attitudes? Susan Welch and Lee Sigelman (1992) looked at exit polls in the United States between 1980 and 1988. They found that gender gaps existed for Hispanics, Blacks, and Whites. Women of all three groups were more liberal than men were, more likely to vote for the Democratic Party, and more likely to vote for Democratic presidential candidates. But the gender gap in these groups often disappeared when differences among men and women (e.g., levels of education, income, and age) were included. And, even though looking at raw differences suggests that the gender gap between White men and White women is larger than the gaps between Black and Hispanic men and women, Welch and Sigelman showed that the gender gap is actually similar in size across all three racial and ethnic groups. That is, White women are as different, on average, from White men as Black women are from Black men and Hispanic women are from Hispanic men.

Similarly, in the recent California recall vote (where Arnold Schwarzenegger was the frontrunner candidate to replace the governor in the case of recall), although all racial and ethnic groups (Black, Latino, and Asian American) were less likely to vote for the recall, a gender gap only appeared between Whites: White women were less likely than White men to vote for the recall. Black women, Latino women, and Asian American women were no less likely than the men of their respective racial and ethnic groups to vote for the recall (Bedolla and Scola 2006).

But focusing on impartial statistics may mask the difficulties experienced by minority women in negotiating political issues. As explained by Mansbridge and Tate (1992:488), "Race constructs the way Black women experience gender; gender constructs the way Black women experience race." Thus, certain political issues may force minority women to choose between supporting minority issues or woman's issues.

On the one hand, Black women demonstrate strong support for women's issues. In fact, their levels of support are even higher than that of White women. Specifically, Black women have given stronger attitudinal support to the women's movement than White women have. In 1972, Black women were more likely than White women to expressive sympathy for the goals of women's liberation groups (67% to 35%) (hooks 1981:148). Black women are also more likely than White women to identify themselves as feminist (Baxter and Lansing 1983; Klein 1984; Mansbridge and Tate 1992). Jane Mansbridge and Katherine Tate (1992) suggested that Black women are more likely to identify as feminist because structural factors have forced them into a situation of relative equality (through economic independence and educational equality) with Black men. Further, because they experience multiple oppressions, Black women better understand what it means to be structurally oppressed and that ending that oppression may require working through a political movement. Clyde Wilcox (1990) also suggested that Black consciousness can lead to increased feminist consciousness.

However, evidence also suggests that despite greater identification with feminist causes, Black women identify more strongly than White women with race than gender (Gay and Tate 1998). This is not to say that gender is irrelevant to Black women. But, like the "double jeopardy" Black women experience as they face both racism and sexism, Black women are in a "double bind" when they must choose between being Black and being a woman (Gay and Tate 1998:171). And when forced, it appears Black women tend to choose race.

As an example, the Clarence Thomas hearings, discussed at the beginning of this chapter and in Chapter 1, put American Black women in a difficult position. Anita Hill was a Black woman accusing Clarence Thomas, a Black man, of sexual harassment. What should a Black woman do? Should she support the interests of Blacks? Or should she support the interests of women? It turns out that Black women sided with Black men on this issue and supported Clarence Thomas. Black women were less likely than White women, and even less likely than White and Black men, to believe Anita Hill (Mansbridge and Tate 1992:489).

Jane Mansbridge and Katherine Tate (1992:488–9) discussed the Thomas nomination:

Why did race trump gender for Blacks in the Thomas nomination? Blacks supported Thomas because of their desire to maintain representation on the Supreme Court. In addition, Blacks favored Thomas because of the complicated history of race and gender relations in this country, which led both Black men and Black women to concern at this historical moment with the public image of a Black woman attacking a Black man. The media and organized interest groups also played important roles in shaping public opinion on this matter. The way the media presented the confrontation between Thomas and Hill did not make clear why she had waited 10 years to bring her story forward and why she had not quit or brought charges at the time. For these reasons, Black leaders had difficulty organizing against Thomas. That paucity of organized opposition greatly benefited his candidacy.

But intersections of gender, race, and ethnicity do not fully explain the nuances of political attitudes. Class differences may also be important. Indeed, Mansbridge and Tate (1992) found that politically active professional Black women appear to have supported Anita Hill more strongly (although too few such women were surveyed for concrete conclusions). And shortly after Clarence Thomas was sworn in on the Supreme Court, more than 1,600 Black university women took out a full-page *New York Times* advertisement expressing support for Professor Hill. Mansbridge and Tate (1992) suggested that working-class women were profoundly suspicious of Hill's decision not to immediately accuse Thomas of sexual harassment when it occurred. In contrast, professional women realized that such accusations could have been profoundly damaging to Hill's career.

International Comparisons

This chapter focused on the United States. By comparing the information in this chapter to previous chapters, there is an implicit comparison between the United States and other countries in women's formal political participation. But how do gender gaps in the United States compare with those in the rest of the world?

Although we do not have as much data across countries and over time as we do in the United States, International IDEA has compiled information about the gender gap in turnout after 1945 across eight democracies: Barbados, Finland, Germany, Iceland, India, Malta, New Zealand, and Sweden (Pintor and Gratschew 2002). In two of these countries, Barbados and Sweden, women have been voting more often than men since even the 1950s. In countries such as Germany, Finland, and Iceland, women voted less often than men in modest numbers during the 1950s and 1960s. But in all of these countries except for India women have closed the voting gap or reversed it. In India, women have long voted in much lower numbers than men, and although women have progressed over time, they remain substantially underrepresented at the polls (Pintor and Gratschew 2002).

Information on men's and women's voting behavior in the 1990s is available for 19 countries across the world. The group of countries includes not only Western industrialized countries but also a small number of

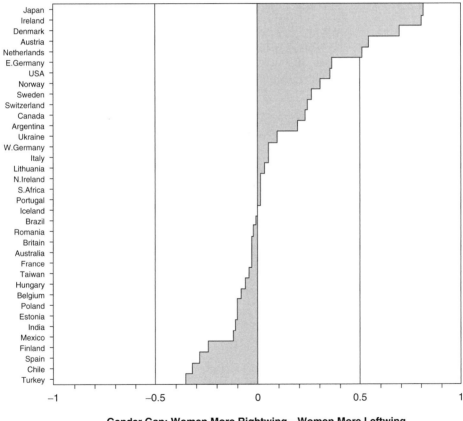

Gender Gap: Women More Rightwing—Women More Leftwing

Figure 9.15   The Gender Gap Around the World

SOURCE: Inglehart and Norris (2000). Reprinted with permission of Sage Publications Ltd.

countries in Latin America, Asia, and Central and Eastern Europe. In most countries, men's and women's participation was close to even. In only one of the countries did women participate at significantly higher rates than men—Sweden. Women reported lower rates of turnout in the newer democracies of Poland, Hungary, and Romania by a margin of 4% to 7% (Pintor and Gratschew 2002).

Similar to the United States, women across the world were historically more conservative than men (Goot and Reid 1975; Inglehart; Klausen 2001; and Norris 2000). In 1960, Seymour Martin Lipset found that "practically every country for which we have data . . . women tend to support the conservative parties more than do men" (p. 221). Similarly, Pulzer (1967:107) argued that in the United Kingdom, "there is overwhelming evidence that women are more conservatively inclined than men." During the 1970s, older women continued to vote more conservatively in the United Kingdom, whereas younger women began to align with the more liberal, or leftist, parties (Klausen 2001).

Also similar to U.S. trends, in the post-1990 period, the gender gap reversed in many advanced industrial societies, and women moved to the left of men (Inglehart and Norris 2000). But women continue to be more conservative than men in postcommunist countries and in the developing world (see Figure 9.15).

In summary, the U.S. gender gap in both voting and party affiliation is currently similar to other advanced industrialized countries. Further, the United States shared with other countries a similar pattern of change in the gender gap over time. Women overtook men in voting rates. And women in the United States, like women in other industrialized countries, switched from voting more conservatively than men to voting more liberally. Thus, as we introduced in the opening of this chapter, the United States is not unusual, exceptional, or unique. Instead, it falls in the middle of the international pack.

10

Where Do We Go From Here?
And How Do We Get There?

We do not have a crystal ball that will allow us to gaze into the future of women in politics. But in this chapter, we review where women have been with an eye to where women may be going. In doing so, we introduce a new measure of women's political representation that accounts for the distribution of the world's population, called the Women Power Index. We also summarize the lessons learned in previous chapters and present several ways for countries and citizens to influence women's incorporation into formal politics in the future.

Where Are We Now?

During the last 100 years, women around the world have made inroads into every area of political decision making. From the scattered and sporadic power of queens and tribal leaders, women are today presidents, prime ministers, parliamentarians, and mayors. In fact, women are not only political leaders but also grassroots activists, revolutionaries, and everyday voters. Truly, the increase in women's political representation over the last century is one of the success stories of the modern world.

But as we have stressed throughout this book, women continue to face substantial barriers to their political equality. As one way to measure

Table 10.1   The Women Power Index, 2005

World	Free	Partly Free	Not Free
14.4%	13.6%	9.6%	17.5%

SOURCES: Freedom House (2006), Inter-Parliamentary Union (2005a), and U.S. Census Bureau (2006).

women's political power, we created the **Women Power Index**. Table 10.1 presents the Women Power Index for 2005. This index focuses on one measure of women's political power, their representation in national legislatures. But unlike a simple world average, the Women Power Index accounts for differences in population across countries. Thus, the index acknowledges that more people (1 billion) live under India's 8% women than the people (4.5 million) who live under Norway's 38% women. The Woman Power Index therefore depicts the level of female representation experienced by the typical person in the world. To calculate the index, take each country's percentage of women in parliament and multiply it by the proportion of the world's population that lives in that country. Then add all countries to give a measure of the percentage of women governing the population of the world.

Overall, the world's population is governed by national legislatures that are 14.4% women. In Table 10.1 we also account for broad differences in governance by creating separate measures for countries that are **free, partly free**, and **not free** (Freedom House 2006). (Territories that are not independent countries are excluded from our calculations, as are countries such as Brunei and Qatar that have no legislatures.) Looking at Table 10.1, one can see that there are significant differences in the Women Power Index across different types of societies. In 2005, citizens of free countries were governed by legislatures that were 13.6% female, whereas partly free societies were more male dominated, living under 9.6% women. Across countries that are not free, the population looked to legislatures that are 17.5% female. These differences provide further evidence of a pattern for women's power that we have seen throughout this book: Women hold a greater share of political positions that are less powerful.

But looking across time, one can see increases in women's political power. Figure 10.1 displays values of the Women Power Index from 1971 to 2000 for free and partly free countries.

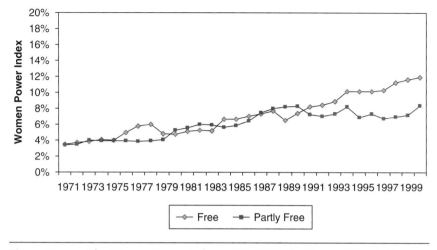

Figure 10.1   The Women Power Index, 1971–2000, for Free and Partly Free
Countries

Overall, Figure 10.1 shows that women have been gaining power over
time, but at a generally slow rate. Women move from a power index value
of about 3.5% in both free and partly free countries in 1971 to just under
12% for free countries and only 8% in partly free countries in 2000. Also,
whereas free and partly free countries were similar in their index scores
until the 1990s, free countries pulled ahead during the 1990s and elected
more women to power.

We can also consider women's political progress across time in other
ways. Table 10.2 presents a snapshot of the number of countries that have
reached certain thresholds of women's representation—10%, 20%, 30%,
40%, and 50%—by mid-year 2005.

Although there are some notable successes, it is clear from this table that
women still have far to go. Although no country has yet achieved 50%
women in parliament, two countries have come close to gender parity,
crossing the threshold of 40% women in parliament (Sweden and Rwanda).
Sixteen countries have at least 30% women in their parliaments, representing all regions of the world except for Asia, the Pacific islands, and North
Africa, and twice that number have passed the threshold of 20%. It is
sobering to see, however, that more than 70% of countries have less than
20% women in parliament, and more than a third of countries have not
even reached 10% women.

Table 10.2   Thresholds of Women's Parliamentary Representation for
185 Countries, June 2005

Threshold	None	10%	20%	30%	40%	50%	Total
Number of Countries	68	67	32	16	2	0	185
Percentage of Total	36.8%	36.2%	17.3%	8.6%	1.1%	0.0%	100.0%

SOURCE: Inter-Parliamentary Union (2005a).

Where Are We Going?

Will women reach 50% of any national legislature in the next 10 years? Will
the United States have a female president in 20 years? Will women in India
ever vote at levels similar to those of men? Obviously, we can only speculate
about the answers to these questions. But some research offers guidance in
thinking about the future of women in politics.

To begin, gender quotas offer a powerful prescriptive for women's future
access to positions of political authority. As we discussed in Chapter 5, the
implementation of quotas has in some countries allowed women to make
large jumps in political representation in a relatively short period of time. In
fact, the "typical picture" of women's acquisition of political power may be
changing from slow and steady progress to fast-tracked power (Dahlerup
and Friedenvall 2005). As Drude Dahlerup (2003:4) explained, "The
Scandinavian experience cannot be considered a model for the 21st century
because it took 80 years to get that far. Today, the women of the world are
not willing to wait that long."

Not only are more countries adopting quotas but quotas are also becoming more effective. Higher quota levels, placement mandates, and sanctions
for noncompliance are creating quotas that better guarantee women a seat
at the table. It is probably safe to say that quotas will continue to increase
levels of women in politics where they are effectively adopted and appropriately enforced. What is less clear is whether some countries will ever feel
comfortable enough with levels of female participation to remove quotas.
We hope that the question of whether to dismantle quotas because they are
no longer needed will be debated sooner rather than later.

Another important trend is the election of female heads of state. Women
are getting elected as presidents and prime ministers at an increasing rate.
It took 20 years for the first five women to be elected as president and
prime minister. The next five were elected in 10 years. Fourteen women
came to power in the 1990s. Even as we wrote this book, we had to revise

Chapter 3's lists of female leaders five times and also incorporate Nancy Pelosi as the newly elected U.S. Speaker of the House. As of March 1, 2006, 4% of the world's governments were headed by women. It is probably safe to say that this number will grow over time but is likely to remain a small percentage of all leaders for some time.

Understanding where various countries of the world are going requires looking at where they have been. In Chapter 3, we introduced five basic historical paths to power: flat, increasing, big jump, small gains, and plateau. Extrapolating forward from these trends suggests certain groups of countries, such as those in the increasing category, where one is likely to see even larger gains in the future. Small gains countries should also be watched because their small gains may turn into long-term increases in women's representation. Another point to remember from our discussion in early chapters is that the West did not necessarily lead the world historically in women's political power and is not currently in the forefront of women's representation. Countries making significant gains in women's representation over the next 10 years are just as likely to be from the global south.

The female leaders of tomorrow are the girls of today. And girls growing up today in most countries are the first generation to see women participating at the highest levels of politics in even moderately large numbers. Apart from a few pioneer countries in Scandinavia and Eastern Europe, women's major gains in politics in most countries of the world occurred in just the last two decades. As Figure 10.1 shows, most women of the free world were living under less than 10% women as recently as 1993. And the average citizen of the partly free world has never lived under more than 10% women in power.

So what will happen when a generation of girls, who see women in political life as normal and appropriate, grows up? Will they participate at even higher levels, helping push the percentage of women in politics to 50% and beyond? We have some help in answering this question in the research of Christina Wolbrecht and David Campbell (2005). Looking across 27 countries, Wolbrecht and Campbell found a pure role model effect of women in politics. In countries with greater numbers of women in parliaments, adolescent girls envisioned themselves participating in politics more often (see also Atkeson 2003; Campbell and Wolbrecht 2006; Koch 1997).

Indeed, Lisa Murkowski, Republican senator from Alaska, experienced some hero worship from young girls:

I am encouraged by the young girls that I see, those still in high school. They are really excited. They are almost giggly, movie-star excited—"Wow! You are a woman in the United States Senate!" You feel kind of silly, but you have to stop and think: This is something that they can look to and say, "I could be there." That is so incredibly important. They can visualize themselves here. (Victor 2005)

A role model effect of women in politics is simultaneously cause for optimism and pessimism. Women around the world generally participate less than men in a variety of political activities. And these sex differences often appear very early among boys and girls (Orum, Cohen, Grasmuck, and Orum 1974; Owen and Dennis 1988). Therefore, if countries with high numbers of women in formal politics produce girls who plan to act politically, then the slow increase in women's political power over the last 100 years might switch to more exponential growth. However, in the countries of the world where women have barely gained a foothold in politics, the prognosis is bleaker. There, it may be generations before girls look at politics and expect a woman's face.

How Do We Get There?

Can one take away any lessons from this book? In this section, we draw on the lessons learned in previous chapters to present ways that countries and citizens can influence women in politics.

Furthering Women's Position in the Social Structure

We discussed that for women to succeed in politics they must have the knowledge, skills, and resources to compete against men. Therefore, organizations, political parties, and governments seeking to empower women politically should work to increase educational and training opportunities for both women and girls. And one must also remember that structural change takes time. Indeed, years will pass before the law student of today becomes the politician of tomorrow. So in the fight for women's representation, the time to arm women with the tools to succeed is now.

A more short-term strategy to improve women's political circumstances is to bolster their financial resources. Running for political office certainly requires money. But countries can level the playing field through public financing of campaigns. Political action organizations, such as EMILY's List, that finance women's campaigns are also key to increasing women's political representation. And individuals seeking to make a difference can contribute to such organizations or to individual female candidates.

Resources such as education and money matter everywhere. But it is also important to remember that the proper solution to the problem of political gender inequality varies depending on the context. And in different countries women must overcome unique barriers. For instance, across parts of the Islamic world, family laws prevent women from effectively participating in the public realm. There, it is the reform of such laws that is the place to start in affecting women's representation.

Influencing Culture

We also explained that changing cultural beliefs may facilitate women's political participation and representation. Although cultural beliefs may seem slow to change (and probably are), change can be enacted when individuals challenge stereotypes and biases when they see them. Beliefs grounded in religion are no exception. When thinking about religion, remember that millions of adherents belonging to all major world religions accept women in politics while maintaining their religious beliefs.

But one must also acknowledge that in some parts of the world, cultural beliefs seem to present almost an insurmountable obstacle to women's political equality. In these contexts, we detailed how the growing interconnectedness of countries across the globe may help to facilitate change. Because countries are part of a global community with global norms and standards, activists and media sources can mobilize information strategically to generate pressure on countries and parties to incorporate women. Further, the international women's movement and the United Nations continue to redefine global norms and standards and to exert pressure on countries. Finally, postconflict reconstruction efforts (such as in Afghanistan and Iraq) may also be places where people can concentrate efforts to benefit women.

Disrupting Politics as Usual

When considering lessons learned about political influences, it is clear that some factors are more amenable to change than others. Although a number of countries have experimented with a variety of constitutional forms, realistically most countries are wedded to their particular electoral system. Still, we encourage citizens to become informed about the variety of electoral systems that exist around the world. Some electoral systems promote not only the representation of women (and other minority groups) but also the representation of a variety of political views.

But even if electoral systems are unchanged, electoral rules may be altered to hasten women's gains in politics. In recent years, quota policies have been adopted in a wide range of countries. But we have learned that the construction of quota laws matters greatly for their efficacy. Therefore, citizen-activists pushing for change should remember that placement mandates and sanctions for noncompliance are critical components of successful gender quota legislation.

In this text, we also argued that political parties serve important functions as gatekeepers to public office. But because political parties operate in a competitive environment, they must be responsive to citizens. Thus, individuals can help women gain political power by expressing their preferences for female candidates to party leaders. And using the power of the vote, citizens can interrupt politics as usual.

Citizens can also look to successful countries for ways to make parliaments and national legislatures more women friendly. For example, in South Africa (with 33% women), the parliamentary calendar was reorganized to match the school calendar. That is, when children are out of school, parliament is out of session. To further recognize that many parliamentarians have family responsibilities, debates end early in the evening and day care is provided (Britton 2006:70). And as we showed, pushing for the formation of women's policy machinery can provide women outside traditional political circles access to government.

Finally, knowing that women are less likely to aspire to or run for public office, we encourage all women to consider running for office at the local, state/regional, or national level. Remember, Fox and Lawless (2004) suggested that women are more qualified than they think. And to men who aspire to public office, Tremblay and Pelletier (2000) remind readers that men can also act as feminists, producing positive action on behalf of women. In the following list are Web resources that can help both men and women further understand women's descriptive and substantive representation:

International IDEA Women in Politics, http://www.idea.int/gender/

IPU Parline Database, http://www.ipu.org/parline-e/parlinesearch.asp

The U.N. Fourth World Conference on Women Platform for Action: Women in Power and Decision-Making, http://www.un.org/womenwatch/daw/beijing/platform/decision.htm

Women's Environment & Development Organization 50/50 Campaign, http://www.wedo.org/campaigns.aspx?mode=5050main

Development Alternatives with Women for a New Era, http://www.dawnorg.org/

Center for American Women and Politics, http://www.cawp.rutgers.edu/index
.html

The White House Project, http://www.thewhitehouseproject.org/index.html

In Conclusion: What Would a 50/50 World Look Like?

In closing, we should stop and consider for a moment what a 50/50 world would look like. What would legislative meetings look like and sound like if 50% of the members were women? What would nuclear arms nonproliferation talks look like and sound like if the leaders negotiating were female? What would the U.S. cabinet and U.S. Supreme Court look like under a string of female presidents?

Anne Phillips (1991:7) provides one vision of a future:

> People are no longer defined through their nature as women or men. In this future scenario, . . . men and women . . . would vary as individuals rather than sexes in their priorities or experience, and would be equally attracted to (or repulsed by!) a political life. In such a context, the notion of the citizen could begin to assume its full meaning, and people could participate as equals in deciding their common goals.

But this 50/50 world is not reality. And we will not know what one looks like until women achieve such levels of power across many countries. And, ultimately, the women of the world need to be educated about their low levels of representation in politics. Kira Sanbonmatsu (2003) found that one area in which women know less about politics than men is in estimating the percentage of women in office. Women are more likely than men to overestimate women's political presence. Sanbonmatsu (2003:367) suggested that "women would be even more supportive of electing women to office if they were as knowledgeable as men about the extent of women's underrepresentation." We hope that this book contributes to this process.

References

Abou-Zeid, Gihan. 2003. "Introducing Quotas in Africa: Discourse in Egypt." Presented at the meeting of the International Institute for Democracy and Electoral Assistance, November 11–12, Pretoria, South Africa.

Abramowitz, Alan I., Brad Alexander, and Matthew Gunning. 2005. "Incumbency, Redistricting, and the Decline of Competition in U.S. House Elections." Prepared for the annual meeting of the Southern Political Science Association, January 6–8, New Orleans, LA.

Abu-Zayd, Gehan. 1998. "In Search of Political Power—Women in Parliament in Egypt, Jordan and Lebanon." *Women in Politics: Beyond Numbers.* Available online at http://archive.idea.int/women/parl/studies1a.htm

Acker, Joan. 1992. "From Sex Roles to Gendered Institutions." *Contemporary Sociology* 21:565–569.

Afghani, Jamila. 2005. "The Current State of Affairs for Afghan Women." Presented at the Afghan Women Leaders Speak Conference, November 16–19, Columbus, OH.

Ahmed, Leila. 1992. *Women and Gender in Islam.* New Haven, CT: Yale University Press.

Alexander, Herbert E. 2001. "Approaches to Campaign and Party Finance Issues." P. 198 in *Foundations for Democracy: Approaches to Comparative Political Finance,* edited by K. Nassmacher. Baden-Baden: Nomos.

Almond, Gabriel Abraham, R. Scott Appleby, and Emmanuel Sivan. 2003. *Strong Religion: The Rise of Fundamentalisms Around the World.* Chicago: University of Chicago Press.

Alqudsi-Ghobra. 2002. "Women in Kuwait: Educated, Modern and Middle Eastern." Available online at http://www.kuwait-info.org/Kuwaiti_Women/women_in_kuwait.html

Alvarez, Sonia. 1990. *Engendering Democracy in Brazil: Women's Movements in Transition Politics.* Princeton, NJ: Princeton University Press.

_____. 1994. "The (Trans)formation of Feminism(s) and Gender Politics in Democratizing Brazil." Pp. 13–63 in *The Women's Movement in Latin America,* edited by J. S. Jaquette. Boulder, CO: Westview Press.

Amnesty International. 2004. "Saudi Arabia: Women's Exclusion from Elections Undermines Progress." Available online at http://news.amnesty.org/index/ ENGMDE230152004

_____. 2005. *Afghanistan: Women Still Under Attack—A Systematic Failure to Protect.* Available online at http://web.amnesty.org/library/pdf/ASA110072005ENGLISH/$File/ASA1100705.pdf

Anderson, Nancy Fix. 1993. "Benazir Bhutto and Dynastic Politics: Her Father's Daughter, Her People's Sister." Pp. 41–69 in *Women as National Leaders,* edited by M. A. Genovese. Newbury Park, CA: Sage.

Antrobus, Peggy. 2000. "Transforming Leadership: Advancing the Agenda for Gender Justice." *Gender and Development* 8(3):50–56.

Araújo, Clara. 2003. "Quotas for Women in the Brazilian Legislative System." Presented at the workshop of the International Institute for Democracy and Electoral Assistance, February 23–24, Lima, Peru.

Arceneaux, Kevin. 2001. "The 'Gender Gap' in State Legislative Representation: New Data to Tackle an Old Question." *Political Research Quarterly* 54:143–60.

Associated Press. 1997. "Marriage No Longer Protects Rapists in Peru." Available online at http://www.newsrx.com/newsletters/Sex-Weekly-Plus/1997-04-21/1997042133315SW .html

———. 2004. "Nobel Laureate Speaks Out for Women." Available online at http://www .yuyu.net/burmanet2-l/archive/0284.html

Atkeson, Lonna Rae. 2003. "Not All Cues Are Created Equal: The Conditional Impact of Female Candidates on Political Engagement." *Journal of Politics* 65:1040–61.

Atwood, Nancy C. 2001. "Gender Bias in Families and Its Clinical Implications for Women." *Social Work* 46:23–36.

Avicenna. [~1000] 1963. "Healing: Metaphysics X." Pp. 98–111 in *Medieval Political Philosophy*, edited by R. Lerner and M. Mahdi, translated by Michael E. Marmura. New York: The Free Press.

Azize-Vargas, Yamila. 2002. "The Emergence of Feminism in Puerto Rico, 1870–1930." Pp. 175–83 in *Latino/a Thought: Culture, Politics, Society*, edited by F. H. Vazquez and R. D. Torres. Lanham, MD: Rowman and Littlefield.

Baker, Paula. 1994. "The Domestication of Politics: Women and American Political Society, 1780–1920." Pp. 85–110 in *Unequal Sisters: A Multicultural Reader in U.S. Women's History*, 2d ed., edited by V. L. Ruiz and E. C. DuBois. New York: Routledge.

Baldez, Lisa. 2003. "Elected Bodies: The Gender Quota Law for Legislative Candidates in Mexico." Presented at the meeting of the American Political Science Association, August 28–31, Philadelphia.

———. 2004. "Elected Bodies: The Gender Quota Law for Legislative Candidates in Mexico." *Legislative Studies Quarterly* 29:231–58.

Ballington, Julie, ed. 2004. *The Implementation of Quotas: Africa Experiences*. Stockholm, Sweden: IDEA.

Barber, E. Susan. 1997. *One Hundred Years toward Suffrage: An Overview*. Available online at http://memory.loc.gov/ammem/naw/nawstime.html

Barnes, Teresa A. 1992. "The Fight for Control of African Women's Mobility in Colonial Zimbabwe, 1900–1939." *Signs: Journal of Women in Culture and Society* 17:586–608.

Bauer, Gretchen. 2004. "'The Hand That Stirs the Pot Can Also Run the Country': Electing Women to Parliament in Namibia." *Journal of Modern African Studies* 42:479–509.

———. 2006. "Namibia: Losing Ground without Mandatory Quotas." Pp. 85–110 in *Women in African Parliaments*, edited by G. Bauer and H. Britton. London: Lynne Rienner.

Baxter, Sandra and Marjorie Lansing. 1983. *Women and Politics: The Visible Majority*. Ann Arbor: University of Michigan Press.

BBC News. 2005a. "Profile: Liberia's 'Iron Lady.'" *BBC News*. November 23.

———. 2005b. "UK Women Earn 27% Less Than Men." *BBC News*. August 30.

Beckwith, Karen. 2005. "The Comparative Politics of Women's Movements." *Perspectives on Politics* 3:583–96.

Bedolla, Lisa García and Becki Scola. 2006. "Finding Intersection: Race, Class, and Gender in the 2003 California Recall Vote." *Politics and Gender* 2:5–27.

Bedolla, Lisa Garcia, Katherine Tate, and Janelle Wong. 2005. "Indelible Effects: The Impact of Women of Color in the U.S. Congress." Pp. 152–175 in *Women and Elective Office:*

Past, Present, and Future, edited by S. Thomas and C. Wilcox. Oxford, UK: Oxford University Press.

Berkman, Michael B. and Robert E. O'Connor. 1993. "Do Women Legislators Matter? Female Legislators and State Abortion Policy." *American Politics Quarterly* 21:102–24.

Berkovitch, Nitza. 1995. "From Motherhood to Citizenship: The Worldwide Incorporation of Women into the Public Sphere in the Twentieth Century." Ph.D. dissertation, Stanford University, Stanford, CA.

————. 1999. *From Motherhood to Citizenship: Women's Rights and International Organizations.* Baltimore: Johns Hopkins University Press.

Beyer, Georgina. 2005. "Biography." Available online at http://www.ps.parliament.govt.nz/mp137.htm

Bielby, William T. and James N. Baron. 1986. "Men and Women at Work: Sex Segregation and Statistical Discrimination." *American Journal of Sociology* 91:759–99.

Binkin, Martin and Shirley J. Bach. 1977. *Women and the Military.* Washington, DC: Brookings Institution.

Birch, Sarah. 2003. "Women and Political Representation in Contemporary Ukraine." Pp. 130–52 in *Women's Access to Political Power in Post-Communist Europe,* edited by R. E. Matland and K. A. Montgomery. Oxford, UK: Oxford University Press.

Black, Jerome H. 2000. "Entering the Political Elite in Canada: The Case of Minority Women as Parliamentary Candidates and MPs." *Canadian Review of Sociology and Anthropology* 37(2):143–66.

Blatch, Harriot Stanton and Alma Lutz. 1940. *Challenging Years: The Memoirs of Harriot Stanton Blatch.* New York: G. P. Putnam's Sons.

Blau, Peter M. 1977. "A Macrosociological Theory of Social Structure." *American Journal of Sociology* 83:26–54.

Blondel, Jean. 1980. *World Leaders: Heads of Government in the Postwar Period.* Beverly Hills, CA: Sage.

————. 1988. "Introduction: Western European Cabinets in Comparative Perspective." Pp. 1–16 in *Cabinets in Western Europe,* edited by J. Blondel and F. Muller-Rommel. London: Macmillan.

————. 1991. "Introduction." Pp. 1–4 in *The Profession of Government Minister in Western Europe,* edited by J. Blondel and J. Thiebault. London: Macmillan.

Bloomfield, David, Teresa Barnes, and Luc Huyse, eds. 2003. *Reconciliation after Violent Conflict: A Handbook.* Halmstad, Sweden: International Institute for Democracy and Electoral Assistance.

Blumberg, Rae L. 1984. "A General Theory of Gender Stratification." *Sociological Theory* 2:23–101.

Bonder, Gloria and Marcela Nari. 1995. "The 30 Percent Quota Law: A Turning Point for Women's Political Participation in Argentina." Pp. 183–93 in *Rising Public Voice: Women in Politics Worldwide,* edited by A. Brill. New York: Feminist Press.

Bonevac, D. W. B. and S. Phillips. 1992. *Beyond the Western Tradition: Readings in Moral and Political Philosophy.* Mountain View, CA: Mayfield.

Booth, Alan R. 1992. "European Courts Protect Women and Witches: Colonial Law Courts as Redistributors of Power in Swaziland 1920–1950." *Journal of Southern African Studies* 18:253–75.

Bop, Codou. 2001. "Women in Conflicts, Their Gains and Their Losses." Pp. 19–34 in *The Aftermath: Women in Post-Conflict Transformation,* edited by S. Meintjes, A. Pillay, and M. Turshen. London: Zed Books.

Borelli, MaryAnne. 2002. *The President's Cabinet: Gender, Power, and Representation.* Boulder, CO: Lynne Rienner.

Boserup, E. 1970. *Women's Role in Economic Development.* London: Allen and Unwin.

Boudreaux, R. 1991. "The Great Conciliator." *Los Angeles Times Magazine,* January 6, Pp. 9–13.

Boxer, Barbara. 1994. *Strangers in the Senate: Politics and the New Revolution of Women in America.* Washington, DC: National Press Books.

Boyd, Rosalind E. 1989. "Empowerment of Women in Uganda: Real or Symbolic." *Review of African Political Economy* 45/46:106–17.

Bratton, Kathleen A. 2005. "Critical Mass Theory Revisited: The Behavior and Success of Token Women in State Legislatures." *Gender and Politics* 1:97–195.

Bratton, Kathleen A., and Kerry L. Haynie. 1999. "Agenda Setting and Legislative Success in State Legislatures: The Effects of Gender and Race." *Journal of Politics* 61:658–79.

Braun, Carol Moseley. 2003. "Giving Life to Declaration of Intent: A Call to Citizenship." Presented at Roosevelt University, February 26, Chicago, IL.

Brickhill, P., C. O. Hoppers, and K. Pehrsson. 1996. *Textbooks as an Agent of Change.* Stockholm, Sweden: SIDA.

British Broadcasting Corporation. 2001. "Candidate Selection." Available online at http://news.bbc.co.uk

Britton, Hannah E. 2001. "New Struggles, New Strategies: Emerging Patterns of Women's Political Participation in the South African Parliament." *International Politics* 38:173–200.

———. 2003. "Coalition Building, Election Rules, and Party Politics: South African Women's Path to Parliament." *Africa Today* 49(4):33–67.

———. 2005. *Women in the South African Parliament: From Resistance to Governance.* Urbana, IL: University of Illinois Press.

———. 2006. "South Africa: Mainstreaming Gender in a New Democracy." Pp. 59–84 in *Women in African Parliaments,* edited by G. Bauer and H. E. Britton. London: Lynne Rienner.

Brown, Barbara A., Thomas I. Emerson, Gail Falk, and Ann E. Freedman. 1971. "The Equal Rights Amendment: A Constitutional Basis for Equal Rights for Women." *The Yale Law Journal* 80:871–985.

Burk, Martha. 2005. "Women Earn Less, Period." *Miami Herald.* April 12. Available online at www.commondreams.org/views05/0412-30.htm

Burn, Shawn Meghan. 2005. *Women Across Cultures: A Global Perspective,* 2d ed. New York: McGraw-Hill.

Burns, Nancy, Kay Lehman Schlozman, and Sidney Verba. 2001. *The Private Roots of Public Action: Gender, Equality, and Political Participation.* Cambridge, MA: Harvard University Press.

Burrell, Barbara C. 1994. *A Woman's Place Is in the House: Campaigning for Congress in the Feminist Era.* Ann Arbor: University of Michigan Press.

———. 1998. "Campaign Finance: Women's Experience in the Modern Era." Pp. 26–37 in *Women and Elective Office: Past, Present, and Future.* Oxford, UK: Oxford University Press.

———. 2004. *Women and Political Participation: A Reference Handbook.* Santa Barbara, CA: ABC-CLIO.

Burundi Parliamentary. 2006. "Burundi Parliamentary." Available online at http://www.burundi.gov.bi/parlement.htm

Bussey, Jane. 2000. "Campaign Finance Goes Global." *Foreign Policy* 118(Spring):74–84.

Byanyima, Karagwa W. 1992. Women in political struggle in Uganda. Pp. 129–42 in *Women Transforming Politics: Worldwide Strategy for Empowerment,* edited by J. M. Bystylzienski. Bloomington: Indiana University Press.

Bystydzienski, Jill M., ed. 1992. *Women Transforming Politics: Worldwide Strategies for Empowerment.* Bloomington: Indiana University Press.

———. 1995. *Women in Electoral Politics: Lessons From Norway.* Westport, CT: Praeger.

Cahill, Spencer E. 1986. "Childhood Socialization as Recruitment Process: Some Lessons from the Study of Gender Development." Pp. 163–86 in *Sociological Studies of Child Development,* edited by P. Adler and P. Adler. Greenwich, CT: JAI Press.

Calasanti, Toni M. and Carol A. Bailey. 1991. "Gender Inequality and the Division of Household Labor in the United States and Sweden: A Socialist-Feminist Approach." *Social Problems* 38:34–53.

Caldwell, John C. 1986. "Routes to Low Mortality in Poor Countries." *Population and Development Review* 12:171–220.

Camp, Roderic A. 1998. "Women and Men, Men and Women: Gender Patterns in Mexican Politics." Pp. 167–78 in *Women's Participation in Mexican Political Life,* edited by Victoria E. Rodriguez. Boulder, CO: Westview Press.

Campbell, David and Christina Wolbrecht. 2006. "See Jane Run: Women Politicians as Role Models for Adolescents." *Journal of Politics* 68:233–47.

Cantor, Dorothy W., Toni Bernay, and Jean Stoess. 1992. *Women in Power: The Secrets of Leadership.* Boston: Houghton Mifflin.

Caprioli, Mary and Mark A. Boyer. 2001. "Gender, Violence, and International Crisis." *The Journal of Conflict Resolution* 45(4):503–18.

Carey, J. M., R. G. Niemi, and L. W. Powell. 1998. "The Effects of Term Limits on State Legislatures." *Legislative Studies Quarterly* 23:271–300.

Carras, Mary C. 1995. "Indira Gandhi: Gender and Foreign Policy." Pp. 45–58 in *Women in World Politics: An Introduction,* edited by F. D'Amico and P. R. Beckman. London: Burgin and Garvey.

Carroll, Susan J. 1984. "Women Candidates and Support for Feminist Concerns: The Closet Feminist Syndrome." *Western Political Quarterly* 37:307–23.

———. 1988. "Women's Autonomy and the Gender Gap: 1980 and 1982." Pp. 236–57 in *The Politics of the Gender Gap,* edited by C. Mueller. Newbury Park, CA: Sage.

Carroll, Susan J. and Debra L. Dodson. 1991. "Introduction." Pp. 1–11 in *Gender and Policymaking: Studies of Women in Office,* edited by D. L. Dodson. New Brunswick, NJ: Center for the American Woman and Politics.

Carroll, Susan J. and Krista Jenkins. 2001. "Do Term Limits Help Women Get Elected?" *Social Science Quarterly* 82:197–202.

Casas-Zamora, Kevin. 2005. "Political Finance Regulation in Guatemala: A Comparative Survey." IFES White Paper II. Available online at http://www.moneyandpolitics.net/researchpubs/pdf/Political_Finance_Guatemala.pdf

Catt, Carrie C. 1918. "Do You Know? Voting Facts About Women." Washington, DC: Library of Congress, Rare Book and Special Collections Division, National American Woman Suffrage Association Collection.

Caul, Miki. 1999. "Women's Representation in Parliament: The Role of Political Parties." *Party Politics* 5(1):79–98.

———. 2001. "Political Parties and the Adoption of Candidate Gender Quotas: A Cross-National Analysis." *The Journal of Politics* 63(4):1214–29.

CBS News. 2006. "Ready for a Woman President." Available online at http://www.cbsnews.com/stories/2006/02/03/opinion/polls/main1281319.shtml

Center for American Women and Politics. 1997. *The Gender Gap: Attitudes on Public Policy Issues.* New Brunswick, NJ: Center for American Women and Politics.
Center for American Women and Politics (CAWP) is an outstanding reference for students of American women in politics. We drew from the data on their Web site and from many of their fact sheets in writing Chapter 9. We suggest that anyone interested in women in American politics bookmark CAWP's site (www.cawp.rutgers.edu) as an essential resource.

_____. 1999. *Gender Gap Evident in Numerous 1998 Races.* New Brunswick, NJ: Center for American Women and Politics.

_____. 2001. *Women State Legislators: Past, Present, and Future.* New Brunswick, NJ: Center for American Women and Politics.

_____. 2004. *Gender Gap Persists in the 2004 Election.* New Brunswick, NJ: Center for American Women and Politics.

_____. 2005a. *The Gender Gap: Party Identification and Presidential Performance Ratings.* New Brunswick, NJ: Center for American Women and Politics.

_____. 2005b. *The Gender Gap: Voting Choices in Presidential Elections.* New Brunswick, NJ: Center for American Women and Politics.

_____. 2005c. *Sex Differences in Voter Turnout.* New Brunswick, NJ: Center for American Women and Politics.

_____. 2006a. *Fact Sheet: Women of Color in Elective Office 2006: Congress, Statewide, State Legislature.* New Brunswick, NJ: Center for American Women and Politics.

_____. 2006b. *Fact Sheet: Women in State Legislatures 2006.* New Brunswick, NJ: Center for American Women and Politics.

_____. 2006c. *Statewide Elected Executive Women 2006.* New Brunswick, NJ: Center for American Women and Politics.

_____. 2006d. *Women Candidates for Governor 1970–2004: Major Party Nominees.* New Brunswick, NJ: Center for American Women and Politics.

_____. 2006e. *Women in the U.S. Congress 2006.* New Brunswick, NJ: Center for American Women and Politics.

Center for Reproductive Rights. 2004. "CEDAW: The Importance of U.S. Ratification." Item F021. Available online at http://www.reproductiverights.org/pub_fac_cedaw.html

Central Intelligence Agency. 2004. "Rwanda." *CIA Factbook 2004.* Available online at http://www.cia.gov/cia/publications/factbook/geos/rw.html

_____. 2005. *The World Factbook.* Available online at http://www.cia.gov/cia/publications/factbook/

_____. 2006a. "Burundi." *CIA Factbook.* Available online at http://www.cia.gov/cia/publications/factbook/geos/by.html

_____. 2006b. *Chiefs of State and Cabinet Members of Foreign Governments.* Available online at http://www.odci.gov/cia/publications/chiefs/

_____. 2006c. "Chile." *CIA Factbook.* Available online at http://www.cia.gov/cia/publications/factbook/geos/ci.html

Chafetz, Janet S. 1984. *Sex and Advantage: A Comparative Macrostructural Theory of Sex Stratification.* Totowa, NJ: Rowman and Allanheld.

_____. 1990. *Gender Equity: An Integrated Theory of Stability and Change.* Newbury Park, CA: Sage.

Chafetz, Janet S. and Anthony Gary Dworkin. 1986. *Female Revolt: Women's Movements in World and Historical Perspective.* Totowa, NJ: Rowman and Allanheld.

Chaney, Elsa. 1973. "Women in Latin American Politics: The Case of Peru and Chile." Pp. 104–39 in *Male and Female in Latin America,* edited by A. Pescatello. Pittsburgh, PA: University of Pittsburgh Press.

Channock, Martin. 1982. "Making Customary Law: Men, Women and Courts in Colonial Northern Rhodesia." Pp. 53–67 in *African Women and the Law: Historical Perspectives*, edited by M. J. Hay and M. Wright. Boston: Boston University.

Charrad, Mounira M. 2001. *States and Women's Rights: The Making of Postcolonial Tunisia, Algeria and Morocco*. Berkeley: University of California Press.

Chazan, Naomi. 1989. "Gender Perspectives on African States." Pp. 185–201 in *Women and the State in Africa*, edited by J. L. Parpart and K. A. Staudt. Boulder, CO: Lynne Rienner.

Chen, Martha A. 1995. "Engendering World Conferences: The International Women's Movement and the United Nations." *Third World Quarterly* 16(3):477–95.

Childs, Sarah. 2002. "Hitting the Target: Are Labour Women MPs 'Acting for' Women?" *Parliamentary Affairs* 55:143–53.

Childs, Sarah and Mona Krook. 2005. "The Substantive Representation: Rethinking the 'Critical Mass' Debate." Presented at the American Political Science Association, September 1–4, Washington, DC.

Childs, Sarah and Julie Withey. 2004. "Women Representatives Acting for Women: Sex and the Signing of Early Day Motions in the 1997 British Parliament." *Political Studies* 52:552–64.

Chilean Government. 2006. "President-Elect Michelle Bachelet Named Her Cabinet." Available online at http://www.chileangovernment.cl/index.php?option=com_content&task=view&id=577&Itemid=2

Chodorow, Nancy. 1978. *The Reproduction of Mothering*. Berkeley: University of California Press.

Chou, B. E. and J. Clark. 1994. "Electoral Systems and Women's Representation in Taiwan: The Impact of the Reserved-Seat System." Pp. 161–170 in *Electoral Systems in Comparative Perspective: Their Impact on Women and Minorities*, edited by Wilma Rule and J. F. Zimmerman. Westport, CT: Greenwood.

Chowdhury, Najma. 2002. "The Implementation of Quotas: Bangladesh Experience—Dependence and Marginality in Politics." Presented at the regional workshop of the International Institute for Democracy and Electoral Assistance, November 11–12, Jakarta, Indonesia.

Christensen, Ray. 2000. "The Impact of Electoral Rules in Japan." Pp. 25–46 in *Democracy and the Status of Women in East Asia*, edited by R. J. Lee and C. Clark. Boulder, CO: Lynne Rienner.

Chuchryk, Patricia. 1991. "Feminist Anti-Authoritarian Politics: The Role of Women's Organizations in the Chilean Transition to Democracy." Pp. 149–84 in *The Women's Movement in Latin America: Feminism and the Transition to Democracy*, edited by J. Jaquette. Boulder, CO: Westview Press.

Cillizza, Chris. 2005. "Emily's List Celebrates Clout as It Turns 20: Pro-Abortion-Rights Candidates Championed." *The Washington Post*, October 18, p. A13.

Cingranelli, David L. and David L. Richards. 2004a. *The Cingranelli-Richards (CIRI) Human Rights Database Coder Manual*. Manual Version 8.01.04. Available online at http://ciri.binghamton.edu/documentation/web_version_7_31_04_ciri_coding_guide.pdf#search=%22The%20Cingranelli-Richards%20coder%20manual%22

———. 2004b. *The Cingranelli-Richards (CIRI) Human Rights Dataset*. Available online at http://www.humanrightsdata.org

Clift, Eleanor. 2003. *Founding Sisters and the Nineteenth Amendment*. Hoboken, NJ: Wiley & Sons.

Coalition on Revival. 1999. *The Christian Worldview of the Family*. Available online at http://www.reformation.net/cor/cordocs/family.pdf

Cole, Judith K. 1990. "A Wide Field for Usefulness: Women's Civil Status and the Evolution of Women's Suffrage on the Montana Frontier, 1864–1914." *American Journal of Legal History* 34:262–94.

Commonwealth Secretariat. 1999. *Women in Politics: Voices From the Commonwealth.* London: Commonwealth Secretariat.

Connell, R. W. 1987. *Gender and Power: Society, the Person, and Sexual Politics.* Cambridge, MA: Polity.

Conover, Pamela Johnston. 1988. "Feminists and the Gender Gap." *Journal of Politics* 50:985–1010.

Conover, Pamela Johnston and Virginia Sapiro. 1993. "Gender, Feminist Consciousness, and War." *American Journal of Political Science* 37: 1079–99.

Conway, M. M., Gertrude A. Steuernagel, and David W. Ahern. 1997. *Women and Political Participation: Cultural Change in the Political Arena.* Washington, DC: CQ Press.

Cook, Elizabeth A. and Clyde Wilcox. 1991. "Feminism and the Gender Gap: A Second Look." *Journal of Politics* 53:1111–22.

Cook, Rebecca J. 1994. "State Accountability Under the Convention on the Elimination of All Forms of Discrimination Against Women." Pp. 228–56 in *Human Rights of Women: National and International Perspectives,* edited by R. J. Cook. Philadelphia: University of Pennsylvania Press.

Coole, Diana H. 1988. *Women in Political Theory: From Ancient Misogyny to Contemporary Feminism.* Sussex, UK: Wheatsheaf Books.

Cornwall, Marie, Eric C. Dahlin, and Brayden G. King. 2005. "Mobilization, Strategies, and Elite Support: An Institutionalist Analysis of State-Level Woman Suffrage Movement Outcomes." Unpublished Manuscript.

Costa, Paul T., Jr., Antonio Terracciano, and Robert R. McCrae. 2001. "Gender Differences in Personality Traits Across Cultures: Robust and Surprising Findings." *Journal of Personality and Social Psychology* 81:322–31.

Craske, Nikki. 1999. *Women and Politics in Latin America.* New Brunswick, NJ: Rutgers University Press.

Crenshaw, Kimberlé. 1991. "Mapping the Margins: Intersectionality, Identity, Politics and Violence Against Women of Color." *Stanford Law Review* 43:1241–99.

———. 1994. "Mapping the Margins: Intersectionality, Identity Politics, and Violence Against Women of Color." Pp. 93–118 in *The Public Nature of Private Violence,* edited by M. A. Fineman and R. Mykitiuk. New York: Routledge.

Critchlow, Donald T. 2005. *Phyllis Schlafly and Grassroots Conservativism: A Woman's Crusade.* Princeton, NJ: Princeton University Press.

Czudnowski, Moshe M. 1975. "Political Recruitment." Pp. 155–242 in *Handbook of Political Science: Micropolitical Theory,* vol. 2, edited by F. I. Greenstein and N. W. Polsby. Reading, MA: Addison Wesley.

Dahlerup, Drude. 1988. "From a Small to a Large Minority: Women in Scandinavian Politics." *Scandinavian Political Studies* 11:275–98.

———. 2002. "Using Quotas to Increase Women's Political Representation." Pp. 91–106 in *Women in Parliament: Beyond Numbers,* edited by A. Karam. Stockholm, Sweden: IDEA.

———. 2003. "Quotas Are Changing the History of Women." Presented at an International Institute for Democracy and Electoral Assistance conference, November 11–13, Pretoria, South Africa.

Dahlerup, Drude and Lenita Friedenvall. 2005. "Quotas as a 'Fast Track' to Equal Representation for Women." *International Feminist Journal of Politics* 7:26–48.

Dahlerup, Drude and Anja Taarup Nordlund. 2004. "Gender Quotas: A Key to Equality? A Case Study of Iraq and Afghanistan." *European Political Science* 3:91–8.

D'Amico, Francine. 1995. "Women National Leaders." Pp. 15–30 in *Women in World Politics: An Introduction,* edited by Francine D'Amico and Peter R. Beckman. London: Bergin and Garvey.

D'Amico, Francine and Peter R. Beckman, eds. 1995. *Women in World Politics: An Introduction*. London: Bergin and Garvey.

Dao, James. 2002. "Senate Panel Approves Treaty Banning Bias Against Women." *New York Times*, July 31, p. A3.

Darcy, R. 1996. "Women in the State Legislative Power Structure: Committee Chairs." *Social Science Quarterly* 77:888–98.

Darcy, R. and James R. Choike. 1986. "A Formal Analysis of Legislative Turnover: Women Candidates and Legislative Representation." *American Journal of Political Science* 30:237–55.

Darcy, R. and Charles D. Hadley. 1988. "Black Women in Politics: The Puzzle of Success." *Social Science Quarterly* 69:629–45.

Darcy, R. and D. L. Nixon. 1996. "Women in the 1946 and 1993 Japanese House of Representatives Elections: The Role of the Election System." *Journal of Northeast Asian Studies* 15:3–19.

Darcy, R. and Sarah Slavin Schramm. 1977. "When Women Run Against Men: The Electorate's Response to Congressional Contests." *Public Opinion Quarterly* 41(Spring):1–12.

Darcy, R., Susan Welch, and Janet Clark. 1994. *Women, Elections, and Representation*. Lincoln: University of Nebraska Press.

Davis, Rebecca. 1997. *Women and Power in Parliamentary Democracies: Cabinet Appointments in Western Europe, 1968–1992*. Lincoln: University of Nebraska Press.

Day, Lynda R. 1994. "The Evolution of Female Chiefship During the Late Nineteenth-Century Wars of the Mende." *The International Journal of African Historical Studies* 27:481–503.

de Figueres, Karen Olsen. 2002. "A People Marching-Women in Parliament in Costa Rica." Available online at http://archive.idea.int/women/parl/studies3a.htm

Denich, Bogdan. 1981. "Women and Political Power in a Revolutionary Society: The Yugoslav Case." Pp. 115–23 in *Access to Power: Cross-National Studies of Women and Elites*, edited by C. F. Epstein and R. L. Coser. London: George Allen & Unwin.

De Pauw, Linda G. 1981. "Women in Combat: 'The Revolutionary War Experience.'" *Armed Forces and Society* 7(2):209–66.

Diamond, Irene. 1977. *Sex Roles in the Statehouse*. New Haven, CT: Yale University Press.

Disney, Jennifer Leigh. 2006. "Mozambique: Empowering Women through Family Law." Pp. 31–57 in *Women in African Parliaments*, edited by G. Bauer and H. Britton. London: Lynne Rienner.

D'Itri, Patricia Ward. 1999. *Cross Currents in the International Women's Movement, 1848–1948*. Bowling Green, OH: Bowling Green University Popular Press.

Dolan, Kathleen. 1997. "Support for Women's Interests in the 103rd Congress: The Distinct Impact of Congressional Women." *Women and Politics* 18:81–94.

———. 1998. "Voting for Women in the 'Year of the Woman.'" *American Journal of Political Science* 42:272–93.

Donahoe, Debra Anne. 1999. Measuring Work in Developing Countries. *Population and Development Review* 25:543–76.

Dowd, Maureen. 1991. "7 Congresswomen March to Senate to Demand Delay in Thomas Vote." *New York Times*, October 9, p. A1.

Dubeck, Paula J. 1976. "Women and Access to Political Office: A Comparison of Female and Male State Legislators." *Sociological Quarterly* 17(1):42–52.

DuBois, Ellen C. 1998. *Women's Suffrage and Women's Rights*. New York: New York University Press.

Duerst-Lahti, Georgia. 1997. "Reconceiving Theories of Power: Consequences of Masculinism in the Executive Branch." Pp. 11–32 in *The Other Elites: Women, Politics, and Power in the Executive Branch*, edited by M. A. Borrelli and J. M. Martin. Boulder, CO: Lynne Rienner.

Dugger, Celia W. 2001. "Abortions in India Spurred by Sex Test Skew the Ratio Against Girls." *New York Times*, April 22, p. 12.

Dutton, M. A. 1992. *Empowering and Healing the Battered Woman*. New York: Springer.

Duverger, Maurice. 1955. *The Political Role of Women*. Paris: UNESCO.

Eagly, Alice H. and Mary C. Johannesen-Schmidt. 2001. "The Leadership Styles of Women and Men." *Journal of Social Issues* 57:781–97.

Eagly, Alice H. and B. T. Johnson. 1990. "Gender and Leadership Style: A Meta-Analysis." *Psychological Bulletin* 108:233–56.

Eagly, Alice H. and S. J. Karau. 2002. "Role Congruity Theory of Prejudice toward Female Leaders." *Psychological Review* 109:573–98.

Eagly, Alice H., M. G. Makhijani, and B. G. Klonsky. 1992. "Gender and the Evaluation of Leaders: A Meta-Analysis." *Psychological Bulletin* 111:3–22.

The Economist. 2005. "A Spoil-the-Men's Party." *The Economist*, April 14. Available online at http://www.economist.com/displayStory.cfm?story_id=3871283

Ehrick, Christine. 1998. "Madrinas and Missionaries: Uruguay and the Pan-American Women's Movement." *Gender and History* 10:406–24.

Einhorn, Barbara. 1991. "Where Have All the Women Gone? Women and the Women's Movement in East Central Europe." *Feminist Review* 39(Autumn): 16–36.

———. 1992. "German Democratic Republic: Emancipated Women or Hardworking Mothers?" Pp. 125–54 in *Superwoman and the Double Burden*, edited by C. Corrin. London: Scarlet Press.

Eisenstein, Zillah R. 1993. *The Color of Gender: Reimaging Democracy*. Berkeley: University of California Press.

Elazar, Daniel J. 1966. *American Federalism: A View from the States*. New York: Harper & Row.

Election World. 2005. *The World Database on Elections*. Available online at http://www.electionworld.org/

Elfin, Margery L. 1982. "Learning From Failures Present and Past." *PS* 15:585–87.

EMILY's List. 2006. "Emily's List." Available online at http://www.emilyslist.org

EMILY's List Australia. 2005. "Welcome to EMILY's List Australia." Available online at http://www.emilyslist.org.au/

England, Paula, Marilyn Chassie, and Linda McCormack. 1982. "Skill Demands and Earnings in Female and Male Occupations." *Sociology and Social Research* 66:147–68.

Enloe, Cynthia. 1980. "Women as the Reserve Army of Labor." *Review of Radical Political Economics* 12(Summer):42–52.

———. 1987. "Feminist Thinking about War, Militarism, and Peace." Pp. 526–47 in *Analyzing Gender: A Handbook of Social Science Research*, edited by Beth B. Hess and Myra Marx Ferree. Newbury Park, CA: Sage.

Etienne, Mona. 1980. "Women and Men, Cloth and Colonization: The Transformation of Production-Distribution Relations among the Baule (Ivory Coast)." Pp. 518–35 in *Women and Colonization: Anthropological Perspectives*, edited by M. Etienne and E. Leacock. New York: Praeger.

Everett, Jana. 1993. "Indira Gandhi and the Exercise of Power." Pp. 103–134 in *Women as National Leaders*, edited by M. A. Genovese. Newbury Park, CA: Sage.

Fallon, Kathleen. 2003. "Transforming Women's Citizenship Rights within an Emerging Democratic State: The Case of Ghana." *Gender and Society* 17:525–43.

Falwell, Jerry. 1980. *Listen America!* Garden City, NY: Doubleday.

"Finnish Women." 1911. *Dawson Daily News*, March 22. Available online at http://www.explorenorth.com/library/vignettes/bl-FinnWomen1911.htm

Fischer, Audrey. 1994. "Winning the Vote for Women." *Library of Congress Information Bulletin*, April 15. Available online at http://www.loc.gov/loc/lcib/9607/suffrage.html

Flexner, Eleanor. 1975. *Century of Struggle: The Woman's Rights Movement in the United States*. Cambridge, MA: Belknap Press.

Flynn, Trisha. 1995. "Corporation Quakes, All Because of a T-Shirt Message." *Rocky Mountain News*, October 15, p. A72.

Fodor, Eva. 2002. "Smiling Women and Fighting Men: The Gender of the Communist Subject in State Socialist Hungary." *Gender and Society* 16:240–63.

Food and Agriculture Organization. 2003. *One Woman's Day in Sierra Leone*. Available online at http://www.fao.org/NEWS/FACTFILE/FF9719-E.HTM

Ford, Lynne E. and Kathleen Dolan. 1999. "Women State Legislators: Three Decades of Gains in Representation and Diversity." Pp. 203–18 in *Women in Politics: Outsiders or Insiders*, edited by Lois Duke Whitaker, 3d ed. Upper Saddle River, NJ: Prentice Hall.

Fox, Richard L. and Jennifer L. Lawless. 2004. "Entering the Arena? Gender and the Decision to Run for Office." *American Journal of Political Science* 48:264–80.

Fox, Richard L. and Zoe M. Oxley. 2003. "Gender Stereotyping in State Executive Elections: Candidate Selection and Success." *Journal of Politics* 56:833–50.

Franceschet, Susan. 2001. "Women in Politics in Post-Transitional Democracies: The Chilean Case." *International Feminist Journal of Politics* 3:207–36.

Freedom House. 2006. *Freedom in the World*. New York: Rowman and Littlefield.

Freeman, Jo. 1987. "Feminist Influence in the Democratic and Republican Parties." Pp. 215–44 in *The Women's Movements of the United States and Western Europe: Feminist Consciousness, Political Opportunity and Public Policy*, edited by M. C. M. Katzenstein. Philadelphia, PA: Temple University Press.

Freidenvall, Lenita. 2003. "Women's Political Representation and Gender Quotas—The Swedish Case." *Stockholm Working Paper Series* 2. Stockholm, Sweden: Stockholm University.

French, Marilyn. 1992. *The War Against Women*. New York: Summit Books.

Friedman, Elisabeth J. 1998. "Paradoxes of Gendered Political Opportunity in the Venezuelan Transition to Democracy." *Latin American Research Review* 33:87–135.

———. 2000. "State-Based Advocacy for Gender Equality in the Developing World: Assessing the Venezuelan National Women's Agency." *Women and Politics* 21:47–80.

———. 2003. "Gendering the Agenda: The Impact of the Transnational Women's Rights Movement at the UN Conferences of the 1990s." *Women's Studies International Forum* 26:313–31.

Furlong, Marlea and Kimberly Riggs. 1996. "Women's Participation in National-Level Politics and Government: The Case of Costa Rica." *Women's Studies International Forum* 19:633–43.

Gabiro, Gabriel. 2004. "Women behind Bars for Genocide." Available online at http://www.hirondelle.org/hirondelle.nsf/0/7f71ee4cc01128aec1256e660077b8f8?Open Document

Gaddie, Ronald Keith and Charles S. Bullock III. 1997. "Structural and Elite Features in Open Seat and Special U.S. House Elections: Is There a Sexual Bias?" *Political Research Quarterly* 50:459–68.

Gal, Susan and Gail Kligman. 2000. *The Politics of Gender after Socialism: A Comparative Historical Essay*. Princeton, NJ: Princeton University Press.

Gallagher, Michael and Michael Marsh, eds. 1988. *Candidate Selection in Comparative Perspective: The Secret Garden of Politics*. Beverly Hills, CA: Sage.

Gamson, William A. 1990. *The Strategy of Social Protest.* Belmont, CA: Wadsworth.

Gardner, Catherine Villanueva. 2006. *Historical Dictionary of Feminist Philosophy.* London: Scarecrow Press.

Gay, Claudine and Katherine Tate. 1998. "Doubly Bound: The Impact of Gender and Race on the Politics of Black Women." *Political Psychology* 19:169–84.

Geisler, Gisela. 1995. "Troubled Sisterhood: Women and Politics in Southern Africa: Case Studies from Zambia, Zimbabwe, and Botswana." *African Affairs* 94: 545–78.

Gelb, Joyce and Marian Lief Palley. 1987. *Women and Public Policies.* Princeton, NJ: Princeton University Press.

General Accounting Office. 2003. "Women's Earnings: Word Patterns Partially Explain Differences between Men's and Women's Earnings." Washington, DC: General Accounting Office.

Genovese, Michael A., ed. 1993. *Women as National Leaders.* Newbury Park, CA: Sage.

Gerami, Shahin. 1996. *Women and Fundamentalism: Islam and Christianity.* New York: Garland.

Gerami, Shahin and Melodye Lehnerer. 2001. "Women's Agency and Household Diplomacy: Negotiating Fundamentalism." *Gender and Society* 15:556–73.

Gerson, Kathleen. 1985. *Hard Choices: How Women Decide about Work, Career, and Motherhood.* Berkeley: University of California Press.

Giddings, Paula. 1996. *When and Where I Enter: The Impact of Black Women on Race and Sex in America.* New York: Quill William Morrow.

Giele, J. Z. and A. C. Smock, eds. 1977. *Women, Roles, and Status in Eight Countries.* New York: Wiley and Sons.

Giriazzo, Alicia. 2004. "Ten Years After: Women in Sandinista Nicaragua." Available online at http://www.epica.org/Library/women/nica_women.htm

Givhan, Robin. 2005. "Condoleezza Rice's Commanding Clothes." *Washington Post.* February 25, p. C01.

Glaser, Kurt and Stefan T. Possony. 1979. *Victims of Politics: The State of Human Rights.* New York: Columbia University Press.

Goetz, Anne Marie. 1995. "The Politics of Integrating Gender to State Development Processes: Trends, Opportunities and Constraints in Bangladesh, Chile, Jamaica, Mali, Morocco, and Uganda." Occasional Paper #2, Fourth World Conference on Women. Geneva, Switzerland: United Nations Research Institute for Social Development.

———. 2003. "Women's Political Effectiveness: A Conceptual Framework." Pp. 29–80 in *No Shortcuts to Power: African Women in Politics and Policy-Making,* edited by A. M. Goetz and S. Hassim. London: Zed Books.

Goetz, Anne Marie and Shireen Hassim, eds. 2003. *No Shortcuts to Power: African Women in Politics and Policy Making.* London: Zed Books.

Goldman, Nancy, ed. 1982. *Female Soldiers—Combatants or Noncombatants? Historical and Contemporary Perspectives.* Westport, CT: Greenwood.

Goldstein, Joshua S. 2001. *War and Gender: How Gender Shapes the War System and Vice Versa.* Cambridge, UK: Cambridge University Press.

Goot, Murray and Elizabeth Reid. 1975. *Women and Voting Studies: Mindless Matrons or Sexist Scientism.* Beverly Hills, CA: Sage.

Gordon, Rosemary. 1998. "'Girls Cannot Think as Boys Do': Socialising Children Through the Zimbabwe School System." *Gender and Development* 6:53–58.

Goven, Joanna. 1993. "Gender Politics in Hungary: Autonomy and Anti-Feminism." Pp. 224–40 in *Gender Politics and Post-Communism: Reflections from Eastern Europe and the Soviet Union,* edited by N. Funk and M. Mueller. New York: Routledge.

Gray, Tricia J. 2003. "Electoral Gender Quotas: Lessons from Argentina and Chile." *Bulletin of Latin American Research* 22:52–78.

Green, Jennifer L. 2004. "Uncovering Collective Rape: A Comparative Study of Political Sexual Violence." *International Journal of Sociology* 34:97–116.

Grey, Sandra. 2002. "Does Size Matter? Critical Mass and New Zealand's Women MPs." *Parliamentary Affairs* 55:19–29.

Grimshaw, Patricia. 1994. "Women's Suffrage in New Zealand Revisited: Writing from the Margins." Pp. 25–41 in *Suffrage and Beyond: International Feminist Perspectives*, edited by Caroline Daley and Melanie Nolan. New York: New York University Press.

Gronlund, Paula. 2003. "Women Members of Finland's Parliament." Available online at http://www.eduskunta.fi/efakta/opas/tiedotus/naisede.htm

Haavio-Mannila, Elina, and Torild Skard, eds. 1985. *Unfinished Democracy: Women in Nordic Politics*. Oxford, UK: Pergamon Press.

Hadassah. 2004. "Focus On: Women's Rights Worldwide." Available online at http://www.hadassah.org/news/content/per_american/archive/2004/04summer/focus.html

Hale, Sondra. 2001. *Liberated, But Not Free: Women in Post-War Eritrea*. London: Zed Books.

Halperin-Kaddari, Ruth. 2004. *Women in Israel: A State of Their Own*. Philadelphia: University of Pennsylvania Press.

Hancock, Ange-Marie. 2005. "When Multiplication Doesn't Equal Quick Addition: Examining Intersectionality as a Research Paradigm." Presented at the annual meeting of the American Political Science Association, September 1–4, Washington, DC.

Hannam, June, Mitzi Auchterlonie, and Katherine Holden. 2000. *International Encyclopedia of Women's Suffrage*. Santa Barbara, CA: ABC-CLIO.

Hansen, Karen V. 1994. *A Very Social Time: Crafting Community in Antebellum New England*. Berkeley: University of California Press.

Harris, Kenneth. 1988. *Thatcher*. London: Weidenfeld and Nicolson.

———. 1995. "Prime Minister Margaret Thatcher: The Influence of Her Gender on Her Foreign Policy." Pp. 59–70 in *Women in World Politics: An Introduction*, edited by F. D'Amico and P. R. Beckman. London: Burgin and Garvey.

Hassim, Shireen. 2004. "Nationalism, Feminism, and Autonomy: The ANC in Exile and the Question of Women." *Journal of Southern African Studies* 30:433–55.

Haub, Carl and Diana Cornelius. 2000. *2000 World Population Data Sheet*. Washington, DC: Population Reference Bureau.

Hawkesworth, Mary, Kathleen J. Casey, Krista Jenkins, and Katherine E. Kleeman. 2001. "Legislating by and for Women: A Comparison of the 103rd and 104th Congresses." New Brunswick, NJ: Center for the American Woman and Politics.

Hayward, Clarissa R. 2000. *De-Facing Power*. Cambridge, UK: Cambridge University Press.

Heath, Roseanna Michelle, Leslie A. Schwindt-Bayer, and Michelle M. Taylor-Robinson. 2005. "Women on the Sidelines: Women's Representation on Committees in Latin American Legislatures." *American Journal of Political Science* 49:420–36.

Heckscher, Gunnar. 1984. *The Welfare State and Beyond: Success and Problems in Scandinavia*. Minneapolis: University of Minnesota Press.

Hegel, Georg. 1977. "The Philosophy of Right." Pp. 161–70 in *History of Ideas on Women: A Source Book*, edited by R. Agonito. New York: G. P. Putnam's Sons.

Henig, Ruth and Simon Henig. 2001. *Women and Political Power: Europe Since 1945*. London: Routledge.

Hiers, Cheryl. 2004. "The Nineteenth Amendment and the War of the Roses." Available online at http://www.blueshoenashville.com/suffragehistory.html

High-Pippert, Angela Comer, and John Comer. 1998. "Female Empowerment: The Influence of Women Representing Women." *Women and Politics* 19(4):53–66.

Hill, David B. 1981. "Political Culture and Female Political Representation." *The Journal of Politics* 43:159–68.

Hill Collins, Patricia. 2000. *Black Feminist Thought: Knowledge, Consciousness and the Politics of Empowerment,* 2d ed. New York: Routledge.

Hochschild, Arlie. 1989. *The Second Shift: Working Parents and the Revolution at Home.* New York: Viking.

Hoff, Joan. 1985. "Gallant Warrior for Peace." Presented at the dedication of the Jeannette Rankin's Statue May 1, Washington, DC.

Hogan, Robert E. 2001. "Campaign Spending by Men and Women Candidates for the State Legislature." Presented at the annual meeting of the American Political Science Association, August 29–September 2, San Francisco, CA.

Holm, Jeanne. 1982. *Women in the Military: An Unfinished Revolution.* Novato, CA: Presidio Press.

Holt, Renee. 1991. Women's rights and international law: The struggle for recognition and enforcement. *Columbia Journal of Gender and Law* 1:117–41.

hooks, bell. 1981. *Ain't I a Woman: Black Women and Feminism.* Boston: South End Press.

———. 2000. *Feminist Theory: From Margin to Center,* 2d ed. Boston: South End Press.

Horton, Susan. 1995. *Women and Industrialization in Asia.* New York: Routledge.

Htun, Mala N. and Mark P. Jones. 2002. "Engendering the Right to Participate in Decision-Making: Electoral Quotas and Women's Leadership in Latin America." Pp. 32–56 in *Gender and the Politics of Rights and Democracy in Latin America,* edited by N. Craske and M. Molyneux. Houndmills, UK: Palgrave.

Hughes, Melanie. 2004. "Another Road to Power? Armed Conflict, International Linkages, and Women's Parliamentary Representation in Developing Nations." Presented at the 99th American Sociological Association annual meeting, August 14–17, San Francisco, CA.

———. 2005. "The Continuing Importance of History: The Residual Effects of Colonialism on Women's Parliamentary Participation." Presented at the 100th American Sociological Association annual meeting, August 13–16, Philadelphia, PA.

Human Rights Watch. 1999. *Crime or Custom: Violence Against Women in Pakistan.* New York: Human Rights Watch.

Inglehart, Ronald and Pippa Norris. 2000. "The Developmental Theory of the Gender Gap: Women's and Men's Voting Behavior in Global Perspective." *International Political Science Review* 21:441–63.

International Alliance of Women. 2005. "Declaration of Principles." Available online at www.womenalliance.com/declare.html

International Institute for Democracy and Electoral Assistance. 2005. "Voter Turnout by Gender." Available online at http://www.idea.int/gender/vt.cfm

———. 2006. *Global Database of Quotas for Women.* Available online at http://www.idea.int/quota

Inter-Parliamentary Union. 1995. *Women in Parliaments: 1945–1995: A World Statistical Survey.* Geneva, Switzerland: Inter-Parliamentary Union.

———. 2000. *Politics: Women's Insight.* Geneva, Switzerland: Inter-Parliamentary Union.

———. 2005a. *Women in National Parliaments* [Webpage] http://www.ipu.org. Accessed December 7, 2005.

_____. 2005b. "Women's Suffrage: A World Chronology of the Recognition of Women's Rights to Vote and to Stand for Election." Available online at http://www.ipu.org/wmn-e/suffrage.htm

_____. 2006a. *Parline Database.* Available online at http://www.ipu.org/parline-e/parlinesearch.asp

_____. 2006b. "Women in National Parliament: World and Regional Averages." Available online at http://www.ipu.org/wmn-e/world.htm

Isaksson, Eva, ed. 1988. *Women and the Military System.* Hertfordshire, UK: Havester-Wheatsheaf.

Ishiyama, John T. 2003. "Women's Parties in Post-Communist Politics." *East European Politics and Societies* 17:266–304.

Jalalzai, Farida. 2004. "Women Political Leaders: Past and Present." *Women and Politics* 26:85–108.

Japanese Ministry of Health, Labour, and Welfare. 2005. *Basic Survey on Wage Structure.* Available online at http://web-japan.org/stat/stats/18WME42.html

Jaquette, Jane S. 1994. "Introduction: From Transition to Participation—Women's Movements and Democratic Politics." Pp. 1–11 in *The Women's Movement in Latin America,* edited by J. S. Jaquette. Boulder, CO: Westview Press.

Jaquette, Jane S. and Sharon L. Wolchik, eds. 1998. *Women and Democracy: Latin America and Central and Eastern Europe.* Baltimore: Johns Hopkins University Press.

Jayawardena, Kumari. 1986. *Feminism and Nationalism in the Third World.* London: Zed Books.

Jeannette Rankin Peace Center. 2006. "Jeannette Who?" Available online at http://www.jrpc.org/jeannette_who.html

Jenkins, J. C. 1983. "Resource Mobilization Theory and the Study of Social Movements." *Annual Review of Sociology* 9:527–53.

Jeydel, Alana and Andrew J. Taylor. 2003. "Are Women Legislators Less Effective? Evidence from the U.S. House in the 103rd–105th Congress." *Political Research Quarterly* 56:19–27.

Joachim, Jutta. 2003. "Framing Issues and Seizing Opportunities: The UN, NGOs and Women's Rights." *International Studies Quarterly* 47:247–74.

Johnson, Deb with Hope Kabuchu, and Santa Vusiya Kayonga. 2003. "Women in Ugandan Local Government: The Impact of Affirmative Action." *Gender and Development* 11(3):8–18.

Jones, Mark P. 1998. "Gender Quotas, Electoral Laws, and the Election of Women: Lessons from the Argentine Provinces." *Comparative Political Studies* 31(1):3–21.

_____. 2004. "Quota Legislation and the Election of Women: Learning From the Costa Rican Experience." *The Journal of Politics* 66:1203–23.

Jones, Mark P. and Patricio Navia. 1999. "Assessing the Effectiveness of Gender Quotas in Open-List Proportional Representation Electoral Systems." *Social Science Quarterly* 80(2):341–56.

Jorgensen-Earp, Cheryl R., ed. 1999. *Speeches and Trials of the Militant Suffragettes: The Women's Social and Political Union, 1903–1918.* London: Associated University Presses.

Josephson, Hannah. 1974. *Jeannette Rankin: First Lady in Congress.* New York: Bobbs-Merrill.

Kabeer, Naila. 1994. *Reversed Realities: Gender Hierarchies in Development Thought.* London: Verso.

Kahn, Kim Friedkin. 1996. *The Political Consequences of Being a Woman: How Stereotypes Influence the Conduct and Consequences of Political Campaigns.* New York: Columbia University Press.

Kanter, Rosabeth Moss. 1977. *Men and Women of the Corporation.* New York: Basic Books.

Karam, Azza. 1999. "Strengthening the Role of Women Parliamentarians in the Arab Region: Challenges and Options." Available online at http://www.pogar.org/publications/gender/karam2/section5.html

Karvonen, Lauri and Per Selle. 1995. "Introduction: Scandinavia: A Case Apart." Pp. 3–23 in *Women in Nordic Politics: Closing the Gap,* edited by L. Karvonen and P. Selle. Aldershot, UK: Dartmouth.

Kathlene, Lyn. 1994. "Power and Influence in State Legislative Policymaking: The Interaction of Gender and Position in Committee Hearing Debates." *American Political Science Review* 88:560–76.

————. 1995. "Alternative Views of Crime: Legislative Policymaking in Gendered Terms." *Journal of Politics* 57:696–723.

Kathlene, Lyn, Susan E. Clarke, and Barbara A. Fox. 1991. "Ways Women Politicians Are Making a Difference." Pp. 31–8 in *Gender and Policymaking: Studies of Women in Office,* edited by D. L. Dodson. New Brunswick, NJ: Center for the American Woman and Politics.

Kawamara-Mishambi, Sheila and Irene Ovonji-Odida. 2003. "The 'Lost Clause': The Campaign to Advance Women's Property Rights in the Uganda 1998 Land Act." Pp. 160–87 in *No Shortcuts to Power: African Women in Politics and Policy-Making,* edited by A. M. Goetz and S. Hassim. London: Zed Books.

Keck, Margaret E. and Kathryn Sikkink. 1998. *Activists Beyond Borders: Advocacy Networks in International Politics.* Ithaca, NY: Cornell University Press.

Kelber, Mim. 1994. *Women and Government: New Ways to Political Power.* Westport, CT: Praeger.

Kelly, Liz. 2000. "Wars Against Women: Sexual Violence, Sexual Politics and the Militarised State." Pp. 45–65 in *States of Conflict: Gender, Violence, and Resistance,* edited by Susie Jacobs, Ruth Jacobson, and Jen Marchbank. London: Zed Books.

Kenworthy, Lane and Melissa Malami. 1999. "Gender Inequality in Political Representation: A Worldwide Comparative Analysis." *Social Forces* 78:235–68.

King, Brayden G. and Marie Cornwall. 2004. "Specialists and Generalists: Learning Strategies in the Woman Suffrage Movement, 1866–1918." Unpublished Manuscript.

King, James D. 2002. "Single-Member Districts and the Representation of Women in American State Legislatures: The Effects of Electoral System Change." *State Politics and Policy Quarterly* 2:161–75.

Kirkpatrick, Jeane. 1974. *Political Women.* New York: Basic Books.

Kishor, Sunita and Kiersten Johnson. 2004. *Profiling Domestic Violence: A Multi-Country Study.* Columbia, MD: ORC Macro.

Kiss, Yudit. 1991. "The Second 'No': Women in Hungary." *Feminist Review* 39 (Autumn): 49–57.

Klausen, Jytte. 2001. "When Women Voted for the Right: Lessons for Today From the Conservative Gender Gap." Pp. 209–28 in *Has Liberalism Failed Women: Assuring Equal Representation in Europe and the United States,* edited by J. Klausen and C. S. Maier. New York: Palgrave.

Klein, Ethel. 1984. *Gender Politics: From Consciousness to Mass Politics.* Cambridge, MA: Harvard University Press.

Knight, Louise W. 2004. "Educating Women Worldwide." *International Higher Education* 37(Fall):15–16.

Koch, Jeffrey. 1997. "Candidate Gender and Women's Psychological Engagement in Politics." *American Politics Quarterly* 25:118–33.

Koester, David. 1995. "Gender Ideology and Nationalism in the Culture and Politics of Iceland." *American Ethnologist* 22:572–88.

Kohn, W. S. 1980. *Women in National Legislatures: A Comparative Study of Six Countries.* New York: Praeger.

Kostova, Dobrinka. 1998. "Women in Bulgaria: Changes in Employment and Political Involvement." Pp. 203–21 in *Women and Democracy: Latin America and Central and Eastern Europe,* edited by J. S. Jaquette and S. L. Wolchik. Baltimore: Johns Hopkins University Press.

Kristof, Nicholas. 2004. "Sentenced to Be Raped." *New York Times,* September 29, p. A25.

————. 2005. "Raped, Kidnapped, and Silenced." *New York Times,* June 14, p. A23.

Krook, Mona. 2003. "Not All Quotas Are Created Equal: Trajectories of Reform to Increase Women's Political Representation." Presented at the European Consortium for Political Research, Joint Sessions of Workshops, March 28–April 2, Edinburgh, Scotland.

————. 2004a. "Gender Quotas as a Global Phenomenon: Actors and Strategies in Quota Adoption." *European Political Science* 3(3):59–64.

————. 2004b. "Promoting Gender-Balanced Decision-Making: The Role of International Fora and Transnational Networks." Pp. 205–20 in *Crossing Borders: Re-mapping Women's Movements at the Turn of the 21st Century,* edited by H. R. Christensen, B. Halsaa, and A. Saarinen. Odense, Denmark: University Press of South Denmark.

Krupavicius, Algis and Irmina Matonytė. 2003. "Women in Lithuanian Politics: From Nomenklatura Selection to Representation." Pp. 81–104 in *Women's Access to Political Power in Post-Communist Europe,* edited by R. E. Matland and K. A. Montgomery. Oxford, UK: Oxford University Press.

Krupskaya, Nadezhda K. 1938. "Introduction." Pp. 5–10 in *Women and Society,* edited by V. I. Lenin. New York: International Publishers.

Kumar, Krishna, ed. 2001. *Women and Civil War: Impact, Organizations, and Action.* Boulder, CO: Lynne Rienner.

Kunovich, Sheri. 2003. "The Representation of Polish and Czech Women in National Politics: Predicting Electoral List Position." *Comparative Politics* 35:273–91.

Kunovich, Sheri and Pamela Paxton. 2005. "Pathways to Power: The Role of Political Parties in Women's National Political Representation." *The American Journal of Sociology* 111:505–52.

Kvennalistinn. 1987. *Aims of the Women's Alliance.* Available online at http://www.mith2 .umd.edu/WomensStudies/GovernmentPolitics/InternationalDirectory/Europe/iceland

LaFraniere, Sharon. 2005. "Entrenched Epidemic: Wife-Beatings in Africa." *New York Times,* August 11, p. A1.

Lane, Amanda. 2001. "Promoting Voter Awareness among Jordanian Women and Youth." *The Network Newsletter* 23:6–7.

Larson, Taft A. 1965. "Woman Suffrage in Wyoming." *Pacific Northwest Quarterly* 56(2):57–66.

Lavrin, Asuncion. 1994. "Suffrage in South America: Arguing a Difficult Case." Pp. 184–209 in *Suffrage and Beyond: International Feminist Perspectives,* edited by C. Daley and M. Nolan. New York: New York University Press.

Lawless, Jennifer L. and Sean M. Theriault. 2005. "Women in the U.S. Congress: From Entry to Exit." Pp. 164–81 in *Women in Politics: Outsiders or Insiders?* 4th ed., edited by Lois Duke Whitaker. New York: Prentice Hall.

Lerner, Gerda. 1986. *The Creation of Patriarchy.* New York: Oxford University Press.

Lindberg, Staffen. 2004. "Women's Empowerment and Democratization: The Effects of Electoral Systems, Participation, and Experience in Africa." *Studies in Comparative International Development* 39:28–53.

Lindeke, William A. and Winnie Wanzala. 1994. "Regional Elections in Namibia: Deepening Democracy and Gender Inclusion." *Africa Today* 41(4):5–15.

Lipman-Blumen, Jean. 1973. "Role De-Differentiations as a System Response to Crisis: Occupational and Political Roles of Women." *Sociological Inquiry* 43: 105–29.

Lipset, Seymour M. 1960. *Political Man.* London: Heinemann.

Liswood, Laura A. 1995. *Women World Leaders: Fifteen Great Politicians Tell Their Stories.* London: HarperCollins.

Lithwick, Dahlia. 2001. "Double Dipping at the Waffle House." Available online at http://www.slate.com/id/117140/

Little, Thomas H., Dana Dunn, and Rebecca E. Deen. 2001. "A View from the Top: Gender Differences in Legislative Priorities Among State Legislative Leaders." *Women and Politics* 22:29–49.

Longman, Timothy. 2006. "Rwanda: Achieving Equality or Serving an Authoritarian State?" Pp. 133–50 in *Women in African Parliaments,* edited by G. Bauer and H. Britton. London: Lynne Rienner.

Lorber, Judith. 2003. "'Night To His Day': The Social Construction of Gender." Pp. 33–47 in *Feminist Frontiers,* 6th ed., edited by L. Richardson, V. Taylor, and N. Whittier. New York: McGraw-Hill.

Lovenduski, Joni. 1993. "Introduction: The Dynamics of Gender and Party." Pp. 1–15 in *Gender and Party Politics,* edited by J. Lovenduski and P. Norris. Newbury Park, CA: Sage.

Luciak, Ilja A. 2001. *After the Revolution: Gender and Democracy in El Salvador, Nicaragua, and Guatemala.* Baltimore: Johns Hopkins University Press.

Lukes, Steven. 1974. *Power: A Radical View.* London: Macmillan.

MacKinnon, Catharine. 1989. *Toward a Feminist Theory of the State.* Cambridge, MA: Harvard University Press.

Mair, Lucille. 1991. "Religion as Catalyst for Female Activism." Pp. 155–59 in *Women, Politics, and Religion,* edited by H. L. Swarup and S. Bisaria. Etawah, India: A. C. Brothers.

Mann, Michael. 1986. "A Crisis in Stratification Theory? Persons, Households/ Families/Lineages, Genders, Classes and Nations. Pp. 40–56 in *Gender and Stratification,* edited by R. Crompton and M. Mann. Cambridge, UK: Polity Press.

Manninen, Merja. 2004. "Women's Status in Finland." Available online at http://virtual.finland.fi/netcomm/news/showarticle.asp?intNWSAID=25736.

Mansbridge, Jane J. 1986. *Why We Lost the ERA.* Chicago: University of Chicago Press.

————. 1999. "Should Blacks Represent Blacks and Women Represent Women? A Contingent 'Yes.'" *Journal of Politics* 61:628–57.

Mansbridge, Jane and Katherine Tate. 1992. "Race Trumps Gender: The Thomas Nomination in the Black Community." *PS: Political Science and Politics* 25:488–92.

Manza, Jeff and Clem Brooks. 1998. "The Gender Gap in U.S. Presidential Elections: When? Why? Implications?" *American Journal of Sociology* 103(5):1235–66.

Margolis, Diane Rothbard. 1993. "Women's Movements Around the World: Cross-Cultural Comparisons." *Gender and Society* 7:379–99.

Martin, Janet M. 1997. "Women Who Govern: The President's Appointments." Pp. 51–72 in *The Other Elites: Women, Politics, and Power in the Executive Branch,* edited by M. A. Borrelli and J. M. Martin. Boulder, CO: Lynne Rienner.

Martin, Patricia Yancy. 2004. "Gender as a Social Institution." *Social Forces* 82:1249–73.

Mathew, G., ed. 2000. *Status of Panchayati Raj in the States and Union Territories of India, 2000.* New Delhi, India: Institute of Social Sciences, Concept Publication.

Matland,^v Richard E. 1993. "Institutional Variables Affecting Female Representation in National Legislatures: The Case of Norway." *The Journal of Politics* 55:737–55.

_____. 1998. "Women's Representation in National Legislatures: Developed and Developing Countries." *Legislative Studies Quarterly* 23:109–25.

_____. 2002. "Enhancing Women's Political Participation: Legislative Recruitment and Electoral Systems." Pp. 65–90 in *Women in Parliament: Beyond Numbers*, edited by A. Karam. Stockholm, Sweden: IDEA.

_____. 2003. "Women's Representation in Post-Communist Europe." Pp. 321–42 in *Women's Access to Political Power in Post-Communist Europe*, edited by R. E. Matland and K. A. Montgomery. Oxford, UK: Oxford University Press.

Matland, Richard E. and Deborah D. Brown. 1992. "District Magnitude's Effect on Female Representation in U.S. State Legislatures." *Legislative Studies Quarterly* 17:469–92.

Matland, Richard E. and Kathleen A. Montgomery, eds. 2003. *Women's Access to Political Power in Post-Communist Europe.* Oxford, UK: Oxford University Press.

Matland, Richard E. and Donley T. Studlar. 1996. "The Contagion of Women Candidates in Single-Member District and Proportional Representation Systems: Canada and Norway." *Journal of Politics* 58:707–33.

McAdam, Doug. 1982. *Political Process and the Development of Black Insurgency, 1930–1970.* Chicago: University of Chicago Press.

_____. 1983. "Tactical Innovation and the Pace of Insurgency." *American Sociological Review* 48:735–54.

McAdam, Doug, John D. McCarthy, and Mayer N. Zald. 1996. *Comparative Perspectives on Social Movements.* Cambridge, UK: Cambridge University Press.

McCammon, Holly J. 2001. "Stirring Up Suffrage Sentiment: The Formation of the State Woman Suffrage Organizations, 1866–1914." *Social Forces* 80:449–80.

_____. 2003. "'Out of the Parlors and into the Streets': The Changing Tactical Repertoire of the U.S. Women's Suffrage Movements." *Social Forces* 81:787–818.

McCammon, Holly J. and Karen E. Campbell. 2001. "Winning the Vote in the West: The Political Successes of the Women's Suffrage Movement, 1866–1919." *Gender and Society* 15:55–82.

McCammon, Holly J., Karen E. Campbell, Ellen M. Granberg, and Christine Mowery. 2001. "How Movements Win: Gendered Opportunity Structures and U.S. Women's Suffrage Movements, 1866 to 1919." *American Sociological Review* 66(1):49–70.

McDonagh, Eileen L. and H. Douglas Price. 1985. "Woman Suffrage in the Progressive Era: Patterns of Opposition and Support in Referenda Voting, 1910–1918." *The American Political Science Review* 79:415–35.

McFarlane, Stewart. 1994. "Chinese Religions." Pp. 158–67 in *Women in Religion*, edited by J. Holm with J. Bowker. London: Pinter.

McGlen, Nancy E., Karen O'Connor, Laura van Assendelft, and Wendy Gunther-Canada. 2002. *Women, Politics, and American Society.* New York: Longman.

McGlen, Nancy E. and Meredith Reid Sarkees. 1993. *Women in Foreign Policy: The Insiders.* New York: Routledge.

Meier, Petra. 2000. "From Theory to Practice and Back Again: Gender Quotas and the Politics of Presence in Belgium." Pp. 106–16 in *Deliberation, Representation and Association*, edited by M. Saward. London: Routledge.

Meyer, John W., John Boli, George M. Thomas, and Francisco O. Ramirez. 1997. "World Society and the Nation State." *The American Journal of Sociology* 103(1):144–81.

Meyer, Katherine, Helen Rizzo, and Yousef Ali. 1998. "Islam and the Extension of Citizenship Rights to Women in Kuwait." *Journal for the Scientific Study of Religion* 37:131–44.

Meznaric, Silva. 1994. "Gender and an Ethno-Marker: Rape, War, and Identity Politics in the Former Yugoslavia." Pp. 76–97 in *Identity Politics and Women: Cultural Reassertions and Feminisms in International Perspective*, edited by V. M. Moghadam. Boulder, CO: Westview Press.

Mill, John Stuart. 1859. *On Liberty*. London: J. W. Parker.

_____. 1861. *Considerations on Representative Government*. London: Parker, Son and Bourn.

_____. 1869. *On the Subjugation of Women*. London: Dent.

Minor v. Happersett, 21 Wallace, U.S. Reports. (1835).

Mission, Gina. 1998. "Their Own Worst Enemies: Gender Politics in the Philippines." Available online at http://www.geocities.com/Wellesley/3321/win8d.htm

Moghadam, Valentine. 1994. *Gender and National Identity: Women and Politics in Muslim Societies*. London: Zed Books.

_____. 1997. "Gender and Revolutions." Pp. 137–67 in *Theorizing Revolutions*, edited by J. Foran. New York: Routledge.

_____. 2003. "Engendering Citizenship, Feminizing Civil Society: The Case of the Middle East and North Africa." *Women and Politics* 25(1/2):63–88.

_____. 2005. *Globalizing Women: Transnational Feminist Networks*. Baltimore: Johns Hopkins University Press.

Molyneux, Maxine. 1985a. "Legal Reforms and Socialist Revolution in Democratic Yemen: Women and the Family." *International Journal of the Sociology of Law* 133:147–72.

_____. 1985b. "Mobilization without Emancipation? Women's Interests, the State, and Revolution." *Feminist Studies* 11:227–54.

_____. 1998. "Analysing Women's Movements." *Development and Change* 29:219–45.

Moncrief, Gary F., Peverill Squire, and Malcolm E. Jewell. 2001. *Who Runs for the Legislature? Real Politics in America*. Upper Saddle River, NJ: Prentice Hall.

Montgomery, Kathleen A. 2003. "Introduction." Pp. 1–18 in *Women's Access to Political Power in Post-Communist Europe*, edited by R. E. Matland and K. A. Montgomery. Oxford, UK: Oxford University Press.

Moore, Gwen and Gene Shackman. 1996. "Gender and Authority: A Cross-National Study." *Social Science Quarterly* 77:273–88.

Moraes, Dom. 1980. *Indira Gandhi*. Boston: Little, Brown.

Morgan, Robin. 1984. *Sisterhood Is Powerful: An Anthology of Writings From the Women's Liberation Movement*. New York: Random House.

Morokvasic, Mirjana. 1998. "The Logics of Exclusion: Nationalism, Sexism, and the Yugoslav War." Pp. 65–90 in *Gender, Ethnicity and Political Ideologies*, edited by N. Charles and H. Hintjens. London: Routledge.

Moser, Robert G. 2003. "Electoral Systems and Women's Representation: The Strange Case of Russia." Pp. 153–72 in *Women's Access to Political Power in Post-Communist Europe*, edited by R. E. Matland and K. A. Montgomery. Oxford, UK: Oxford University Press.

Moses, Claire G. 1984. *French Feminism in the Nineteenth Century*. Albany: State University of New York Press.

Moskowitz, D. W., E. J. Suh, and J. Desaulniers. 1994. "Situational Influences on Gender Differences in Agency and Communion." *Journal of Personality and Social Psychology* 66:753–61.

Murdock, George P. 1967. "Ethnographic Atlas: A Summary." *Ethnology* 7:109–236.

National Center for Education Statistics. 2006. *Number of Bachelor's Degrees Earned by Women, by Field of Study.* Available online at http://nces.ed.gov/

Nechemias, Carol. 1987. "Changes in the Election of Women to U.S. State Legislative Seats." *Legislative Studies Quarterly* 12(1):125–42.

Newland, K. 1979. *The Sisterhood of Man.* New York: Norton.

Niven, David. 1998. "Party Elites and Women Candidates: The Shape of Bias." *Women and Politics* 19(2):57–80.

Noonan, Rita K. 1995. "Women Against the State: Political Opportunities and Collective Action Frames in Chile's Transition to Democracy." *Sociological Forum* 10(1):81–111.

Norderval, Ingunn. 1985. "Party and Legislative Participation Among Scandinavian Women." *Women and Politics in Western Europe* 18(4):71–89.

Nordlund, Anja Taarup. 2004. "Demands for Electoral Gender Quotas in Afghanistan and Iraq." Working Paper Series 2004:2. Available online at http://www.statsvet.su.se/quotas/a_nordlund_wps_2004_2.pdf

Norrander, Barbara and Clyde Wilcox. 2005. "Change and Continuity in the Geography of Women State Legislators." Pp. 176–96 in *Women and Elective Office: Past, Present, and Future,* 2d ed., edited by S. Thomas and C. Wilcox. Oxford, UK: Oxford University Press.

Norris, Pippa. 1985. "Women's Legislative Participation in Western Europe." *West European Politics* 8:90–101.

————. 1993. "Conclusions: Comparing Legislative Recruitment." Pp. 309–30 in *Gender and Party Politics,* edited by J. Lovenduski and P. Norris. Newbury Park, CA: Sage.

————. 1997. *Passages to Power: Legislative Recruitment in Advanced Democracies.* Cambridge, UK: Cambridge University Press.

Norris, Pippa and Ronald Inglehart. 2001. "Cultural Obstacles to Equal Representation." *Journal of Democracy* 12:126–40.

Norris, Pippa and Joni Lovenduski. 1995. *Political Recruitment: Gender, Race and Class in the British Parliament.* Cambridge, UK: Cambridge University Press.

Odunjinrin, O. 1993. "Wife Battering in Nigeria." *International Journal of Gynaecology and Obstetrics* 41:159–64.

Okin, Susan Muller. 1979. *Women in Western Political Thought.* Princeton, NJ: Princeton University Press.

————. 1999. "Is Multiculturalism Bad for Women?" Pp. 7–26 in *Is Multiculturalism Bad for Women?* edited by J. Cohen, M. Howard, and M. C. Nussbaum. Princeton, NJ: Princeton University Press.

Okonjo, Kamene. 1994. "Women and the Evolution of a Ghanaian Political Synthesis." Pp. 286–97 in *Women in Politics Worldwide,* edited by B. J. Nelson and N. Chowdhury. New Haven, CT: Yale University Press.

Olafsdottir Bjornsson, Anna. 2001. "Homepage: The Women's Alliance." Available online at http://www.itn.is/~annari/kveensk.htm

Opfell, Olga. 1993. *Women Prime Ministers and Presidents.* London: McFarland.

Orum, Anthony M., Roberta S. Cohen, Sherri Grasmuck, and Amy W. Orum. 1974. "Sex, Socialization, and Politics." *American Sociological Review* 39:197–209.

Owen, Diana and Jack Dennis. 1988. "Gender Differences in the Politicization of American Children." *Women and Politics* 8:23–43.

Oxley, Zoe M. and Richard L. Fox. 2004. "Women in Executive Office: Variation Across American States." *Political Research Quarterly* 57(1):113–20.

Pankhurst, Donna. 2002. "Women and Politics in Africa: The Case of Uganda." *Parliamentary Affairs* 55(1):119–28.

Parpart, Jane L., Shirin M. Rai, and Kathleen Staudt. 2002. "Rethinking Em(power)ment, Gender and Development: An Introduction." Pp. 3–21 in *Rethinking Empowerment: Gender and Development in a Global/Local World*, edited by J. L. Parpart, S. M. Rai, and K. Staudt. London: Routledge.

Pateman, Carole. 1988. *The Sexual Contract*. Cambridge, UK: Polity.

_____. 1989. *The Disorder of Women: Democracy, Feminism, and Political Theory*. Cambridge, UK: Polity.

Paxton, Pamela. 1997. "Women in National Legislatures: A Cross-National Analysis." *Social Science Research* 26:442–64.

Paxton, Pamela and Hein Goemans. 2006. "Four Myths about Female Leaders." Working Paper. Columbus: Ohio State University and University of Rochester.

Paxton, Pamela, Melanie Hughes, and Jennifer Green. 2006a. "The International Women's Movement and Women's Political Representation, 1893–2003." *American Sociological Review* 71:898–920.

_____. 2006b. *Women in Parliament, 1893–2003. Dataset*. Unpublished dataset.

Paxton, Pamela and Sheri Kunovich. 2003. "Women's Political Representation: The Importance of Ideology." *Social Forces* 81(5):87–114.

Pesonen, Pertti. 1968. *An Election in Finland: Party Activists and Voter Reactions*. New Haven, CT: Yale University Press.

Pettman, Jan J. 1996. *Worlding Women: A Feminist International Politics*. London: Routledge.

Phillips, Anne. 1991. *Engendering Democracy*. University Park: Pennsylvania State University Press.

_____. 1995. *The Politics of Presence: The Political Representation of Gender, Ethnicity and Race*. Oxford, UK: Clarendon Press.

Pinto-Duschinsky, Michael. 2002. "Financing Politics: A Global View." *Journal of Democracy* 13(4):69–86.

Pinto-Duschinsky, Michael and Alexander Postnikov, in collaboration with Christian Nadeau and Robert Dahl. 1999. "Campaign Finance in Foreign Countries: Legal Regulation and Political Practices (A Comparative Legal Survey and Analysis)." Washington, DC: International Foundation for Election Systems.

Pintor, Rafael L. and Maria Gratschew. 2002. *Voter Turnout Since 1945: A Global Report*. Stockholm, Sweden: International IDEA.

Pitkin, Hanna F. 1972. *The Concept of Representation*. Berkeley: University of California.

Powley, Elizabeth. 2003. *Strengthening Governance: The Role of Women in Rwanda's Transition*. Available online at http://www.un.org/womenwatch/osagi/meetings/2004/EGMelectoral/EP5Powley.PDF#search=%22%22elizabeth%20powley%22%22

Prestage, Jewel L. 1991. "In Quest of African American Political Woman." *Annals of the American Academy of Political and Social Science* 515:88–103.

Public Broadcasting System. 2002. "Japanese Women in Politics: Forging Ahead." *To the Contrary*. Available online at http://www.pbs.org/ttc/politics/japanese_women.html

Pulzer, P. G. J. 1967. *Political Representation and Elections in Britain*. London: Allen and Unwin.

Putnam, Robert D. 1976. *The Comparative Study of Political Elites*. Englewood Cliffs, NJ: Prentice Hall.

_____. 1994. *Making Democracy Work: Civic Traditions in Modern Italy*. Princeton, NJ: Princeton University Press.

Quesada, Ana I. G. 2003. "Putting the Mandate into Practice: Legal Reform in Costa Rica." Presented at the workshop for the International Institute for Democracy and Electoral Assistance, February 23–24, Lima, Peru.

"Quote of the Day." 2005. *The Independent,* May 17, p. 25.

Qusti, Raid. 2004. "Women Driving Cars Is a Sinful Thing: Al-Qarni." *Arab News,* January 25. Available online at http://www.arabnews.com/?page=1&section=0&article=38586 &d=25&m=1&y=2004

Rai, Shirin. 2002. "Class, Caste, and Gender—Women in Parliament in India." Pp. 115–23 in *Women in Parliament: Beyond Numbers,* edited by A. Karam. Stockholm, Sweden: International IDEA.

Raman, Vasanthi. 2002. "The Implementation of Quotas for Women: The Indian Experience." Presented at regional workshop The Implementation of Quotas: Asian Experiences, September 25, Jakarta, Indonesia.

Ramirez, Francisco O., Yasemin Soysal, and Suzanne Shanahan. 1997. "The Changing Logic of Political Citizenship: Cross-National Acquisition of Women's Suffrage Rights, 1890 to 1990." *American Sociological Review* 62(5):735–45.

Randall, Margaret. 1981. *Sandino's Daughters: Testimonies of Nicaraguan Women in Struggle.* Vancouver, Canada: New Star Books.

Randall, Vicky. 1987. *Women and Politics: An International Perspective.* London: Macmillan.

Rehn, Elisabeth and Ellen Johnson Sirleaf, eds. 2002. *Women War Peace: The Independent Experts' Assessment. Progress of the World's Women, Vol. I.* Available online at http://www.parliament.gov.za/pls/portal30/docs/folder/parliamentary_information/publications/unifem/index.htm

Reingold, Beth. 1992. "Concepts of Representation Among Female and Male State Legislators." *Legislative Studies Quarterly* 14(4):509–37.

Remmert, Consuelo. 2003. "Rwanda Promotes Women Decision-makers." *UN Chronicle* 4:25.

Reskin, Barbara F. and Heidi I. Hartmann. 1986. *Women's Work, Men's Work: Sex Segregation on the Job.* Washington, DC: National Academy Press.

Reskin, Barbara and Patricia Roos. 1993. "Sex Segregation in the Workplace." *Annual Review of Sociology* 19(1):271–300.

Reuther, Rosemary Radford, ed. 1974. *Religions and Sexism: Images of the Women in the Jewish and Christian Traditions.* New York: Simon & Schuster.

Reynolds, Andrew. 1999. "Women in the Legislatures and Executives of the World Knocking at the Highest Glass Ceiling." *World Politics* 51:547–72.

Reynolds, Andrew, Ben Reilly, and Andrew Ellis. 2005. *Electoral System Design: The New International IDEA Handbook.* Stockholm, Sweden: International Institute for Democracy and Electoral Assistance.

Ridgeway, Cecelia L. 2001. "Gender, Status, and Leadership." *Journal of Social Issues* 57:637–55.

Ridgeway, Cecilia and Lynn Smith-Lovin. 1999. "The Gender System and Interaction." *Annual Review of Sociology* 25:191–216.

Risman, Barbara J. 2004. "Gender as a Social Structure: Theory Wresting with Activism." *Gender and Society* 18:429–50.

Rizzo, Helen, Katherine Meyer, and Yousef Ali. 2002. "Women's Political Rights: Islam, Status and Networks in Kuwait." *Sociology* 36(3):639–62.

Robertson, Claire. 1986. "Women's Education and Class Formation in Africa, 1950–1980." Pp. 92–113 in *Women and Class in Africa,* edited by C. Robertson and I. Berger. New York: Africana.

Rosenthal, Cindy Simon. 1998a. "Determinants of Collective Leadership: Civic Engagement, Gender or Organizational Norms?" *Political Research Quarterly* 51:847–68.

_____. 1998b. *When Women Lead: Integrative Leadership in State Legislatures*. Oxford, UK: Oxford University Press.

_____. 2005. "Women Leading Legislatures: Getting There and Getting Things Done." Pp. 197–212 in *Women and Elective Office: Past, Present, and Future*, 2d ed. Oxford, UK: Oxford University Press.

Rowlands, Jo. 1997. *Questioning Empowerment: Working with Women in Honduras*. Oxford, UK: Oxfam Publications.

Ruddick, Sara. 1989. *Maternal Thinking*. Boston: Beacon Press.

Rueschemeyer, Marilyn. 1994. "Difficulties and Opportunities in the Transition Period: Concluding Observations." Pp. 225–37 in *Women in the Politics of Postcommunist Eastern Europe*, edited by M. Rueschemeyer. Armonk, NY: M. E. Sharpe.

Rule, Wilma. 1981. "Why Women Don't Run: The Critical Contextual Factors in Women's Legislative Recruitment." *Western Political Quarterly* 34:60–77.

_____. 1987. "Electoral Systems, Contextual Factors and Women's Opportunity for Election to Parliament in Twenty Three Democracies." *Western Political Quarterly* 20:477–98.

_____. 1990. "Why More Women Are State Legislators. A Research Note." *The Western Political Quarterly* 43:437–48.

_____. 1994. "Parliaments of, by, and for the People: Except for Women?" Pp. 15–31 in *Electoral Systems in Comparative Perspective: Their Impact on Women and Minorities*, edited by W. Rule and J. F. Zimmerman. Westport, CT: Greenwood Press.

_____. 1999. "Why Are More Women State Legislators?" Pp. 190–202 in *Women in Politics: Outsiders or Insiders?* 3rd ed., edited by L. D. Whitaker. Upper Saddle River, NJ: Prentice Hall.

Rupp, Leila J. and Verta Taylor. 1999. "Forging Feminist Identity in an International Movement: A Collective Identity Approach to Twentieth-Century Feminism." *Signs* 24:363–86.

Ruppert, Uta. 2002. "Global Women's Politics: Towards the 'Globalizing' of Women's Human Rights." Pp. 147–59 in *Common Ground or Mutual Exclusion? Women's Movements and International Relations*, edited by M. Braig and S. Wolte. London: Zed Books.

Ruthven, Amanda. 2005. "Women in Washington: Will Women Ever Be Adequately Represented in Congress?" *Feminist Uproar*. Available online at http://www.democracy matters.org/press/spring2005feministuproar.php

Saint-Germain, Michelle. 1989. "Does Their Difference Make a Difference? The Impact of Women on Public Policy in Arizona Legislature." *Social Science Quarterly* 70:956–58.

_____. 1993. "Women in Power in Nicaragua: Myth and Reality." Pp. 70–102 in *Women Heads of State*, edited by Michael Genovese. Newbury Park, CA: Sage.

Sambanis, Nicholas. 2002. "A Review of Recent Advances and Future Directions in the Literature on Civil War." *Defense and Peace Economics* 13:215–43.

Sanbonmatsu, Kira. 2002a. *Democrats, Republicans, and the Politics of Women's Place*. Ann Arbor: University of Michigan Press.

_____. 2002b. "Gender Stereotypes and Vote Choice" *American Journal of Political Science* 46:20–34.

_____. 2002c. "Political Parties and the Recruitment of Women to State Legislators." *Journal of Politics* 64:791–809.

_____. 2003. "Gender-Related Political Knowledge and the Descriptive Representation of Women." *Political Behavior* 25:367–88.

Sandburg, Carl. 1939. *Abraham Lincoln: The War Years, Volume I*. New York: Harcourt, Brace.

Sapiro, Virginia. 1982. "Private Costs of Public Commitments or Public Costs of Private Commitments? Family Roles versus Political Ambition." *American Journal of Political Science* 26:265–79.

Sawer, Marian. 1990. *Sisters in Suits: Women and Public Policy in Australia*. Sydney, Australia: Allen and Unwin.

———. 2000. "Parliamentary Representation of Women: From Discourses of Justice to Strategies of Accountability." *International Political Science Review* 21:361–80.

Saxonberg, Steven. 2000. "Women in East European Parliaments." *Journal of Democracy* 11:145–58.

Schlozman, Kay Lehman, Nancy Burns, and Sidney Verba. 1994. "Gender and the Pathways to Participation: The Role of Resources." *The Journal of Politics* 56(4):963–990.

Schmidt, Gregory D. and Kyle L. Saunders. 2004. "Effective Quotas, Relative Party Magnitude and the Success of Female Candidates: Peruvian Municipal Elections in Comparative Perspective." *Comparative Political Studies* 37:704–34.

Schroeder, Patricia. 1998. *24 Years of Housework . . . and the Place Is Still a Mess: My Life in Politics*. New York: Andrews Mcmeel.

Schwindt-Bayer, Leslie A. 2006. "Still Supermadres? Gender and the Policy Priorities of Latin American Legislators." *American Journal of Political Science* 50:570–85.

Segal, David R., Mady Wechsler Segal, and Xiaolin Li. 1992. "The Role of Women in the Chinese People's Liberation Army." Pp. 115–26 in *Armed Forces in the USSR and the PRC*, edited by E. Sandschneider and J. Kuhlmann. Munich, Germany: Forum International.

Seitz, Barbara. 1991. "Songs, Identity, and Women's Liberation in Nicaragua." *Latin American Music Review* 12(1):21–41.

Seltzer, Richard A., Jody Newman, and Melissa Voorhees Leighton. 1997. *Sex as a Political Variable: Women as Candidates and Voters in U.S. Elections*. Boulder, CO: Lynne Rienner.

Sen, Amartya. 1990. *More Than 100 Million Women Are Missing*. Available online at http://ucatlas.ucsc.edu/gender/Sen100M.html

Shapiro, Robert Y. and Harpreet Mahajan. 1986. "Gender Differences in Policy Preferences: A Summary of Trends from the 1960s to the 1980s." *Public Opinion Quarterly* 50:42–61.

Sharfman, Daphna. 1994. "Women and Politics in Israel." Pp. 381–95 in *Women and Politics Worldwide*, edited by B. J. Nelson and N. Chowdhury. New Haven, CT: Yale University Press.

Shaul, Marnie S. 1982. "The Status of Women in Local Governments: International Assessment." *Public Administration Review* Nov./Dec.:491–500.

Shayne, Julie D. 2004. *The Revolution Question: Feminisms in El Salvador, Chile, and Cuba*. New Brunswick, NJ: Rutgers University Press.

Shehadeh, Lamia. 1998. "The Legal Status of Married Women in Lebanon." *International Journal of Middle East Studies* 30:501–19.

Shelton, Beth Anne. 1990. "The Distribution of Household Tasks: Does a Wife's Employment Status Make a Difference?" *Journal of Family Issues* 11:115–35.

Sherwani, Haroon Khan. 1977. *Studies in Muslim Political Thought and Administration*, 4th ed. Philadelphia, PA: Porcupine Press.

Shvedova, Nadezhda. 2002. "Obstacles to Women's Participation in Parliament." Pp. 57–63 in *Women in Parliament: Beyond Numbers*, edited by A. Karam. Stockholm, Sweden: International IDEA.

Sideris, Tina. 2001. "Rape in War and Peace: Social Context, Gender, Power, and Identity." Pp. 142–58 in *The Aftermath: Women in Post-Conflict Transformation*, edited by S. Meintjes, A. Pillay, and M. Turshen. London: Zed Books.

Siemienska, Renata. 2003. "Women in the Polish Sejm: Political Culture and Party Politics versus Electoral Rules." Pp. 217–44 in *Women's Access to Political Power in Post-Communist Europe*, edited by R. E. Matland and K. A. Montgomery. Oxford, UK: Oxford University Press.

———. 2004. "Gender Party Quotas in Poland." Presented at the workshop of the International Institute for Democracy and Electoral Assistance, October 22–23, Budapest, Hungary.

Simmons Levin, Leah. 1999. "Setting the Agenda: The Impact of the 1977 Israel Women's Party." *Israel Studies* 4(2):40–63.

"The Single Victim at the Border Sacrifices." 1885. *The Book of Rites. Part I. Book IX. Sacred Books of the East, Vol. 27.* Translated by James Legge. Available online at http://www.sacred-texts.com/cfu/liki/liki09.htm

Skjeie, Hege. 1991. "The Rhetoric of Difference: On Women's Inclusion into Political Elites." *Politics and Society* 19:233–63.

———. 2002. "Credo on Difference—Women in Parliament in Norway." Pp. 183–89 in *Women in Parliament: Beyond Numbers*, edited by A. Karam. Stockholm, Sweden: International IDEA.

Smith, Eric R. A. N. and Richard L. Fox. 2001. "The Electoral Fortunes of Women Candidates for Congress." *Political Research Quarterly* 54(1):205–21.

Sobritchea, Carolyn I. 1990. "Gender Inequality and Its Supporting Ideologies in Philippine Society." Pp. 8–17 in *And She Said No! Human Rights, Women's Identities and Struggles*, edited by L. Bautista and E. Rifareal. Caloocan City: National Council of Churches in the Philippines.

Sohoni, Neera Kuckreja. 1995. *The Burden of Girlhood: A Global Inquiry into the Status of Girls*. Oakland, CA: Third Party Publishing.

Solheim, Bruce O. 2000. *On Top of the World: Women's Political Leadership in Scandinavia and Beyond*. Westport, CT: Greenwood Press.

Sorush, Lisa. 2005. "Women's Leadership and Religion." Presented at the Afghan Women Leaders Speak Conference, November 16–19, Columbus, OH.

Soule, Sarah A. and Brayden King. 2006. "Stages of the Policy Process and the Equal Rights Amendment, 1972–1982." *American Journal of Sociology* 111:1871–1909.

Soule, Sarah A. and Susan Olzak. 2004. "When Do Movements Matter? The Politics of Contingency and the Equal Rights Amendment." *American Sociological Review* 69:473–97.

Sperling, Valerie. 1998. "Gender Politics and the State During Russia's Transition Period." Pp. 143–65 in *Gender, Politics, and the State*, edited by V. Randall and G. Waylen. London: Routledge.

Squires, Judith. 1996. "Quotas for Women: Fair Representation?" Pp. 73–90 in *Women and Politics*, edited by J. Lovenduski and P. Norris. Oxford, UK: Oxford University Press.

———. 2004. "Gender Quotas: Comparative and Contextual Analyses." *European Political Science* 3(3):51–58.

———. 2005. "The Implementation of Gender Quotas in Britain." Available online at http://www.quotaproject.org/CS/CS_Britain_Squires.pdf

Stanton, Elizabeth Cady. 1848. *Declaration of Sentiments and Resolutions*. Seneca Falls, NY. Available online at http://usinfo.state.gov/usa/women/rights/sentimnt.htm

Stanton, Elizabeth C., Susan B. Anthony, and Matilda Joslyn Gage, eds. 1887. *History of Woman Suffrage, Volume I*. Rochester, NY: Susan B. Anthony.

Staudt, Kathleen. 1986. "Stratification: Implications for Women's Politics." Pp. 197–215 in *Women and Class in Africa*, edited by C. Robertson and I. Berger. New York: Africana.

———. 1998. *Policy, Politics, and Gender: Women Gaining Ground*. Bloomfield, CT: Kumarian.

Stepen, F. 2001. "Empowering Women in Gram Panchayats through Training." In *Building Women's Capacities*, edited by M. K. Ranjani. Thousand Oaks, CA: Sage.

Sternbach, Nancy Saporta, Marysa Navarro-Aranguren, Patricia Chuchryk, and Sonia E. Alvarez. 1992. "Feminisms in Latin America; From Bogota to San Bernardo." *Signs* 17:393–434.

Stetson, Dorothy McBride. 1995. "The Oldest Women's Policy Agency: The Women's Bureau in the United States." Pp. 254–71 in *Comparative State Feminism*, edited by D. M. Stetson and A. G. Mazur. Thousand Oaks, CA: Sage.

Stetson, Dorothy McBride and Amy G. Mazur, eds. 1995. *Comparative State Feminism*. Thousand Oaks, CA: Sage.

Sumbul, Aysha. 2004. "Women's Reservation Bill—A Critique." *PUCL Bulletin*. Available online at http://www.pucl.org/Topics/Gender/2004/womens-reservation-bill.htm

Susan B. Anthony List. 2006. "What's New?" Available online at http://www.sba-list.org/

Susskind, Yifat. 2004. "Colombia's Conflict: The Basics." Available online at http://www.madre.org/articles/lac/colombiabasics.html

Swers, Michele L. 1998. "Are Women More Likely to Vote for Women's Issue Bills Than Their Male Colleagues?" *Legislative Studies Quarterly* 23:435–48.

———. 2002a. *The Difference Women Make: The Policy Impact of Women in Congress*. Chicago: University of Chicago Press.

———. 2002b. "Transforming the Agenda: Analyzing Gender Differences in Women's Issue Bill Sponsorship." Pp. 260–83 in *Women Transforming Congress*, edited by C. S. Rosenthal. Norman: University of Oklahoma Press.

Szyber, Caroline. 2005. "Giving Voice to the Voiceless: A Field Study from India about Capacity Building towards Women in Panchayats as an Instrument for Empowerment." Stockholm, Sweden: UNPAN.

Tahri, Rachida. 2003. "Women's Political Participation: The Case of Morocco." Presented at the conference Implementation of Quotas: African Experiences, November 11–12, Pretoria, South Africa.

Tamale, Sylvia. 1999. *When Hens Begin to Crow: Gender and Parliamentary Politics in Uganda*. Boulder, CO: Westview Press.

Taylor-Robinson, Michelle M. and Roseanna Michelle Heath. 2003. "Do Women Legislators Have Different Policy Priorities Than Their Male Colleagues? A Critical Case Test." *Women and Politics* 24:77–101.

The Telegraph. 2004. "The New Amazons." *The Telegraph*, August 15. Available online at http://www.telegraphindia.com/1040815/asp/look/story_3622999.asp

Thomas, Sue. 1991. "The Impact of Women on State Legislative Priorities." *The Journal of Politics* 53:958–76.

———. 1994. *How Women Legislate*. Oxford, UK: Oxford University Press.

———. 1998. "Introduction: Women and Elective Office: Past, Present, and Future." Pp. 1–14 in *Women and Elective Office: Past, Present, and Future*, edited by S. Thomas and C. Wilcox. Oxford, UK: Oxford University Press.

_____. 2003. "Scenes in the Writing of 'Constance Lytton and Jane Warton, Spinster: Contextualising a Cross-Class Dresser." *Women's History Review* 12(1):51–71.

Thomas, Sue and Susan Welch. 1991. "The Impact of Gender on Activities and Priorities of State Legislators." *The Western Political Quarterly* 44:445–56.

Thompson, Seth. 1995. "Golda Meir: A Very Public Life." Pp. 135–60 in *Women as National Leaders,* edited by M. A. Genovese. Thousand Oaks, CA: Sage.

Tinker, Irene and Jane Jacquette. 1987. "The UN Decade for Women—Its Impact and Legacy." *World Development* 15:419–27.

Towns, Ann. 2004. *Norms and Inequality in International Society: Global Politics of Women and the State.* Ph.D. Dissertation, University of Minnesota, Minneapolis.

Tremblay, Manon. 1993. "Political Party, Political Philosophy and Feminism: A Case Study of the Female and Male Candidates in the 1989 Quebec General Election." *Canadian Journal of Political Science* 26:507–22.

Tremblay, Manon and Rejean Pelletier. 2000. "More Feminists or More Women? Descriptive and Substantive Representations of Women in the 1997 Canadian Federal Elections." *International Political Science Review* 21:381–405.

Tripp, Aili Mari. 1994. "Gender, Political Participation, and the Transformation of Associational Life in Uganda and Tanzania." *African Studies Review* 37:107–31.

_____. 2001. "Women's Movements and Challenges to Neopatrimonial Rule: Preliminary Observations from Africa." *Development and Change* 32:33–54.

_____. 2003. "The Changing Face of Africa's Legislatures: Women and Quotas." Presented at the workshop of the International Institute for Democracy and Electoral Assistance, November 11–12, Pretoria, South Africa.

_____. 2006. "Uganda: Agents of Change for Women's Advancement?" Pp. 111–32 in *Women in African Parliaments,* edited by G. Bauer and H. E. Britton. Boulder, CO: Lynne Rienner.

Tripp, Aili M. and Alice Kang. 2006. "Quotas: The Fast Track to Increasing Female Legislative Representation around the World." Working paper.

Truth, Sojourner. 1851. "Ain't I a Woman?" Available online at http://www.suffragist.com/docs.htm#truth

Tucker, Judith E. 1993. *Arab Women: Old Boundaries, New Frontiers.* Bloomington: Indiana University Press.

Tymoshenko, Yulia. 2005. "Biography of Yulia Tymoshenko." Available online at http://ww2.tymoshenko.com.ua/eng/about/

UNESCO. 2005. *Education for All Global Monitoring Report.* Paris: UNESCO.

UNIFEM. 2005. "Fiji." Available online at http://www.womenwarpeace.org/fiji/fiji.htm

United Nations. 1946. "Political Rights of Women." *General Assembly Resolution* 56(1).

_____. 1979. "Convention on the Elimination of All Forms of Discrimination against Women." Available online at http://www.un.org/womenwatch/daw/cedaw/text/econvention.htm

_____. 1995. "Fourth World Conference on Women Beijing Declaration." Available online at http://www.un.org/womenwatch/daw/beijing/platform/declar.htm

_____. 1998. *Too Young to Die: Genes or Gender?* New York: United Nations.

_____. 2000a. *Women Go Global* [CD-ROM]. New York: United Nations.

_____. 2000b. *Women in Asia and the Pacific: High-Level Intergovernmental Meeting to Review Regional Implementation of the Beijing Platform for Action, 26–29 October 1999.* New York: United Nations.

_____. 2004. *World Population Prospects: The 2004 Revision and World Urbanization Prospects: The 2003 Revision.* New York: United Nations.

United Nations Development Programme. 1995. *Human Development Report*. New York: Oxford University Press.

————. 2000. *Women's Political Participation and Good Governance: 21st Century Challenges*. New York: United Nations Development Programme.

————. 2004a. *Human Development Report 2004: Cultural Liberty in Today's Diverse World*. New York: United Nations Development Programme.

————. 2004b. "UN Report on China: Mixed Gains for Women." Available online at http://www.undp.org/dpa/pressrelease/releases/2004/march/prChina25mar04.html

United Nations High Commissioner for Human Rights. 2003. *Fact Sheet 23: Harmful Practices Affecting Women and Children*. Available online at http://www.unhchr.ch/html/menu6/2/fs23.htm#i

United Nations Population Fund. 2005. "The Promise of Equality: Gender Equality, Reproductive Health and the MDGs." Available online at http://www.unfpa.org/swp/2005/english/ch1/index.htm

Urdang, Stephanie. 1989. *And Still They Dance: Women, War, and the Struggle for Change in Mozambique*. New York: Monthly Review.

U.S. Census Bureau. 2001. *Population by Race and Hispanic or Latino Origin, for the United States, Regions, Divisions, and States, and for Puerto Rico: 2000*. Washington, DC: U.S. Census Bureau.

————. 2006. *International Data Base*. Available online at http://www.census.gov/ipc/www/idbnew.html

U.S. Department of State. 2005. "Background Note: Uganda." Available online at http://www.state.gov/r/pa/ei/bgn/2963.htm

Verba, Sidney, Nancy Burns, and Kay Lehman Schlozman. 1997. "Knowing and Caring about Politics: Gender and Political Engagement." *The Journal of Politics* 59:1051–72.

Victor, Kirk. 2005. "Still an Old Boys Club?" *National Journal* 37:748.

von Hippel, Theodor Gottlieb. 1792. *On Improving the Status of Women*. Translated by T. F. Sellner. Detroit, MI: Wayne State University Press.

Wakoko, Florence and Linda Labao. 1996. "Reconceptualizing Gender and Reconstructing Social Life: Ugandan Women and Path to National Development." *Africa Today* 43:307–22.

Walby, Sylvia. 1996. "The 'Declining Significance' or the 'Changing Forms' of Patriarchy?" Pp. 19–33 in *Patriarchy and Economic Development: Women's Positions at the End of the Twentieth Century*, edited by V. M. Moghadam. Oxford, UK: Clarendon Press.

Walecki, Marcin. 2005. "Political Money and Corruption." International Foundation for Election Systems Political Finance, White Paper Series. Available online at http://www.moneyandpolitics.net/researchpubs/pdf/Money_Corruption.pdf

Wangnerud, Lena. 2000. "Testing the Politics of Presence: Women's Representation in the Swedish Riksdag." *Scandinavian Political Studies* 23:67–91.

Ward, Kathryn B. 1984. *Women in the World-System: Its Impact on Status and Fertility*. New York: Praeger.

Wartenberg, Thomas E. 1990. *The Forms of Power: From Domination to Transformation*. Philadelphia, PA: Temple University Press.

————. 1992. *Rethinking Power*. Albany: State University of New York.

Waylen, Georgina. 1994. "Women and Democratization: Conceptualizing Gender Relations in Transition Politics." *World Politics* 46:327–54.

————. 1996. *Gender in Third World Politics*. Boulder, CO: Lynne Rienner.

Weber, Max. 1978. *Economy and Society: An Outline of Interpretive Sociology*. Translated by E. Fischoff. Berkeley: University of California Press.

Weir, Sara J. 1999. "The Feminist Face of State Executive Leadership: Women as Governors." Pp. 248–59 in *Women in Politics: Outsiders or Insiders?* 3rd ed., edited by L. D. Whitaker. Upper Saddle River, NJ: Prentice Hall.

Wejnert, Barbara. 1996. "Introduction: The Dynamics of Societal Macro Changes: Implications for the Life of Women." Pp. xiii–xvii in *Research on Women in Russia and Eastern Europe, Volume 2: Women in Post Communism,* edited by B. Wejnert and M. Spencer. Greenwich: JAI Press.

Welch, Susan. 1978. "Recruitment of Women to Public Office." *Western Political Quarterly* 31:372–80.

Welch, Susan and Lee Sigelman. 1992. "A Gender Gap among Hispanics? A Comparison with Blacks and Anglos." *The Western Political Quarterly* 45:181–99.

Weldon, S. Laurel. 2002a. "Beyond Bodies: Institutional Sources of Representation for Women in Democratic Policymaking." *The Journal of Politics* 64:1153–74.

_____. 2002b. *Protest, Policy and the Problem of Violence Against Women: A Cross-National Comparison.* Pittsburgh, PA: University of Pittsburgh Press.

Welter, Barbara. 1966. "The Cult of True Womanhood: 1820–1860." *American Quarterly* 18:151–74.

West, Candace and Don H. Zimmerman. 1987. "Doing Gender." *Gender and Society* 1:125–51.

Wetherell, Elizabeth. 1851. "How May an American Woman Best Show Her Patriotism?" *The Ladies Wreath* III:313.

The White House. 1998. "Remarks by the President and the First Lady on International Women's Day." Available online at http://clinton4.nara.gov/WH/ New/html/19980311-14543.html

White House Project. 2006. "Elect a President." Available online at http://www.the whitehouseproject.org/v2/programs/pipeline/electapresident/index.html

Whitney, Catherine. 2000. *Nine and Counting: The Women of the Senate.* New York: HarperCollins.

Wilcox, Clyde. 1990. "Black Women and Feminism." *Women and Politics* 10:65–84.

Wilcox, Clyde, Beth Stark, and Sue Thomas. 2003. "Popular Support for Electing Women in Eastern Europe." Pp. 43–62 in *Women's Access to Political Power in Post-Communist Europe,* edited by R. E. Matland and K. A. Montgomery. Oxford, UK: Oxford University Press.

Wilford, Rick. 1998. "Women, Ethnicity and Nationalism: Surveying the Ground." Pp. 1–22 in *Women, Ethnicity and Nationalism: The Politics of Transition,* edited by R. Wilford and R. L. Miller. Oxford, UK: Routledge.

Williams, Melissa S. 1998. *Voice, Trust, and Memory: Marginalized Groups and the Failings of Liberal Representation.* Princeton, NJ: Princeton University Press.

Winess, Michael. 1991. "How the Senators Handled the Professor's Accusations." *New York Times,* October 8, p. A22.

The WISH List. 2006. "Women in the Senate and House." Available online at http://www .thewishlist.org

Wolbrecht, Christina and David Campbell. 2005. "Do Women Politicians Lead Adolescent Girls to Be More Politically Engaged? A Cross-National Study of Political Role Models." Presented at the annual meeting of the American Political Science Association, September 1–September 4, Washington, DC.

Wolchik, Sharon. 1981. "Eastern Europe." Pp. 252–77 in *The Politics of the Second Electorate: Women and Public Participation,* edited by J. Lovenduski and J. Hills. London: Routledge and Kegan Paul.

_____. 1994. "Women and the Politics of Transition in the Czech and Slovak Republics." Pp. 3–27 in *Women in the Politics of Postcommunist Eastern Europe,* edited by M. Rueschemeyer. Armonk, NY: M. E. Sharpe.

Wollstonecraft, Mary. 1792. *A Vindication of the Rights of Woman.* Printed at, Faust's Statue, Boston, 45 Newbury Street. Available online at http://www.bartleby.com/144/

Women for Women International. 2004. "Women Taking a Lead: Progress Toward Empowerment and Gender Equity in Rwanda." Women for Women International Briefing Paper, September. Available online at http://womenforwomen.org/nrrwpap.html

Women in World History. 2006. *Women and Confucianism.* Available online at http://www .womeninworldhistory.com/lesson3.html

Women of Uganda Network. 2005. "Search WOUGNET." Available online at http://www .wougnet.org/search.html

Wong, Pansy. 1997. "Maiden Statement." Available online at http://www.pansywong.co.nz/eng

Woods, Harriet. 2000. *Stepping Up to Power: The Political Journey of American Women.* Boulder, CO: Westview Press.

World Values Survey Association. 2000. *World Values Surveys and European Values Surveys, 1981–1984, 1990–1993, and 1995–1997* [Computer file]. ICPSR version. Ann Arbor, MI: Institute for Social Research and Inter-university Consortium for Political and Social Research.

Wright, Erik Olin, Janeen Baxter, and Gunn Elizabeth Birkelund. 1995. "The Gender Gap in Workplace Authority: A Cross-National Study." *American Sociological Review* 60:407–35.

Yarr, Linda F. 1996. "Gender and the Allocation on Time: Impact on the Household Economy." Pp. 110–22 in *Vietnam's Women in Transition,* edited by K. Barry. New York: St. Martin's Press.

Yoder, Janice D. 1991. "Rethinking Tokenism: Looking Beyond Numbers." *Gender and Society* 5:178–92.

Yoon, Mi Yung. 2001. "Democratization and Women's Legislative Representation in Sub-Saharan Africa." *Democratization* 8(2):169–90.

Young, Iris M. 1990. *Justice and the Politics of Difference.* Princeton, NJ: Princeton University Press.

Yuval-Davis, Nira. 1997. "Women, Citizenship and Difference." *Feminist Review* 57:4–27.

Zarakhovich, Yuri. 2005. "Ukraine's Iron Lady: Yuliya Tymoshenko Still Has to Convince Doubters That She's the Right Choice to Be the New Prime Minister." *Time Europe.* January 30.

Zetkin, Clara. 1920. "Lenin on the Women Question." Transcribed by S. Ryan. Available online at http://www.marxists.org/archive/zetkin/1920/lenin/zetkin1.htm

Zinsser, Judith P. 1990. "The United Nations Decade for Women: A Quiet Revolution." *The History Teacher* 24(1):19–29.

Zubaida, Sami. 1987. "The Quest for the Islamic State: Islamic Fundamentalism in Egypt and Iran." Pp. 25–50 in *Studies in Religious Fundamentalism,* edited by L. Caplin. Albany: State University of New York Press.

Glossary/Index